A Level Religious Studies for Eduqas

Philosophy of Religion

LIBBY AHLUWALIA

OXFORD
UNIVERSITY PRESS

OXFORD
UNIVERSITY PRESS

Great Clarendon Street, Oxford, OX2 6DP, United Kingdom

Oxford University Press is a department of the University of Oxford.
It furthers the University's objective of excellence in research, scholarship,
and education by publishing worldwide. Oxford is a registered trade mark of
Oxford University Press in the UK and in certain other countries

British Library Cataloguing in Publication Data
Data available

978-1-382-02898-1

978-1-382-02899-8 (ebook)

10 9 8 7 6 5 4 3 2 1

Paper used in the production of this book is a natural, recyclable product
made from wood grown in sustainable forests.

The manufacturing process conforms to the environmental regulations of the
country of origin.

Printed in Great Britain by Bell and Bain Ltd, Glasgow

The publisher would like to thank Julie Haigh for help preparing this book
for publication, and James Helling for the index.

This resource has been reviewed against WJEC Eduqas'
endorsement criteria. As this resource belongs to a
third party, there may be occasions where a specification
may be updated and that update will not be reflected
in the third party resource. Users should always refer
to WJEC Eduqas' specification and Sample Assessment
Materials to ensure that learners are studying the most
up to date course.

It is recommended that teachers use a range of resources
to fully prepare their learners for the exam and not rely
solely on one textbook or digital resource.

WJEC, nor anyone employed by WJEC has been paid for
the endorsement of this resource, nor does WJEC receive
any royalties from its sale.

Contents

Introduction

Religious Studies is a fascinating subject. Not only does it involve learning facts about other people's opinions, beliefs and practices, but it also raises some very deep and important questions that have excited thinkers for centuries. What does it mean to be a good person? Is there a God? Why is there evil and suffering in the world? If one religion is true, must other religions, therefore, be false? What is the best method of making moral decisions? Is there a truth 'out there' to be discovered? Is there a reason why the universe exists, and why humanity exists? Questions like these really matter for all of us as human beings; this subject is not just a means to getting a good grade, it will draw your attention to some of the most important aspects of human life.

Following a course in Religious Studies will enrich your thinking and help you to develop your skills in a wide range of ways. It will help you cultivate a questioning disposition, expand your debating skills, and help you write more thoughtfully and persuasively. You will learn to be a better listener and to develop your own opinions using reasoning, so that you can justify your point of view while being open to hearing the views of others. All of these skills will help you in adult life, and are excellent preparation for many degree courses and career choices.

Although you will gain a great deal from Religious Studies, regardless of the exams, you are probably keen to achieve the best grade you can, to reflect your abilities and recognise all you have achieved. This section of this book will give you some guidance about the exams, showing you what to expect and what examiners will be looking for when they read your work.

Features

This book has been written to help you with the Philosophy of Religion component of your course.

The first part of each chapter takes you through the AO1 content you need to cover for each theme in the specification. It introduces you to key issues and thinkers, and explains ideas that may be new

to you. Throughout the AO1 section, you will see activities that will help you develop your knowledge and understanding. For example:

AO1 activity 3
Explain in your own words why an inductive argument can lead to probable conclusions but can never lead to a definite final proof.

The second part of each chapter concentrates on the AO2 skills of analysis and evaluation, inviting you to consider different points of view in relation to the issues and perspectives in the specification. For each discussion question, you are given contrasting points of view with reasons people could give to support them. Scholars that do not appear in the specification are mentioned to help with your evaluation; these scholars will not be named in an exam question. The AO2 activities encourage you to weigh up the different points of view and decide which you find the most convincing. For example:

AO2 activity 1
On balance, how persuasive do you find inductive arguments for the existence of God? Do you think there are some observable phenomena for which the best explanation is God? Give reasons to support your answer.

Some of the vocabulary in this course may be unfamiliar to you, and so key words have been identified and defined. For example:

Key term

inductive argument: an argument based on evidence that comes from observations and experience; an argument constructed on possibly true premises reaching a logically possible and persuasive conclusion

Definitions are closely based on the official Eduqas glossary (https://www.eduqas.co.uk/umbraco/surface/blobstorage/download?nodeId=13812) but have sometimes been condensed or split up into smaller entries, and we've added some additional definitions to help you. All the key words are also collected together at the back of the book in the glossary, so you can refer to them throughout the course.

Many areas of the course have connections within and across themes, and within and across components. These connections are highlighted with the 'Synoptic link' feature, so you can revisit different parts of the course and see how ideas are connected. For example:

Synoptic link

Link to *A Level Religious Studies for Eduqas: Religion and Ethics*, Chapter 3: Deontological ethics: Aquinas' Natural Law. Aquinas' ideas on combining faith and reason can be clearly seen in his ethical theory of Natural Law.

This feature of the book will be particularly useful when you revise.

Quotations from a range of scholars are used in the book to help you clarify your understanding, and to give you opportunities to read scholars' ideas in their own words. If you plan to go on to further study after A Level, it will be useful for you to begin reading passages from scholars' original writings. The quotations in this book stand out from the rest of the text to make them more obvious. For example:

> *Every being which begins has a cause for its beginning; now the world is a being which begins; therefore, it possesses a cause for its beginning.*
>
> Al-Ghazali, *Incoherence of the Philosophers*

It can help you to demonstrate your knowledge and understanding if you sometimes use quotations from scholars, but you do not need to learn every passage by heart as if you were going to be performing it in a play. An occasional well-chosen short phrase or sentence is plenty for a quotation in an essay; there is no need to quote entire paragraphs.

The Exam support sections at the end of each chapter introduce you to some past paper questions, and give you some guidance about how to tackle them in an exam. There are example paragraphs to demonstrate what good responses could look like, sometimes in comparison with example paragraphs that would not score so highly. These are intended to be used as possible models for your own writing, but they are not 'perfect answers' to be learned or copied. Instead, look at them to see how the writer of the paragraph has tailored their response to meet the assessment objectives. The work has been highlighted in different colours to help you see the different skills displayed. There are also other activities in the Exam support section to help you improve your skills, as well as more questions from past papers to help you practise.

Exam support

How is the course structured?

In this course, you will explore three components: A Study of Religion (where you will focus on one of the six major world religions); Philosophy of Religion; Religion and Ethics.

Each component is worth one-third of the total marks. For A Level, you will study four themes for each component, and for AS Level, you will study fewer themes in less detail.

What will the exams be like?

For A Level, you will sit three papers, one for each component. All of the assessment tasks will be essays; there are no multiple-choice questions, short-answer questions, or coursework tasks.

Sections A and B

Each A Level paper will have two parts: Section A and Section B. Section A contains two questions, usually both from the same theme, and you must choose just one of them to answer. Section B will contain three questions taken from anywhere else in the component, and you must choose one of them. You must answer parts (a) and (b) of the same question; you cannot choose to answer part (a) from one question and part (b) from a different question. When you are choosing which questions to tackle, read the question as a whole, and make sure you are confident about tackling both parts before you begin.

The papers are divided into two sections, to make sure you cover all of the course when you are learning and revising. Sometimes, students realise that they have left their revision too late. They think they can cut down the amount of work they need to do by trying to guess what the questions will be, and then only revise thoroughly for those selected topics. This is a very bad idea, because those students may have chosen to ignore the theme that appears in Section A, and then they will not be able to answer either question in that section. By choosing one compulsory theme for Section A, and not letting you know in advance which theme it will be, the question setters make sure that you cover all the course when you learn and revise. Any theme can be chosen for Section A, including a theme that has appeared in recent past papers.

Timing in the exam

Make sure you allow equal time to answer both questions. Some students make the mistake of allowing too much time to answer the question from Section A, and not enough time to answer the questions from Section B; this can mean their Section B answers are rushed, short or even missing.

At A Level you have 2 hours, or 120 minutes, to answer both questions (unless you have extra time). Plan your time carefully, giving yourself enough time to settle, read the questions carefully, and plan your answers to the questions you choose.

Understanding the Assessment Objectives

At A Level, your work is assessed against two different criteria. It is important to understand what examiners are looking for, so that you can present your knowledge and your skills in a way that helps them reward you. During your course, your teacher will use the same criteria to mark your work and give you feedback so that you can see how to improve.

Assessment Objective 1 (AO1) requires you to demonstrate your knowledge and understanding of the material in the course. You need to show that you understand religious and philosophical ideas and teachings. You need to show an understanding of the contributions that different thinkers have made to the issues in the course, as well as the challenges these contributions present and the views of people who disagree with them. In every question in the exam, for every component, part (a) assesses this knowledge and understanding, using 'Explain', 'Examine', 'Compare', 'Apply' and – if you are sitting an AS examination – 'Outline' to tell you what you need to do.

For high marks in AO1, your work needs to demonstrate knowledge and understanding that is relevant to the specific question. Make sure you read the question carefully so that you can address exactly what it is asking; your response needs to be thorough and accurate. Where possible, you should use examples to clarify your response, and you should support the claims you make with evidence.

If appropriate, you should make reference to sacred texts. Sometimes, it can be appropriate to show that there are links between the issue in the question and issues in other areas of the course. You should demonstrate a good knowledge and understanding of a range of scholarly views, and you should aim to use the specialist terms that theologians and philosophers use confidently and accurately in your writing. AO1 is about demonstrating what you know; you do not need to give your own views in responses to part (a) questions.

The marks for part (a) are worth 40% of the question total at A Level.

Assessment Objective 2 (AO2) requires you to analyse and evaluate the different issues and perspectives in the course. You need to show that you understand why there are different opinions about an issue, and develop an opinion of your own that you can justify with reasoned argument. In part (b) responses, you do not need to give lengthy descriptions and explanations; you should concentrate on analysis and evaluation.

Analysis involves unpacking a claim or an argument to explore its structure; you need to consider the chains of reasoning that have been used to justify a view.

Evaluation involves weighing up an argument or a point of view, deciding whether or not it is persuasive, and making a reasoned judgement. You could conclude that an argument is flawed, or effective, or that an issue is significant, for example. You need to develop your own views, and not just describe the opinions of others.

For high marks in AO2, your response needs to address the question asked specifically. You need to show that you understand the issues raised by the question, and focus your answer on those issues, rather than discussing more generally. There may be opportunities in part (b) to show how the issues in the question have connections with other areas of the course. And, as with AO1, you should use specialist language accurately and with confidence where appropriate.

Thinking for yourself is important here. However, avoid simply giving your own view without making any reference to scholarly thinking. Aim to show which side of the debate you prefer, while at the same time making it clear that you have a good understanding of key thinkers and the contribution each has made to the debate. You should use the ideas of different scholars or different schools of thought in your response; but the emphasis should be on *using* them, and not just on *listing* them. You should show how scholar X's thinking is more persuasive than scholar Y's thinking, or how there are flaws in scholar Z's reasoning that make their argument ineffective, rather than simply saying, 'X said this, but Y said that'.

As you answer the question and analyse scholars' views, you should aim to use reasoning and evidence to support the evaluations you make.

Think of approaching AO2 as you would approach attending a meeting. Your role is not the role of a secretary: you are not there simply to record who says something and what they say, while keeping quiet yourself. You are a participant, so you have a voice. Pay attention to the views of scholars, as you would listen to the other people in the meeting. In part (a) of your answer, you are asked to explain, examine, outline, or compare different ideas that others have put forward. However, part (b) is your own turn to speak: refer to what others have said, and then make it clear what your opinion is: 'I agree with A and B because …, I agree with C, but only up to a point because …, I think D and E are wrong because . . .; and, therefore, I conclude with *this* judgement.' Make sure that your judgements are backed up with reasoning, and are not just asserted as though it is obvious that you are right and your opinion does not need explaining.

When you study this course, you may have strong beliefs of your own, either as a religious believer or as someone who thinks religion is wrong; or you may be undecided about many of the questions that the subject raises. Although Religious Studies courses are intended to help you think about and shape, your own beliefs, in an exam it is your reasoning that is awarded not your beliefs. You should focus on telling the examiner how your reasoning leads to your conclusions; you will not gain marks by telling the examiner about your personal religious or non-religious beliefs.

There are lots of ways you can improve your performance in AO1 and AO2:

- Reading is always important. The course is quite detailed, and you may feel you do not have a lot of time for additional reading; but try, if possible, to read more than just one textbook or resource. Reading will enrich your knowledge and help you to feel more confident about the subject matter. If you read good-quality writing, your own written style will improve, as you will become more familiar with the kind of language professional writers and philosophers use to express what they want to say. When possible, read extracts from philosophers in their own words; some are more accessible than others. Reading and note-taking is a valuable skill to practise if you hope to go on to further study after your A Levels.

- Involving yourself in class discussions is very helpful. You will remember ideas more clearly if you have engaged in debates about them. If you strongly agree or disagree with thinkers, you are more likely to remember their names. Discussion will help you develop your own opinions so that you can articulate them clearly; it will help you find ways to challenge the views of those you disagree with; it will help you respond to challenges and defend your own views against criticism. It will also help you to develop useful skills for later life, as you learn to speak with confidence, listen to others, and work through differences of opinion in a civilised and constructive way.

- For AO2, make a habit of thinking about different ideas when they are presented to you in class, rather than simply writing them down. Ask yourself whether you agree with the idea, or whether you think the scholar or school of thought is wrong, and think about why you agree or disagree.

- This book gives you plenty of activities to help you develop your skills in AO1 and AO2.

Command words

Command words are the words in exam questions that tell you want you need to do, such as 'Explain' or 'Evaluate'.

For AO1 – part (a) – different command words are used. These include:

- **Apply:** This command word requires you to show how a principle, theory, or teaching might be used in relation to an issue or a situation; for example, how Utilitarianism might be applied to animal experimentation for medical research. To gain high marks, you must show how the theory works to decide which actions are right or wrong in the specific moral dilemma mentioned in the question.

- **Compare:** This command word requires you to explain the similarities and differences between two things, perhaps two arguments, two scholars' perspectives, or two theories. To gain high marks, you need to avoid simply describing one and then the other; you should concentrate on drawing out ways in which they are similar and different.

- **Explain:** This command word asks you to write a full and detailed account of a topic. The question will tell you what to explain, and you need to pay careful attention to exactly what you are being asked to do. For example, the question could say 'Explain the significance of …', in which case you need to concentrate on giving reasons why the thing is significant, rather than simply describing the thing. You might be asked to explain how a thinker deals with an issue, or why someone criticises a view.

- **Examine:** This command word asks you to give an account of one or more aspects of something fairly complex. In Religion and Ethics, for example, you might be asked to examine a particular aspect of Aquinas' theory of Natural Law such as his use of reason. Or in Philosophy of Religion, you could be asked to examine selected features of Irenaeus' approach to the problem of evil, such as his ideas about growing into the likeness of God. An 'examine' question asks you to go into depth about a narrower topic, while an 'explain' question asks for a broader range of detail.

- **Outline:** AS questions sometimes use the command word 'outline'. For this, you need to identify the key features of the thing you are describing; try to draw a picture of it in words as if you are teaching the examiner about it.

For AO2 – part (b) – the same command word is always used:

- **Evaluate:** The question might be phrased as follows: *'Here is a statement asserting a position.' Evaluate this view.*

Alternatively, it might say: *Evaluate the view that (followed by a point of view).*

You need to weigh up a variety of arguments and ideas, making reference to scholars where appropriate, and making a reasoned judgement about them. You must include a conclusion, showing what you think of the idea you were asked to evaluate.

Structuring your responses

There is no single right way to structure your answers. Eduqas does not have a formulaic essay template that you should follow. As long as your essays meet the assessment objectives, you can structure them in whatever way you think best.

However, some students struggle to know where to start and how to proceed with presenting material or an argument, and so teachers sometimes offer them essay structures to use. (They might have mnemonics to help you remember them, such as PEREL: Point Explain Response Evaluate Link.) These structures can be useful, in the same way that stabilisers can be useful when learning to ride a bicycle; but not everyone will find them helpful, and there will come a time when you find you write more naturally and fluently without them.

For part (a), you do not need an introduction or a conclusion, because you are not making any judgements that require summing up. However, you do need to organise your material so that it follows an orderly structure. It could make sense to present the material in chronological order, showing what early thinkers said and then how later thinkers developed those ideas. If you are explaining a theory or one thinker's ideas, it may not matter which order you choose to present the different facets of the material. Sometimes the question will require you to explain the thinking of two or three different people, or to give two different arguments, and then it would make sense to explore each in turn, rather than going back and forth between them.

For part (b), you must have a conclusion because you are being asked for your judgement, so you need to say what that judgement is. You could begin your response with your own judgement, or put it at the end, or have a series of mini-conclusions throughout your answer.

One structure that can work quite well for part (b) responses is to set up the points of view that you disagree with, say why you think they are wrong, and then present views you prefer and say why you find them stronger. This is one of the ways people present arguments in everyday life. If your friend is asking for your advice about what to wear to a wedding, you might say: 'Not the red dress: the colour is too shouty and you will look as if you want to be the centre of attention. Not the blue dress either: it is too short for a religious ceremony and the bride's mother is wearing exactly the same colour. I think you should wear the green one: the colour suits you and you have a nice jacket that goes with it in case the weather is cool.' For each of the options, you are giving reasons to support your opinion, resulting in a persuasive argument.

Another structure that can work well is an 'ABCD' approach. In each paragraph, you give an **A**rgument. Then you **B**ack it up with reasons. Next you offer a **C**ounter-argument. And, finally, you **D**ecide which view is stronger. This can be a good approach because you are displaying analysis and evaluation in every paragraph, so if you were to run out of time, you have demonstrated all the AO2 skills despite not finishing. You may find other structures that work well for you; there is no need to pick just one and stick to it rigidly.

Making essay plans

Your essays will be more coherent and more thorough if you plan them before you begin writing. If you are writing an essay for homework, you will have the time to make a more detailed essay plan. In an exam, you will have time only for a few brief notes to remind yourself of the key points you want to make.

Your plan functions like a shopping list. It reminds you of the ingredients you need for your essay, so that you avoid missing out something essential. A good shopping list also organises the ingredients, so all the fruit and vegetables are together, and all the dairy items together and so on; so that, in the shop, you do not waste time going back and forth for individual items, but can make an efficient single circuit of the supermarket and save time. Your essay plan should organise your material in a similar way, so that you know what you want to say first, and where you want to end up, and the route you plan to take between the two. With a good plan in place, you will be able to write a thorough, easy-to-follow essay with more confidence.

As you go through the course, practise making plans for the past paper questions in the Exam support sections of each chapter. When you revise, look at past paper questions on the Eduqas website and practise making plans for them.

In the exam, choose your questions carefully, making sure that you can answer both parts of the questions you choose. Once you have chosen your two questions, write all four plans before beginning to write your first essay. This will help you keep calm, as you will begin writing knowing that you have both questions under control; you will not be worrying about the second question while you are trying to concentrate on the first one.

Using band descriptors and mark schemes

If you look at Eduqas' website (www.eduqas.co.uk), you will find past papers and mark schemes to help you with your learning.

Mark schemes contain what is called 'indicative content'. They show you the kinds of things examiners were expecting candidates to write. They are not a checklist. Examiners do not try to match your response against the mark scheme, nor do they take marks away from you if your response does not include some of the indicative content. Instead, the mark schemes are a useful guide to show you the level of detail required for a top-level response. If you are writing a practice essay, it can be useful to look at the mark scheme for some guidance about what to include, but you do not need to follow it exactly. Examiners will credit relevant material in your essay that does not appear in the mark scheme, and they will award you appropriately if you have taken a different approach, or used different thinkers to demonstrate your skills instead of the ones in the mark scheme, provided they are relevant to the question that was asked.

Band descriptors are used to determine the quality of your answer and show the examiners which marks to give you. The examiner decides whether your answer is 'thorough, accurate and relevant', for example, or 'satisfactory' or 'limited', and awards you the appropriate mark. These band descriptors

will help you understand the marks your teacher gives the essays you write during the course, and you can use them to help you improve your work. When your marked essays are returned to you, look at the band descriptors to see what your mark means, and also look at the description in the band above, to see where you need to improve. You may need to make your work more accurate, for example, or make better use of scholarly thought, or be more thorough in your analysis.

Revision

Revision is essential for success in your A Levels. You need to allow plenty of time for it. The February half term before your exams is a good time to start organising your notes and recapping the work you did at the start of the course. You can also do things throughout the course to help you prepare for your revision:

- Make a regular habit of revisiting your notes and reading the material you have covered, rather than leaving all your revision to the end of the course.
- Try making flash cards with key bullet points whenever you finish a unit of study. The process of picking out the key points and making the cards is very useful for embedding the content in your memory and developing your understanding.
- Try setting yourself quick quiz questions as you finish each unit of study. Writing the questions will help you remember the key information, and you could put the questions aside so that you can test yourself when you come to revise.

Remember to revise for AO2 as well as for AO1. When you are revising for AO1, you will be noting and memorising the content you have covered. For AO2, rehearse the arguments you will put forward when you are asked for your view on an issue. Many students concentrate their revision too heavily on AO1 and forget to revise for AO2; but if you were a lawyer defending a client, you would not go into court without an idea of what you were going to say in the client's defence; you would have rehearsed your argument carefully. You can do the same for AO2, reminding yourself of the reasons why you reached your current opinion as you do your revision.

1 Arguments for the existence of God: inductive

The question of the existence of God is one of the most important philosophical questions that there is. However, it is not an easy one to answer. How do people who believe in God know that God exists? Is their belief founded on solid arguments and solid evidence?

Some people believe that the existence of God is not a matter for reasoned argument at all, but a matter for faith. Perhaps the question of God's existence cannot be answered through reason. It is not something that we can work out for ourselves. We cannot collect evidence for or against God's existence in order to come to a reasoned judgement. Perhaps God is not something that can be known with reason, but instead is something to be experienced through faith, supported by revelation from God.

Other people argue, however, that it is part of human nature to want at least some reasons to support religious belief. We need to know that our beliefs are not totally irrational. Even if we cannot prove with any certainty that God either does or does not exist, we need to have reasons to support our theism or atheism.

For many religious believers, the existence of God is obvious. They argue that you only need to look around you to see the work of God in the beauty of nature, in the variety of species, and in the ways that the natural world seems to work so well as a system. Even the very existence of the universe points to the existence of a God who planned and created it. However, for people without belief in God, the existence of God is not obvious at all. Scientific explanations tell us why the natural world works as a system and how the universe first came into being, and there seems to be too much evil, suffering, and chaos in the world for it to be obvious that God exists.

Is the beauty of the natural world best explained by the existence of a loving God?

In this chapter, we will be exploring some examples of arguments for the existence of God that use inductive reasoning. Inductive reasoning involves looking at the evidence and working out what is the best explanation for the things we observe.

- Can the existence of God be demonstrated through finding evidence, using our observation?
- Is the existence of the universe best explained by the existence of God?
- Does the natural world provide evidence for the existence of God?
- How strong are inductive arguments for God's existence?
- How useful are inductive arguments in supporting reliable conclusions?

This section of the chapter will enhance your **knowledge** and **understanding** of the topic and help you develop your AO1 skills.

What is an inductive argument?

An **inductive argument** is an argument that is based on evidence. An argument from induction starts with an observation: we see something happening often, and we assume that it probably always happens. Based on our previous experience, we make inferences and draw conclusions. The more reliable data we have, the more confident we can be about our conclusions.

We use inductive reasoning to make predictions: 'Whenever I've been in the sea in the UK in March, it's been too cold for me. It's March now, so the sea will probably be too cold for me.' We also use it to infer cause and effect: 'I left my phone charger here and now it's missing. My brother has probably taken it again.'

When we use inductive reasoning, we are looking for the most probable explanation to match our observations. An important feature of inductive arguments is that there is always the possibility that we could be wrong. Our conclusions are whatever we think is the most likely explanation, the one that fits best with the information we have available to us, but other explanations are also possible. Perhaps this March the sea will be unusually warm. Perhaps someone else took the phone charger, or I misremembered where I left it.

Examples of the use of inductive reasoning to draw conclusions can be found within the sciences and other academic disciplines. For example, scientists make an observation, then they set up tests with repeat experiments or measurements, and try to work out what is the best explanation for their findings. Their conclusions are always provisional; there is always the possibility that they could be wrong. Some new piece of data could emerge that makes them have to rethink their previous conclusions and find a better explanation, or a new piece of equipment could be invented that helps to get more accurate data. Doctors, mechanics, and other people who fix things use inductive reasoning all the time; they use observation to see that something is wrong, and they use their past experience and the information they have available to work out what the cause might be.

> **Key term**
>
> **inductive argument:** an argument based on evidence that comes from observations and experience; an argument constructed on possibly true premises reaching a logically possible and persuasive conclusion

People in Europe used to think that all swans were white, because all the swans they had ever seen were white. When they went to Australia and saw black swans, they had new information and had to change their previous conclusion.

AO1 activity 1

Here are some examples of inductive reasoning. The first sentence shows an observation, and the second shows the inductive reasoning based on the observation.

- Something has eaten all the pumpkin seedlings in the greenhouse. It was probably mice.
- The fish van was at the market last week and the week before.
  It will probably be there again this week.
- There is a train pass on the pavement. Someone must have dropped it.

Now think of three examples of your own to illustrate inductive reasoning.

Some people argue that inductive arguments can be used to demonstrate the existence of God. There are a number of different inductive arguments for God's existence, including:

1. Cosmological arguments: these arguments take the existence of the universe and conclude that the best explanation for the universe's existence is God.
2. Teleological arguments: these look at order, purpose, and beauty in the natural world and conclude that the best explanation for this must be a supernatural intelligence or 'designer', which is God.
3. Moral arguments: these try to find an explanation for our sense of morality. Why do we feel guilty when we do something wrong, even if nobody saw us? The arguments conclude that our moral sense most probably comes from God.
4. Arguments from religious experience: these try to find the reason why many people claim to have had an experience of God, and conclude that it is probably because God exists.
5. Arguments from miracles: these look at evidence of incidents where something wonderful that cannot be easily explained by science happened, and conclude that they were most probably done by God.

In this chapter, we will be exploring the first two of these inductive arguments: cosmological arguments and teleological arguments, and weighing up whether the conclusions of these arguments are persuasive.

What is *a posteriori* knowledge?

Philosophers often classify different ways of constructing arguments, and one way of classifying them is to make a distinction between **a priori** and **a posteriori** knowledge, a distinction that goes back at least a thousand years.

A priori arguments use knowledge that is independent of experience to draw a conclusion based upon principles of logic. If someone tells you that James is a bachelor then logic tells you that he is unmarried, because 'unmarried' is what 'bachelor' means. We do not need to meet James, or meet lots of examples of bachelors, to draw our conclusion; we can easily work out that James is unmarried from the knowledge that he is a bachelor. 4 + 5 = 9 is another example of reasoning using *a priori* knowledge, as mathematics depends on logic. We do not need to keep experimenting with fours and fives to draw our conclusion. '*A priori*' literally means 'from what is before'.

Key terms

a priori: (Latin) without, or prior to, experience; used of an argument, such as the ontological argument, which is based on acquired knowledge, independent of, or prior to, experience

a posteriori: (Latin) on the basis of experience; *a posteriori* knowledge is based on experience, observation, and empirical evidence

Based on the premises before the conclusion, we can use logic to reach our answer. This is called deductive reasoning.

A posteriori arguments use knowledge that is derived from observation and experience to draw conclusions. Our conclusions are justified by experience, and are open to being revised when new information comes along. It means 'from what comes after'; we use the after-effects of something as the basis for our reasoning. For example, the after-effects of sneezing and a rash might be used to reason that this person has an allergy. Inductive arguments use *a posteriori* reasoning.

Inductive arguments for the existence of God: cosmological

Cosmological arguments try to demonstrate the existence of God by asking the question 'Why is there something rather than nothing?'. They look at the existence of the universe (the cosmos) as something we can observe, and try to work out what must have caused it. The existence of the universe, it is claimed, requires an explanation, and according to cosmological arguments the best explanation is the existence of God.

Cosmological arguments are inductive arguments, because they look at the evidence and try to find the most probable explanation for it. They use *a posteriori* knowledge, because they start with the end result (the existence of the universe) and look back to try to work out what brought it about.

Thomas Aquinas' first Three Ways

Aquinas and Aristotle

Thomas Aquinas was one of the greatest of all philosophers and theologians. He lived in the thirteenth century at the time of the Crusades, when the Christian Church decided to regain control of the Holy Land from Islamic rule by force. This led Aquinas to produce some ground-breaking writing about how Christians should conduct themselves in wartime: his Just War theory is one of his best-known ideas. Aquinas also became very interested in the works of the Greek philosopher Aristotle.

Aristotle lived five hundred years before Aquinas, but his works had been lost to the Christian world. They had, however, been preserved by Arabic scholars. When the Crusades took place and Christian soldiers raided Islamic libraries, Aristotle's writings were rediscovered by European Christians and caused a stir among leaders of the Church. Aristotle was hugely intelligent, had an immense general knowledge, and an insatiable appetite for learning. His curiosity and methodology laid the foundations for science as we know it today. Meteorology, psychology, biology, scientific classification, and many other aspects of science that we take for granted began with Aristotle. Aristotle was the first to be firm in the opinion that the Earth is spherical. He also advocated the scientific method of making observations and conducting repeatable experiments with controlled variables in order to

> **AO1 activity 2**
> Explain in your own words, and using your own examples, what is meant by *a priori* knowledge and *a posteriori* knowledge.

> **AO1 activity 3**
> Explain in your own words why an inductive argument can lead to probable conclusions but can never lead to a definite final proof.

> **Key terms**
>
> **cosmological:** to do with the universe
>
> **cosmological argument:** an argument for the existence of God that claims God's creativity is the best explanation for the existence of the universe

produce theories. Along with many other intelligent people, Aquinas could see the attraction of Aristotelian thought, but there were problems with it.

The Church was worried. Aristotle's common-sense approach to logic and observation, and the range of his work, was seen as a threat to Christianity. Aristotle was offering attractive answers to questions such as 'How did the universe come into existence?' without any reference to the Christian God. Some of Aristotle's conclusions, presented with reasoned explanations, were contrary to the teaching of the Church. Should Church leaders ban Christians from reading Aristotle, in case they turned away from faith and chose science instead?

Aquinas was one of the thinkers at the time who believed that this would be a mistake. He thought it was necessary to show that scientific Aristotelian reason and logic could be compatible with Christian belief. As a Christian monk, he did not want his fellow believers to be put in a position where they felt forced to choose between religious faith and common-sense science. Aquinas wanted to show, in his writings, that faith and reason can work alongside each other. Reason can be used to support faith, and logical arguments can be put forward to show that Christian beliefs are true. Reason comes from God, argued Aquinas, and our abilities to explore the world around us and to ask questions are given by God.

Aquinas wanted to use some of Aristotle's own arguments to demonstrate how they supported the teachings of the Bible and of the Church. In doing so, Aquinas not only helped Christians to develop a more reasoned faith, but also helped science to develop in Europe.

Aquinas and his Five Ways

Aquinas presented 'Five Ways' of showing that God exists because he was convinced that although the existence of God is not self-evident (in other words, it is not blindingly obvious), it can be demonstrated with logical thought based on evidence.

Aquinas wrote about these Five Ways in his book *Summa Theologica*, which was written for Christian believers rather than written with the intention of persuading others to convert. The book, which was never finished, is over 4000 pages long, and only two of these pages are devoted to the arguments for the existence of God. However these, along with the Just War theory, have become some of Aquinas' most famous ideas.

The first three of these Five Ways are cosmological arguments. Each uses observation of the way the universe works to come to the conclusion that the best explanation for it is God.

- **The First Way: motion or change, the Unmoved Mover**

    In his first way of demonstrating the existence of God, Aquinas drew attention to motion and change. When we observe the world around us, we see that everything is in a state of motion or a state of change. Things grow or decay, or get warmer or colder. The days get longer or shorter, the tide goes in and out, the seasons change. Even non-living things change over time: the chair you are sitting in does not look exactly the same as it did when it was new. This was an observation that bothered

Synoptic link

Link to *A Level Religious Studies for Eduqas: Religion and Ethics*, *Chapter 3: Deontological ethics: Aquinas' Natural Law*. Aquinas' ideas on combining faith and reason can be clearly seen in his ethical theory of Natural Law.

Aquinas said that faith combined with reason can give five ways of demonstrating the existence of God.

the ancient Greek philosophers: how can we gain true knowledge of anything when everything is in a constant state of change?

Aquinas was particularly interested in changes of state, which he spoke of in terms of things moving from 'potentiality' to 'actuality'. Things have the potential to become something else, and then the potential is 'actualised' when, for example, ice melts into water or water becomes steam.

Aristotle had observed this constant change too, and Aquinas used some of Aristotle's arguments in his reasoning. Although Aquinas lived a long time before Isaac Newton, he realised, like Newton, that things stay the same unless a force acts upon them to make them change or move. There must be something that moves or changes to make the next thing move or change, and then the next thing after that, and so on. But if everything in motion is dependent for its motion on some other moving thing, where did all this movement and change originally come from?

Aquinas wrote that the whole chain of movement could not be traced back infinitely, with no beginning. There must be, he concluded, a 'first mover' that could initiate the motion and change in everything else, but it would have to be something that was itself unmoved. Aquinas' First Way is often known as 'the Unmoved Mover', and Aquinas argued that this Unmoved Mover must be God. Aquinas wrote:

> *Therefore, whatever is in motion must be put in motion by another. If that by which it is put in motion be itself put in motion, then this also must needs be put in motion by another, and that by another again. But this cannot go on to infinity, because then there would be no first mover, and, consequently, no other mover; saying that subsequent movers move only inasmuch as they are put in motion by the first mover; as the staff moves only because it is put in motion by the hand. Therefore it is necessary to arrive at a first mover; put in motion by no other; and this everyone understands to be God.*
>
> Thomas Aquinas, *Summa Theologica*

- **The Second Way: cause and effect, the Uncaused Causer**

The second way of demonstrating the existence of God is very similar to the first, except that this time, Aquinas started with an observation of cause and effect, rather than motion. Every 'effect', Aquinas said, must have a 'cause'; there must have been some kind of activity that brought it about. (Aquinas refers to this as an '**efficient cause**', using terminology from Aristotle.) Everything we observe is here because something else made it happen. Somebody made it or built it, or it is the result of reproduction or glaciation or the weather, or any number of other reasons; nothing exists without a cause, or an 'agent', to explain how it got here. But, said Aquinas, we cannot trace this chain of cause and effect back infinitely; there cannot be an **infinite regress**. This is because if we tried to trace back the whole chain of cause and effect infinitely and there was never a beginning, then there would have been nothing to start off the whole cause-and-effect process, therefore nothing would exist; and our observation tells us that things do exist.

Key terms

efficient cause: the activity that brings about changes

infinite regress: a sequence that can be traced back and back but never comes to an end

Therefore, there must be some 'first cause', something that does not have a cause itself but is nevertheless capable of producing effects. The Second Way is often known as the 'Uncaused Causer', and Aquinas argued that the Uncaused Causer must be God. Aquinas wrote:

> In the world of sense we find there is an order of efficient causes. There is no case known (neither is it, indeed, possible) in which a thing is found to be the efficient cause of itself; for so it would be prior to itself, which is impossible. Now in efficient causes it is not possible to go on to infinity, because in all efficient causes following in order, the first is the cause of the intermediate cause, and the intermediate is the cause of the ultimate cause, whether the intermediate cause be several, or only one. Now to take away the cause is to take away the effect. Therefore, if there be no first cause among efficient causes, there will be no ultimate, nor any intermediate cause. But if in efficient causes it is possible to go on to infinity, there will be no first efficient cause, neither will there be an ultimate effect, nor any intermediate efficient causes; all of which is plainly false. Therefore it is necessary to admit a first efficient cause, to which everyone gives the name of God.
>
> Thomas Aquinas, *Summa Theologica*

- **The Third Way: argument from contingency and necessity**

Aquinas' Third Way is given several different names, the most common being the 'argument from contingency'.

Aquinas argued that when we use our observation, we find things in nature that come into existence and then stop existing. It is obviously possible that they can exist (because we can observe them), and it is also possible that they might not exist; there was a time when they did not exist, and there will be a time in the future when they no longer exist. These things are **contingent**, in other words they are dependent: their existence depends on other factors. Plants and animals, for example, depend on the Sun, water, reproduction, the climate, a suitable habitat, an absence of disease, and they have a naturally limited life-span. Artificial objects depend on someone having put them together, and they last until they wear out or are destroyed.

Aquinas asks us to suppose that every being is a contingent being. So, for every contingent being, there was a time when it did not exist; therefore, it is impossible that a contingent being could be everlasting. There could have been a time when no things existed at all, and so, at that time, there would have been nothing to bring contingent beings into existence. And this chain of reasoning leads us to conclude that there is nothing in existence now; but, clearly, this is an absurd conclusion because things do exist and we are here observing them.

Therefore, Aquinas argued, not every being is a **contingent being**. There must be something that exists 'of its own necessity'; in other words something that does not depend on anything else for its existence, and this **necessary being** is God.

> **AO1 activity 4**
> Explain how Aquinas' first two Ways are different.

> **Key terms**
>
> **contingent:** dependent on other things or other circumstances
>
> **contingent being:** a being that depends upon something else for its existence; it need not be or could have been different
>
> **necessary being:** a being that is not dependent on something for its existence

Aquinas wrote:

> *The third way is taken from possibility and necessity, and runs thus. We find in nature things that are possible to be and not to be, since they are found to be generated, and to corrupt, and consequently, they are possible to be and not to be. But it is impossible for these always to exist, for that which is possible not to be at some time is not. Therefore, if everything is possible not to be, then at one time there could have been nothing in existence. Now if this were true, even now there would be nothing in existence, because that which does not exist only begins to exist by something already existing. Therefore, if at one time nothing was in existence, it would have been impossible for anything to have begun to exist; and thus even now nothing would be in existence — which is absurd. Therefore, not all beings are merely possible, but there must exist something the existence of which is necessary. But every necessary thing either has its necessity caused by another, or not. Now it is impossible to go on to infinity in necessary things which have their necessity caused by another, as has been already proved in regard to efficient causes. Therefore we cannot but postulate the existence of some being having of itself its own necessity, and not receiving it from another, but rather causing in others their necessity. This all men speak of as God.*
>
> Thomas Aquinas, *Summa Theologica*

AO1 activity 5

a) Explain what is meant by a 'contingent being' and a 'necessary being'.
b) Explain how Aquinas arrived at the conclusion that there must be a necessary being, which is God.

The Kalam cosmological argument

'Kalam' is the Arabic word for mediaeval theology; it literally means 'to argue' or 'to discuss'. The **Kalam cosmological argument** is a version of the cosmological argument that developed in the Muslim world. It has become popular for discussion again in recent years because of a reformulation by William Lane Craig.

William Lane Craig

William Lane Craig, an American philosopher, was born in 1949. He became a Christian in 1965 after a profound religious experience, and went to a theological college in Chicago where he became interested in the cosmological argument. Craig decided to focus on this argument for his PhD, and came to the UK to study under Professor John Hick at the University of Birmingham. While he was studying the argument, Craig became fascinated by its historical roots and the way it had developed in Muslim literature. He also noticed what he thought were striking similarities between the cosmological argument and the discoveries of modern science.

Craig spotted a potential weakness in Aquinas' cosmological argument. Aquinas had asserted that infinite regress was impossible: it was impossible for motion, or cause and effect, or contingency to be part of a chain that went back into infinity without a beginning. But Aquinas had perhaps not

Key terms

Kalam cosmological argument: a form of the cosmological argument from Muslim culture; it concentrates on the idea that the universe must have had a beginning in time, and therefore must have been caused by something outside of time

made a very good case for this impossibility, because there was plenty of debate that continued for centuries about whether the universe was infinite or whether it had a beginning. Using the Kalam argument, Craig set out to provide solid evidence to justify that the universe really cannot be infinite and must have had a beginning, and must therefore have been caused by God.

The Kalam argument's roots in Muslim theology

Craig called his version of the cosmological argument 'the Kalam cosmological argument' because of its basis in mediaeval Islamic thought, and in particular, the thought of Al-Ghazali.

Al-Ghazali was a twelfth-century Muslim thinker from Persia, which is modern-day Iran; he was well-known for his expertise in philosophy, theology, and Islamic law. Al-Ghazali believed that Muslim theology had become too heavily influenced by ancient Greek philosophy, particularly when it came to questions about cause and effect. Al-Ghazali, in his book *Incoherence of the Philosophers*, thought that the ancient Greeks had put too much emphasis on science and not enough on God's agency in the world. He put forward the view that all causes are caused by God, and that nothing happens unless God wills it to happen. When cotton catches fire, he said, it might look as though the fire causes the cotton to burn, but in fact it is God that causes the fire to burn the cotton, and without God's will, the fire would not be able to burn anything.

Al-Ghazali's argument was that the universe must have a beginning, because the idea of a universe with no beginning is absurd. Since nothing begins without a cause, there must be a creator of the universe.

> *Every being which begins has a cause for its beginning; now the world is a being which begins; therefore, it possesses a cause for its beginning.* "
>
> Al-Ghazali, *Incoherence of the Philosophers*

Craig's development of the Kalam cosmological argument

Craig developed the argument by first looking at the idea that everything has a cause for its beginning. He dismissed as absurd the idea that things can just pop up without any cause, saying that nobody sincerely believes that is a possibility. Even if we think that something could appear by magic, it is caused by magic. If we cannot accept that anything could appear without a cause, then the idea of an entire universe appearing without a cause is even more absurd.

He argues that, if the universe *can* appear without a cause, then we need an explanation of why nothing else seems to appear without a cause. Why would only universes appear from nowhere, for no reason, but not ordinary objects around us? The idea makes no sense.

Craig also points out that modern science agrees that nothing exists without a cause. The science of cosmogony looks at the possible ways in which the universe might have begun and what could have caused it. Sometimes critics of the cosmological argument point out that, on a subatomic level, elementary particles in an accelerator can come into being without any apparent cause; but Craig responds to this criticism by saying that in this example, there is a conversion of one type of matter into another, not the bringing into existence of new matter out of nowhere.

Having established that everything has a cause for its beginning, Craig looked at the idea that the universe began to exist at some point, which is more controversial and has been the subject of debate. Did the universe have a beginning, or has it always existed, eternally, going back in time infinitely? This is where the Kalam cosmological argument is distinctive. It looks very closely at the idea of infinite regress, and puts up arguments to reject it. Without the possibility of infinite regress, the universe must have had a beginning, in time, and therefore it must have been caused. The argument says that God is the best explanation as the cause of the universe.

Like Al-Ghazali, Craig makes a distinction between 'potential infinites' and 'actual infinites'. He says that there is not a problem with potential infinites. When people refer to potential infinites, infinity is a kind of ideal limit that is never reached, and a useful idea for understanding mathematics. Infinity is used as if it were a number, but it is actually a shorthand way of saying '… and goes on forever without reaching an end'.

Actual infinites, however, are a different matter. As you can never arrive at the 'infinitieth' number in a series, you can never reach an actual infinity. This distinction between potential and actual infinites is important because it means that, in reality, there cannot be an infinite number of days before this one or we would never have arrived at today, and yet here we are.

Craig's best-known example to show the absurdity of an actual infinity is to ask us to imagine a library containing an infinite number of books. Then he asks us to imagine that there are only two colours of book, some red and some black. He writes:

> *We would probably not balk if we were told that the number of black books and the number of red books is the same. But would we believe someone who told us that the number of red books in the library is the same as the number of red books* plus *the number of black books?*
>
> William Lane Craig, *The Kalam Cosmological Argument*

Craig then goes on to ask us to imagine that the books come in three different colours, or four, or five, and asks if we can really believe that the total of all the books together is the same as the total of books of just one of those colours. If there were an infinite number of colours, there would not just be one book of each colour but an infinite number of books of each colour, and each collection of a single colour would number the same as the whole library containing all the books of all the colours. If people borrowed or returned books, the number of books in the library would never change. Clearly, Craig argues, this is absurd; an actual infinity is not possible.

If actual infinity is impossible, Craig argues, then the universe cannot actually be infinite. It must have a beginning: and as everything that begins has a cause, the universe must also have a cause. The most likely cause for the beginning of the universe, he concludes, is God.

Craig argues that the cause of the universe is a personal being, on the grounds that the creation of the universe must have involved choice:

> If the universe began to exist, and the universe is caused, then the cause of the universe must be a personal being who freely chooses to create the world.
>
> William Lane Craig, *The Kalam Cosmological Argument*

It is important for Craig's argument that the universe is created by a personal being rather than, for example, a physical force. He argues that physical forces and other laws of nature could not have created the universe because before the universe existed, there were no physical forces. There is no such time as 'before the universe was created', because time began when the universe began; therefore a mindless force of nature could not have acted to cause the universe to come into being.

The universe must have been created, he argues, by something with decision-making powers that does not exist only within time, but transcends time. It must have been a being that is not constrained by 'before' and 'after', a being that creates and controls time. Craig concludes that the universe must have been created by a transcendent, omnipotent, and intelligent being, which is God.

Leibniz and the principle of sufficient reason

Gottfried Leibniz lived in the seventeenth and eighteenth centuries, and was one of the mathematicians who developed calculus. He offered an alternative form of the cosmological argument, in which he tried to avoid the problems raised by the suggestion of an infinite regression. Leibniz argued that even if the universe has always existed, this still does not give us an explanation of *why* it exists. According to Leibniz, everything has to have a 'sufficient reason', or a good enough reason, to give a satisfactory explanation. The principle of sufficient reason states that there must be reasons to explain facts. There must be an explanation, even if we do not yet know what it is, or even if it is beyond human comprehension.

Craig explains his Kalam cosmological argument by asking us to imagine a library containing an infinite number of books.

AO1 activity 6

Look up the puzzle of Achilles and the tortoise, one of the paradoxes of the Greek philosopher Zeno. What would happen, in real life, if Achilles raced the tortoise?

AO1 activity 7

Explain in your own words why Craig thought that the universe must have been created by a personal being, rather than by some kind of physical force of nature.

Inductive arguments for the existence of God: teleological

Teleological arguments attempt to demonstrate the existence of God from the evidence of order and purpose in the world around us. According to teleological arguments, when we look at the world we see examples of order, beauty, purpose, and complexity, and these are things that cannot just arrive as the result of chance; therefore there must be some being, outside the universe, that designed the world to be this way.

The word **teleological** means to do with end goals or outcomes. *'Telos'* literally means 'tail' in Greek, and the word is used to refer to ends, or purposes, or outcomes. Teleological arguments for the existence of God look at the outcome – order and purpose in the natural world – and use inductive reasoning to reach the conclusion that the best explanation for the outcome is God.

Teleological arguments are often powerful because they are based on the commonly-shared experience of the awe and wonder that we often feel when we observe the natural world, for example when we look at the night sky, or when we notice small details on flowers or seashells, or watch a TV program about spectacular animals.

The eighteenth-century German philosopher Immanuel Kant wrote:

> *This proof always deserves to be mentioned with respect. It is the oldest, the clearest, and the most accordant with the common reason of mankind.* 99
>
> Immanuel Kant, *Critique of Pure Reason*

Although Kant respected teleological arguments for God's existence, he did not think they actually worked.

Thomas Aquinas' Fifth Way

The last of Thomas Aquinas' Five Ways takes up a version of the design argument for the existence of God. In the Fifth Way, Aquinas said that nature seems to have an order and a purpose to it. He suggested that nothing inanimate is purposeful without the aid of a 'guiding hand'. What Aquinas means here is that no non-living thing can have its own purpose. A river cannot decide to flow to the sea because a river has no mind, and yet it does flow to the sea. The Sun cannot decide to rise in the morning and make each day the right length, and yet it does rise and set with regularity.

Aquinas used the example of an archer shooting an arrow at a target. If we see an arrow flying towards a target, we know that someone must have aimed and fired it with the intention that it should go towards the target. In the same way, when we look at the world around us and the purposiveness of inanimate objects, we can conclude that the guiding hand of God must be behind it. Therefore, everything in nature which is moving but has no intelligence must be directed to its goal by God.

AO1 activity 8

Collect some pictures that show order, purpose, beauty, and/or complexity in the natural world; for example of nautilus seashells or ferns.

Key term

teleological: from the Greek word *telos*; to do with end goals or outcomes

AO1 activity 9

Read Psalm 104 in the Bible. Make a list of some of the things the writer of the Psalm attributes to God. For example, they say that it is God that makes the grass grow.

> *The fifth way is taken from the governance of the world. We see that things which lack knowledge, such as natural bodies, act for an end, and this is evident from their acting always, or nearly always, in the same way, so as to obtain the best result. Hence it is plain that they achieve their end, not fortuitously, but designedly.*
>
> *Now whatever lacks knowledge cannot move towards an end, unless it be directed by some being endowed with knowledge and intelligence; as the arrow is directed by the archer. Therefore, some intelligent being exists by whom all natural things are directed to their end; and this being we call God.*
>
> Thomas Aquinas, *Summa Theologica*

In this argument, Aquinas presents two strands of reasoning. Firstly, he says we notice that there is a regularity in the way the world operates. Things that 'lack knowledge' or, in other words, things that are incapable of decision-making (such as tides and stars and rivers and seasons) act with a regularity that we can predict. We can observe the different phases of the Moon and we know what will come next. These things follow patterns, and Aquinas says this is 'not fortuitously, but designedly', meaning that it is not a result of a chance accident, but because they were designed that way. When Aquinas refers to 'the governance of the world', he means that the world is being governed, or supervised, by an authority.

Secondly, Aquinas says we notice that objects with no minds of their own seem to act with a purpose. They have an 'end' or a goal, are moving in order to achieve that goal, and yet cannot have made up their own minds to act in the way they do because they have no minds. Aquinas concludes that the best explanation for regularity and purpose in inanimate objects is God.

William Paley's watchmaker analogy

William Paley was an English clergyman, an excellent mathematician, a keen campaigner against the slave trade, and the author of one of the best-known teleological arguments for the existence of God. He lived at an exciting time for science, when rapid progress was being made in areas such as botany and zoology. Physicists, following Isaac Newton, were discovering the rules that determine the forces of the natural world, including gravity and motion. The invention of the microscope allowed people to observe the structure of cells that were invisible to the naked eye. For many Christian believers, the more people learned about the world around them, the more plainly they could see that it was all the work of an intelligent creator.

In his book *Natural Theology* written in 1802, Paley put forward his version of the design argument, using an analogy. He asks us to imagine someone walking across a heath, when they discover a watch lying on the ground. The person who discovers the watch notices how well it is put together in order to tell the time and how complex its mechanism is, and concludes that someone must have designed and made the watch. It could not have simply arrived there on the heath without a designer and creator. We do not need to have seen watches being made to realise that this watch had a maker, and the watch does not have to be in perfect working order for us to draw our conclusions.

> **AO1 activity 10**
>
> Explain in your own words what Aquinas meant to demonstrate when he used the example of an arrow moving towards a target.

Paley said that there are similarities between a watch and the natural world. When we look at the movement of the planets, we can see that they work in an orderly manner, just like the workings of a watch. When we look at something like the human body, we cannot help noticing how well it all works together, with different organs performing different functions as if they were all parts of a complex machine. Paley noticed the properties that seeds and animal eggs have to enable reproduction, and the ways in which muscles work to enable joints to move. He compared human and animal skin to clothing, asking us to look closely at the structure of a feather and the way that fur functions to retain heat.

Paley was particularly interested in the function of the eye, comparing it with a telescope as well as with a watch. The eye is made up of complex parts: the iris that moves to regulate the light coming in through the pupil, the retina with cells that receive images, the lens that changes shape to enable us to see near and far objects with clarity, and the optic nerve that sends images to the brain for interpretation. All of these different parts have a function to perform, and work together to form a highly specialised organ that enables us to see.

When we look at the complexity of the natural world and the sophistication of its different systems, we can see that it is even more impressive than a watch.

> *the contrivances of nature surpass the contrivances of art, in the complexity, subtlety, and curiosity of the mechanism.*
>
> William Paley, *Natural Theology*

The analogy between the world and a watch was not Paley's own invention, as other thinkers such as David Hume referred to it before Paley wrote his book; it was a popular way of understanding things. Ever since Isaac Newton, people had been impressed by the way that the universe seemed to be governed by natural laws. Physics was uncovering laws of gravity, motion and thermodynamics, and (it seemed) was uncovering the ways in which the universe worked like a giant machine, or like the cogs in a watch.

Paley came to the conclusion that the world contains clear evidence of design and 'contrivance' (indicating that things had deliberately been put together in a certain way, for a purpose); and in order for there to be design, there must be a designer, which is God. Paley went on to argue that we have evidence not only of God's existence, but also of God's goodness, because the designs in nature are beneficial. Even pain is beneficial, Paley pointed out. When we look at the care that must have been taken in the design of tiny things, such as insects, and the way in which each one is carefully made, we can conclude that God is caring. The Designer of the insect has millions of insects to design, but does not slack off because of the scale of the task. The world contains a huge variety of creatures, but God is not distracted from the one being designed just because there are so many others to design. We have evidence of God's attention to detail, argued Paley, and therefore we can have confidence that God will care for each one of us.

> *The hinges in the wings of an earwig, and the joints of its antennae, are as highly wrought, as if the Creator had nothing else to finish. We see no signs of diminution of care by multiplicity of objects, or of distraction of thought by variety. We have no reason to fear, therefore, our being forgotten, or overlooked, or neglected.*
>
> William Paley, *Natural Theology*

AO1 activity 11
Explain how, in Paley's view, the human eye is like a machine.

Design qua *purpose and design* qua *regularity*

Paley's teleological argument has two strands, which are expressed as 'design *qua* purpose' and 'design *qua* regularity':

- Design *qua* purpose: the argument that everything in the universe has been designed to fulfil a purpose; for example earthworms aerate the soil, bees pollinate flowers, and the pupil in the eye widens and narrows to respond to light levels.
- Design *qua* regularity: the argument that the universe and everything in it works with an orderly regularity, following patterns.

F.R. Tennant's anthropic and aesthetic arguments

Frederick Robert Tennant (1866–1957) was a scientist and theologian who lived at a time when Darwin's theory of evolution through natural selection was new, exciting, and challenging for Christian faith. Charles Darwin's work put forward the view that animals and plants evolved gradually through a process of natural selection. Living things only work as well as they do because the ones that failed to work died out. It might look as though the world is full of marvellous design but, according to Darwin's theory, this apparent design is simply the result of chance. The fittest survived, so it is hardly surprising that when we look at nature we see animals and plants that are fit for their environments.

Thomas Huxley, Darwin's friend and colleague, gave lectures presenting the substantial scientific evidence supporting Darwin's theory of evolution. Tennant went to hear Huxley, and was both impressed and convinced. Tennant could see that the design argument for the existence of God needed a new direction and a new emphasis, because the idea that God was the best explanation for the complexity of the natural world was seriously threatened. Science might seem to provide a better explanation, but Tennant thought that evolution could be used to support the design argument, rather than undermine it.

Tennant thought that evolution is entirely consistent with design arguments because of the way in which evolution itself seems to have a purpose. In the evolutionary process, creatures do not just randomly evolve this way and that, according to Tennant. Progress is being made all the time, with the development of life forms that are ever more complex, ever more intelligent, and have an increasing amount of moral awareness. In Tennant's view, as he explains in his book *Philosophical Theology*, evolution has a purpose. As evolution is a process that does not have a mind of its own to have any goals or purposes, it must be guided by God.

> *The multitude of interwoven adaptations by which the world is constituted a theatre of life, intelligence, and morality, cannot reasonably be regarded as an outcome of mechanism, or of blind formative power, or aught but purposive intelligence.*
>
> F.R. Tennant, *Philosophical Theology*

For Tennant therefore, evidence supporting the theory of evolution was also further evidence for the existence of God. Tennant believed that if something is moving towards some kind of a goal, there must be a 'guiding hand' behind it, just as Aquinas had argued in his Fifth Way. Tennant saw evolution as movement towards an end goal, and therefore believed it to be evidence of the governance of God.

Tennant's teleological argument put forward two strands of thought: an anthropic argument and an aesthetic argument.

Tennant's anthropic argument

Tennant was the first philosopher to use the expression '**anthropic principle**'. '*Anthropos*' is a Greek word meaning 'man' or 'humanity', and Tennant's argument was that the world has been designed in such a way that it is perfect for human life.

If the laws of gravity were very slightly different, or the balance of gases in the atmosphere were very slightly different, then human life (or any other kind of life) would not be able to flourish. Tennant looked at a range of scientific evidence to illustrate his argument. The chances of everything on Earth being so perfectly fine-tuned for human existence are against all the odds, and yet everything is in place so that we can live in the world and flourish. Tennant thought that it was too unlikely that this fine-tuning happened on its own. It is not just 'as though' the Earth had been prepared in order for life to flourish. A much better explanation is that the world really has been prepared for human life by God.

Tennant also drew attention to the way in which the functioning of the universe is available to human understanding. People have been endowed with intelligence, and some are gifted in the natural sciences so that they can engage with the mechanisms of the universe and work out the laws that govern it for human benefit. The fact that we can understand gravity and thermodynamics, for example, leads us to be able to invent flying machines. In Tennant's view, this availability of the universe to human understanding was further evidence to support the anthropic principle. God had clearly designed the world for our benefit.

> **Key term**
>
> **anthropic principle:** the principle that everything in the universe has been designed to allow human existence to flourish

Tennant's aesthetic argument

Tennant also presented an **aesthetic** argument for the existence of God. This inductive argument considers the beauty of the world and the human ability to appreciate it, and looks for an explanation for it.

Tennant argued that beauty is not a necessary part of the evolutionary process, and is not necessary for our survival. It cannot be explained away by science; it is what Tennant called 'a biologically superfluous accompaniment of the cosmic process'. The natural world is full of beauty on a scale that people can never imitate, argued Tennant. Even though human artists and designers can make beautiful things, their very best work is never as good as the beauty that appears everywhere in the natural world.

Beauty does not perform a utilitarian function within the evolutionary process, therefore there is no reason for there to be so much of it in the world, unless it is put there by God for the purposes of human enjoyment, and for God to enjoy during and after the creative process.

Tennant's arguments lead him not only to conclude that God exists, but also to conclude that God's benevolent and caring nature is revealed in the design of the world. God wants us to flourish, and wants us to enjoy life.

> **Key term**
>
> **aesthetic:** relating to beauty

AO1 activity 12

a) Explain Tennant's anthropic argument in your own words.
b) Explain Tennant's aesthetic argument in your own words.
c) Explain why Tennant thought that teleological arguments still had strength, even when he believed that Darwin was right about evolution through natural selection.

Challenges to inductive arguments

David Hume's challenges to inductive arguments

David Hume was an eighteenth-century Scottish philosopher who had a great influence on Western philosophy. He presented challenges to cosmological and teleological arguments, and also to inductive arguments as a whole.

The problem of induction

The 'problem of induction', as it is known, was given its best-known formulation by Hume. The problem, Hume pointed out, is that when we use inductive reasoning, we make a big assumption. We assume that the future will resemble the past. However, Hume said, we have no good reason to make this assumption. Just because something has always happened up until now is no guarantee that it will continue to happen.

We assume that there is a connection between different things because we have always seen them connected in the past. Heat makes water boil, gravity makes objects fall to the ground, night follows day. We think we know such things for certain, but Hume argued that we just assume them to be true because that has been our experience up until now. We have no way of knowing for certain that the same laws of nature will continue in the same way in the future.

Bertrand Russell, the twentieth-century mathematician and philosopher, summed up the problem of induction with a tragic little story. The turkey at a turkey farm is fed by the farmer every morning at 9:00am. Every day the farmer comes to feed the turkey, whatever the day of the week and whatever the weather. The turkey eventually feels comfortably certain in its conclusion that the farmer will always come to feed it; until it is proved wrong, on Christmas Eve.

The problem of induction is important for arguments for the existence of God because, like all other inductive arguments, they make the assumption that the future will resemble the past. As far as we know, nothing we have observed exists without a cause … yet. Complex design always means that someone intelligent must have designed it, because that is how the complex designs we have experienced have always originated … so far.

Hume recognised that we cannot go through life wondering whether everything we assume to be true will continue. We do not doubt that gravity will continue as normal, that the world outside the room will look the same when we go out again, that fire will continue to burn, and that summer will follow spring. However, we have no really solid, logical justification for our certainty.

Hume's criticisms of cosmological and teleological arguments

In his book *Dialogues Concerning Natural Religion* published in 1779 after Hume's death, Hume put forward a series of criticisms of inductive arguments for the existence of God. This book came out before Paley's *Natural Theology*, and it is likely that Paley had read Hume's arguments but did not think them a serious challenge.

Dialogues Concerning Natural Religion is written as a dialogue in which three men, called Demea, Philo, and Cleanthes, debate the existence of God. Demea and Cleanthes put forward versions of teleological and cosmological arguments, along with other arguments too, and Philo points out some of the problems with their reasoning. Philo's views are the closest to Hume's own.

Hume's criticisms of the cosmological argument include:

1. The cosmological argument makes the assumption that every effect must have a cause. If we observe the universe, the argument says, then we must realise that it has been caused by something else. But Hume's view, using the problem of induction, was that cause and effect is uncertain. We cannot be sure that A causes B just because whenever we have seen A in the past, B follows. Our empirical observation, in other words using our five senses, can tell us what is happening, but it cannot

> **AO1 activity 13**
> Summarise the problem of induction in your own words.

tell us what causes the things that we observe. Cause and effect is an assumption not a certainty, and the whole cosmological argument is based on the shaky assumption that the universe must have a cause.

2. Hume challenged the cosmological argument that the universe must have a cause. Even if everything in the universe has a cause, it does not follow that the universe *as a whole* must also have a cause. Bertrand Russell made a similar point in the twentieth century, illustrating that just because every human being has a mother, this does not mean that the human species as a whole has a mother. It is overstepping the rules of logic to move from individual causes of individual things, to the view that the totality has a cause. This kind of mistake is known as a 'fallacy of composition'. Something that is true of one part is not necessarily true of the whole. Other examples of fallacies of composition include: 'If you sit in the front row of the class, you will get more attention from the teacher. Therefore, everyone in the class should sit in the front row and then they will all get more attention from the teacher', or 'Every country in the world has a capital city. Therefore, the world as a whole has a capital city'.

AO1 activity 14

a) Explain how Hume used the problem of induction to challenge cosmological arguments.

b) Explain how Hume showed that inductive arguments make the logical error of using a fallacy of composition.

Hume's criticisms of the teleological argument include:

1. Hume said that the analogy between a watch and the world is a weak analogy. It is not obvious to everyone that the world is like a watch, regularly formed and fit for a purpose. We can see purpose and order in a watch, but these characteristics are not nearly so obvious in the world. We only make watches because there is nothing natural that is like a watch. We would only stop on a heath to pick up a watch because we know it could not have arrived there naturally, because such design is not seen in nature.

    There is no case, thought Hume, for saying that the world is very much like a human-designed machine because the similarities are not obvious. Hume argued that it could just as easily be said that the world is like an enormous crustacean, or like a floating vegetable.

2. Hume said that order in the world does not necessarily mean that someone must have had a design idea, and then made the world to that design. We do not know with certainty that all order comes about because of an intelligent idea. Therefore, if we can see order in the world, this does not entitle us to leap to the conclusion that there must be a designer which is God. Also, in our experience, intelligent thought does not, on its own, bring material things into existence. We therefore

Hume said that the analogy between the world and a watch is a weak analogy.

have no reason to assume that the mind of God could produce a whole universe out of nowhere.

3. We do not know if this world is particularly well-ordered. We have no other worlds to compare it with to see if it is orderly or not. Perhaps there are other worlds much more orderly than this one, which would lead us to conclude that there is very little order in our world. In other aspects of our experience, we see the same thing occurring often so it is reasonable to make an assumption (for example, smoke usually indicates a fire and to it is reasonable to think there must be a fire when we see smoke). But we have only seen one universe, so we cannot use the same reasoning because we have only one example.

4. If we do have order, said Hume, then this might only be because order is a necessary part of the world's existence. If everything were chaotic then the world would soon cease to exist; any world will look designed, but this could be only by chance.

5. Even if the world is designed, this does not entitle us to conclude that God must have designed it. In order to reach this conclusion, we would have to be able to show that order in the world could not come about by any other means than God's design. (Hume was writing a long time before Charles Darwin published his theory of evolution by natural selection. Darwin's theories appear to support what Hume was saying: apparent design could have come about by chance or through natural processes, and God is not the only possible explanation.)

6. Hume said that even if we do decide that the best explanation for the world is a creator, there is no reason to imagine that this creator must be the God of Christianity. Our finite, imperfect world gives no justification for assuming it must have been made by an infinite, perfect God. Theistic claims about the nature of God are not supported by teleological arguments. Also, we have no reason to assume that even if God did make the world, that God is still around. God might have made the world and then gone away.

7. Hume uses the example of a pair of old-fashioned kitchen scales, the kind that has weights on one side to balance whatever it is you want to weigh. He said that trying to work out what caused the universe or the apparent design of the world is like trying to work out what is on a pair of scales if one side is hidden from us. We can see that whatever is hidden is heavier than the thing we can see, but we do not know if it is only just heavier or many times heavier, or even infinitely heavier. In the same way, when we look at the world, we can see only the effect. We have no way of being able to work out what the cause is because it is hidden from us. We do not know whether the cause is God. And, if it is God, we do not know whether God is clever or loving or good.

8. Hume goes on to say that when we see a ship, we think how magnificent it is, and how ingenious the builder must have been. But if we go into a ship yard and watch the ship builders at work, we see a 'stupid mechanic' who has copied the work of others and taken a long time to learn how to do the job, making a lot of mistakes along the way. How do we know, asked Hume, that the world might not have been made in a

AO1 activity 15

Explain in your own words Hume's reasons for saying that we cannot look at the world and conclude it must have been made by an infinitely wise and loving God.

similar way? Perhaps it was made by some kind of apprentice god, who had tried and failed many times before. Perhaps it was made by a team or a committee of gods, or even by demons.

Hume's criticisms can be applied to all kinds of inductive arguments for the existence of God. He is arguing that it is too much of a stretch to jump from our observations of the world around us to the conclusion that the universe must have been caused by God.

Scientific challenges to cosmological arguments

In addition to Hume's criticisms, other challenges have also been presented to cosmological arguments, from scientists. The Big Bang theory presents a challenge to cosmological arguments because it offers a different account of the origin of the universe, based entirely on science and without any reference to God.

The Big Bang theory

The Big Bang theory was developed as a result of the observation that other galaxies are apparently moving away from our galaxy and from each other, at great speed. The universe is expanding, with stars and planets getting further and further apart, in the way that dots drawn on a deflated balloon will get further apart when the balloon is blown up. Scientists realised that they could use this observation to help them understand how the universe began if they imagined the process in reverse. They imagined the universe getting closer and closer together, instead of expanding, and they concluded that there must have been a time when all matter was very tightly packed into an unimaginably hot zone of infinite density called the 'singularity'. Using Einstein's theory of relativity, it seemed that about 14 billion years ago, there was a massive inflation of energy and heat, and matter was thrown out in all directions, in what is known as the Big Bang.

Before the Big Bang, there was nothing: no space and no time. The matter did not fly out into an empty space, because space and time were caused at the moment of the Big Bang. Space and time began as the universe began, with space getting bigger and bigger as the universe expanded.

Scientists are not sure why the Big Bang happened, or why the singularity was there. Why did matter go from being packed tightly in the singularity to flying out and creating the universe as it went? Some people see this as a nonsensical question, because it is asking what happened just before the Big Bang, when there could have been no 'before' because there was no time. Some scientists believe that the Big Bang just happened, without a cause, and others are drawn to looking for a reason to explain it.

There is quite strong **empirical** evidence to support the Big Bang theory, from astronomers and physicists, most of whom agree that there was some kind of beginning to the universe. For example, the hypothesis that matter was extremely hot in the beginning is supported by the discovery of cosmic background radiation.

> **Key term**
>
> **empirical:** based on, and verifiable, using our five senses; empirical knowledge comes from things that can be experienced or observed

For some, the Big Bang theory, supported as it is by evidence, presents a plausible explanation for the beginning of the universe, and removes the need to add God as a part of the explanation. For others, the theory still leaves questions, and they still find God to be the most likely answer to those questions.

Scientific challenges to teleological arguments

Science also presents challenges to teleological arguments, by offering an alternative explanation of why animals and plants seem to be so well suited to the environments in which they live.

Darwin's theory of evolution by natural selection

The work of Charles Darwin is considered by many to present design arguments with their greatest challenge. For people like Paley, the complex features of different plants and animals provided clear evidence of a divine designer, carefully fashioning every creature so that it can survive and flourish in its environment. But Darwin's work challenged this view, offering evidence that these different features developed gradually, and that there are plenty of creatures that did not survive and became extinct because they lacked the features that could have helped them survive.

Ideas about evolution had been brewing among scientists before Darwin published his famous book *On the Origin of Species* in 1859, and some had published books about evolution already, including one anonymous work that caused a great deal of excitement and gossip about who the author might be. Darwin's book, however, was the one that caused the most excitement because, unlike his predecessors, he produced solid evidence to back up his theory. Darwin's predecessors had also made sure to point out that God was in charge of evolutionary processes, but Darwin did not feel able to say this with any confidence.

Charles Darwin's work was written as a result of his voyages on a ship called *The Beagle*. He had been invited to join a five-year expedition to South America, during which the crew studied the rocks, plants, and animals they found. What caught Darwin's imagination was the similarities and differences between the characteristics of different species that lived in slightly different environments, and the ways in which these characteristics related to fossil evidence. He collected all kinds of data, including specimens and detailed drawings, and eventually presented his theory of evolution. This was developed and refined by scientists who came after him, and is widely accepted today as the best explanation for the variety of species and their suitability to their habitats.

According to the theory of evolution through **natural selection**, life first began in a very simple form. When a species reproduced, the offspring were not all the same; they had slight variations. Those that survived the longest, and therefore had the opportunity to reproduce the most, were those with the strongest characteristics such as sharper vision or greater speed or better camouflage from predators. Those with the weakest characteristics did not live so long, and

AO1 activity 16
Find out more about the latest developments in scientific theories about the origins of the universe. Explain how these might be seen as a challenge to traditional cosmological arguments for the existence of God.

Key term

natural selection: the process by which evolution is said to take place, through the survival of the fittest who pass on their genes to the next generation

did not get to reproduce as much, and so eventually died out. The remaining stronger ones were then in competition with each other, and those with strongest characteristics outlived and reproduced more than those with the weaker characteristics, and so the process continued. Over many generations, different species evolved and continue to evolve, with greater and greater degrees of complexity. As scientists gained a better understanding of geology and fossils, and of genetics, Darwin's theory gained more and more support.

Darwin did not attack design arguments explicitly. He was worried about the effects that his findings would have on Christian belief, because they contrasted sharply with Biblical creation stories and with traditional Christian views about God as creator. Darwin recognised that he had provided a different explanation for order, purpose and complexity in the natural world, and he knew that many people would see it as more plausible than the idea that the best explanation is God.

Challenges to Tennant's teleological arguments

Although Tennant tried to present a version of the design argument that took into account Darwin's theory of evolution, his argument has not been without criticism.

Tennant's anthropic argument has been challenged:

- Some people think that the anthropic principle has no meaning at all, and just states the obvious. We are here because the universe is suitable for us to be here, not the other way around; the universe does not exist for us, it just so happens that it sustains human life, and therefore there is human life. Douglas Adams, author of the 1978 comedy *The Hitchhiker's Guide to the Galaxy*, made fun of the anthropic principle in 2002. He wrote:

> This is rather as if you imagine a puddle waking up one morning and thinking, 'This is an interesting world I find myself in – an interesting hole I find myself in – fits me rather neatly, doesn't it? In fact it fits me staggeringly well, it must have been made to have me in it!'
>
> Douglas Adams, *The Salmon of Doubt*

- Some thinkers argue that there could be an infinite number of universes in existence. If this is the case, then it is not amazing that everything fell into place on Earth for human life, as there would also be an infinity of universes where this did not happen. Given infinite possibilities, the existence of a planet with everything balanced so that human life can flourish is to be expected, along with every other kind of universe, and is not amazing at all.
- It can be argued that it does not make sense to say the universe is structured in the way it is in order that human life can exist. The argument gives humanity a special status which is unwarranted. If the universe were structured differently, cockroaches would not be here either, and so the argument could equally well be made that the universe is designed for the existence of cockroaches, or even that the universe is designed for the existence of cancer or coronaviruses.

Darwin's studies led him to produce his theory of evolution through natural selection.

AO1 activity 17

Explain why Darwin's theory of evolution through natural selection is seen as a challenge to design arguments for the existence of God.

Douglas Adams made fun of arguments that employ the anthropic principle, using the example of a puddle surprised to find that it fits exactly into the hole in the ground that it finds itself in.

- It might be highly unlikely that the structure of the universe allows for our existence, but everything that ever happens is highly unlikely, when considered alongside all the other possibilities of what might have happened instead. Think of all the odds against the building you are in having been built. The architect could so easily have never been born or could have chosen a different career, the land could easily have been used for something else, and there were probably lots of other designs for the building that could have been chosen instead. When you throw dice, whatever score you get, the odds are against it. For many people, the argument that 'the universe is just right, against such high odds' does not prove the existence of God, but simply demonstrates how chance works.

Tennant's aesthetic argument has also been challenged:

- There are many people who argue that beauty is a matter of taste and opinion, and not an objective quality that we all agree is found in the natural world. Different cultures have different ideas about beautiful faces or décor or music. Tennant writes about beauty in the world as if it is an objective fact, but others disagree and think that beauty is something subjective, an interpretation given by the human mind rather than something inherent in the world.
- The natural world might contain things that are beautiful, but it also contains things that are, in most people's opinions, ugly. Charles Darwin was particularly revolted by a species of insect that exists by laying its eggs inside the living body of another species; the eggs hatch, eat their way out, and destroy their host. Although most people can see beauty in the world, there are also ugly plants and creatures, bad smells, unpleasant noises and tastes, diseases, decay, and cruelty. If we need an explanation for why the world is so beautiful, perhaps we also need an explanation for why the world is so ugly.

Challenges from the problem of evil

One of the biggest challenges to design arguments for the existence of God is the problem of evil. Paley wrote about how we can look at the care God has taken in the design of the world, and conclude that God must care for each one of us and will not allow us to be forgotten or overlooked. But when we look at the world around us, we see people who do seem to have been forgotten or overlooked by God. The world is full of illnesses that can cause horrible suffering and sometimes early death. The structure of the world does not seem to be entirely fit for human flourishing; there are volcanos, earthquakes, tsunamis, hurricanes, droughts, and floods that take life or make it very difficult for people to grow crops or raise livestock.

Hume, and many others before and since, have noted that if God designed the world, then there is evidence to suggest that God is cruel to have made a world in which bad things happen to good people, where it is difficult to survive, and where there is a lot more pain and suffering than is necessary.

Synoptic link

Link to *Chapter 3: Challenges to religious belief: the problem of evil and suffering*. Look at the question of whether the existence of a loving God is compatible with the evil and suffering in the world.

This section of the chapter will enhance your ability to analyse and evaluate the topic and help you develop your AO2 skills. For each question, think about the different positions you might take, and decide which you find most persuasive and why. It is not enough to memorise a list of 'for and against' points; you need to develop an argument.

To what extent are inductive arguments for God's existence persuasive?

This question invites discussion of the use of inductive reasoning to demonstrate God's existence (in other words, whether the things we observe can be best explained by concluding that God exists).

The view that inductive arguments for God's existence are persuasive

Inductive arguments for the existence of God are very popular, and could be considered persuasive.

Many of them, such as the cosmological and teleological arguments, are based on solid evidence that we can see for ourselves. Most people have been struck by the infinite scale of the universe or by the beauty of the natural world at some time in their lives, or how different life forms are suited to their environments in ways that seem ingenious. We like to have firm evidence to justify our beliefs that we can produce if people challenge us, and that we can turn to if we start to doubt. The existence of God could seem both the simplest and the best explanation for the evidence we experience.

Cosmological arguments, in particular, can be seen as persuasive because it is very difficult to doubt that the universe exists, and scientific explanations for the origins of the universe fail to explain why anything exists at all. The explanation that God created the universe appears at least plausible. Design arguments can also be seen as persuasive because even when there are scientific explanations to show how, for example, cells multiply to form a human baby, the processes and beauty of the development of a new person are still wonderful. Even if we can see how natural processes happen and explain them in terms of chemical formulae, we might still be persuaded that the fact they happen at all is evidence of the existence of God.

Other inductive arguments for God's existence, such as the argument that religious experience is evidence for the existence of God, can also be persuasive. Those who believe they have encountered God personally are likely to find their own experiences very persuasive.

> **Synoptic link**
>
> Link to *Chapter 6: Religious experience (part two)*. This chapter explores questions of whether apparent encounters people have with God are evidence that God really exists.

The view that inductive arguments for God's existence are not persuasive

Inductive arguments can only lead to probable conclusions, and can never prove anything with certainty. This could be seen as an advantage in arguments for the existence of God, because religious belief necessarily involves faith. People have to make a decision one way or the other about religious belief, but if the existence of God could be proved with complete certainty, there would be no room for faith or for decisions to make a personal commitment to a religion.

It could be argued that religious belief does not often come about through persuasive argument. Although people need to be reassured that their beliefs are not illogical nonsense and that a rational defence can be made of them, they do not tend to arrive at religious faith by weighing up evidence for and against, like a jury, and then deciding what to believe. Perhaps the strength of inductive arguments for the existence of God lies in their ability to support existing faith, rather than in their ability to change people's minds.

Whether or not people accept that God is the most probable explanation for the existence of the universe, and the apparent design in it, depends heavily on whether they find the concept of God plausible in the first place. If they start with the view that God is a made-up superstition, they are unlikely to accept that God is a reasonable conclusion to draw from any kind of evidence. Many people are unlikely to be persuaded that there is evidence for the existence of God; if there are observable phenomena that science cannot explain, they are likely to take the view that science needs to continue to work to find an explanation which, when found, will be more probable than any conclusion that God was involved.

Hume's criticisms of inductive arguments have been very influential. Hume was keen to show the limitations of induction as a method of reasoning. We all use inductive reasoning because we could not carry on our daily lives without it. But Hume pointed out we should be very aware that when we use inductive reasoning, there is always the possibility that we could be wrong.

Cosmological and teleological arguments for the existence of God, along with other inductive arguments, can only offer God as the most probable explanation for the evidence we see around us; they can never prove God's existence, and there will always be people who think that other explanations are more likely than the view that there is a God. However, it is important to note that scientific criticisms of inductive arguments can also never be proven, because they too are based on inductive reasoning.

AO2 activity 1

On balance, how persuasive do you find inductive arguments for the existence of God? Do you think there are some observable phenomena for which the best explanation is God? Give reasons to support your answer.

To what extent is the Kalam cosmological argument convincing?

William Lane Craig's cosmological argument takes a fresh look at the arguments produced by Aquinas and medieval Islamic scholars. This question invites consideration of whether this formulation of the cosmological argument is successful.

The view that the Kalam cosmological argument is convincing

- The evidence that Craig uses in the Kalam cosmological argument is the existence of the universe, which very few people would disagree with. Although there are some who claim that everything physical is an illusion, it is difficult to maintain this position seriously while continuing to live your daily life.
- It is an argument that is supported by many centuries of scholarship in different religious traditions. It is a modern argument, taking into account modern developments in science and mathematics to support its case. Craig puts up a strong argument to support the view that the universe cannot be infinite, because actual infinity is impossible.
- Modern science supports the view that the universe had a beginning, and it also supports the idea that nothing can begin without a cause.
- Craig's argument leads to a personal God, which many find attractive.

The view that the Kalam cosmological argument is unconvincing

- If actual infinity is impossible and absurd, then it is difficult to argue that the universe was created by an actual infinite God. It makes the argument self-contradictory.
- If nothing can exist without a cause, then this begs the question of who or what caused God. Craig has not offered a convincing reason for supposing that God can exist infinitely without a cause.
- Hume's arguments show that God is not the only possible explanation for the existence of the universe. The Big Bang theory is an explanation for the existence of the universe that does not require the existence of God; it uses only physical factors in its explanation.
- Bertrand Russell's argument that questions about the origin of the universe have no meaning could be considered a strong challenge to the Kalam cosmological argument.
- Although infinite regress is challenging for us to conceptualise, it could still happen. Some people argue that the Kalam cosmological argument misunderstands the nature of infinity, and that infinity has to exist in actuality even if we cannot imagine it.

How convincing are cosmological arguments for the existence of God? Is God the best explanation for the existence of the universe?

- It could be argued that there is no need for there to have been an agent making a choice between having a universe and not having one. The universe could just have begun, at random, by accident, without any conscious choice being made.
- Even if the Kalam cosmological argument is accepted, it does not provide evidence for the existence of a God with all the qualities and characteristics that theists claim God has. Craig acknowledges, at the end of his book, that the argument does not go as far as to defend the qualities traditionally attributed to God.

AO2 activity 2

On balance, do you find the Kalam cosmological argument for the existence of God convincing, or not? What seems to you to be its main strengths and weaknesses? Write a paragraph explaining why you are, or are not, persuaded by the argument.

How effective are cosmological and teleological arguments for God's existence?

This question asks for a consideration of whether cosmological and teleological arguments succeed in demonstrating the existence of God.

The view that cosmological arguments are effective

In some people's view, the cosmological argument is highly effective as an argument for the existence of God.

- The cosmological argument is a very old argument which has stood the test of time and centuries of scientific advances. The cosmological argument could be seen to be compatible with the Big Bang theory, because the Big Bang theory is an explanation of the physics of the origin of the universe, while the cosmological argument explains why the universe happened at all. This makes it a more effective argument, as people do not have to disregard science in order to agree with it.
- Science generally supports the idea that the universe had a cause.
- Everyone can agree that the evidence is there – the universe does exist – and it is difficult to call that into question.
- Scientific explanations of the origins of the universe, such as the Big Bang theory, leave many questions unanswered. It stretches credibility to expect people to accept that the Big Bang happened out of nowhere, for no reason.

The view that cosmological arguments are not effective

Other people find the cosmological argument less effective.

- Even if the cosmological argument successfully supports the idea that the universe has a cause, this does not show that the cause must be God, and even less the God of Christianity. It does not demonstrate whether the universe was created by a good God, or a God who continues to take an interest in creation, or one single God working alone.

- Aquinas makes assumptions about the existence of God that people today might find questionable. Some thinkers, such as Bertrand Russell, argue that the idea of the universe having a cause or a reason is meaningless.
- The cosmological argument depends on the premise that nothing exists without a cause, but then claims that God does exist without a cause, which is self-contradictory.
- The question of whether infinite regress is possible is still debatable; it could be that the universe simply does go back infinitely.
- The best any inductive argument can do is to lead to a probable cause. Scientific explanations of the origins of the universe are more plausible than explanations that introduce supernatural miracles of creation into serious discussion. The scientific explanations work well on their own.

The view that teleological arguments are effective

- Some might argue that teleological arguments remain effective and persuasive. We can all see the evidence for ourselves: we can see that the world contains order, purpose, and beauty.
- The beauty and wonder of the natural world still evoke a powerful emotional response from us, even when we have scientific explanations for the order and beauty of the world. It could be the case that God created and designed the world, using scientific processes, as Tennant suggests.
- Although scientific theories provide an explanation of order and purpose in the world, these theories are also inductive and could be shown to be wrong as more evidence emerges.

The view that teleological arguments are ineffective

Others argue that teleological arguments are less effective.

- Hume's challenges to inductive arguments are strong and thorough; it is difficult to maintain that the teleological argument succeeds in the face of his criticisms. Also, Darwin's theory of evolution through natural selection is more plausible to many than the idea that God designed every creature on Earth.
- The teleological argument relies on weak analogies; the world is not very much like a man-made machine. It is not reasonable to assume that because machines have designers, the world must also have a designer.
- Some argue that the teleological argument is for people who find it hard to cope with adult life and want to believe that everything has a purpose, because it is a comforting thought; in reality, the world just happens to be the way that it is.

AO2 activity 3

On balance, do you find the cosmological argument convincing? Give reasons for your answer.

AO2 activity 4

In your view, how effective are cosmological and teleological arguments? Do you find one of them more effective than the other, or are they equally effective or ineffective?

How far are cosmological and teleological arguments for God's existence persuasive in the twenty-first century?

Cosmological and teleological arguments for the existence of God have endured for centuries, and are still debated today. Modern advances in science have shed new light on the possible origins of the universe, and on the theory of evolution. Religious beliefs have also changed over time. More people live in multi-faith societies and recognise that there are belief systems other than Christianity; fewer people consider themselves to have a firm religious belief. Consequently, some will argue that cosmological and teleological arguments for God's existence are still extremely persuasive, and others that they are less persuasive or not persuasive at all.

The view that cosmological and teleological arguments are persuasive in the twenty-first century

It can be argued that cosmological and teleological arguments remain persuasive, or are more persuasive, in the twenty-first century. Some scientific arguments made in the twentieth and twenty-first centuries support these arguments for the existence of God rather than undermining them.

- The physicist Paul Davies points out in his 2007 book *Cosmic Jackpot* (also titled *The Goldilocks Enigma* in reference to how Goldilocks found everything 'just right') that the world is 'just right' for our existence and that this is a coincidence that points towards a divine intelligence. He argues that if the relative strengths of nuclear and electromagnetic forces were even slightly different, carbon atoms could not exist in nature. His work provides supporting evidence for Tennant's anthropic principle, although Davies himself does not arrive specifically at the God of Christianity as an explanation for the world being 'just right' for human existence.
- Roger Penrose, a Nobel Prize winner in physics, calculates in his book *The Emperor's New Mind* (1989) that the statistical improbability of the universe being as 'fine-tuned' as it appears to be is one in 10 billion, multiplied by 123. Penrose does not consider himself to be a believer in God, but he thinks the universe has a purpose, and that there is something much deeper about its existence than just blind chance.
- William Lane Craig argues that the Kalam cosmological argument has 'quite amazing connections' to contemporary astronomy and cosmology, with the findings of science adding more and more support to the idea that the universe cannot just have come from nowhere.
- Michael Behe, an American professor of biochemistry, argues in his book *Darwin's Black Box* (1996) that biochemistry supports the idea of '**intelligent design**' or, in other words, that features of the world exist because of the intelligence of God in designing them. He argues that there are many aspects of life that are 'irreducibly complex'. Paying particular attention to the structure of the eye, he says that

> **Key term**
>
> **intelligent design:** the theory that the world and universe cannot have been created by chance but were made by a supernatural intelligence

the eye is made up of many components in a complex way, and that all the components are needed if the eye is to work at all. The pupil is necessary to let in the light, the retina is necessary to receive images, and the optic nerve is necessary to pass images to the brain for interpretation. Without any one of these component parts, the eye would be useless. This complexity, Behe argues, shows that there are gaps in Darwin's thinking. How could an eye develop gradually? If it did not work, it would give the creature no advantages in the competition for food.

- Behe thought that a wing could also not develop gradually through natural selection, as a wing is only of any advantage to a creature if it can get the creature off the ground, or help it to swim. Early stages of wing development would not help the creature at all, and so Behe thought that wings cannot have evolved slowly and gradually through natural selection. In his book, Behe also explains the complexities involved in the clotting of blood so that injuries do not lead to complete blood loss but seal themselves. His conclusion is that the evidence all points to an intelligent designer, which is God, and not to evolution as a completely random process governed only by chance.

The view that cosmological and teleological arguments are not persuasive in the twenty-first century

Other modern thinkers and scientists, however, disagree that the cosmological and teleological arguments are persuasive.

- Bertrand Russell, who was a philosopher and mathematician, discussed the cosmological argument in a radio debate in 1948. Russell's view was that the whole question of the universe having a cause is meaningless. It made no sense to him to look at the universe and demand an explanation. He thought that the existence of the universe was a simple 'brute fact': it just exists, and that was all there is to say about it.
- Stephen Hawking, one of the greatest modern physicists, sometimes suggested that there was the possibility of God. However, in his 2010 book, *The Great Design*, Hawking said that he did not think God was necessary to explain the origins of the universe. He thought that the laws of physics were sufficient on their own. He also questioned the idea that a creator of the universe could be a personal God, interested in the activities of individual human beings, saying that he thought it very unlikely.
- Richard Dawkins, a modern biologist, puts forward criticisms of teleological arguments in several of his books. He titled one of them *The Blind Watchmaker* (1986), arguing against Paley's idea that God designed the world as a watchmaker designs a watch. In Dawkins' view, apparent design comes about through evolutionary processes, and there is nothing out there with the ability to imagine the design in its mind's eye. Natural selection has no purpose and no mind's eye; it is a

Stephen Hawking did not think God was necessary to explain the origins of the universe.

'blind watchmaker'. In *River out of Eden* (1996), Dawkins explains how Crick and Watson's work on DNA shows that there is no mysterious soul or divine spark that gives life. DNA can explain the most fundamental causes of life, and there is no need to resort to God as an explanation for the world as we experience it.

Some argue that, in the modern age, there is less need for people to turn to God as an explanation for our experiences. This is often called the 'God of the gaps'; God is used as an explanation to fill in the gaps in our understanding and knowledge. As we learn more, we need God less to account for things we do not understand. We are able to turn to science instead, so that God gets smaller and smaller, and eventually disappears.

Others, however, argue that this shows a misunderstanding of religious belief. Religious believers do not think of God simply in terms of an alternative to saying 'I don't know' to scientific questions. Faith is much deeper and more complex than that, and meets many more needs than just our need to understand natural processes.

AO2 activity 5
On balance, do you think that modern science supports cosmological and teleological arguments for the existence of God? Give reasons for your answer.

How effective are the challenges to the cosmological and teleological arguments for God's existence?

This question is asking for an evaluation of the challenges made to cosmological and teleological arguments for the existence of God. The challenges are effective if they succeed in showing flaws in the arguments, and if they show that the flaws undermine the arguments to a considerable extent.

The view that the challenges to cosmological and teleological arguments are ineffective

It can be argued that challenges made to cosmological and teleological arguments are not very effective. The arguments use inductive reasoning, but the challenges also use inductive reasoning; so although they often present alternative explanations for the universe and for the natural world, those explanations could also be wrong. Even if a good scientific explanation is presented to show how the universe might have originated, or how a different species came to be the way they are, these do not rule out the possibility that God was in control, and remains in control.

Hume's criticisms of inductive arguments are powerful, but they do not disprove. They show that God is not the only possible explanation for the existence of the universe and of order in the world, but they are not able to demonstrate that God does not exist.

The challenge presented by the problem of evil could be said to be ineffective because the existence of evil and suffering in the world does not demonstrate that God cannot exist, even if it raises questions about God's actions.

The view that the challenges to cosmological and teleological arguments are effective

Conversely, it can be argued that the challenges to cosmological and teleological arguments are highly effective. They highlight flaws in reasoning in these traditional arguments, and show that there is no need to introduce God into explanations. They give better explanations for the origins of the universe and the origins of species, using empirical observation rather than faith in the supernatural.

The challenges show that even if it is possible that the world came about through the agency of God, this does not say anything about what kind of God or gods the creator must be, or whether God is still in existence, or whether God takes any interest in the world.

To what extent are scientific explanations more persuasive than philosophical explanations for the universe's existence?

For this question, you need to think about scientific explanations for the existence of the universe (such as the Big Bang theory), and also scientific explanations for apparent design, order, and purpose in nature (such as Darwin's theory of evolution). The question asks for a consideration of whether the scientific explanations are more convincing than philosophical arguments in accounting for the universe and the order within it.

The view that scientific arguments are more persuasive

Some people find scientific explanations more persuasive than philosophical explanations for the universe's existence because they are supported by solid empirical evidence (evidence that can be experienced with the senses). People can see the data for themselves and can look at the calculations. Science has an accepted methodology and is open to peer review: in other words, different scientists criticise each other's work and offer suggestions and alternatives to keep scientific discovery in a continual state of progress. Philosophical and religious points of view, in contrast, depend on reasoning and on faith rather than on empirical evidence, and it is not possible for others to examine the evidence in the same kind of way as they do with science.

The different methodologies used by science and philosophy therefore make science more persuasive.

The view that scientific arguments are not more persuasive

Although there are many scientists, such as Dawkins and Hawking, who argue that the world can be explained without any reference to God, there are also many other scientists who find philosophical and religious arguments convincing, and who do not see a need to choose between either science or religion. Scientists such as Michael Behe, Paul Davies, and Isaac Newton before them, argue that science actually supports cosmological and teleological arguments. They argue that the more we gain scientific knowledge about the origins of the world and the complexities of nature, the more we can see the hand of God in creation. Thinkers such as these argue that science and religion do not need to be viewed as competitors, but that each discipline has its own contribution to make to human understanding.

Others argue that philosophical explanations for the existence of the universe, especially if they are also religious, are more persuasive than scientific explanations. Some thinkers argue that scientific conclusions will always be fallible because they are the work of human minds, whereas the truth about the origins of the universe has been revealed by God through sacred writings. Where science and religion disagree, the word of God will always be more reliable than the theories of human minds, however clever the scientists might be.

In the end, the persuasiveness of the arguments depends on a person's previously-held beliefs. Those who think that God is an outdated superstition are unlikely to find anything persuasive in inductive arguments for the existence of God. Those who already have a religious faith are likely to find their belief is supported when they consider the scale of the universe and the complexities of nature, and see it as the work of an intelligent creator.

Practising AO1 questions

The following question is an example question taken from a past exam paper. All of the questions in the exam are divided into two parts, part (a) and part (b), Part (a) questions always target AO1 and require you to demonstrate knowledge and understanding.

AO1 questions begin with one of a range of possible command words (see pages 8–9 for more detail). The following question begins with the word 'Outline'. 'Outline' questions require you to cover the broad topic area in the question in some detail, structuring your answer so that you cover the material in a sensible and logical way. You do not need to consider the quality of the arguments or offer any views about them.

Outline the different teleological arguments for the existence of God presented by Aquinas, Paley, and Tennant.

(Eduqas AS Level Religious Studies, Summer 2018, Component 2: An Introduction to the Philosophy of Religion, Question 2a)

Example 1

Paley's[6] argument says that the world is like a watch[1]. One day, someone was walking across a heath when he found a watch on the ground.[3] He picked the watch up, and wondered who had made it. Paley[6] said that the world is like a watch[2] because it works like a machine, and all the different parts of the world fit together like the cogs in a watch, and each part of the world has its own job to do. Paley[6] said that this proves the existence of God[2].

1 This is a weak paragraph, because the writer does not have a very clear understanding of Paley's argument, and has not remembered it particularly well. There is limited knowledge and understanding, and only a basic level of accuracy.

2 The writer addresses the question because they are writing about Paley's teleological argument, and have correctly identified this as a design argument using the analogy of a watch.

3 This paragraph does not use any evidence or examples; it just provides a description of what the writer thinks Paley said.

4 You should include references to sacred texts where an opportunity arises naturally, but this should not be forced. It is acceptable for this to be absent if it is not appropriate to the question.

5 Connections with other areas studied should be included only where appropriate; connections should not be forced.

6 The writer appropriately references Paley's thinking in this paragraph.

7 There is no specialist language included in this paragraph; other paragraphs in the response must include the use of specialist language in context.

Example 2

Paley's[6] teleological argument uses an[2] analogy[7], comparing the world with a watch[2]. Using inductive reasoning[7], Paley[6] asks us to imagine someone finding a watch while walking across a heath. The walker sees that the watch has been deliberately designed, because of its complexity, its order, its beauty and the fact that it clearly has a purpose or 'telos'[7]. They would be right to conclude that it must have been made deliberately, by an intelligent mind[2]. In Paley's[6] view, we can see the same characteristics in the natural world around us[1]. We can see complexity[7] in things like the human eye, order in the way the planets move, beauty even in small details and purpose in even the tiny hinges on the wings of an insect[3]. Paley[6] argued that, just as we can see a watch must have a designer, we can also see that the natural world must have been designed by an intelligent mind[1].

Activity

1. Read 'Using band descriptors and mark schemes' on page 10. Then go to www.eduqas.co.uk and look at the mark schemes for the past paper questions below. Familiarise yourself with the level of detail that examiners expect to see in excellent answers.

2. The past paper question on page 45 asks for knowledge and understanding of three different teleological arguments: Aquinas' argument, Paley's argument, and Tennant's argument. The two example paragraphs, above and on page 45, are about Paley. Choose either Aquinas or Tennant, and write one or two paragraphs explaining the teleological argument of the thinker you have chosen. Example 1 is much weaker than example 2, so try to give your answer the same qualities as Example 2, or better.

1 This writer understands Paley's analogy better, providing more detail, and showing how Paley uses ideas like complexity and purpose to make his case.

2 The writer addresses the question well, correctly identifying Paley's argument and describing it without giving their own opinion about it.

3 The writer uses Paley's own examples well in this paragraph.

4 There is no reference made here to sources of wisdom and authority, but this is fine because they would not be appropriate here.

5 This paragraph does not make connections with other areas of study, but that is fine; it's important not to force a connection where there isn't one.

6 The writer appropriately references Paley's thinking in this paragraph.

7 The writer uses specialist vocabulary with accuracy and confidence.

AO1 practice question 1

Now it is your turn. Have a go at answering the following question. There are some points to remember to help you if you are not sure how to start.

> *Explain Aquinas' cosmological arguments for the existence of God.*
>
> (WJEC AS Level Religious Studies, Summer 2017, AS Unit 2: An Introduction to Religion and Ethics and the Philosophy of Religion, Question 3a)

Points to remember

- The question asks you to 'Explain', so you need to give a detailed description of Aquinas' thinking. Show how he arrived at his conclusion that God must exist.
- Remember that Aquinas gave three versions of a cosmological argument in his Five Ways. It would be good to take each of them in turn, and show how they are similar but have different emphases.
- Try to use key vocabulary such as 'contingency' and 'infinite regress'.

AO1 practice question 2

Now try this question by yourself.

> *Explain the different teleological arguments for the existence of God presented by Aquinas and Tennant.*
>
> (WJEC AS Level Religious Studies, Summer 2018, AS Unit 2: An Introduction to Religion and Ethics and the Philosophy of Religion, Question 4a)

Practising AO2 questions

When writing a response to an AO2 question, you must remember that you are being examined on your ability to analyse and evaluate effectively. Analysis involves a detailed examination of something, and you should pick apart the concept to look for its strengths and weaknesses. Evaluation involves judging the quality or importance of the concept. You are expected to analyse and evaluate throughout the whole of your response; you are not expected to include long passages explaining knowledge and understanding.

The questions below are taken from past exam papers. All the questions in the exam are divided into two parts, part (a) and part (b). Part (b) questions always target AO2 and require you to demonstrate analysis and evaluation.

Activity

1. Read 'Making essay plans' on pages 9–10. Then, make a few planning notes for each of the bullets below. You do not need to write a lot of detail; just jot down some bullet points to outline what you would say.

   - Plan what you would argue if you were asked whether Darwin's ideas show Paley's teleological argument is wrong.
   - Plan what you would argue if you were asked whether Tennant's anthropic teleological argument is convincing.
   - Plan what you would argue if you were asked whether Hume gives effective challenges to cosmological arguments.

2. Read the two example paragraphs below and on page 49 and write a brief summary to the student who wrote Example 1, explaining how their paragraph needs to improve and giving them clear guidance about what to do when rewriting it.

'Paley's view of the teleological argument is convincing.'
Evaluate this view.

(Eduqas AS Level Religious Studies, Summer 2018, Component 2:
An Introduction to the Philosophy of Religion, Question 2b)

Example 1

Paley[4] presented a design argument for the existence of God by saying that the world seems to have been designed, and that God is the best explanation for the design[2]. He asks us to imagine someone finding a watch on a heath, and says that we would notice how well designed it was and conclude that someone intelligent must have made it. In the same way, when we look at the natural world, we can see how well designed it is and how it has order and purpose[6]. This leads us to conclude that the natural world must have been designed by God, because without God there would not be any order or purpose. I do not think this is a good argument[1], because it has been disproved by[3] Darwin[4].

---

1. The writer accurately describes Paley's analogy, but an AO2 response should focus on analysis and evaluation. There is a little evaluation, but it is underdeveloped. The writer simply asserts their point of view without going into detail about their reasons.

2. An attempt has been made to identify the issues raised in the question, but it is done too descriptively. It would be better if the writer's point of view was set out at the beginning of the paragraph and not tacked on at the end as an afterthought.

3. The paragraph contains a reason to justify the point of view given, but the writer needs to provide more detail to explain how the views of Darwin challenged teleological arguments.

4. The writer makes reference to an appropriate scholar (Darwin) as well as using the thinking of Paley.

5. Appropriately, there is no reference to connections with other areas of study in this paragraph.

6. There is a little use of specialist terminology in this paragraph.

Example 2

Paley's[4] argument is not convincing, because[2] he does not successfully show that the world is like a watch. The philosopher David Hume[4] criticised arguments that compare the world with a watch or with other machinery, saying that there is very little similarity at all, and he was right to make this criticism[1]. Although many aspects of the natural world are complex and seem to have a purpose, this does not mean that they work in the way that machines work; and, even if they did, we would not be able to draw the conclusion that they must have been made by a supernatural[3] intelligent designer[6] which has to be the God of Christianity.[3] There are many other possible explanations which are more likely.[1] Darwin's[4] theory of evolution[3] provides a better, more plausible explanation[1] of apparent design in the natural world, because he has scientific[3], empirical[6] evidence to support his views[3]. Thinkers such as[5] Dawkins[4] use Darwin's[5] theory of evolution[6] to criticise design arguments and make a case for[5] atheism[6].

1 This paragraph contains detailed and confident analysis and evaluation. Their opinion is clearly expressed, and the reader is in no doubt which opinion the writer holds and their reasons for their view.

2 The issues in the question are clearly identified and addressed.

3 The views given are sustained and clearly supported with reasoning and evidence.

4 This paragraph contains reference to appropriate scholarly views.

5 The writer has made an appropriate connection with another area of study, by referring to Dawkins and New Atheism.

6 There is some good, confident use of specialist vocabulary in this section of the essay.

AO2 practice question 1

Now it is your turn. Have a go at answering the following question. There are some points to remember to help you if you are not sure how to start.

> *'Cosmological arguments for God's existence are not persuasive.' Evaluate this view.*
>
> (WJEC AS Level Religious Studies, Summer 2017, AS Unit 2: An Introduction to Religion and Ethics and the Philosophy of Religion, Question 3b)

Points to remember

- Remember to start by thinking about your own point of view. Do you find cosmological arguments persuasive or not? What are your reasons?
- Plan your answer carefully, thinking about which scholars you might use, how you could use specialist vocabulary, and how you will justify your argument.
- Notice that the question asks only about cosmological arguments, so you do not need to introduce ideas about teleological arguments.

AO2 practice question 2

Now try this question by yourself.

> *'Scientific explanations for order in the universe are more persuasive than teleological arguments.' Evaluate this view.*
>
> (Eduqas AS Level Religious Studies, Summer 2017, Component 2: An Introduction to the Philosophy of Religion, Question 2b)

Mark schemes for all exam questions can be found at www.eduqas.co.uk and www.wjec.co.uk.

2 Arguments for the existence of God: deductive

The ontological argument for the existence of God is unusual. Other arguments for God's existence are inductive, relying on the evidence of sense experience. However, the ontological argument is deductive: it is based only on reason and logic. It is quite a difficult argument to understand straight away, but well worth the effort. The argument started with a very intelligent, very devout monk who went on to become Archbishop of Canterbury shortly after the Norman Conquest, and it has continued to fascinate people for a thousand years.

- Is it possible to demonstrate the existence of God simply through reasoned argument, without any need for supporting evidence?
- What, if anything, are the flaws in the ontological argument?
- Does the ontological argument really prove the existence of God beyond any doubt, or is just some kind of trick that has been played with words?
- Does the ontological argument lead to the God of Christianity specifically, or could it be used to support belief in any religious faith?

Anselm of Canterbury (born in the eleventh century) was the first to introduce the idea that God's existence can be demonstrated through reason.

AO1

This section of the chapter will enhance your **knowledge** and **understanding** of the topic and help you develop your AO1 skills.

Deductive arguments: the origins of the ontological argument

Deductive proofs and the concept of *a priori*

Unlike other arguments for the existence of God, the **ontological argument** is based on deductive reasoning. A **deductive argument** is based in logic and this means that, if the premise is true, the stages of the argument follow each other logically and the conclusion formed is necessarily true, working in a similar way to mathematics. The ontological argument is based in *a priori* knowledge and is deductive in form.

The traditional example of deductive reasoning is:

> All men are mortal.
>
> Socrates is a man.
>
> Therefore, Socrates is mortal.

If we know that the first two statements are true, then we can work out, using logic, that the conclusion must also be true. The first two statements are examples of premises. In logic, a **premise** is an assumption made in an argument that is used to justify the conclusion. Here the premises are that all men are mortal, and that Socrates is a man. If we could show that one or both of those premises is not true, then the conclusion does not follow; but if the premises of our argument are true, then the conclusion is certain. There are no other, alternative conclusions that could be drawn.

We use deductive reasoning in our daily lives. For example, we might think:

> My keys are either on the kitchen table or in my coat pocket.
>
> My keys aren't on the kitchen table.
>
> Therefore, they must be in my coat pocket.

The quality of a deductive argument depends on whether its premises are true. Is it true that those are the only two places I could have left my keys? Are they really not on the kitchen table, or could they be there, hidden under the post? If the premises are true, the conclusion is correct; if not, the conclusion is false.

Key terms

ontological argument: an argument that uses the idea of God to establish the reality of God

deductive argument: an argument that relies on reason and logic; if the premises are true, then the conclusion must be true

premise: an assumption that is claimed to be true, and is used to justify the conclusion of an argument

With inductive reasoning, we have to decide whether the conclusion is the most probable explanation for the things we observe, therefore it is the conclusion that is open for discussion. However, with deductive reasoning, we have to decide whether the premises of the argument are true. With the ontological argument, then, we need to look closely at its premises, and consider whether there are any mistakes in logic, in order to make a judgement about the argument's success or failure.

AO1 activity 1

Look back to pages 13 and 14 of Chapter 1 to help you answer the following questions.

a) Explain what *a priori* means, and how it is different from *a posteriori*.

b) Explain what deductive reasoning is, and how it is different from inductive reasoning.

Anselm's ontological argument

Who was Anselm?

Anselm was born in 1033 in what was then the kingdom of Burgundy, now in Italy. He was a very devout Christian from a young age, applying to a local monastery to become a monk when he was in his teens. Anselm's application was refused because his father would not give permission, but he eventually entered monastic life when he was 27. Anselm soon became

the leader of his monastery in Bec, Normandy, where, despite his youth, he became well known for his rigorous commitment to the spiritual life. The monastery developed under Anselm's leadership into a centre for learning in Europe, attracting students from across France and Italy, and Anselm was famed for his kindness and discipline with the young monks, and for his intellect.

Anselm's duties included teaching the other monks, and he also wrote prayers and devotions. He would send these to monks in other monasteries, and to noblewomen who wanted to develop their faith. His writings covered a wide range of theological topics, including the problem of evil, human nature and free will, God's relationship with time, and the nature of virtue. The best-known of his writings is his ontological argument for the existence of God, which he wrote in a work called ***Proslogion*** in 1078.

Anselm wrote his ontological argument for the existence of God when he was prior of Bec Abbey in Normandy.

Later in his life and following the Norman Conquest, Anselm travelled to England, where he was appointed Archbishop of Canterbury. This appointment was overshadowed by constant conflict with the king,

Key term

Proslogion: (Latin) discourse

William Rufus. Anselm asked the Pope if he could stand down, but the Pope, recognising Anselm's abilities, would not let him. William Rufus sent Anselm into exile to Rome, which allowed him to continue his writing, and he returned to England after the king's death. Anselm died in 1109, and is considered a saint by the Catholic Church and the Church of England.

Faith seeking understanding

Anselm presented his ontological argument for the existence of God in terms of 'faith seeking understanding'. His work is known as *Proslogion*, which means '*discourse*' in Latin, and it is it written in the form of a meditation or a prayer in which Anselm addresses God directly. The ontological arguments that Anselm presents appear at the end of Chapter 2 of *Proslogion*. He was not, he implied, trying to convert unbelievers to Christian faith, but instead was giving an argument that would help people who already had Christian faith to be confident that God must exist, and to understand more about the infinite nature of God.

It is usually agreed that Anselm presented his ontological argument in two different forms, although they are so closely related that some think the second argument was just Anselm saying the same thing again in other words, for clarity.

Anselm began both strands of his argument by giving a definition of the God of Christianity: 'a being than which nothing greater can be conceived'. By 'greater', Anselm clearly meant 'most perfect' rather than 'biggest'. God is understood as a being so perfect that we could not even imagine a more perfect being. This definition of God becomes the first premise of Anselm's argument.

Anselm referred to the Psalms when he made his argument, quoting Psalms 14:1 and 53:1:

> The fool says in his heart,
>   'There is no God.' **"**
>
> Psalms 14:1 and 53:1, *Holy Bible (NIV)*

In exploring this verse, Anselm's opinion was that someone has to be a fool if they say there is no God, because they obviously have a concept of God in order to know what it is that they do not believe in. And if they have a concept of God, then they just need to think about that concept and what it logically entails to realise that God must exist. They are a fool if they have not done this, and have simply rejected God without giving God's existence proper consideration. Anselm took his readers through the thought processes that got him from a concept of God to the existence of God.

God as the greatest possible being (Proslogion 2)

In his first premise, Anselm proposed that we can all agree on a definition of God. God is 'that than which no greater can be conceived' (sometimes translated as 'that than which no greater can be thought'). This definition is very important, and Anselm worded it carefully. When we think about God, Anselm was saying, whether we believe in God or not, we all understand that the term 'God' refers to the greatest being that could possibly be imagined. It would be impossible for anything to exist that is greater than God.

Then, Anselm made a distinction between existing in the mind only, and existing in reality as well. This is called **in intellectu** *(in the mind)* and **in re** *(in reality)* in Latin. In his second premise, Anselm proposed that God exists *in intellectu*: everyone, even the 'fool', accepts that there is such a thing as a concept of God.

If something exists only in the mind but not in reality, Anselm said, then we can conceive of something greater: that same thing, existing both in the mind and in reality too. Anselm's third premise is therefore: something that exists in reality is greater than something that exists only as a concept; *in re* as well as *in intellectu* is greater than *in intellectu* alone.

This took him to his conclusion: We have already agreed that God is that than which nothing greater can be conceived, so God cannot exist only in the mind. God must exist in reality as well.

> *If then that-than-which-a-greater-cannot-be-thought exists in the mind alone, this same that-than-which-a-greater-cannot-be thought is that-than-which-a-greater-can-be-thought. But this is obviously impossible. Therefore there is absolutely no doubt that something-than-which-a-greater-cannot-be-thought exists both in the mind and in reality.*
>
> Anselm, *Proslogion 2*

Anselm was asking us to accept that it is 'greater' to exist in reality than to exist in the mind only. We might think of a marvellous invention that could save everyone a lot of time and trouble, but the idea of this invention, just as an idea, is not as great as having the actual invention in reality and being able to use it. We might imagine a lovely meal with all our favourite foods, but this imaginary meal is not as great as actually having the food on a plate in front of us and being able to enjoy it in reality.

Therefore Anselm's first argument, set out in terms of premises and a conclusion, is:

> God is that than which no greater can be thought. (Even the 'fool' will accept that this is what the concept of God is.)
>
> Existence in reality is greater than existence in the mind alone.
>
> God cannot exist in the mind alone, because 'God is that than which no greater can be thought'.
>
> Therefore, God must exist in reality.

Key terms

in intellectu: (Latin) in the mind

in re: (Latin) in reality

Anselm seems to be taking 'existing in the real world' as a property or characteristic of something, and he sees existence as a property that makes something great.

God has necessary existence (Proslogion 3)

In his second version of the argument, Anselm gave his argument again, but this time he wrote about God's existence in terms of **necessary existence**.

As before, Anselm started with the premise that God is that than which nothing greater can be conceived. Anselm then explained:

> We can imagine, if we try, a being that cannot possibly not exist (a necessary being).
>
> We can also imagine a being that can possibly not exist (a contingent being).
>
> A necessary being is greater than a contingent being.
>
> God is that than which no greater can be conceived.
>
> Therefore, God is a being that cannot possibly not exist, and therefore God exists, necessarily.

Anselm was saying that the 'fool' who says in his heart that there is no God (or in other words fundamentally does not believe in God) is a fool because he does not realise that God exists by definition. Once we understand what God is, we realise (argued Anselm) that God must exist, because it is the nature of God to exist.

Developments of the ontological argument

Compared with cosmological and teleological arguments for the existence of God, which date back to at least the philosophers of ancient Greece, the ontological argument is relatively new. It was overtaken in popularity by Aquinas' Five Ways, probably because they are easier to understand. However, interest in the ontological argument was revived in the seventeenth century by René Descartes. His reformulation of the argument sparked a debate that continues to the present day.

René Descartes

René Descartes was a French philosopher and mathematician who is often considered to be the father of modern philosophy. He was particularly interested in a branch of philosophy called epistemology, which is the philosophy of knowledge. What can be known for certain, if anything? How do we know the things that we know? These questions became a focus for much of Western Philosophy in what became known as the 'Age of Reason'.

AO1 activity 2

Explain in your own words the premises and the conclusion of the first version of Anselm's ontological argument.

Key term

necessary existence: God must exist and God's existence is necessary so it is also impossible for God not to exist

AO1 activity 3

Explain how Anselm uses the idea of God existing necessarily to make his ontological argument.

Descartes had an unpromising start to life. His mother died shortly after giving birth to him, and as a baby he was not expected to survive as he was always considered delicate. As he grew up, it became clear that Descartes was an astonishingly able mathematician and physicist, and he began working on ways to apply principles of mathematics to physics, in order to make progress in engineering. In 1619, Descartes had a series of dreams or visions in which he came to the understanding that all truth was essentially linked. He formulated the principles of analytic geometry as a result, and also came up with his most famous idea: '*Cogito ergo sum*', or 'I think, therefore I am', explained in his *Discourse on the Method*, which was published in 1637.

For Descartes, this idea was the answer to his question about what we can know for certain. Can we be certain even of our own existence, or could we be in some kind of dream? Using a method known as 'hyperbolic doubt', Descartes set about assuming that we need to doubt everything we think we know, and then test it, so that we can work out what is certain and what is only probable. He questioned all his sense experiences, realising that our senses sometimes deceive us, until he arrived at the question of his own existence. The answer to the question of whether or not we can be certain of our own existence is yes, we can: because here we are, thinking about that very question. The fact of our thinking about it demonstrates that we exist: 'I think, therefore I am'.

Part of Descartes' philosophy was the belief that we have innate ideas. These, for Descartes, are ideas that are with us from birth, engraved on our minds. We start off with them, rather than learning them gradually as we explore the world. Descartes thought that people are born with ideas about number, shape, equality, and cause; he also thought that we are born with the idea of God. We understand, from birth, that God is the supreme being with every perfection. In Descartes' view, this idea of God could not be something that we gradually learn through sense experience, because we are fallible human creatures with temporary, imperfect lives, and God is not available directly to sense experience. We would not be able to conceive of such a being as God, unless God put the idea into our nature from birth, because our minds are not capable on their own of conceiving such perfection. The existence of the idea of God was, for Descartes, demonstration that God must exist to have put it there.

> *Certainly, the idea of God, or a supremely perfect being, is one that I find within me just as surely as the idea of any shape or number.* 99
>
> René Descartes, *Fifth Meditation* in *The Philosophical Works of Descartes*

AO1 activity 4

Explain how Descartes came to the conclusion that we have an innate knowledge of God.

Synoptic link

Link to *Chapter 4: Challenges to religious belief: religious belief as a product of the human mind*. Psychologists such as Jung have revisited Descartes' idea that some of our knowledge and beliefs are with us from birth.

René Descartes is often considered the father of modern philosophy.

Descartes' concept of God as a supremely perfect being

Descartes understood the idea of God in terms of a supremely perfect being. By this, he understood that God has every positive quality in its most perfect form. This means that God has perfect power, perfect love, perfect mercy, and so on; and for Descartes, it also meant that God has perfect existence.

René Descartes put forward a new version of the ontological argument, bringing it back into fashion. In his version of the argument, he concentrated on the idea that 'existence' is a quality that makes something great. Anselm had argued that something which exists in reality is greater than something which exists only in the mind. Descartes took up this point and made it a more prominent part of the argument. He explained:

As individuals, we can know for certain that we exist.

We have an innate idea of God as a supremely perfect being.

A supremely perfect being has every perfection.

Existence is a predicate of a supremely perfect being.

Therefore, God exists in the most perfect way.

Descartes, like Anselm, viewed existence as being a characteristic, or a quality, of what is known in philosophical terms as a '**predicate**'. Being green is a predicate of grass; tallness is a predicate of giants; softness is a predicate of marshmallows. What Descartes wanted to argue was that existence is a predicate of God.

Descartes thought that the defining nature of everything includes particular predicates. There are certain features, or predicates, of a cat that make it a cat rather than a dog, predicates of an oak tree that make it an oak tree rather than a walnut tree, and so on. Predicates help us to identify things, telling us about their essential nature. If you were to look in a book about British wildflowers. you would find it full of predicates telling you that borage flowers are blue and have five triangular-pointed petals, and that ragwort is bright yellow and has unpleasant-smelling leaves. Similarly, God has predicates, or defining features, and one of those features is necessary existence. And because necessary existence is a feature of God, then God must exist.

Descartes' analogies of triangles and mountains

Descartes made his ontological argument using a triangle as an analogy. A defining predicate of a triangle is that it has three internal angles that add up to two right-angles. Without this predicate, it would not be a triangle. We could not imagine a triangle without its defining characteristics, because what we were imagining , if anything at all, would not be a triangle; having three angles that add up to two right-angles is essential to the nature of triangles. Descartes argued that, in the same way, existence is a predicate of God. We cannot imagine a supremely perfect being that does not have the characteristic of existence, because existence is an essential part of perfection.

> **Key term**
>
> **predicate:** the part of a sentence that gives information about the subject; it adds to our understanding of the subject by giving us extra detail

> ## AO1 activity 5
> Explain, using your own examples, what is meant by a 'predicate'.

Descartes also used the analogy of a mountain. We cannot even imagine a mountain, he said, without imagining a valley as well. (It could be argued that some mountains, such as Table Mountain or Uluru, do not have valleys, but Descartes is perhaps better translated as saying that it is impossible to think of a slope that slopes upwards but does not, at the same time, slope downwards.) Descartes argued that 'having a valley' is a predicate of a mountain; the idea of a mountain intrinsically includes the idea of a valley, just as the idea of God intrinsically includes existence.

> *I clearly see that existence can no more be separated from the essence of God than can its having three angles equal to two right-angles be separated from the essence of a triangle or the idea of a mountain from the idea of a valley; and so there is not any less repugnance to our conceiving a God (that is, being supremely perfect) to whom existence is lacking (that is to say, to whom a certain perfection is lacking), than to conceive of a mountain which has no valley.*
>
> René Descartes, *Fifth Meditation* in *The Philosophical Works of Descartes*

For Descartes, the existence of God is self-evident. It could be described as an axiom, similar in logic to a mathematical axiom, such as a straight line being the shortest distance between two points. If you understand the concept of God, it is self-evident that God exists.

Norman Malcolm

In the eighteenth century, Immanuel Kant challenged Descartes' ontological argument by saying that existence is not a predicate. Norman Malcolm, writing in the twentieth century, accepted Kant's criticism, agreeing that existence cannot be used as a predicate. However, Malcolm argued that the idea of God's *necessary* existence, as put forward in Anselm's second formulation, can still be used to make a successful ontological argument for the existence of God. Malcolm used a kind of reasoning known as modal logic, often used in mathematics, when he explained how deductive reasoning can lead us to the existence of God.

Norman Malcolm was an American philosopher, who came to the UK as a graduate to study philosophy at Cambridge just before the Second World War. He studied with Ludwig Wittgenstein, and the two became lifelong friends. In 1960, Malcolm wrote his defence of the ontological argument, taking into account criticisms that had been made of it.

Norman Malcolm's concept of God as an unlimited being

Malcolm's argument starts at the same familiar point as Anselm's: God is a being than which no greater can be conceived. It follows from this, Malcolm said, that God must therefore be an unlimited being. If we are conceiving the greatest possible being, we would obviously agree that an unlimited being is greater than a limited one.

Malcolm then takes us through three possibilities. God's existence could be impossible, in which case there is definitely no God. God's existence could be possible, in which case there might or might not be a God. Or God's existence could be necessary, in which case God definitely exists.

AO1 activity 6

a) Explain how Descartes used the analogies of triangles and mountains to show that God must exist.

b) Think of some other examples of features that make a thing what it is (it would not be that thing without this feature). For example, we cannot imagine a needle without an eye; if there is nowhere to thread it, it would not be a needle.

Malcolm argues that God's existence is not impossible. It would only be impossible if it were self-contradictory. For example, a square circle is impossible because it is contradictory for a square to be a circle. We could not entertain the idea of a square circle, or imagine one in our minds, because it is an absurdity. But there is nothing self-contradictory about the nature of God; therefore, Malcolm argues, God is not impossible.

Then, Malcolm looks at the idea that God's existence could be possible. A being that is possible rather than necessary is a contingent being, and a contingent being is one that at some point came into existence and has not always existed. Contingent things begin to exist as the result of a cause, or perhaps by blind chance without a cause. But a being that depends on either an external cause or on blind chance is a limited being, limited by needing something else to bring it into existence, and God is not a limited being. A possible God would not be God at all.

Therefore, the only possibility that remains is that God exists necessarily.

Malcolm did not consider himself to have created a new ontological argument, but to have rephrased Anselm's argument to make it more comprehensible to modern people: saying that 'God is a being than which a greater cannot be thought' is equivalent to saying 'God is an unlimited being'. Malcolm did not think that his argument would convince atheists, but even so, he thought it was worthwhile so that the believer would understand the complete necessity of God's existence, and the way in which everything that exists depends on God.

> **AO1 activity 7**
> Write a summary to show how Malcolm arrived at the conclusion that God is neither impossible nor possible.

Challenges to the ontological argument

The ontological argument faces different challenges from those put to cosmological and teleological arguments, because it uses deductive reasoning. Rather than trying to find counter-evidence to undermine the conclusion, critics need to demonstrate that the premises of the argument are not true. Two of the most famous critics of the ontological argument are Gaunilo and Kant, each of whom took issue with the premises of the ontological argument.

Gaunilo's reply to Anselm

The first critic of Anselm's ontological argument was a monk called Gaunilo. He lived at the same time as Anselm, but at a different monastery at Marmoutiers in France. Very little is known about Gaunilo except for his discussion with Anselm. Although a Christian himself, Gaunilo thought that he saw flaws in Anselm's reasoning, and so sent Anselm a reply called 'On Behalf of the Fool' ('*Pro Insipiente*'). This was not because Gaunilo did not believe in God, but because he thought that Anselm's reasoning was not logically secure.

Gaunilo used an argument known in philosophy as *reductio ad absurdum*. This is when a challenge is made to an argument by pointing out its absurd logic, or showing how it would lead to ridiculous consequences if the logic were extended. For example, it is easy to criticise a claim such as, 'Nobody goes to concerts anymore because they are always so crowded,' using a *reductio ad absurdum* challenge. How can concerts be crowded if nobody goes? Similarly, we could challenge the claim, 'All children of below average height should be given growth hormones by their doctors,' by showing that this would lead to absurd consequences where, at any one time, half the children in the country would be on growth hormones and the average height would keep rising.

Gaunilo argued that the problems in Anselm's thinking become clear if we substitute the word 'God' in the argument with the idea of a 'perfect island', to see the absurdities in the logic. Gaunilo need not have chosen an island; he could have chosen anything. The point Gaunilo was making was that we could use Anselm's argument to argue for the existence of anything at all, and therefore the argument is absurd. We cannot just make things up and then argue them into existence. If we go through the argument again, replacing the idea of God with the idea of an island, then the problems in the ontological argument become obvious, Gaunilo said.

Imagine the most perfect, the most excellent, island. We can do this; we understand, in our minds the concept of a most perfect island, and so the idea of the most perfect island exists as a concept in our understanding. Using Anselm's logic, we might then go on to say that this most perfect island, existing in our minds only, is inferior to that same island existing in reality. If our island is truly the most perfect, it cannot have the inferiority that comes from it being a concept only. In order for it really to be that most perfect island, it must exist in reality. Now, Gaunilo argued, clearly this is ridiculous. We cannot make something such as an island exist and expect to be able to find it and visit it, merely by imagining it and adding 'most perfect' or 'most excellent' to our definition of it.

Gaunilo said that the flaws in Anselm's reasoning become clear if we substitute the concept of God for the concept of an island.

> *When someone tells me there is such an island, I easily understand what is being said, for there is nothing difficult here. Suppose, however, he then goes on to say: you cannot doubt that this island, more excellent than all lands, actually exists somewhere in reality … I would think he were joking; or if I accepted the argument, I do not know whom I would regard as the greater fool, me for accepting it or him for supposing that he had proved the existence of this island with any kind of certainty.*
>
> Gaunilo, quoted in Anselm, *Opera Omina*

Gaunilo closed his reply to Anselm by praising the rest of his work and the brilliance of his mind, and said that Anselm had made a great contribution to Christian understanding.

Anselm was impressed with Gaunilo's argument, and included it in later versions of *Proslogion*, along with his response. Anselm agreed that Gaunilo was right that reasoning based on the ontological argument does not demonstrate that the most excellent island exists. It makes no sense to assume an excellent island exists just because you define it as excellent. But, he argued, Gaunilo's objections do not work when they are applied to the existence of God. Referring to the second version of his own argument, Anselm said that this difference is because an island only has contingent existence, whereas God has necessary existence. There cannot be such a thing as a perfect island, because we can always think of something else that we could add to the island to make it even better; and one person's idea of a perfect island might not be the same as another's. An island is something that comes into being through volcanic activity perhaps, or ceases to exist through rising sea levels, because it is by its nature contingent.

If we think seriously about the concept of God, however, then we realise that God must have the most superior kind of existence, which is necessary existence; and if God has necessary existence, then God exists, necessarily. This unique kind of existence, applicable only to God, is the whole point of the ontological argument. Anselm had been arguing that a being than which no greater can be thought cannot possibly be imagined not to exist; but this only applies to God, and not to islands or to any other contingent thing, as they can easily be imagined not to exist.

Later on, in the thirteenth century, another monk made a contribution to the debate. This was Bonaventura, a Franciscan monk who took his degree alongside Thomas Aquinas, and who, like Aquinas, had been very much influenced by the writings of Aristotle. Bonaventura took Anselm's side, arguing that God is 'the highest truth' and so cannot be thought not to exist. He put forward the idea that was later taken up by Descartes: the idea that existence is a part of the nature of God. Bonaventura also expressed Anselm's argument in terms of 'the best', saying that we all accept that the best is exactly that: the best. The best being must be a being that is absolutely complete, and this absolute completeness involves existence. God is the absolute best, and therefore God must exist, by definition.

Immanuel Kant's objection

Immanuel Kant raised an objection to the ontological argument which is considered by many people to be fatal to it. He was addressing Descartes' revived version of the ontological argument, and so Kant, like Descartes, concentrated his attentions on the idea of existence as a defining characteristic, or predicate, of God.

Kant's objection to the ontological argument was that existence is not a predicate. Predicates describe what something is like, telling us about its characteristics. It might be shiny, or yellow, or salty to taste. Its predicates make it different from other things, so that we can identify it when we see it. But 'existence', Kant said, is not a predicate, and should not be used in the

AO1 activity 8
a) Explain, in your own words, Gaunilo's criticism of Anselm's argument.
b) How did Anselm reply to Gaunilo?

same way as words that describe something's characteristics. When we say that something exists, we are not saying that it has the quality of existence, in addition to its other qualities. What we are saying is that the thing we are thinking of, with all of its characteristics, has been 'actualised': that there is at least one example of it in the real world.

Kant's objection can be better understood if we think about it in other contexts. Imagine someone putting up a notice at school saying, 'Lost: art folder – it's black with a zip, it exists, it's got lots of charcoal drawings inside, it's A3 in size.' Or, imagine someone writing in a job application, 'I have three years' experience in retail, I have a full UK driving licence, I exist, and I am fluent in English and Punjabi.' The reference to existence immediately jumps out as something that does not belong in a list of characteristics or qualities. Predicates, argued Kant, add something to our understanding of the nature of the thing we are describing, and existence does not do this. Instead, it tells us whether the thing we are describing, with all its characteristics, is real.

Kant gave his own example, asking us to imagine 100 thalers, which were large coins used in the currency of some eighteenth-century European countries. He suggested that it makes no difference at all, when describing the size, shape and material of the thalers, if you add 'exists' to the list of descriptors; not a single coin is added or taken away. Of course, if we actually had the money, we would be richer than if the coins were only imaginary, but the status of the coins as either real or imaginary does nothing to describe them.

A further objection Kant made was to question Descartes' analogy of the triangle. It is true that a triangle by definition must have these three angles that add up to two right-angles. But this does not mean that we have to accept the existence of triangles. We could just reject the whole concept of triangles, definition and all. Similarly with mountains: we could agree that mountains necessarily slope down if they slope up, but we do not also have to accept that there are such things as mountains in the real world. Kant's point might be more easily understood if we use the example of unicorns. We might say a unicorn, by definition, must have one horn, otherwise it would not be a unicorn; and everyone might agree with our definition, that unicorns do indeed have to have one horn. However, accepting the definition of a unicorn is very different from accepting that unicorns actually exist in the real world. Kant was arguing that even if we accept the definition of God that Descartes offers, we could simply reject the whole idea that there is a God who necessarily exists in reality with all the perfections.

It made no sense, to Kant, to use the ontological argument to demonstrate the existence of God because the argument, especially in the way Descartes presents it, focuses on the idea that existence is one of God's characteristics. In Kant's view, this is not logically sound.

Kant uses the example of thalers, which were coins in the currency he used.

AO1 activity 9

Explain why Kant thought that existence is not a predicate.

To what extent are *a priori* arguments for God's existence persuasive?

To recap, arguments for God's existence, like other arguments, can be classified as *a priori* or *a posteriori*. *A priori* arguments depend entirely on logical reasoning and not on sense experience. They do not need any kind of experiment or evidence to back them up. Instead, they work like mathematics: if you have understood the terms correctly and done the workings correctly, the conclusion is certain. Most arguments for the existence of God are inductive, *a posteriori* arguments, but the ontological argument is a deductive, *a priori* argument. How persuasive do you find this kind of argument?

The view that *a priori* arguments for God's existence are persuasive

A priori arguments depend only on logic, and not on sense experience. Sense experience is not always reliable; we sometimes think that we saw or heard something, and then find out we were mistaken. Sense experience is different for different people; we see colours differently, we have different views about whether things sound or taste good, and we interpret what we experience differently depending on our previously-held beliefs. With *a posteriori* arguments, new information might be discovered that makes us have to change our minds. But with *a priori* arguments, if the premises are true, then the conclusion is inescapably true as well. It is not a question of the conclusion being persuasive or otherwise. With a sound argument, the conclusion is a certainty, just as in mathematics there is no persuasion involved in accepting the conclusion that $a + b = b + a$.

The fact that *a priori* arguments do not rely on experience can be seen as an advantage, because it means that people of different cultures and belief systems can reach the same conclusions. People in the twenty-first century live in very different cultural environments to the cultural environments experienced by Anselm and Descartes, but this does not affect the strength of their ontological arguments; we do not have to tell ourselves 'people understood science differently in those days' or 'the world was a different place when they were alive' when we are assessing their thinking.

The view that *a priori* arguments for God's existence are not persuasive

A priori arguments are only as good as their premises. If the premises are unsound then the whole argument falls apart. For example, I could give the argument:

> If my front door is red, there are lemons on Mars.
>
> My front door is red.
>
> Therefore, there are lemons on Mars.

There is nothing wrong with the logical structure of this argument, but the premises are false: the colour of my front door has nothing to do with whether or not there are lemons on Mars and, incidentally, my front door is not red. The premises are false and the conclusion is absurd. In the case of the ontological argument, the premises are debatable, and an *a priori* argument will only convince if the premises are true. Some people will argue that its premises are logically unsound, and so they will not be persuaded by it.

A priori arguments are abstract and conceptual, and this does not appeal to everyone. Many people, whether they have faith in God or not, find the ontological argument to be little more than an intellectual puzzle that is playing with words and has little relevance to everyday questions of belief. Some argue that ontological arguments are merely circular: they require us to accept a definition of God before we can even begin, and then we are forced to agree with the definition we started with in the conclusion, and we have not really got anywhere. Many prefer to base their beliefs on their experiences, perhaps feeling a sense of wonder at the beauty of the world or the existence of the universe, or a sense that there is a greater power guiding them in their lives. They argue that *a posteriori* arguments are more persuasive because they are based on evidence that is available to everyone.

Anselm himself recognised that the *a priori* nature of his argument would be unlikely to convince the unbeliever, instead referring to it as 'faith seeking understanding'. It is, he thought, a meditation on the concept of God to give Christians a deeper spiritual understanding of the faith they already have, and not an argument that will bring a relationship with God into the real everyday lives of people who previously had no belief.

> ### AO2 activity 1
> How persuasive do you find *a priori* arguments for the existence of God, in comparison with *a posteriori* arguments? Give reasons to support your answer.

To what extent do different religious views on the nature of God impact on arguments for the existence of God?

This question is asking whether arguments for the existence of God depend on a particular understanding of what God is like, and whether different views of God might make the arguments more or less effective.

Ontological, cosmological, and teleological arguments for the existence of God tend to come from the monotheistic religious traditions of Christianity and Islam, and to an extent, Judaism. These religions share belief in a God who is omnipotent (all-powerful), omnibenevolent (all-loving or all-good), and omniscient (all-knowing). They also share belief in a God who is personal, in other words a being with intentions who is capable of having relationships rather than a blind force.

The ontological argument

The ontological argument depends completely on accepting an understanding of God in which God has all the perfections, is the best, and a being than which nothing greater can be thought. A different kind of religious belief, without the belief that God is that than which no greater can be thought, would not give the ontological argument the premises it needs in order to begin. Buddhist belief, for example, has many variants, but there are Buddhists who believe that there is no ultimate God. Belief in God, for some Buddhists, is a step on the way to enlightenment, but should in the end be discarded. The ontological argument would not work for these Buddhists because they would not agree that God exists in reality, just as a concept. Similarly, a religious belief system that involves a range of deities, with virtues and with flaws, is not compatible with the ontological argument, as the ontological argument is set up to demonstrate the existence of one supremely perfect being. Belief in a God that has elements of both good and evil is also incompatible with the ontological argument, as we can imagine a greater and more perfect God, one that is wholly good.

Within the Christian tradition, too, Aquinas questioned the ontological argument's definition of the nature of God, because in Aquinas' view, the nature of God is beyond human understanding. We cannot know the nature of God and, therefore, we cannot all agree on a definition of God as our first premise. In his writing, Aquinas pointed out that people have different religious beliefs; some, for example, believe that God has a physical body, which means that Anselm's definition is not universally accepted.

> *Perhaps not everyone who hears the name 'God' understands it to signify something than which nothing greater can be thought, seeing that some have believed God to be a body.*
>
> Thomas Aquinas, *Summa Theologica*

Different religious views on the nature of God impact greatly on the ontological argument because the argument only gets off the ground if we agree at the beginning on a definition that God is supremely perfect.

The cosmological argument

The cosmological argument depends on an understanding of God as a being with ultimate power, who is capable of creating something out of nothing. The cosmological argument does not necessitate God having other attributes, such as kindness or wisdom. It does, however, depend on an idea of a God who exists necessarily, without a cause. The argument can still work for people whose idea of God is that God is an impersonal force, or that God transcends the universe and does not interact with it, or that God started the universe and then left. But there are other understandings of God that would not work well with the cosmological argument. Some people believe that God is a kind of pictorial way of expressing human hope (and so would not exist if there were no people to have the hope); they think of God in terms of a concept that helps people understand the world and their place in it, but is perhaps not a being that exists 'out there'. The cosmological argument does nothing to support this kind of understanding of God, as it focuses on the idea of God as an all-powerful supernatural cause that existed before there were any people to conceptualise God. For those who hold the view that God is a pictorial way of understanding reality, the cosmological argument is of little importance or relevance.

The cosmological argument is also incompatible with the idea that, instead of one God, there are a range of gods and spirits of varying limited abilities who inhabit the natural world. It would also not work for those whose religious beliefs are that the physical world is ultimately an illusion, as the cosmological argument starts with the premise that the universe exists.

Different religions have different understandings of the nature of God, which may not be supported by the traditional Christian arguments for God's existence.

Teleological arguments

Teleological arguments depend on an understanding of one God with ultimate power, in the sense that they point to the existence of a designer that was not itself designed. However, they could be compatible with religious beliefs in many gods, as it could be held that different things in the world are attributable to the creative activity of different deities; there is no need to assume that if the world is designed, it must have all been designed by one single intelligence, as Hume noted in his criticisms.

Design arguments point to a personal God (or gods) who is creative and who makes decisions, but they do not necessarily point to a loving God. In fact, some people argue that the design of the natural world suggests an uncaring or even a cruel God, who deliberately makes creatures that cause others to suffer, and who makes a natural world in which there are disasters and hardships.

Most religions teach that God, or the gods, are responsible for creating and designing the world, and so design arguments are compatible with most belief systems. However, religions that teach that the world is ultimately an illusion (such as some schools of Buddhism) have no need of design arguments; and those that teach that God too is ultimately an illusion have no need of any arguments asserting God's existence in reality.

AO2 activity 2

How far do you think religions other than Christianity are supported by ontological, cosmological, and teleological arguments for the existence of God?

How effective is the ontological argument for God's existence?

In answering this question, we need to consider what 'effective' means. Anselm's ontological argument was written as a meditation on the nature of God, for use in prayer and contemplation by Christians, and so it is effective if it is used in that way and brings whoever uses it to a greater understanding of their faith. However, if it is understood as an argument for God's existence, then it is effective if it demonstrates that God exists, and ineffective if it does not.

The view that the ontological argument is effective

The ontological argument could be regarded as effective because it is an *a priori* argument and presents a deductive proof. Rather than giving a conclusion that is more or less probable, it could be thought to present an incontrovertible set of logical steps that demonstrate God exists for certain. If the premises are accepted, then the argument is extremely effective. There is nothing that could be said against it, and no new information could be produced to lead to a different conclusion.

The ontological argument could be regarded as effective because it has a thousand-year history, demonstrating that it has stood the test of time and deserves respectful consideration. Although it is an old argument, it can be used with contemporary methods of philosophy, such as Norman Malcolm's modal logic.

Although people have criticised the ontological argument, there are also those who respond to the criticisms. Some scholars, such as Malcolm, argue that although existence is not a predicate of contingent things, necessary existence is a predicate of God. This is because only God has necessary existence. Therefore if we are talking about 'a being with necessary existence' then we can identify this being as God, just from that description.

The ontological argument could be regarded as effective to the extent that it meets its aim of 'faith seeking understanding': it gives theists a deeper understanding of the nature of God and the way in which God exists, which could strengthen their faith as they come to an understanding that God's existence is something that is totally reliable.

The fact that the ontological argument continues to attract the interest of modern scholars shows that it is effective in provoking thought, even if it does not lead people to religious belief. A thousand years after it was first presented, scholars are still debating the ideas it raises.

The view that the ontological argument is not effective

The ontological argument is unlikely to convert people from atheism to Christian faith, however strong it is, because people are not usually converted by logic. Religious belief tends to operate on a more subjective, personal level.

As a rational argument, some people argue that the ontological argument is ineffective because of the criticisms raised by Gaunilo and Kant. Gaunilo's argument, that you cannot make something exist just by defining it with superlatives, seems to many to be a sound criticism. Kant's idea that 'existence is not a predicate' also seems correct to many; existence is not a quality or a characteristic, but instead tells us whether the object in question has been 'actualised': it tells us whether or not there are examples of it in real life.

Some critics object to the ontological argument as put forward by Malcolm. Malcolm argued that God is an unlimited being whose existence is not impossible. As an unlimited being, God cannot have the limits of existing contingently so, in Malcolm's view, God cannot simply be possible but must instead exist necessarily. Critics argue that Malcolm's case is weak: there are plenty of things that do not exist but whose existence is not impossible, such as English words that rhyme with 'orange', or a Porsche that belongs to me. Malcolm may have established that a being meeting the definition of 'God' cannot come in and out of existence, but that is different from saying that God, with all the attributes Malcolm wishes to ascribe to God, might or might not exist. All Malcolm has succeeded in showing is that there may or may not be an unlimited being in reality.

The ontological argument depends on us agreeing at the outset that God is perfect and is superlatively great. To some, this means that we are asked to accept the conclusion of the argument as a premise. We might not want to accept that definition of God. We might, instead, want to define God as 'an imaginary being' or 'a concept that people use to help them make sense of their lives', or any number of other definitions. If we have to accept the conclusion as one of the premises, then the argument is nothing but circular.

> **AO2 activity 3**
> How effective do you think the ontological argument is in demonstrating the existence of God? Give reasons to support your answer.

Is the ontological argument more persuasive than the cosmological and teleological arguments for God's existence?

This question is asking for a comparison between the ontological, cosmological, and teleological arguments for the existence of God. Which, if any, works the best?

The view that the ontological argument is the most persuasive

The ontological argument could be viewed as the most persuasive because of its nature as a deductive argument. If it works, it leads to the inescapable conclusion that God exists. It does not depend on any sense experience, so the conclusion will not change whatever happens. Even if there is a terrible disaster in the world, or we stop seeing any evidence of design or purpose around us, this does not affect the conclusion of the ontological argument. It could be seen as the most rock-solid of any argument that could be offered. The other arguments, in contrast, are inductive in nature and cannot, therefore, lead to the certainty of a deductive argument.

The view that the cosmological argument is the most persuasive

Some find the cosmological argument the most persuasive because it starts with our observation that the universe exists, which is difficult to deny. As it depends on observation rather than logic, it could be seen as more accessible to most people than the ontological argument. It could also be seen as more persuasive than teleological arguments, because in the case of the existence of the universe, science has not presented an alternative explanation that does not need reference to God. It could be argued that the Big Bang theory still lacks a sufficient reason for the cause of the universe; even though it might explain the processes by which the universe came into being, it does not offer any explanation of why these processes happened at all.

The view that teleological arguments are the most persuasive

Teleological arguments cannot lead to certain conclusions, and they face strong challenges from science, especially from the theory of evolution as an alternative explanation of apparent order and purpose in the world. However, there are, nevertheless, many people who feel drawn to teleological arguments, because they have an emotional pull that the other arguments lack. They appeal to the feelings of wonder we have when we see a new-born baby or a spectacular sunset, or when we see a snowflake through a microscope or watch a program about the natural world. Religious belief is about emotion as well as reason and so, while other arguments might have more strength as reasoned arguments, teleological arguments could appeal more to the spiritual side of human nature.

The view that the ontological, cosmological, and teleological arguments are equally persuasive

For many people, the arguments for the existence of God work well together; there is no need to pick a favourite. The arguments are seen to present a cumulative case for God's existence, each adding additional evidence for theistic belief. Some might argue that there are many aspects of the world, available for us to observe, that can support belief in God using inductive reasoning, and the ontological argument adds to this by showing that the God to whom the inductive arguments point is a God who must exist necessarily.

The view that none of the arguments are persuasive

Many argue that none of the arguments persuasively demonstrate the existence of God. The ontological argument depends on our acceptance of premises that we might not want to accept; we might agree with Kant that existence is not a predicate. Cosmological and teleological arguments depend on an agreement that God is the best explanation for the things we observe, but many take the view that science provides a more solid, reliable, testable explanation, and that we need to look no further than scientific explanations to understand the world around us. There are religious believers, too, who do not think the arguments are persuasive. They argue that religious belief is a matter for faith, and that rational arguments cannot produce that.

AO2 activity 4

a) Of the three arguments for the existence of God you have studied, which, if any, do you find the most and the least persuasive?
b) Outline what you consider to be the strong and weak points of each of the three arguments for the existence of God you have studied.

How effective are the challenges to the ontological argument for God's existence?

This question asks for a consideration and evaluation of criticisms of the ontological argument. Gaunilo challenged Anselm's version of the argument, and Kant challenged Descartes'. Both aimed to show that the ontological argument does not work. Have they been successful in showing that the ontological argument has serious flaws?

The view that challenges to the ontological argument are effective

The first challenge made to the ontological argument came from Gaunilo, who argued that it was absurd for Anselm to attempt to move from a definition of God to the proof of a God existing in reality. Those who find this challenge effective would agree that a definition is not able to demonstrate or prove existence. The definition can only show what the nature of something would be if it existed. Gaunilo's use of an island to illustrate his point is seen as effectively demonstrating the absurdity of the ontological argument.

Kant's challenge to the ontological argument could also be considered effective. If Kant is right that existence is not a predicate, then ontological arguments cannot predicate the existence of God and then claim to have demonstrated God's existence. Kant rejects Descartes' analogies of triangles and of mountains, saying that we can accept that this is what triangles or mountains must be like, but we do not have to accept that they also exist in real life; and the same applies to God. The word 'exists' just means that the concept corresponds to something in real life; it does not add anything to our understanding. Kant's example of the 100 thalers can be seen as effective, as it is true that a pile of 100 real thalers and a pile of 100 imaginary thalers have the same number of coins in them.

The twentieth-century philosopher Bertrand Russell supported Kant's view. He criticised the ontological argument in a similar way, by offering the statement, 'The present king of France is bald'. This is not a true statement. However, this does not mean that the present king of France in fact has hair because there is no such person as the present king of France. We can predicate what we like about this imaginary king, but our predicates do nothing to establish his existence. Russell found Kant's objections effective.

Other challenges to the ontological argument include the idea that we do not all agree about what God is and, therefore, we cannot accept the first premise of the ontological argument or move any further forward with it. This could be seen as an effective argument because there are different religions in the world and different kinds of spirituality, and they do not all share a common view of God.

The view that challenges to the ontological argument are not effective

Anselm responded to Gaunilo straight away, to say that Gaunilo had missed the point and that 'an island' cannot be substituted for 'God' in the argument because islands do not have God's necessary existence. The challenge from Gaunilo can be regarded as ineffective because it was readily and immediately countered.

Kant's argument, that existence is not a predicate, could be seen as ineffective. His example of the thalers has been criticised: of course there is a difference between 100 real coins and 100 imaginary ones. If asked which you would prefer, you would of course prefer the real ones. Some argue that existence can be used as a predicate; people talk about things being 'real' in order to distinguish them from the imaginary or the fake. Malcolm, among others, argued that existence can be a predicate of God, if not of contingent things, because God is unique in existing necessarily. We might be able to reject the existence in reality of a triangle or a mountain, but triangles and mountains are contingent.

Challenges to the ontological argument can also be seen as ineffective because they fail to take into account that the purpose of the argument was 'faith seeking understanding'. The challenges are accusing the argument of failing to convince unbelievers, when it was never intended to be used for that purpose.

AO2 activity 5
How effective do you find the challenges to the ontological argument? Do you think they are fair? Give reasons to support your answer.

To what extent are objections to the ontological argument persuasive?

This question raises very similar issues to the previous, in that it asks whether the views that challenge ontological arguments, such as the views of Gaunilo and Kant, put up a strong case. The points discussed for the previous question would be relevant in a response to this question .

The view that objections to the ontological argument are persuasive

The objection that people do not share the same understanding of God can be seen as very persuasive, as there is evidence of many different understandings of God. Some religions are strictly monotheistic, such as Judaism, Christianity, and Islam, and these religions also promote the view that God is all-powerful and perfectly good. However, believers in other religions have different views. For example, in Hinduism, although there is a belief in one God, there is also the belief that God is manifest in many different ways in the form of deities, and there is the belief that God is both creative and destructive, good and evil, kind and cruel. Some schools of Buddhist thought have a belief in God but others see God as, ultimately, an illusion. There are also people with pagan beliefs or animistic beliefs, or beliefs in a creator God who takes no interest in the world, or beliefs in a pantheon of gods rather than a single ultimate deity. Others understand the concept of God from the position of atheism, seeing God as an imaginary support for those who find adult life difficult, or as a means of controlling the working classes by making them think they should accept inequality because God has chosen it for them. All of these different understandings of God are clearly evidenced and, without a common understanding of what God is, the ontological argument does not work.

Gaunilo was right to show that the argument is essentially absurd, and Kant's view that existence is not a predicate is sound. We do not use 'existence' in language as a defining characteristic to tell us more about a subject. Adding the word 'exists' to a description of anything does not change whether or not that thing can be found in reality.

The view that objections to the ontological argument are not persuasive

Those who support the ontological argument will find the objections unconvincing. They might argue that a common understanding of God is not necessary for the argument to work: those who do not understand God to be that than which no greater can be thought are 'fools' who have not given the concept of God sufficient thought.

Supporters of the ontological argument take the view that the objections fail to recognise the necessary existence of God. Necessary existence is a predicate of God, and a proper understanding of God reveals that God exists necessarily; therefore, the conclusion that God exists is certain.

AO2 activity 6

Having studied different versions of the ontological argument and a range of objections to it, which do you think is the strongest version of the argument (if any)? Which is the strongest objection (if any)? Give reasons to support your answers.

Exam support

Practising AO1 questions

AO1 questions begin with one of a range of possible command words (see pages 8–9 for more detail.) The following question begins with the word 'Outline'. 'Outline' questions require you to demonstrate knowledge and understanding of the key features of the topic in the question. You do not need to consider the quality of an argument or offer any views about it.

Activity

Look at the past paper question and the example paragraph taken from a longer answer written in response. Using the example paragraph as a guide, write a second paragraph for this answer in which you outline Kant's challenges to the ontological argument. Try to make your paragraph relevant, and try to use specialist terms such as 'predicate'.

> *Outline the challenges to the ontological argument with reference to Gaunilo and Kant.*
>
> (Eduqas AS Level Religious Studies, Summer 2017, Component 2: An Introduction to the Philosophy of Religion, Question 3a)

Example

Gaunilo[2] was a monk and a contemporary of Anselm. Although he was a Christian himself, he did not think that the ontological argument worked. When he read Anselm's ontological argument, presented in his work *Proslogion*[4], he challenged them with a *reductio ad absurdum*[7] argument, in which he repeated Anselm's argument back to him but changed the subject matter from 'God' to a 'lost island'[6]. He did this to demonstrate that the logic of the ontological argument does not work. The ontological argument is a *deductive*[7] argument, aiming to work from *a priori* premises[7] to a conclusion. If the premises are true and the logic is sound, then the conclusion must be true as well. Gaunilo's reply was meant to demonstrate that the premises are not sound, because Anselm moved from defining God as[1] 'that than which no greater can be conceived'[6] to a conclusion in which he claims to show that God must exist in reality[1] (in re[7]) as well as in the mind[1] (in intellectu[7]).

1 This paragraph contains accurate and relevant knowledge and understanding.

2 This is an extensive and relevant paragraph that responds to the specific demands of the question; it sticks firmly to the subject matter of the question.

3 This paragraph contains excellent use of evidence and examples, with the writer using their own example to demonstrate their understanding.

4 This passage makes accurate reference to *Proslogion* and 'On Behalf of the Fool'.

Gaunilo argued that if we replace the idea of God with the idea of an island, we can imagine our island as being 'the most excellent', but we would not be justified in assuming that, just because we have termed it superlatively excellent, it must exist in reality. Gaunilo called his reply[2] 'On Behalf of the Fool'[4] because he felt he was defending those who do not see how the concept of God leads with certainty to the conviction that God must, therefore, exist.[2] Gaunilo's challenge was that we cannot define something into existence just by calling it 'most excellent' or 'most perfect'.[1] For example, I could define the most perfect house, greater than which no house could be conceived, but it does not exist just because I have defined it as perfect.[3]

5 This passage does not make links with other areas of study, but this is fine because such links would not be appropriate in this part of the answer.

6 This paragraph refers to Gaunilo and to Anselm with accuracy. Gaunilo's challenge is essential for this answer, and the writer has correctly identified that it was Anselm's version of the argument that Gaunoli challenged.

7 The paragraph contains thorough and accurate use of specialist language and vocabulary in context.

AO1 practice question 1

Try answering the following question, using the points to remember to help you construct your answer.

> *Examine different versions of the ontological argument for the existence of God as presented by Anselm and Malcolm.*
>
> (Eduqas A Level Religious Studies, Summer 2018, Component 2: Philosophy of Religion, Question 2a)

Points to remember

- The question asks specifically for Anselm's and Malcolm's versions of the ontological argument, so with limited time in an exam, stick closely to these two versions and do not add in a description of, for example, Descartes' version.
- Provide as much detail as you can; for example, show you understand that Anselm presented his version of the ontological argument in two slightly different ways.
- Try to use specialist vocabulary with confidence. You could use terms such as '*a priori*' and 'necessary existence'.
- This type of question is looking for knowledge and understanding, so you do not need to give your opinion of the arguments or present any objections to them.

AO1 practice question 2

Now try this question on your own.

> *Explain how ontological arguments may be challenged with reference to Gaunilo and Kant.*
>
> (Eduqas A Level Religious Studies, Autumn 2020, Component 2: Philosophy of Religion, Question 2a)

Practising AO2 questions

AO2 questions are designed to assess your ability to evaluate and critically analyse. Concentrate on weighing up different views and identifying the strengths and weaknesses of each view. Avoid spending too much of your response presenting your knowledge in a descriptive way.

Activity

Here is an example of a past paper question and two example paragraphs taken from longer answers written in response.

1. The writer of Example 1 has not properly understood the difference between AO1 and AO2 skills. Using 'Understanding the Assessment Objectives' on pages 6–8 to help you, briefly explain to them how the two Assessment Objectives are different, and how part (b) questions should be answered.

2. Example 2 is part of a good response. Give the writer some detailed feedback, telling them what they have done well using examples from the paragraph. For example, you could say, 'Your use of key terms is very good. You show a clear understanding of the terms "*a priori*" and "*a posteriori*", and you are confident in your knowledge of what a 'premise' is in an argument.' Explain how their answer successfully meets the requirements for AO2.

'A priori *arguments can never prove God's existence.' Evaluate this view.*

(Eduqas A Level Religious Studies, Autumn 2020, Component 2: Philosophy of Religion, Question 2b)

Example 1

Ontological arguments are [2] *a priori* [6] arguments.[2] This means that they work from first principles, starting with[1] premises[6] and then building on the premises to reach a conclusion.[1] They do not rely on sense experience or evidence. Anselm's[4] ontological argument was written in his book *Proslogion*, where he gave two slightly different versions. In his first version, he began with the statement that God is 'that than which nothing greater can be conceived'.[1] He used this to say that existence in the real world is greater than existence in the mind, and so God must exist in the real world[2] (*in re* [6]). In his second argument, Anselm began with the same premise[6], but this time he talked about God existing necessarily[6] rather than contingently[6]. If God exists necessarily then this proves the existence of God.[3]

1 The information is accurate, but the student should be focusing on analysing the strengths and weaknesses of the view presented in the quotation and making evaluative judgements.

2 This paragraph focuses on the subject matter of the quotation, but it does not respond correctly to the command word.

3 The judgement made in this paragraph is only assertive. It should be supported with reasons or examples.

4 There is a reference to an appropriate scholar in this paragraph.

5 This paragraph does not make any connections with other areas of study. This is fine, because connections should not be forced.

6 There is some good, accurate use of specialist vocabulary in this paragraph.

Example 2

Ontological arguments can prove the existence of God, because[2] they are *a priori*[6] arguments that lead to certain conclusions. *A posteriori*[6] arguments, in contrast, can only lead to probable conclusions; they can never prove, because they depend on sense experience and evidence which can be mistaken or can change[3]. With *a priori* arguments, a series of premises[6] lead to a conclusion; if the premises are true then the conclusion must also be true. If any argument for the existence of God can be called 'proof', it is only the ontological argument. Anselm, Descartes, and Malcolm[4] each successfully[1] used *a priori* reasoning to show the existence of God. Anselm's[4] first premise – God is that than which no greater can be conceived – is a sound[1] premise, as anyone who truly understands the nature of God will understand that this is what God must be like. Descartes[4] concentrated on the idea of God's perfection, and similarly used this true premise to make a persuasive and effective case[1] that if God has all the perfections, God must necessarily exist[6]. Malcolm's[4] argument is based on the premise that God's existence is neither impossible nor merely possible, and therefore must be necessary. Each presents an incontrovertible argument that can easily withstand challenges[1]. These arguments are successful because they are logically sound and based on true premises.[3] Those who disagree with the ontological argument need to be able to show that the premises are unsound, and the critics do not do this effectively.

1 Evaluative language is used throughout the paragraph. Right from the start, we are in no doubt which side of the argument the writer prefers.

2 The issue at the heart of the question is successfully identified and addressed.

3 A reason is given to show why *a posteriori* arguments cannot prove something, and a reason is given why ontological arguments are successful.

4 The paragraph contains references to scholarly views that are appropriate and used in the right context.

5 This paragraph does not have connections to other areas of study, as they would not be appropriate here.

6 Specialist vocabulary is used accurately throughout the paragraph.

AO2 practice question 1

Try answering this question. There are some points to remember to help you write your response.

> *'The ontological arguments for God's existence are completely ineffective.' Evaluate this view.*
>
> (WJEC AS Level Religious Studies, Summer 2018, AS Unit 2: An Introduction to Religion and Ethics and the Philosophy of Religion, Question 3b)

Points to remember

- Remember that you are trying to write reasoned analysis and evaluation, rather than description.
- Notice that the question asks about arguments in the plural, so do not confine your discussion to just one thinker.
- Decide whether you think the ontological arguments for God's existence are effective or not, and give your reasons. Rather than just listing what other people have said, make sure you evaluate their contributions to the debate.
- Make references to different scholars where possible, and try to use their arguments and criticisms to support the line of argument you are taking, so that you can lead to a conclusion that you have justified well throughout your response.

AO2 practice question 2

Now try this question on your own.

> *'Kant's challenge to the ontological argument is not effective.' Evaluate this view.*
>
> (Eduqas AS Level Religious Studies, Summer 2018, Component 2: An Introduction to the Philosophy of Religion, Question 3b)

Mark schemes for all exam questions can be found at www.eduqas.co.uk and www.wjec.co.uk.

3 Challenges to religious belief: the problem of evil and suffering

One of the greatest challenges to belief in a loving God is the problem of evil and suffering. If there is an all-powerful, loving God, then why is there evil in the world and why do people suffer? Although most people experience beauty, the kindness of others, good health, and successes, it is also true that most people encounter ugliness, unkindness, illness, and failures; and everyone experiences death. The challenge presented by the problem of evil and suffering is that an omnipotent, omnibenevolent God should have the power to prevent evil and suffering, and ought to want to prevent it out of goodness; and yet evil and suffering exist. Perhaps human experience of evil and suffering indicates that God is not wholly good, or does not have the power to prevent evil or suffering, or perhaps it even shows that there is no God.

This problem is an ancient one. Throughout human history, when people have been faced with suffering and loss, they have had to try to come to terms with it. An accident or an attack can bring lives to an unexpected end or leave people with life-changing injuries. It can seem impossible to cope with infertility, the loss of a child, or the death of a partner or a close friend. Being diagnosed with a serious illness can mean the future suddenly looks very different and plans have to change. For people without religious belief, suffering can be seen as the result of chance; people are in the wrong place at the wrong time, or are just unlucky. But for those with belief in an all-loving, all-powerful God, questions are raised that need answers. Why does God allow suffering? Why does human nature allow some people to inflict suffering on others? Why is God apparently not doing anything when innocent people are in pain?

In this chapter, we will explore two of the most famous ways in which religious thinkers have tried to find answers to the problem of evil and suffering.

Events such as world wars lead people to ask questions about why God allows evil and suffering in the world.

- Does the existence of evil and suffering in the world undermine arguments for the existence of God, providing evidence that a good God cannot exist?
- Does evil and suffering demonstrate that, if God exists, God is not all-powerful?
- Might God have reasons for allowing evil and suffering?
- Could any argument provide a satisfactory answer to the question of why people suffer?

This section of the chapter will enhance your **knowledge** and **understanding** of the topic and help you develop your AO1 skills.

The problem of evil and suffering

Suffering presents difficulties for everyone, no matter what their religious beliefs. Most people hope for a life in which they and their families and friends experience the minimum of suffering, with good health, a comfortable standard of living, contentment and good relationships, a long life, and a peaceful and painless death. This does not always happen, and then people have to find ways of coming to terms with their circumstances and getting through hard times, both practically and emotionally.

However, for religious believers, suffering and evil present more than just practical and emotional challenges: they also present a serious challenge to faith. The problem is particular to those who believe in the 'God of **Classical Theism**', which is a term used to describe God as understood by Judaism, Christianity, and Islam. In other religious traditions, such as Hinduism, God is both good and evil, both creative and destructive. But the God of Classical Theism is described as having attributes which make the existence of evil in the world difficult to understand.

The God of Classical Theism

According to Christian belief, God is perfect. God is the one supreme being who has no rivals (so is not, for example, challenged by a Devil who has equal power). Four of the traditional attributes of God are particularly relevant when considering the problem of evil.

Creator

Christians believe that everything in existence was created by God. The Bible teaches that 'In the beginning, God created the heavens and the earth' (Genesis 1:1, *Holy Bible (NIV)*), and 'Through him all things were made; without him nothing was made that has been made' (John 1:3, *Holy Bible (NIV)*). This means that God deliberately made and designed everything, out of nothing, which is known as ***creatio ex nihilo***. God did not have to work with material that was already in existence and make the best of it; God started from nothing and designed everything from scratch, unconstrained by anything and able to use whatever materials and designs God chose. God made all of the natural processes in the world, and God made the human body and human nature; God gave people their abilities to reason, to make choices, to feel pain, and to inflict pain.

This is an important consideration in discussions of the problem of evil and suffering, because it raises questions about why God designed the world in such a way that there are earthquakes, tsunamis, droughts and disease, when presumably it could have been made differently. The traditional view

> **Key terms**
>
> **Classical Theism:** a term used to refer to belief in one eternal creator God who has attributes of omnipotence, omniscience, and omnibenevolence
>
> ***creatio ex nihilo:*** (Latin) creation out of nothing

of God as creator implies that God did not only make the wings of a butterfly and cause the seasons to enable crops to grow, but also created viruses, cancers, and disabilities. It also raises questions of whether God was right to create the world at all, given the amount of suffering in it.

Omnipotence

Belief in God's omnipotence means belief that God has ultimate power. God has the power to create whole universes out of nothing. Within the philosophy of religion, there are debates about what it means to say that God is **omnipotent**. There are ancient philosophical puzzles about the power of God, such as, 'Can God create a stone too heavy for God to lift?' This is a paradox because whichever answer is chosen, yes or no, it places apparent limits on God's power. Either God can create such a stone (and God is limited because God cannot lift it) or God cannot create such a stone (and God is limited from the outset); in both cases we have allegedly found something God cannot do, and demonstrated that there can be no such thing as absolute omnipotence. This is known as the Paradox of Omnipotence, and some thinkers have argued that omnipotence as a concept does not make sense. There is not just an argument about whether God's omnipotence is compatible with God's other attributes, but about whether omnipotence is a characteristic that is logically possible.

Some philosophers, such as René Descartes, argued that in spite of such paradoxes, God is totally omnipotent and can do absolutely anything at all; there is literally nothing that is beyond God's power, nothing that is too hard for God. The traditional Paradox of Omnipotence can be answered by saying, 'Yes, God can do the logically impossible'. God can create the unliftable stone and can also lift it. Even if it makes no sense to us, it is not impossible for God. We might not be able to see how it could be done, but that is because we are not omnipotent.

Other thinkers, however, such as Aquinas, have argued for a more qualified understanding of the omnipotence of God. If God can do absolutely anything at all, then it follows that God must be able to do evil, and to do unwise things and unloving things; but this does not fit with the idea of a perfect and omnibenevolent God. So, in the view of Aquinas, as well as many other Christian thinkers, God's omnipotence is qualified to mean that God can do anything that is within God's nature, and anything that does not imply a contradiction. God cannot, therefore, commit a wrong act, or fail in any way. Aquinas argued that this does not limit the power of God, because God can still do anything God wants. None of God's choices are impossible for God to do – God has the power to act in whatever way God wants – but God would just never choose to do evil.

God's omnipotence is an important consideration in discussions around the problem of evil and suffering because it raises questions about whether God has the power to prevent suffering by, for example, stopping a tsunami or a pandemic. It raises questions of whether God was forced into making a world in which there is suffering, in order for some greater purpose to be

Key term

omnipotent: all-powerful

achieved, or whether God could have achieved that purpose simply through power and could have avoided the suffering.

Omniscience

Christians believe that God is **omniscient**, or all-knowing. This idea includes both knowledge and wisdom; God knows everything that there is to know, and always knows and does the right thing. Philosophers of religion debate whether omniscience means that God knows the future as well as the past. Those who take the view that God exists eternally, outside time, argue that God sees and knows the whole of the universe from beginning to end, and is in all times and all places. Anselm, for example, argued that God is in the future as well as the past because time does not exist in the same way for God as it does for us. Just as we are limited to being in one geographical location and God is everywhere at once, we are limited to being in one time in history and God is in all times at once. The God of Classical Theism exists in this eternal way, outside time and having full knowledge of the future as well as of everything else.

But this, too, raises questions for the problem of evil and suffering. It suggests that God knew that humanity would disobey God's commandments and fall into sin, even before the creation of the world (although this too is problematic: can there be such a thing as 'before' for a timeless God?). It suggests that God knew about acts of genocide, terrorist attacks and serial killings, as well as natural disasters and personal tragedies, for all time – and yet still let them happen. It can be difficult to blame moral evil entirely on human fault, if God not only created people the way that they are, but also knew even before they were born what they would do. Included in the concept of an eternal God is the idea that God knows, even before people are born, what their destiny will be: whether they will go to heaven after death, or to hell. The implication of this is that God knows from the beginning of time that some people will be immoral, and will cause suffering to others, and will not repent and turn to Christ, and yet creates them anyway.

Some thinkers have, therefore, rejected the eternal God of Classical Theism, and have instead proposed that God moves along the same timeline that we do. God is omniscient in the sense that God knows everything that can be known, but the future cannot be known because it has not happened yet. Some philosophers, such as Charles Hartshorne and Richard Swinburne, argue that the problem of evil and suffering, and questions of human **free will**, can only be understood if this aspect of the God of Classical Theism is qualified to mean that God knows everything that has happened and everything that can be known, but not everything absolutely.

Omnibenevolence

In Classical Theism, God is understood to be **omnibenevolent**. This is understood to mean that God is perfectly loving and perfectly good. All love, wherever it is found, and all goodness, comes from God. Everything that God is, thinks, and does is perfectly good. This raises questions of whether God's goodness places limitations on God's omnipotence, as there

The God of Classical Theism is said to have attributes of perfection, which are challenged by the problem of evil.

appear to be all sorts of things that God cannot do because they are wrong. Aquinas answered this by saying that God's power is unlimited but that God's nature means God will never do evil.

It is an important consideration in discussions of the problem of evil and suffering because many people argue that a perfectly good, perfectly loving God should want to destroy evil and remove all suffering. In discussions of the problem of evil and suffering, God's omnibenevolence is a quality that religious believers have not wanted to suggest is in any way limited.

The types of evil: moral and natural

Traditionally, evil and suffering in the world have been divided into two kinds: moral evil and natural evil.

Moral evil is the name given to the kinds of evil and suffering that are the result of human wrongdoing. It includes things like bullying, murder, war, theft, deceit, and terrorism. Moral evil is considered to refer to deliberate acts that have a wrong intention behind them. They can be 'acts of commission' when a person chooses a course of action and then does it (for example, breaks into a house and commits a burglary), or they can be 'acts of omission' when someone could have done something good but chooses not to (for example, seeing that someone has fallen in the street but not bothering to check on them, or knowing that building materials are unsafe and not using a safer, more expensive alternative).

Natural evil, in contrast, is sometimes called 'non-moral evil', and it refers to suffering and harm that happens because of the workings of the natural world rather than human agency. Natural evil includes things like droughts and floods, earthquakes and volcanoes. It also includes suffering from diseases and from mental illness, and pain cause by the natural processes of childbirth and old age. These are events that do not seem to have any intention behind them and do not target specific individuals, but nevertheless cause suffering.

Evil and suffering are divided into these two types because each type raises different questions and challenges. Natural evil presents questions of why the world should be designed in such a way that it sometimes causes harm and loss of life. It also raises questions about why the human body is so fragile and why there are disabilities, diseases, and psychological traumas. If God is all-loving and all-powerful, why did God create a world in which suffering is a part of nature, when presumably it could have been created differently? Religious believers are left with difficult choices: they have to show that natural evil is in some way the fault of humanity or caused by the Devil, or show that God had good reasons for creating it, or show that natural evil does not really exist.

Responses to the problem of evil and suffering are known as theodicies. '**Theodicy**' comes from two Greek words, *theos* meaning 'God' and *dike*

AO1 activity 1

Create a table or a mind-map illustrating the key attributes of the God of Classical Theism, making sure that you include definitions of unfamiliar terms.

Key terms

moral evil: the kinds of evil and suffering that are brought about through human agency, through wrongdoing

natural evil: the kinds of evil and suffering that are not the fault of humanity but happen because of the way the world is made

theodicy: an attempt to defend and justify the God of Classical Theism given that there is evil and suffering in the world

meaning 'justice', and the philosopher Gottfried Leibniz came up with the word 'theodicy' to describe the justifications that people put forward to explain how God can be defended even though evil and suffering exist in the world.

Moral evil might seem easier to explain, because the blame for suffering can be placed on humanity rather than on God. However, there is still the issue of why God created human nature in such a way that people want to be cruel to each other. Theists often argue that moral evil is the result of free choice: God gave people free will to make their own decisions, rather than creating them as obedient puppets, and because of this free will, people sometimes make wrong choices. This position still leaves difficult questions to answer. Could God not just have given us free will, but also a human nature that was more inclined to choose good? Or given us free will, but a more limited capacity to cause harm? Why does God not stop people who are about to do something terrible and cause great suffering?

Earthquakes are considered to be examples of natural evil, because they happen without any human agency.

Some philosophers point out that the distinction between moral and natural evil is not always sharp, and that the two can overlap. Brian Hebblethwaite, for example, in his book *Evil, Suffering and Religion* (1976) pointed out that even though human sin causes suffering through war, the suffering happens because of the natural way in which people are made. We are conscious and sentient beings, and so have the capacity to suffer. Moral evil starts the war, but natural evil accounts for the disabilities caused by injuries and the psychological problems of PTSD. It is because we have pain receptors and emotions that we are able to feel injuries and suffer bereavement; our bodies are naturally made in such a way that limbs do not grow back and scars are permanent. Some aspects of suffering can be blamed on human moral failure, but not all of them. The same applies to many illnesses; although some are caused through over-eating or lack of exercise or smoking, the natural way our bodies are made enables the suffering.

Both natural and moral evil raise serious questions about why God designed and created a world in which so much pain is possible, when God could have created a world with much less pain, or even chosen not to make a world at all.

> **AO1 activity 2**
> List four examples of evil and suffering that could be classified as moral evil, and four that could be classified as natural evil. Make some notes to explain the difference.

The logical problem of evil: Epicurus

The logical problem of evil is often attributed to the Greek philosopher Epicurus, who lived from 341–270 BCE. Although there is no record of the problem in Epicurus' surviving writings, traditionally the logical problem of evil is known as the Epicurus Dilemma or the Epicurean Paradox.

Epicurus presented the problem of evil in the following way, with premises leading to a conclusion:

If God is all-powerful, then God is able to prevent evil.

If God is all-loving, then God will want to prevent evil.

Evil exists: therefore there cannot be an all-powerful, all-loving God.

The Epicurean problem of evil is a logical problem, because it concentrates on the contradictory nature of belief in an all-loving, all-powerful God when there is evil in the world; it says that it is logically inconsistent to believe in such a God while at the same time recognising that there is evil and suffering. A God who is omnipotent and omnibenevolent cannot exist if there is evil in the world, in the same way that a square circle cannot exist. This version of the argument uses deductive reasoning.

David Hume refers to the Epicurean version of the problem of evil in his 1779 book, *Dialogues Concerning Natural Religion*:

> *Epicurus' old questions are yet unanswered. Is He [God] willing to prevent evil, but not able? Then He is impotent. Is He able, but not willing? Then He is malevolent. Is He both able and willing? Whence then is evil?*
>
> David Hume, *Dialogues Concerning Natural Religion*

Because the problem is presented in the form of deductive reasoning, critics need to show that one or more of the premises of Epicurus' argument is untrue. Usually, philosophers such as William Lane Craig take issue with the premise that if God is all-loving, then God will want to prevent evil. They try, in various ways, to show that allowing evil is in some way more loving than not allowing it to exist.

The evidential problem of evil

The problem of evil can also be considered as an evidential problem. In this way of understanding the problem, people look at their experience of evil and suffering, and use inductive reasoning to decide whether the evidence best supports theism or atheism.

William Paley looked at apparent design in the world and saw evidence of a good and loving God, but not everyone has drawn the same conclusions. Some, such as Charles Darwin, observed the way that some creatures can only exist by causing suffering to others, and wondered how a good God could have created them in such a way. John Stuart Mill, the nineteenth-century philosopher best known for his work on Utilitarianism, argued in an essay called 'On Nature' that if we look at the way the world works, we see evidence of something very different from a wise and loving creator. Nature does all the things we consider criminal offences because of the harm it causes. Mill wrote of the devastation caused by 'a trifling chemical change in an edible root', referring to the Great Irish Famine that was within living memory for his readers.

Synoptic link

Link to *Chapter 1: Arguments for the existence of God: inductive*. The design argument suggests that looking at the world reveals the goodness of God; the problem of evil and suffering suggests the opposite.

> *The order of nature, in so far as unmodified by man, is such as no being, whose attributes are justice and benevolence, would have made with the intention that his rational creatures should follow it as an example … In sober truth, nearly all the things which men are hanged or imprisoned for doing to one another are nature's every-day performances. Killing, the most criminal act recognised by human laws, Nature does once to every being that lives; and, in a large proportion of cases, after protracted tortures such as only the greatest monsters whom we read of ever purposely inflicted on their living fellow creatures … Next to taking life (equal to it according to a high authority) is taking the means by which we live; and Nature does this too on the largest scale and with the most callous indifference. A single hurricane destroys the hopes of a season; a flight of locusts, or an inundation, desolates a district; a trifling chemical change in an edible root starves a million of people … Everything, in short, which the worst men commit either against life or property is perpetrated on a larger scale by natural agents.*
>
> John Stuart Mill, 'On Nature', from *Three Essays on Religion: Nature, the Utility of Religion and Theism*

Bertrand Russell, a leading philosopher and mathematician of the twentieth century, also drew attention to the evidential problem of evil in a lecture given between the two world wars, provocatively entitled 'Why I Am Not a Christian':

> *When you come to look into this argument from design, it is a most astonishing thing that people can believe that this world, with all the things that are in it, with all its defects, should be the best that omnipotence and omniscience has been able to produce in millions of years. I really cannot believe it. Do you think that, if you were granted omnipotence and omniscience and millions of years in which to perfect your world, you could produce nothing better than the Ku-Klux-Klan or the Fascists?*
>
> Bertrand Russell, 'Why I Am Not a Christian'

Many people argue that the sheer scale and intensity of suffering in the world amounts to substantial evidence against the existence of an all-powerful, all-loving God. Because the evidential problem of evil is presented using inductive reasoning, those defending religious belief need to show that the balance of evidence is in favour of the existence of the God of Classical Theism; at the very least, they need to show that, in the end, the good outweighs the evil. They also still have to address the question of why there is any evil at all, on whatever scale.

John Stuart Mill used the example of the Great Irish Famine of the mid-nineteenth century to illustrate the evidential problem of evil.

Developments of the problem of evil

The problem of evil and suffering is an issue that is often revisited in discussions of religious belief. The two world wars of the twentieth century made many people question belief in the God of Classical Theism. For example, J.L. Mackie considered the problem in terms of its logic; William Rowe and Gregory Paul looked at the evidential form of the problem of evil and suffering.

AO1 activity 3
Explain in your own words how the logical problem of evil and the evidential problem of evil are different.

J.L. Mackie

J.L. Mackie was an Australian philosopher, perhaps best known for his work on ethical language. He put forward a case for atheism in an essay called 'Evil and Omnipotence', first published in *Mind* in 1955, in which he discussed the implications of the problem of evil for religious belief. The essay was published only ten years after the end of the Second World War, when many people had lost family members as casualties of fighting, had been bombed out of their homes, and had lived on food rations for years. People had seen newsreels of the Nazi concentration camps and the devastating effects of the dropping of atomic bombs on Hiroshima and Nagasaki. The problem of evil and suffering has always been a problem, but for Mackie's generation, it was particularly acute.

In this essay, Mackie argued that the traditional arguments for the existence of God fail, and showed that it is not possible to establish God's existence through reasoned argument. The believer has to resort to the position that God is known in some other way, not through reason but through faith. However, Mackie argued, the truth is not that God's existence can be known through faith rather than reason, in some non-rational kind of way; instead, the truth is that belief in God is actually irrational. Belief in God depends on believing contradictory things at the same time, and simply does not make sense.

Mackie put forward three beliefs that are held by Christians, and referred to them as the 'inconsistent triad', using a phrase from David Hume. These three beliefs are:

1. God exists and is omnipotent.
2. God exists and is omnibenevolent.
3. Evil exists.

These beliefs are called the inconsistent triad because, according to Mackie and others, all three cannot be true at the same time. If God is all-powerful and all-loving, then it does not make sense for evil to exist in the world, because a God who is all-loving would want to eliminate evil. If that same God is all-powerful, then God has the power to eliminate evil. Theists have to deny the existence of evil, or else claim that God's power is limited or that God is not always loving. If we accept that there is evil and suffering in the world, Mackie argued, then it is impossible to also maintain a rational belief in the God described by Classical Theism.

Mackie looked at some of the different solutions to the problem of evil that have been offered by religious believers. He argued that the problem can only be resolved if people are prepared to give up one of the propositions of the inconsistent triad. Mackie recognised that there have been various attempts to justify God despite the existence of evil and suffering in the world but, he argued, if we look at these possible solutions, it is easy to see that people have given up on one of the propositions in the inconsistent triad.

Some, for example, argue that God has to allow evil into the world in order for there to be human free will, or that evil is necessary as a counterpart to good. Mackie argued that this kind of position means that belief in God's omnipotence has been abandoned: God is constrained, God's intentions for humanity cannot be carried out without some concessions. Believers have to say that God is omnipotent but under the control of logic (rather than that God has power over logic). Mackie referred to this sort of religious explanation as 'half-hearted' because these same religious believers, he said, are not willing to qualify God's omnipotence in other contexts. He said that the solution in which God's omnipotence is constrained may be adequate as a solution, but it is rarely sincerely adopted; people say it in the context of the problem of evil and suffering, but elsewhere they continue to claim that God's power is absolute.

Then there are those who argue that the universe is a better place with evil in it. Mackie argued that this sort of solution to the problem of evil weakens the idea of God's omnipotence. It seems that God's plans cannot be fulfilled unless there is evil: God is constrained; there is something that God cannot do, namely achieve God's aims for humanity while not allowing evil into the world. It also weakens the idea of God as omnibenevolent: God has plans and will stop at nothing to achieve them, even if it means people suffer along the way, making God seem callous.

Mackie concluded by noting a fundamental difficulty with religious belief and the problem of evil. If people really have free will to make their own choices, this has to mean that even God cannot control what they do. But if God cannot control what they do, then God cannot be omnipotent. The Paradox of Omnipotence makes it impossible to defend the concept of an omnipotent God.

William Rowe

William Rowe was an American philosopher of religion, whose 1979 paper 'The Problem of Evil and Some Varieties of Atheism' presents the challenge of the problem of evil and suffering as a reason for being an atheist.

In contrast to Mackie's essay, Rowe's development of the problem of evil focused on the evidential problem of evil, rather than on the logical problem of evil. He argued that while it might, up to a point, seem reasonable for God to allow some suffering in order for people to learn to cope with challenge, there seems to be no understandable excuse for what he termed 'intense suffering'.

Rowe thought that the evidential presentation of the problem of evil presents a stronger challenge to theism than the logical presentation. His view was that the logical presentation makes assumptions that we cannot possibly know to be true. As we are not omniscient, we do not know whether a particular example of suffering might bring about greater good, and so there is no need to accept the premise that an all-loving God will always eliminate evil. It could be that something that causes us to suffer temporarily is a necessary part of God bringing about a much greater good, or preventing a much worse evil. The logical presentation of the problem fails because it is not water-tight; we can question its premises.

AO1 activity 4
Summarise Mackie's views on the problem of evil in your own words. Try to use key terms with accuracy, including: omnipotent, Paradox of Omnipotence, omnibenevolence, logical problem of evil.

However, Rowe argued, if we look at the evidence and weigh up probabilities, it seems highly likely that the God of Classical Theism does not exist. He focused on examples of intense suffering, where it is hard to imagine what eventual good result could possibly make the suffering acceptable. Rowe discussed animal suffering to illustrate his point. He asked us to imagine a forest fire in which a fawn is trapped and horribly burned. It dies slowly and in great pain, over several days. Rowe said that this kind of suffering seems pointless: there does not seem to be any good that can eventually come out of such suffering, or any bad that is being prevented. There does not seem to be any reason why the animal should have died slowly rather than straight away. The animal is not capable of learning from its suffering and, with no witnesses, no one else is going to learn from it either. Rowe argued that events like this do happen, and an omnipotent, omniscient being could prevent them. If there is an omnipotent, omniscient God, then God should be able to see that intense suffering is about to happen and step in to prevent it.

Rowe accepted that, perhaps, there is a reason somewhere for intense suffering but concludes that, on balance, it seems more likely that the atheist is right.

> *The theist may point out that some suffering leads to moral and spiritual development impossible without suffering. But it's reasonably clear that suffering often occurs in a degree far beyond what is required for character development. The theist may say that some suffering results from free choices of human beings and might be preventable only by preventing some measure of human freedom. But again, it's clear that much intense suffering occurs not as a result of human free choices.*
>
> William Rowe, 'The Problem of Evil and Some Varieties of Atheism'

Rowe's argument, then, starts with the observation that intense suffering happens. It seems that an omniscient and omnibenevolent God would only allow suffering to happen if there was some point to it, some purpose to be achieved that could not be achieved without the suffering. However, much intense suffering appears to be pointless. Therefore, it is probable that there is no omnipotent, omnibenevolent God.

Rowe termed himself a 'friendly atheist'. He did not reject theistic answers to the problem of evil completely, but considered that the evidence gives a strong indication that the God of Classical Theism does not exist.

Gregory S. Paul

Gregory S. Paul is an American freelance writer, scientist, and artist. He specialises in dinosaurs and in illustration, but is also interested in theology and sociology, particularly because his academic specialism of palaeontology has brought him into disagreement with those who believe that the theory of evolution is false and that the world was created as described in the Bible. Paul has attracted the interest of the media because of his article published in the journal *Philosophy and Theology* in 2007, where he used statistical evidence to argue that an omnibenevolent God cannot exist. The article is called, 'Theodicy's Problem: A Statistical Look

AO1 activity 5

Explain why Rowe chose to use the example of animal suffering to make his point, rather than choosing the suffering of an adult human being.

at the Holocaust of the Children and the Implications of Natural Evil for the Free Will and Best of All Worlds Hypothesis'.

Paul writes that the problem of evil often comes into the foreground of philosophical thought after a natural disaster such as the Indian Ocean tsunami of 2004, but then fades back into the background after a while. However, Paul argues, there is a problem far more serious than even the most severe natural disasters, and that problem is the sheer scale of the number of children throughout history who have died before reaching what is often thought of as 'the age of reason'. He is referring to children whose lives were so short that they had not reached a stage at which they could have made a mature decision about Christian faith. Paul suggests that a good way of assessing God's 'moral management' of the world is to measure the results of God's management, using statistics. Then, taking a somewhat scientific approach, these statistics can be used to judge whether or not God appears to be good.

Paul estimates that in total, some 100 billion humans have been born, and the number of conceptions is much higher: 'this figure may be as high as or even exceed half a trillion'. Many pregnancies do not reach full term, resulting in miscarriage or stillbirth, and a large number of pregnancies have also resulted in maternal death. Then, even in developed countries, the number of children who died in infancy was as high as 25 per cent in 1900 and, before 1800, at least half of all children died before they reached maturity. In developing countries, record-keeping has not been as thorough but it appears that at least one-quarter of births have resulted in the death of the baby, and more than half the number of live births have resulted in infant death. Most died of diseases, Paul notes, and 'Christian children died off as rapidly as those of other faiths'. Therefore, since humans first appeared, the number of infants who died before reaching the age of reason exceeds 50 billion. If you add in the number of conceptions that did not lead to the birth of a live baby, the number of childhood deaths exceeds the number of people who survived into adulthood by around 7:1. On top of that, there is also a relatively small number of children who die through moral evil: war, genocide, preventable famine, and so on. The leading cause of death among children is microbial disease, in particular malaria, where young children are particularly susceptible because their immune systems are immature. Paul refers to these statistics as the 'Holocaust of the Children'.

> *If a creator exists, then it has chosen to fashion a habitat that has maximised the level of suffering and death among young humans that are due to factors beyond the control of humans over most of history.*
>
> Gregory S. Paul, 'Theodicy's Problem: A Statistical Look at the Holocaust of the Children and the Implications of Natural Evil for the Free Will and Best of All Worlds Hypothesis'

Synoptic link

Link to *Chapter 1: Arguments for the existence of God: inductive*. Paul challenges thinkers such as Tennant who have argued that the universe is 'just right' for human life.

Paul considers the ways in which religious believers often justify natural evil, and rejects them. He rejects the view that a world that contains some suffering is necessary in order that we are able to learn, grow and make free decisions, because so many children never get to do those things. Many religious thinkers argue that human free will is so important that some suffering is necessary: we need to have real choices between good and evil, and real challenges to face, otherwise we would just be puppets or automata, and life would not be worth living. But Paul argues that this cannot be used to justify natural evil because of the sheer number of very young people who do not ever get those free mature choices and opportunities to learn. Free will is a bogus argument, he insists, and the way humanity is designed is grossly wasteful and causes needless suffering on a huge scale. Even if people assume that those 50 billion children went straight to heaven after death, this does not resolve the question of why they had to suffer in their short lives. Why were they given such poor immune systems with which to face the world? Why are female bodies made in such a way that birth is so dangerous?

Paul challenges those who claim that the universe has been fine-tuned so that it is exactly right for human life and human flourishing, saying that the statistics show that in fact the world is a death-trap for children. He concludes that if a God exists who created and designed everything, which he doubts, then such a God is not worthy of worship.

> **AO1 activity 6**
> In your own words, explain how Paul uses statistical evidence to present a challenge to religious belief.

Religious responses to the problem of evil: Augustinian-type theodicy

Who was Augustine?

Augustine of Hippo, who lived in North Africa from 354–430 CE, was one of the leading figures of Christianity, and had a great influence on the development of its doctrines. He wrote a great deal, and a substantial amount of his writing survives, giving us an insight into his mind and thought processes in a way that is hard to achieve for other thinkers who are known only by repute. Augustine's thinking drew heavily on his own wrongdoing and his own experiences of evil and suffering, described in his work *Confessions* and *City of God*. Augustine's mother Monica was a Christian, which was unusual at the time; his parents were relatively well-off and were able to educate Augustine, who learned to express himself fluently in the Roman art of rhetoric.

As a young man, Augustine began a relationship with a woman in Carthage, with whom he had a son. Augustine spent about ten years as a Manichaean; the Manichee faith involved belief in equal powers of good and evil that were engaged in a cosmic battle and pulling people to behave well or badly. This was to have a lasting influence on Augustinian thought, as Augustine struggled with ideas about evil and free will in later life. Monica had never approved of Augustine's relationship with the mother of his child, and

> **Synoptic link**
> Link to *A Level Religious Studies for Eduqas: Religion and Ethics, Chapter 8: Determinism and free will: free will*. Augustine's idea were very influential for Christian ethics, particularly on the theme of free will.

eventually she persuaded him to break it off, although Augustine did not recover easily from this. Augustine became a Christian after reading Paul's letter to the Romans, and from then on he became a well-known preacher and writer.

Augustine's theodicy

Augustine was firmly of the belief that God is perfectly good and, therefore, it cannot be the case that God deliberately created evil; yet there is evil in the world that requires explanation. Augustine took an idea from the Greek philosopher Aristotle, in which evil is understood not as a 'substance' in itself, but as a lack of goodness. Aristotle understood goodness in terms of something fulfilling its purpose, seeing things as less good if they fall short of what they were meant to be or have not completely met their potential. Using this idea, Augustine wrote of evil in terms of a ***privatio boni*** or a lack of goodness. (A 'privation' is a lack of something that ought to be there, so a car with only two wheels would have a privation of wheels, but we would not say that a rock has a privation of sight.)

> **Key term**
>
> ***privatio boni:*** (Latin) a lack of goodness

Evil, according to Augustine, is not a 'thing', but a lack, just as a shadow is a lack of light. Augustine saw that in the world, there is a great deal of variety: some trees have edible fruit, some have cones; some people are tall and others are short; some people are male and some are female; some days are hot and others are cold. Augustine believed that this variety is part of the goodness of God's creation, providing us with richness of experience and new things to discover and appreciate every day. However, a rich variety necessarily means that some things will lack attributes that others have. These differences are not evils, but simply the result of the wonderful variety of creation.

Augustine's theodicy – his argument to justify God in the face of evil and suffering – was based heavily on a literal understanding of the Bible, as well as some non-Biblical mythology. According to Augustine, God is not responsible for human sin. When God made the angels, Augustine said, they were all made perfect, as everything God does is perfect, but God gave some of them less grace than others as part of the rich variety of creation. However, some of the angels had too little grace to be willing worshippers of God. (Grace is understood in Christian terms as the assistance that God gives humanity to enable them to become more holy.) These angels wanted to be more independent, and so they fell away from God as a direct result of their own free will. Fallen angels then started to wreak havoc on humanity. They tempted Adam and Eve in the Garden of Eden to disobey the commandment that God had given them. God had made Adam and Eve perfect, and given them a wonderful garden in which to live, and they had been told not to eat the fruit of the tree in the middle of the garden. However, they were

The Fall of Adam and Eve, when they chose to disobey God, is central to Augustinian theodicy.

tempted to disobey and they did eat the fruit, using the free will God had given them. This disobedience to God is known as the Fall, and the story of the Fall is told in the Bible in Chapters 2 and 3 of Genesis.

According to Augustine, the Fall changed everything. It corrupted not only Adam and Eve but all of their descendants, so that every human life is tainted with 'original sin'. Augustine taught that sin became 'seminally present' in human nature after the Fall – in other words, the seeds of sin are in all of humanity because they are inherited from Adam and Eve. People since Adam and Eve have corrupted and corruptible natures, and are no longer able to see and feel God's presence easily. They misuse their free will and make bad choices. The Fall was so catastrophic that it also disrupted the created natural world. Growing crops became difficult, so that people had to work hard to grow food. Women had pain in childbirth, and people became mortal. Natural disasters are all attributable to the introduction of sin into the world through the Fall. Both moral and natural evil, then, are seen by Augustine as a consequence of sin.

According to Augustine, using the ideas of the New Testament, Christ came into the world as a 'second Adam', to put right humanity's relationship with God. Christ's death on the cross was an act of salvation, as Christ was without sin and paid the price for human sin by sacrificing himself for the good of humanity. In Matthew's gospel in the Bible, at the point of Jesus' death, the curtain in the temple that was meant to keep people out of the holiest part of the building was torn in two, showing that the barrier between God and humanity had been broken down. Those who use their free will to accept Christ as their saviour have the opportunity to repair their relationship with God and be saved. This theodicy is sometimes known as a **soul-deciding theodicy**, because people have the choice to decide whether or not to accept Christ, and God decides whether they will go to heaven or to hell.

For Augustine, then, God cannot be blamed for evil because it was brought into the world through the free choices made by the angels and humanity, and not because God put it there. God did not just ignore the damage done by the Fall: God sent his own Son as a sacrifice on the cross to overcome evil.

Aquinas and the problem of evil

Thomas Aquinas followed the thinking of Augustine on the problem of evil, up to a point. In Aquinas' view, Augustine was right to consider evil in terms of a falling away from good, and right to point out that variety in nature is necessary as a reflection of the infinite nature of God. However, Aquinas also said that in creating the world, God had to create something contingent, because everything that is created is contingent by definition. Contingent things are not perfect and, therefore, God could not have created a perfect world, because that is not logically possible. There are also aspects of Aquinas' argument that are similar to the theodicy of Irenaeus, as Aquinas argues that evil is necessary in order for there to be second-order goods.

Key term

soul-deciding theodicy: a term used to describe the kind of theodicy which proposes that evil and suffering allow people to make a personal choice about faith

AO1 activity 7

Read the story of the creation of humanity and the Fall, in Chapters 2 and 3 of Genesis, to familiarise yourself with their influence on Augustine's thought.

AO1 activity 8

Summarise the key features of this Augustinian-type theodicy, using as many key terms as you can.

Challenges to Augustinian-type theodicies

Augustine's thinking has been very influential in Christian thought, but his theodicy and other theodicies like it have been challenged.

- Augustine based his views very heavily on a literal interpretation of Chapters 2 and 3 of Genesis. However, these chapters do not mention angels, except as guards of the garden after the Fall, and they do not say that Adam and Eve were tempted by fallen angels. The serpent has traditionally been interpreted as the Devil or a fallen angel, but the Bible only says it was a serpent.

- Many people today do not interpret the Genesis stories literally. Instead, many religious believers argue that they are meant to be interpreted as myth. They are memorable, lively fictional stories with underlying messages, designed to convey truths about God and the relationship between God and humanity. Treating them as accurate accounts of historical events misses the point. Understanding the stories in a figurative rather than a literal way challenges Augustinian theodicy because Augustine based his argument on the premise that the Fall was a real-life event.

- Augustinian-type theodicies could be challenged on scientific grounds. There is no evidence to suggest that the whole of humanity descended from a single pair, and that these two people were the first human beings, created within a week of the creation of the Earth. If the idea of humanity inheriting sin from Adam and Eve is meant to be understood in terms of genetics, then this does not cohere with modern biological understanding of genetics. Genes have been found to account for inherited illness such as cystic fibrosis and muscular dystrophy, but nobody has found a 'sin gene'.

- Geological and biological evidence does not support the idea that there used to be a perfect world which then became chaotic following a single event. Augustine's theodicy depends on the idea that God made a world that was perfect before it was corrupted by human sin, so people who accept Augustinian-type theodicies have to reject the scientific evidence.

- In Augustine's theology, those who are not saved by the cross of Christ are condemned to hell for eternity. Some people, such as John Hick, have questioned this idea, arguing that an all-loving God would not create hell and would not allow anyone to go there forever, with no hope of escape. The problem is particularly acute if it is presented alongside the belief that God is omniscient, as Augustine does. God must know, for all time and before humanity was even created, that some people would sin and never be saved, which raises questions about why a morally perfect God would make those people at all.

- Critics argue that Augustine's theodicy is not compatible with the view that God has perfect knowledge and is perfectly wise. If God has perfect knowledge, then God should have known that some of the angels were going to fall from grace; and there is no reason why they should have done. They could not have made a wrong choice because, before they fell, there was allegedly no wrong to choose. God should have known that Adam and Eve would fall, because God knows everything, and you do not need to be omniscient to see that it is unwise to place temptation within reach if yielding to that temptation is going to bring catastrophic results.

- Thinkers such as Gregory S. Paul argue that the sheer scale of human suffering and premature death cannot be brushed aside as *privatio boni*, a lack of good. It is far more serious than that.
- Others also argue that the argument that there is variety in nature does have some strengths, but can appear glib and insensitive to those who have to cope with significant congenital disadvantages.

AO1 activity 9

Create a two-column table showing key features of Augustine's theodicy in one column, and how each feature has been challenged in the other column. For example:

Augustinian-type theodicy	Challenges to Augustinian-type theodicy
Augustine based his theodicy on the story of the Fall in Chapters 2 and 3 of Genesis.	Critics argue that the story of the Fall is not meant to be taken literally.

Religious responses to the problem of evil: Irenaean-type theodicy

Who was Irenaeus?

Irenaeus lived earlier than Augustine, from about 130–202 CE, and was a leading Christian theologian in the second century. He was born somewhere in Asia Minor, and was brought up in one of the very earliest Christian families. According to many sources, Irenaeus heard the preaching of Polycarp (or perhaps studied under him), who knew John the apostle as a very old man; Irenaeus lived at a time when Christianity was still very new. He helped to form the New Testament with his opinions on which writings genuinely deserved a place in the Bible, and is sometimes cited as a scholar who divided the Bible into the Old and New Testaments. Much of his work was dedicated to clarifying Christian doctrine.

Not a great deal is known about Irenaeus' personal life, as there is little evidence beyond legend. He became a bishop in Gaul, and was there when the Roman Emperor Marcus Aurelius ordered a mass slaughter of Christians in 177 CE. Persecution of Christians because of their faith was very real for people in Irenaeus' time, and so the issue of how a God of love and power could allow such suffering was naturally a topic to which Christian thinkers turned. It is possible that Irenaeus was eventually killed because of his faith.

Irenaeus' theodicy

Irenaeus did not attempt to show that evil and suffering were not real, and he admitted that God appears to allow evil and suffering in the world without preventing them. Irenaeus argued, instead, that evil and suffering must exist in the world because they serve some greater purpose. God deliberately created the world with a mixture of good and evil, to allow people to make genuinely free choices and to develop and grow in their relationship with God. This is sometimes referred to as a **soul-making theodicy**.

Humans are not created perfect, according to Irenaeus, but have to learn and grow in order to become the people God wants them to be. In his writings, Irenaeus referred to the book of Genesis, where God created Adam and Eve. God decided to make people:

> Then God said, 'Let us make mankind in our image, in our likeness'
>
> Genesis 1:26, *Holy Bible (NIV)*

Later theologians have used Irenaeus' ideas to make a distinction between God's image and God's likeness. Being made in God's image means being born with the potential for divine spiritual qualities, whereas being in the likeness of God is when those qualities have been made real and the potential has been actualised. God made humanity in God's own image, Irenaeus said, which meant that people have some of the attributes of God: they have the ability to know right from wrong, they have reason and intelligence, and they have freedom to make choices, just like God. But people have to grow into the likeness of God, according to later thinkers. As people become adults and face challenges, they have free choices to make and, in making these choices and coping with difficulties, people have the opportunity to grow into likeness of God. Some people explain this thinking by making a comparison with adults commenting that a baby is 'the image of his father'. Of course, they do not mean that the baby has wrinkles or a hairy chest or size eleven feet; instead, they mean they can see the father in the baby and predict that, as the child grows, it will resemble its father more and more, growing into its father's likeness.

Irenaeus argued that there has to be evil in the world for us to be able to appreciate good. Challenges and hardships are necessary in order for us to develop qualities such as compassion and patience. If God simply gave us goodness at birth, then this goodness would not mean anything. Part of being good is making an effort of will, turning down temptation to do wrong and choosing to do the right thing even if it is sometimes difficult. If God gave us no opportunity to make such choices, it would remove our freedom and prevent us from being able to learn from our mistakes.

This process, in which something bad has to happen in order to bring about good results, is sometimes referred to in terms of 'first-order evils' and '**second-order goods**'. The good effects – such as patience, wisdom, and generosity – come second, but they are argued to be worth having and, therefore, the first-order evils are justified as a means of achieving them. These virtues and qualities could not exist without at least some degree of suffering and evil. We would not be patient if we always get what we want immediately, and we would not be generous if nobody else needed anything, or brave if we never encountered danger.

Key terms

soul-making theodicy: a term used to describe a theodicy that proposes people grow into spiritual maturity through encountering suffering

second-order goods: virtues and qualities that can only exist if there is evil in the world, such as compassion

Irenaeus used the example of Jonah from the Bible to illustrate his point. Jonah was called by God to be a prophet but was not keen on the idea, so he ran away to sea, hoping to be able to avoid God. But Jonah brought bad luck on the ship's crew, or so they thought, and they threw him overboard where he was swallowed by a big fish. Jonah suffered from being in the fish's stomach for a few days, but eventually the fish threw him up at a location called Nineveh, which was exactly where God had wanted Jonah to go and preach all along. Jonah realised his dependence on God and that he had had a narrow escape, and he was able to learn from his mistakes. Jonah's temporary suffering, wrote Irenaeus, was all for the good in the end, and helped Jonah to develop his relationship with God.

Irenaeus used the analogy of God as a craftsman, which is an image that appears in various places in the Bible. Human beings are the material that God has to work with, and they are shaped into the form that God has always wanted them to become through God's activity.

Irenaeus used the imagery of a craftsman to convey the idea that we are God's material to be shaped by the experiences God gives us.

> *Yet you, Lord, are our Father.*
> *We are the clay, you are the potter;*
> *we are all the work of your hand.*
>
> Isaiah 64:8, *Holy Bible (NIV)*

Central to Irenaean thought is the concept of eternal life with God after death. Irenaeus saw evil and suffering as a necessary means to an end, and that end goal is heaven. After enduring suffering in this world, making genuine free choices and learning from their mistakes, people are brought to God after death where they can have the relationship with God that they have freely chosen. Augustine thought that people were destined for heaven or hell, and that those who had turned away from God through sin were eternally doomed, but Irenaeus seems to have thought that God's mercy and forgiveness continues in the afterlife.

The Italian story of Pinocchio, written by Carlo Collodi in 1883 and made into a Disney animated film, has a lot of similarities with Irenaean theodicy. Pinocchio is created as a wooden puppet, but he wants to become a real boy. He does not want to have his strings pulled by his creator: he wants to make his own free choices. He goes off into the world and, because he is not perfect, he makes all kinds of mistakes, especially as he has a tendency to enjoy bad company and to tell lies. But, by suffering the consequences of his mistakes, he learns to listen to his conscience and, eventually, Pinocchio returns to his father, ready to have a relationship of genuine freely-chosen love rather than control.

AO1 activity 10

Summarise Irenaeus' theodicy in a list of bullet points, showing how his reasoning led to his conclusions.

Developments of Irenaean theodicy

Irenaeus did not write a book or an essay focusing on the problem of evil and theodicy. His thoughts on the subject have to be pieced together from comments in his surviving writings on other topics. More modern scholars have taken Irenaeus' ideas about the world as a place for spiritual growth and expanded on them, fleshing them out with details and addressing some possible counter-arguments in what are known as Irenaean-type theodicies.

John Hick

John Hick takes an Irenaean approach to the problem of evil and suffering, and develops it further in his important 1985 book *Evil and the God of Love*. Hick argued, along with Irenaeus, that if we never faced any kind of challenge we would not be able to learn anything morally. When we learn at school, we develop as students as we are faced with increasingly challenging tasks; we do not carry on doing the same kinds of activities we did in Year 1 without ever being given anything harder to do. We need to be given problems to solve, sometimes tough ones, and we need to experience failure if we are to make any kind of progress; as we build on our past experience, we learn. Hick argued that in life, we need to face real challenges and real dangers:

> *A world which is to be a person-making environment cannot be a pain-free paradise but must contain challenges and dangers, with real possibilities of many kinds of accident and disaster, and the pain and suffering which they bring.*
>
> John Hick, *Evil and the God of Love*

Hick borrowed a phrase from the English poet John Keats, describing the world as a 'vale of soul-making'. Keats was a young poet, full of promise and just becoming well-known, when he developed tuberculosis at the age of only 25 and subsequently died in 1821. His short life was full of sadness; his father died of a head injury when John Keats was quite young, and then his mother died of tuberculosis, as did his brother Tom. John was a medical student and knew, when he developed symptoms himself, that there was no cure. Writing a letter to his friend, he described the world as a 'vale of soul-making', in other words saying that this life is like a dark valley – the 'valley of the shadow of death' described in Psalm 23 – which develops our souls as we travel through it. Keats was not being pessimistic by describing the world as a vale of soul-making; he rejected the idea common in the early-nineteenth century that the world was a 'vale of tears'. Instead, as a vale of soul-making, Keats saw that second-order goods would result from his suffering and that of those around him.

Using this term, Hick described how this world is deliberately made by God as the best place for us to develop our souls. Humans are imperfect when they are created, and through making mistakes and learning from those mistakes, they mature and become wiser. By facing challenges, we learn to make better decisions and understand our dependence on God, so second-order goods come out of first-order evils. In a vale, the mountains block the view and shadows are cast, but valleys do not go on forever; eventually we travel through them and emerge into the light where we are able to see further and more clearly.

In answer to the question of why God's purposes are not clearer to us in this life, Hick writes about **epistemic distance**, by which he meant a distance in knowledge or a distance in understanding. Hick thought that God has to keep a distance from us and remain partially hidden in this world because, otherwise, our choices would not be genuinely free. We need to learn to trust God, thought Hick, by taking a chance and having faith. Religious belief needs to be a choice. If God was obvious to us then we would have to believe, without having the freedom to decide not to. Therefore, part of the point of evil and suffering in the world is to keep things 'religiously ambiguous', so that we can make up our own minds without being forced.

In Hick's theodicy, the idea of life after death is more fully developed than in the writings of Irenaeus. Hick believed that, after death, people are not judged immediately and sent to heaven or hell; they are able to continue their spiritual journey. This is important to Hick, because it provides a response to the question of what happens to people who die young and are unable to do all the learning and growing that they should be able to do in a normal lifespan. Hick proposed that after death, people can carry on developing their relationships with God. They will understand the reasons for evil and suffering, and will be able to put right any wrong choices they made in their lives. Those who were a long way away from religious faith in their lifetimes will, over time, be able to see the truth more clearly and, eventually, everyone will get to be with God. Hick's proposal is one of universal salvation: he thought that in the end, everyone will be saved, whichever religion they followed during their earthly lives and regardless of any lack of belief or any wrongdoing. Hick did not think that a God of love would send anyone to hell, because it is in God's nature to be loving and forgiving.

Life after death is an important part of Irenaean theodicy, and for Hick in particular. Hick thought that life after death was necessary so that the puzzle of why there is evil and suffering in the world could finally be understood. We cannot fully understand suffering in this life, Hick thought, but there will be **eschatological** justification. By this, he meant that in the afterlife (known as the 'eschaton'), we will be given understanding and be able to see the reasons why things happened the way that they did, and will realise that everything happened for the best. The apparent injustices of this world will be put right in the afterlife.

Richard Swinburne

Richard Swinburne is another modern philosopher of religion who has adopted an Irenaean-type theodicy. In his 1979 book *The Existence of God*, Swinburne argues that God had a range of possibilities for the kind of world that could be created. God could have chosen to create a limited number of immortal beings with free will, who only had a small amount of work to do to improve the world before it reached perfection, for example; or an unlimited number of such beings, with an unlimited amount to do; or an unlimited number of such beings who were also capable of reproduction; or God could have made the world with unlimited mortal beings, capable

Key terms

epistemic distance: a distance of knowledge; a phrase used by John Hick in his development of Irenaeus' theodicy to refer to the distance of knowledge between God and humankind, which allows human beings to choose freely

eschatological: to do with the end of time, life after death and judgement for humanity

AO1 activity 11
Explain what Hick meant by 'universal salvation', and explain why he thought that this is what happens after death.

of reproducing and with an unlimited amount of work to do to perfect the world. God chose this last option, a world with mortal beings who have an unlimited amount of work to do to make the world perfect.

Swinburne argues that this allows people the opportunity to exercise genuine freedom. With more limited life spans, people have more reason to get on with doing what they can to improve the world. A limited life span limits the suffering people will face and limits the amount of suffering they can inflict on others, while allowing them to develop second-order goods such as compassion, courage and perhaps also self-sacrifice. Swinburne argues that a world with more limited suffering and fewer opportunities to improve the world would just be a 'toy world'. It was never beyond God's power to make an apparently better world for human life, but other kinds of world would have given people less freedom and less opportunity.

> **AO1 activity 12**
> Explain what Swinburne meant by a toy world, and why he thought this was to be avoided.

Challenges to Irenaean-type theodicies

Although Irenaean-type theodicies tend to be more popular than Augustinian-type theodicies, they have been met with many criticisms and challenges.

- Many object to the idea of first-order evils being used to justify second-order goods. Evil and suffering should not, it is argued, be used by God as a means to an end, even if the end is worth having. If God is omnipotent and omnibenevolent, God should be able to, and want to, achieve those ends without causing suffering. God could have given us the virtues of compassion and courage as part of human nature, rather than leaving us to try to achieve them through suffering. Furthermore, using evil and suffering to achieve greater goods makes evil and suffering only seem bad, while really they are good in disguise. This idea of evil as good in disguise can be seen as morally repugnant, blurring the lines between good and evil, right and wrong. There are many acts and motivations that are just plain wrong.
- It can seem very glib and insensitive to tell people who have experienced great suffering that there is a good reason for it and that good things come out of suffering. Parents who have lost a child in dreadful circumstances are not likely to want to hear about how their suffering has helped others appreciate their own children more, or allowed their friends to show compassion.
- Irenaeus' interpretation of Genesis 1:26, where God makes humanity in his own image and likeness, is an unusual interpretation and, according to many, not an interpretation that can easily be justified. It seems more likely that the writer of Genesis did not intend to make any distinction between 'image' and 'likeness' but was instead using the literary device of repetition to emphasise the point that humanity is endowed with some of the qualities of God. If Irenaeus is wrong in his interpretation of this verse then his theodicy is undermined.
- Many find the concept of universal salvation, developed by John Hick, to be unjust. Hick argued that eventually, with everyone's spiritual

journeys continuing after death, everyone will be saved. On the surface this might seem to be what an omnibenevolent God would do, loving everyone, forgiving everyone and shutting no one out of heaven. However, if people are all going to end up in heaven no matter what they do, it removes much of the religious incentive for leading a good life on Earth; we can behave just as we like, be totally selfish or even cruel, and remain happy in the knowledge that we will go to heaven regardless. There is no particular reward for faith or good works, or punishment for terrible crimes. Those brave people who sacrificed their own lives to save Jews during the Nazi Holocaust, or who worked the so-called underground railway to free people from enslavement in the US, will end up side-by-side in heaven with those who caused their suffering. Hick is criticised because this part of his theodicy is not biblical. Passages such as the Parable of the Sheep and the Goats in Matthew 25 make it clear that the good will be rewarded, while those who have not cared about the suffering of others will go to eternal punishment. Finally, the concept of universal salvation is seen to be inconsistent with the central teachings of Christianity. If everyone is going to heaven in the end, it makes the suffering of Christ on the cross pointless. There was no need for Christ to atone for the sin of humanity if we would all have gone to heaven anyway, regardless of whether Christ came into the world or not. There is no need to encourage others to turn to Christ if they will go to heaven whatever they believe.

- The presentation of the problem of evil given by Gregory S. Paul presents a modern challenge to Irenaean-type theodicies, as he points to the frequency with which the end result of achieving a mature relationship with God is not realised. A huge number of human lives are very short, through no fault of humanity, which undermines the idea that suffering is necessary for longer-term 'soul-making'. If God means for us to go through suffering and challenges in this life for soul-making reasons, this fails, because so many people do not get to live their lives. If soul-making continues after death for all the children who did not survive to adulthood, then why could God not restrict soul-making to the afterlife and give us contented and trouble-free lives while we are on Earth?

- The sheer scale of suffering seems too great to be justified with Irenaean-type theodicies. Surely God could achieve second-order goods without allowing people to suffer quite so much. There are people who lose all their children and their homes in house fires, there are stories in newspapers of entire families being killed in plane crashes, or of people suffering one tragedy after another. These events draw attention to a related challenge, which is that evil and suffering do not seem to be fairly distributed. Some live long lives in good health, with a comfortable standard of living, happy relationships and successful children, and feel thoroughly content nearly all the time; others seem to have suffering, disappointment and disaster heaped on them. Does this mean that God does not want everyone to develop their souls in equal measure?

- In addition to the fact that many people die in infancy or before birth, Irenaean theodicy has also been challenged (by thinkers such as D.Z. Phillips) on the grounds that in real life, second-order goods do not always arise as a result of suffering. Struggling with poverty can make people bitter or dispirited; it can force them to turn to crime and it can destroy family relationships. Living with pain can make people short-tempered or self-centred, or less optimistic than they would be if they enjoyed full health. Personal tragedy can make people lose their faith in God. Some people suffer who are not capable of learning from their suffering, such as those with Alzheimer's Disease or severe learning difficulties, or new-born babies. Animals suffer, but they are not capable of rationalising and learning from pain. It simply is not the case that evil is always worth it in the end, for its good results in developing virtue, or at least not in this life.

- Irenaean-type theodicies depend on the idea that there is an afterlife in which God will make everything better. People will understand the reasons for suffering and will be compensated for their losses; the whole picture will be revealed, it is claimed. However, there is no evidence of other lives beyond this one, others argue. There is no evidence that we have immortal souls or that there is any kind of life after death. The whole idea of life after death, critics argue, is just wishful thinking, made up to help people cope with pain and injustice.

- Critics of Irenaean theodicy argue that an omnipotent God should not need to do things this way. Although the theodicy claims that human free will is so important that evil is a price worth paying, not everyone agrees. Some people argue that the suffering people experience is too extreme, and that God could have taught the same lessons with a lesser degree of pain. For some people, even if suffering is worthwhile in terms of the lessons it might teach people, it would have been better if God had never made the world. Dostoevsky, in his novel *The Brothers Karamazov*, presented the argument that the price we are expected to pay to have free will is just too high. In the novel, Ivan Karamazov speaks to his brother, Alyosha, who is a novice monk. Ivan draws Alyosha's attention to reports of innocent suffering: the cruel treatment of animals, for example, and the torture of a child. Ivan says that it is not the existence of God that he doesn't accept, it is just that he 'returns his entrance ticket'; he wants no part in a world where the price of free will is so high. Devastatingly, Ivan asks Alyosha if he would have created a world which was perfect except that it demanded, for its existence, the suffering of just one tiny child, and Alyosha has to admit that, no, he would not have created a world on those terms.

AO1 activity 13

As you did with Augustinian-type theodicies, create a two-column table showing key features of Irenaean theodicy in one column and how each feature has been challenged in the second column.

This section of the chapter will enhance your ability to **analyse** and **evaluate** the topic and help you develop your AO2 skills. For each question, think about the different positions you might take, and decide which you find most persuasive and why. It is not enough to memorise a list of 'for and against' points; you need to develop an argument.

To what extent is the classical form of the problem of evil a problem?

This question is asking for a consideration of whether or not the problem of evil is an issue that matters. It could be that it matters to some people more than others, or that it is more significant in some contexts than in others. Perhaps it presents a very significant barrier to faith, or perhaps it is something that does not concern people to any great extent.

The view that the classical form of the problem of evil is not a significant problem

For those who have no belief in God, or those who believe that God is not all good, the problem of evil in its classical form does not arise. Evil and suffering need to be addressed on practical and emotional levels: people have to find ways of coping with difficulties and failures, and have to come to terms with loss and pain, but the problem of reconciling this experience with belief in God does not exist for those who do not have theistic belief. There is no need to find an answer to the question of why God allows evil if there is no God.

Religious believers might argue that although the problem of evil cannot be ignored, there are responses to it which allow them to continue in their faith without difficulty. They could adopt the Irenaean view that suffering is necessary to allow us free will and to develop our characters, so that we can have a mature relationship with God through faith. They could also argue that, without God's omniscience, humanity cannot understand the reason for every evil and every instance of suffering, but faith leads them to believe that God has everything under control and does not make mistakes. Christians argue that although they do not always know the reason for suffering, they know that God came into the world in Jesus Christ, to share in the human condition and to share in human suffering; so they can be confident that God is not indifferent to people when they suffer, and that everything is part of God's plan. They might argue that the problem of evil is difficult to resolve but, nevertheless, it does not present a significant barrier to faith.

Alternatively, religious believers might argue that the problem of evil is a problem but it is not *our* problem. They might argue that God is, by nature, beyond human comprehension, and that we should not expect to know God's reasoning or be able to understand it. In the Bible, the book of Job focuses on the problem of innocent suffering. It tells the story of a man called Job who is good, honest, and faithful to God. God decides to test him, and Job suffers many tragedies: all his cattle dies, his family die, his house falls down, he becomes very ill. Throughout all his suffering, Job does not lose his belief in God – but he does want answers. He cannot understand why he is suffering so much, and wants to know if he has done something wrong. Job demands an audience with God so that he can have an explanation. But the response he gets is not what he expects. God shows Job the wonders of creation: the seasons, the amazing animal life, God's absolute control over the sea and the planets. God asks Job:

> *Where were you when I laid the Earth's foundation?*
>   *Tell me, if you understand.*
>
>   Job 38:4, *Holy Bible (NIV)*

Job realises that God has total power and total authority, and that he, as a finite human being and part of God's creation, has no right to question God and no right to demand answers.

> *Then Job answered the Lord:*
> *'I am unworthy—how can I reply to you?*
>   *I put my hand over my mouth.*
> *I spoke once, but I have no answer—*
>   *twice, but I will say no more.'*
>
>   Job 40:3–5, *Holy Bible (NIV)*

The view that the classical form of the problem of evil is a significant problem

Although some religious believers argue, along with Job, that evil and suffering in the world are mysteries that humanity cannot understand, there are many others who argue that we do need to have at least some understanding of why an omnipotent and omnibenevolent God appears to allow evil to exist. Scholars such as John Hick argue that although people will never have a full understanding of God, and especially not in this life, it is not unreasonable for them to want some kind of understanding. Hick argues, in *Evil and the God of Love*, that the problem of evil is a legitimate topic for Christians to explore. Moral evil is known to religious believers as sin: a term that refers to deliberate disobedience to God, to turning away from God's commandments. The idea of sin coming into the world and Christ atoning for the sins of humanity is absolutely central to Christian belief and, therefore, Hick argues, people should be allowed to explore what it means, including asking why evil and suffering happen.

The Epicurean Paradox is a problem for those who believe in the God of Classical Theism. Those who believe that God is omnipotent, omniscient, and omnibenevolent have to try to find a way of reconciling this belief with the existence of evil in the world, and this is not easy to do. It is a problem that has been recognised since at least the time of the ancient Greek philosophers, and has not gone away. Modern warfare, acts of terrorism, and natural disasters continue to raise the same question: Why would an all-loving God allow such suffering, if at the same time God has the power to stop or prevent it? The problem of evil seems to demonstrate that it is irrational to believe in an omnipotent and omnibenevolent God.

Some people who take an atheist position do so because of the problem of evil, arguing that it is the main reason why they find religious belief impossible to accept. The logical form of the problem makes the issue clear, and it cannot be resolved without modifying or rejecting at least one aspect of the inconsistent triad. None of the theodicies offer a solution to the logical problem; instead, they have to back down on the belief that God is completely omnipotent, or on the belief that evil is ultimately a bad thing.

Personal tragedy can also lead people to lose a faith they previously had, drawing them to the conclusion that their suffering shows there cannot be an all-loving, all-powerful God after all. The evidential form of the problem, arguing that there is just too much suffering in the world to make the existence of God a probability, is a serious and significant barrier to faith.

The view that the classical form of the problem of evil raises a meaningless question

Followers of a philosophical position known as Logical Positivism would argue that questions of why God allows suffering are meaningless. Logical positivists argue, following Hume, that meaningful discussion takes place when something is available to empirical testing; in other words, when it is available to the senses and can be experienced by everyone. The only statements with any meaning are those that can be tested using the senses, or those that are about definitions, according to Logical Positivism. Discussions about what God might or might not be able to do, or the reasons God might have for acting in one way or another, are considered meaningless.

Synoptic link

Link to *Chapter 7: Religious language (part one)*. Logical positivists argue that all kinds of talk about God are meaningless, because religious claims cannot be tested using the senses.

AO2 activity 1

Do you think that the classical form of the problem of evil raises significant issues, or not? Give reasons to support your answer.

How effective are modern problem of evil arguments in proving that God does not exist?

This question invites a consideration of the problem of evil and suffering as an argument for the non-existence of God. Some people claim that the existence of evil and suffering in the world demonstrates clearly that there is no God, or at least not the God of Classical Theism, and several modern thinkers have rephrased the problem to show that it still presents a significant challenge. How successful are these claims?

The view that modern problem of evil arguments are very effective in proving God does not exist

Some people argue that the problem of evil has always demonstrated that God does not exist, since the time of Epicurus. But modern versions of this challenge are particularly effective, because they show that the problem has not gone away or been successfully resolved. Although humanity has made significant technological and scientific progress since the time of Epicurus, we still have pandemics, natural disasters such as tsunamis and earthquakes, incurable illnesses, and we experience all kinds of intense suffering: we have not found a solution to natural evil. The wars and terrorist attacks of the twentieth and twenty-first centuries also demonstrate the extent to which humanity is capable of great moral evil.

Mackie's argument is often considered highly effective because it is presented as a logical, deductive argument; therefore, if the premises are true, then the conclusion must necessarily follow. It is difficult for theists to challenge the view that an omnipotent God has the power to remove evil, and that an omnibenevolent God should want to eliminate sin and suffering. Therefore, the conclusion follows that given there is evil in the world, there cannot be an omnipotent and omnibenevolent God.

William Rowe's focus on intense suffering can also be seen to present an effective demonstration of the non-existence of God. His argument is that even if suffering exists in order to bring about some kind of greater good, there cannot be any need for the suffering to be so widespread, intense, and apparently pointless. His example of animal suffering is particularly challenging, as animals cannot expect to be able to reason and learn through suffering.

Gregory S. Paul's argument is also viewed as highly effective. He challenges theodicies that argue suffering is necessary for people to grow and develop into a mature relationship with God. By focusing on the deaths of children too young to have been able to learn from their suffering, Paul shows that a very significant amount of human suffering cannot achieve this supposedly good aim and, therefore, the free will defence does not work.

The view that modern problem of evil arguments are not very effective in proving God does not exist

Mackie's argument has been criticised on the grounds that he made assumptions about what God should or should not do, but these are things we cannot know. Mackie assumed that an omnibenevolent God would want to eliminate evil, arguing that 'a good thing always eliminates evil as far as it can'. However, defenders of theism argue that because we are fallible, finite people who lack omniscience, we are not capable of understanding the ways of God. We cannot say that an omnibenevolent God always eliminates evil, or always wants to eliminate evil, because we do not have enough understanding of the nature of God to know that. There is also the point that we do not have any other gods with which to compare God, so we have no grounds for assuming anything about what good gods always do, or always ought to do.

Rowe and Paul have put forward serious challenges, but they do not succeed in *proving* that God does not exist, because they present inductive arguments, based on experience, to arrive at a conclusion using the balance of probabilities. Inductive arguments cannot prove anything with certainty. Religious believers might answer their challenges by pointing out that although there is intense suffering in the world and great loss of life, there is also intense joy and new birth. If the challenge is using the balance of probability to assess the problem of evil, then an assessment should also consider the extent of love, goodness, beauty, and happiness in the world.

Are Augustinian-type theodicies relevant in the twenty-first century?

Augustinian-type theodicies are attempts to justify God, using ideas about the Fall of humanity and the introduction of original sin into the world. This question invites consideration of whether this kind of argument is out of date in the modern world, or whether it still has something important to say, or whether perhaps it was never useful. How relevant are Augustinian-type theodicies for people today?

The view that Augustinian-type theodicies are not very relevant in the twenty-first century

Those who follow a logical positivist approach to knowledge will argue that Augustinian-type theodicies, along with every other kind of theodicy, are not relevant because they are meaningless. They will argue that we cannot test with our senses whether there is a good God, or even whether evil exists, and so the whole debate is pointless.

Others might argue that Augustinian-type theodicies have not stood the test of time. They belong to an era in which people took the Bible literally and believed that Adam and Eve were real people. Although there are still many Christians who try to take the Bible literally, there are also many who do not, particularly in academic discussion. Ideas about angels and the Devil seem to belong to the past, and are more relevant to a so-called mythological age when people were more willing to believe in invisible supernatural forces. In the modern world, people expect theories to be backed up by scientific evidence, and there is no evidence for the existence of angels or the Devil.

Augustine's view that all are descendants of Adam cannot be understood literally, as it has no scientific basis. The idea that everyone is born with original sin because it is inherited from Adam cannot work in anything but a metaphorical sense. The theory of evolution through natural selection is not compatible with an Augustinian theodicy, because it says that humanity evolved gradually and shares common ancestors with primates. It does not

AO2 activity 2

Give the problem of evil argument put forward by Mackie a star rating out of five. Explain your rating in a short review: Why did you give him the number of stars you awarded? What was good about his argument, and where does it fall short? Do the same for the criticisms of theodicies presented by Rowe and by Paul.

support the view that humanity began with Adam and Eve, right at the start of creation.

The view that natural evil is a result of sin is difficult for someone in the twenty-first century to accept, unless they interpret the Bible very literally. Scientific evidence supports the assertion that the world is very much older than humanity, and it also supports the view that earthquakes, ice ages, floods, and volcanic eruptions were happening long before people inhabited the Earth and were able to choose sin, so there cannot be a direct causal link between sin and these natural events. Augustine's teaching about the Fall lacks any kind of scientific or historical evidence to support the view that the world was once perfect within the lifetime of humanity as a species.

Many Christians argue that other theodicies, such as that of Irenaeus, are more plausible than the account given by Augustine, because they fit in better with modern views about personal autonomy, and because they do not depend on outdated Biblical mythology.

It can be difficult for modern people to accept that natural disasters, such as floods, are the result of human sin.

The view that Augustinian-type theodicies are relevant in the twenty-first century

Some might argue that Augustinian-type theodicies succeed for all time because they are based on the Bible. Augustinian's theodicy succeeds and is relevant because its starting point is the word of God, and it follows the teachings of the Bible about how sin came into the world and how Christ atoned for human sin. This is teaching that does not go out of date, because God's word lasts forever. Christ's sacrifice in atoning for the sins of Adam and Eve was an event of cosmic significance, for all time.

Christians could argue that Augustine's understanding of evil and suffering as the result of human sin is relevant today because we are learning more and more about the consequences of human selfishness for the future of the planet. The connection between human choice about how natural resources are used and climate change is well established, and this could be seen to support the view that the natural world is affected by the things humanity decides to do and the poor choices people make.

The modern American philosopher Alvin Plantinga also claims that we should accept the possibility that evil in the world is caused by the Devil or demonic agencies, even in the twenty-first century. Natural evil, he argues, could be the result of the Devil's free decision to fall away from the presence of God and corrupt the world. The Devil made a free decision to turn away from God, to tempt humans to sin and to disrupt nature, and God could not intervene to prevent this without removing the ability to act freely from the angels and from humans. Plantinga does not see this as a limitation of God's omnipotence, but as a necessary consequence of allowing the greater good of free will.

AO2 activity 3

How relevant do you think Augustine's theodicy is in the present day? Give reasons to support your answer.

To what extent does Augustine's theodicy succeed as a defence of the God of Classical Theism?

This question is asking whether Augustine's theodicy does a good job of showing that God can still be considered to have all the characteristics of the God of Classical Theism, despite the existence of evil and suffering. Augustine tries to show that God is not to blame for evil and suffering. Does he present a convincing argument?

The view that Augustine's theodicy succeeds as a defence of the God of Classical Theism

Augustine's theodicy could be understood as a successful defence of the God of Classical Theism. Augustine kept closely to Christian doctrine and the Bible, and did not make concessions about the goodness of God or the omnipotence of God. The blame for evil and suffering in the world is placed on the Fall and not on God.

Augustine defended the goodness of God by saying that evil and suffering came into the world through sin and disobedience, and not through God's own choice. God demonstrated goodness and love by giving people free will, as well as giving free will to the angels. The choice to disobey was not God's own but was a falling away from God. Augustine can, therefore, be considered to have succeeded in defending God against accusations of causing innocent suffering, as no one is innocent once they are tainted with the sin of Adam.

Augustine's understanding of evil as a *privatio boni* could also be seen as a successful part of his theodicy. In understanding evil as a falling away from good, rather than as a force in itself, Augustine avoided the question of why God created evil. In Augustine's view, nothing created evil because evil is not a 'thing'. In this way, Augustine's theodicy is able to maintain the classical theistic idea that God created everything.

Augustine defended the power of God by putting forward the view that everything is God's creation. God, according to Augustine, created everything exactly as planned, and God was not forced into making imperfections just because God also chose to give humanity free will. In Augustine's theodicy, God gives free will without any limitations on God's omnipotence. This can be seen as a successful defence of the God of Classical Theism.

The view that Augustine's theodicy does not succeed as a defence of the God of Classical Theism

Although Augustine tried hard to defend the God of Classical Theism, it can be argued that his theodicy is a failure.

The *privatio boni* understanding of evil is not consistent with most people's experience of evil and suffering. Some suffering, such as missing someone after they have died, might possibly be understood in terms of a lack of goodness, but most kinds of suffering and evil seem to have a very definite power of their own. Aggressive illnesses, such as cancers and motor neurone disease, are experienced as a lot more real, powerful, and frightening than just a lack of health. Acts of terrorism, where someone deliberately targets and kills random people, demonstrate a lot more than just a lack of good will. It is difficult to accept that pain, cruelty, and sickness do not have a reality of their own. Even if we accept that evil is just a lack of perfection, we are still left with the question of why God allowed this lack of perfection into the world.

Augustine's theodicy raises a lot of questions that do not have adequate answers. Why did God give some of the angels less grace than others, so little in fact that they fell into sin? How were they able to make wrong choices, unless the bad option was already there to be chosen, and how could this happen in an allegedly perfect world? Why did God make the angels, and humanity, with the capacity for disobedience, instead of making them so that they would always freely choose the good? If God is omniscient, why did God not see what was going to happen before angels and humanity were created and given free will? The theologian Friedrich Schleiermacher argued cogently, in the nineteenth century, that it is impossible to find a reason why the angels fell into sin, unless they were created imperfectly by God in the first place. Augustine leaves a great deal unexplained.

The view that nobody is innocent, because of original sin, does not explain the suffering of innocent animals.

The defence of God with regard to natural evil also lacks coherence. It is difficult to see how human choice to disobey God could be so disastrous as to cause floods and earthquakes, unless God had a hand in making it happen. It is also difficult to see why God could not simply undo the harm that was done by the Fall, rather than letting it happen; this seems inconsistent with God's omnipotence. Augustinian theodicy suggests that God has been left with a world that was not meant to happen. Christians argue that God did undo sin, by coming into the world as Jesus Christ and paying the price for sin by dying on the cross. However, this begs the question, why was that necessary? And why did God not use infinite power to turn the clock back as soon as Adam and Eve sinned, or to magic away the disastrous consequences of sin, or at least make them a lot less drastic?

Finally, Augustine's theodicy seems unduly pessimistic. In Augustine's view, human nature is corrupted by sin and many people are condemned to hell for eternal punishment. The grace of God will allow only a few into heaven. This, too, does not cohere with the notion of an all-loving, all-powerful God as it leads to questions about why there is a hell at all and why God cannot save everyone.

AO2 activity 4

On balance, do you think that Augustine's theodicy succeeds as a defence of Classical Theism? Write a paragraph or two to explain your reasoning, making it clear as you write that you understand the traditional attributes of God (creator, omnipotence, omniscience, and omnibenevolence).

Are Irenaean-type theodicies credible in the twenty-first century?

This question draws attention to the modern world. It asks whether a theodicy from the first century is believable for people today, and also whether other theodicies of the same type as Irenaeus' can work for people today.

The view that Irenaean-type theodicies are credible in the twenty-first century

Irenaean-type theodicies tend to be more popular in the modern world than Augustinian-type theodicies, largely because they do not require a literal interpretation of the Bible and a rejection of the theory of evolution. They do not expect us to believe that the world was perfect before the arrival of humanity, and that earthquakes and volcanoes came historically later than human life on Earth. Instead, they accept that the world has been the way it is since it was first formed. Therefore, Irenaean-type theodicies can be seen as compatible with ideas about evolution, because they are all about learning and developing, and making progress.

Irenaean-type theodicies fit more comfortably with modern views about respecting the beliefs and values of others. For Hick, everyone achieves salvation, regardless of their religion and beliefs; this fits with modern ideas about multiculturalism, and moral and religious Relativism. It shows that there are different paths to the truth, and that people should not assume their way of thinking is the only right way.

People today like the idea of personal autonomy, of taking responsibility for their own actions. They are less inclined towards beliefs that demand unquestioning obedience to authority. Irenaean-type theodicies focus on human free will and developing as an individual.

Irenaean-type theodicies are optimistic, reassuring people that everything will be all right in the end, which remains a popular way of coping with wars, pandemics, and long-term illnesses.

The view that Irenaean-type theodicies are not credible in the twenty-first century

Irenaean-type theodicies depend on some ideas that do not cohere well with modern thinking.

Central to Irenaean-type theodicies is the view that there will be eschatological justification; everything will be all right in the afterlife, when all suffering will disappear and everything will be justified. Many modern thinkers, such as Antony Flew, point out the total lack of evidence for an afterlife and say that the idea of surviving your own death is nonsensical. Others, such as Karl Marx and Bertrand Russell, have argued that ideas about life after death are just promoted to discourage people from making a fuss about earthly injustice, or only exist because people are not brave enough to cope with the fact that one day their lives will end.

Modern philosophers and some neuroscientists question the idea that people have genuine free will. The philosopher Daniel Dennett, for example, argues that our freedom to do whatever we want is much more limited than we might imagine, and others argue that free will is fundamentally an illusion. We are controlled by our genetics and by external factors to such an extent that we could not choose to do anything other than make the choices we make, even if we feel we are acting freely. Twenty-first century doubts about the genuineness of human free will challenge Irenaean-type theodicies, which focus on the idea that evil is necessary because free will is a greater good.

Twenty-first century thinkers such as Rowe and Paul argue that the sheer scale of suffering, especially apparently pointless suffering, make Irenaean-type theodicies difficult or impossible to accept.

AO2 activity 5

How credible do you find Irenaean-type theodicies in the present day? In other words, how believable are the ideas to people with modern ways of thinking and with access to modern scientific knowledge? Write a paragraph or two to explain your views, with reasons.

To what extent does Irenaeus' theodicy succeed as a defence of the God of Classical Theism?

This question is inviting an evaluation of the theodicy of Irenaeus. He has tried to show that although there is evil and suffering in the world, it exists for a good reason and will benefit people as, by facing challenges, they will become more spiritually mature. How convincing do you find Irenaeus' argument?

The view that Irenaeus' theodicy succeeds as a defence of the God of Classical Theism

Irenaeus' theodicy is popular, and can be argued to give a successful defence of the God of Classical Theism:

- The theodicy gives the religious believer confidence that God has everything under control and has not accidentally been left with an imperfect world that was not meant to happen. The idea of God as creator is preserved with this theodicy: everything is just the way God intended.
- The idea of God as omnibenevolent is maintained. When there is evil and suffering, it is because a good result will come out of it, and that is what God wants for us. God gave us free will out of love, instead of creating us all as automata programmed only to do good. Universal salvation demonstrates a good and loving God who will not condemn anyone to hell for eternity.
- The idea of God as omnipotent is also maintained. The world is exactly as God wants it, and God has the power to make everything turn out well in the end. Instances of evil and suffering do not happen despite God, as if God can do nothing about them or is limited in choice because of them: they are all a part of God's loving plan.

The view that Irenaeus' theodicy does not succeed as a defence of the God of Classical Theism

Others argue that Irenaeus' theodicy, and others of the same type, do not give a successful defence of the God of Classical Theism:

- The idea that God put things like war in the Middle East, the Nazi Holocaust, slavery, and cancer into the world on purpose is unpalatable and inconsistent with the idea of an all-loving God. If evil and suffering are necessary to bring about a greater good, God should not have made the world at all, as the price is not worth paying. There cannot be any ultimate good that justifies the suffering of children.
- The arbitrariness of suffering challenges the idea of God's omnibenevolence. Some people suffer a great deal more than others, which does not suggest a God in control who loves everyone equally and unconditionally.
- The idea that God has to allow evil and suffering to give people free will challenges belief in God's omnipotence. An omnipotent God should be able to do anything, including giving humanity free will without evil. It should not be necessary for a totally powerful being to have to use means to an end: God should want us to have the virtues and so we should have them, without having to jump through hoops to achieve them.
- Aspects of Irenaean theodicy are unbiblical, such as the idea that there will be salvation for all, and the idea that after death we might continue to face challenges as we continue our spiritual journey. In many passages, the Bible teaches that salvation is only for those who have faith in Christ, that there is a hell, and that in heaven there will be no more suffering or pain.

AO2 activity 6

Do you think that Irenaeus successfully defends the God of Classical Theism? Make a list of the traditional attributes of God and, by each one, explain whether you think Irenaeus has or has not successfully defended it.

Practising AO1 questions

AO1 questions begin with one of a range of possible command words (see pages 8–9 for more detail.) The following question begins with the word 'Explain'. 'Explain' questions require you to demonstrate knowledge and understanding of the key features of the topic in the question by writing a systematic and comprehensive account. You do not need to consider the quality of an argument or offer any views about it.

Activity

Here is an example of a past paper question and two example paragraphs taken from longer answers written in response.

1. Imagine you have advised the student who wrote the first example paragraph that they need to expand on and develop their responses to exam questions. They are not sure what you mean by 'expand and develop'. Explain what it means to write a more developed response. Use the second example paragraph to help you.
2. Write a more developed paragraph explaining the views of John Hick on the problem of evil, with the same kind of level of detail as in the second paragraph.

Explain how Irenaean-type theodicies offer a solution to the problem of evil.

(Eduqas AS Level Religious Studies, Summer 2017, Component 2: An Introduction to the Philosophy of Religion, Question 4a)

Example 1

Irenaean-type theodicies[7] offer a solution to the problem of evil which focus on the idea of the world as a[2] vale of soul-making.[7] Irenaeus[6] argued that evil is a part of the world because God designed the world that way, so that people could have the maximum opportunity to learn and grow[1]. Irenaeus[6] argued that we are made in the image of God, but have to grow into God's likeness, using[1] Genesis 1:26[4]. We can only become more like God by having genuine free choice, and that free choice necessarily involves having real evil as an option.[1] John Hick[6] and Richard Swinburne[6], among others, developed Irenaean-type theodicies.

1 This paragraph shows accurate and relevant knowledge, but it could be more detailed.

2 This paragraph focuses on the question asked.

3 A good paragraph should contain at least one piece of evidence or one example. This doesn't contain either.

4 There is an accurate reference to a sacred text, which is used well in the context of the question.

5 This paragraph does not make any links with other areas of study. Links should not be forced and so this is acceptable.

6 There are references to scholarly views, but the references to Hick and Swinburne's views are only mentioned in passing and not developed in this paragraph.

7 There is some accurate use of specialist language and vocabulary.

Example 2

The problem of evil is often expressed in terms of the[2] inconsistent triad[7]: God is[2] omnipotent[7], God is[2] omnibenevolent[7], and yet evil exists. This is seen as a challenge to faith in the God of[2] Classical Theism[7] because it is hard, if not impossible, to believe all three parts of the triad at once.[2] Irenaean-type theodicies[7] offer a solution to the problem of evil which focuses on the idea of the world as a[1] vale of soul-making[7]. This means that the world is designed so that people develop their characters when they encounter challenges, by learning virtues such as patience, fortitude and compassion.[1] Irenaeus[6] argued that evil is a part of the world because God designed the world that way, so that people could have the maximum opportunity to learn and grow and could exercise genuine free choice, rather than being forced to do good because no other options are available. Irenaeus argued that we are made in the image of God, but have to grow into God's likeness, using[1] Genesis 1:26[4] to show that God gave people[1] moral autonomy[7] and rationality at creation.[1] In order to grow, in the sense of making spiritual progress, we need to meet challenges and cope with failures. This will lead to virtues as second-order goods[7] which we could not achieve without encountering evil; for example, we could not develop compassion if nobody was ever in trouble or in pain[3].

1 This paragraph shows thorough, accurate, and relevant knowledge and understanding.

2 This paragraph focuses on the question asked.

3 There is some use of evidence and example in this paragraph.

4 There is an accurate reference to a sacred text, which is used well in the context of the question.

5 Links with other areas of study should not be forced and so it is acceptable that none appear in this paragraph.

6 There are appropriately developed references to scholarly views.

7 There is extensive and confident use of specialist language and vocabulary.

AO1 practice question 1

Try answering the following question, using the points to remember to help you write a developed response.

Examine the problem of evil with reference to Mackie and Rowe.

(Eduqas AS Level Religious Studies, Summer 2018, Component 2: An Introduction to the Philosophy of Religion, Question 4a)

Points to remember

- The question asks you to examine two different thinkers, so make sure you allow roughly equal time for each.
- Mackie presented a logical form of the problem of evil, whereas Rowe presents an evidential form. Make this clear in your answer and show how the two approaches are different.
- Give as much detail as you can about the views of Mackie and Rowe, showing that you know and understand the examples they use and the structure of their arguments.

AO1 practice question 2

Now try this question by yourself.

> *Outline Augustinian-type and Irenaean-type theodicies.*
>
> (Eduqas AS Level Religious Studies, Summer 2019, Component 2:
> An Introduction to the Philosophy of Religion, Question 1a)

Practising AO2 questions

AO2 questions are designed to assess your ability to evaluate and critically analyse. Concentrate on weighing up different views, and identifying the strengths and weaknesses of each view. Avoid spending too much of your response presenting your knowledge in a descriptive way.

Activity

1. Read the guidance about Assessment Objective 2 in 'Understanding the Assessment Objectives' on pages 7–8. When you are studying, make time to stop and think about your own opinions, as well as learning about the views of others, and rehearse what you would say if you were asked to give your view. Give each of the following a star rating out of five, depending on how convincing you think the argument is, and write a line or two to explain why you have chosen your rating:
   - Augustine's ideas about fallen angels
   - Irenaeus' view that we need challenges to grow into God's likeness
   - Paul's claim that statistics demonstrate there cannot be a loving God
   - Hick's view that everyone will achieve salvation in the end.

2. Look at the example of a past paper question and two example paragraphs taken from longer answers written in response below and on page 118. Both example paragraphs present the view that Augustine's theodicy does fail, although the first example paragraph concentrates too heavily on just one reason.

Write another paragraph to continue the first example answer, showing that you understand a different point of view: show why some people think Augustine succeeds, and try to give a range of reasons, as in the second example.

'Augustinian-type theodicies fail to solve the problem of evil.'
Evaluate this view.

(Eduqas AS Level Religious Studies, Summer 2019, Component 2:
An Introduction to the Philosophy of Religion, Question 1b)

Example 1

Augustinian-type theodicies fail to solve the problem of evil[2] because[1] they depend too heavily on a literal interpretation[6] of the Bible. In Augustine's[4] view, God created the world to be perfect, but[1] the disobedience of Adam and Eve caused the Fall[6] and this led to the whole world being corrupted. Human nature was corrupted, and so was the natural world, so natural disasters started to happen. If[1] we take the Bible literally then we might agree with Augustine[4], but most people today do not believe in Adam and Eve as real people[1]. The Bible is better understood as myth[6] rather than history. If the Genesis story is not literally true then Augustine's[4] theodicy falls apart. If people are not descended from Adam and Eve but instead evolved gradually, sharing a common ancestor with primates, then there cannot have been a time when they lived in a perfect garden and chose to disobey God.[3] Augustine[4] is basing his whole theory on a myth; it's as if someone is using the story of Cinderella as evidence in court when we all know it is just a story[3].

1 The paragraph contains confident analysis and evaluation throughout.

2 The paragraph focuses on the issues raised by the question throughout.

3 There is good use of reasoning, evidence, and examples to support the argument being made.

4 Augustine is referred to in this paragraph. The rest of the response should reference other scholars.

5 This part of the answer does not make any reference to other areas of study. Perhaps the writer will go on to refer to areas such as the use of myth in religious language in future paragraphs.

6 This paragraph contains specialist language and vocabulary in context.

Example 2

Augustinian-type theodicies fail for a number of reasons. Firstly[2], Augustine[4] followed Aristotle[4] in considering evil to be no more than a *privatio boni*[6] or lack of goodness. This aspect of his theodicy fails, because our experience of evil is a lot more sinister than just a lack of goodness.[1] If someone has an inoperable brain tumour it does not help to regard it as just a lack of health.[3] Secondly[2], Augustine[4] does not succeed in maintaining a strong defence of the[1] God of Classical Theism[6], because he leaves many questions unanswered[1]. Augustine[4] does not give a satisfactory explanation of why the angels were given too little grace[6], or why people were tempted to turn away from God, when they were meant to have been created perfectly. As Schleiermacher[4] noted, there is no reason why a perfect creature in a perfect world would fall from grace. Augustine's[4] theory challenges the idea of God's[1] omniscience[6], because God should have known[3] that giving people free will[6] to choose evil would lead them into disobedience. If God can see the future as well as the past, God should know[3] before we are born whether or not we will be saved, and that should inform God's choices[3] about whether or not to make us at all. God's[1] omnipotence[6] is also challenged[1], as Augustine[4] implies that once the Fall[6] had happened, there was nothing God could do about it; and God's[1] omnibenevolence[6] is challenged because[1] Augustine's[4] view is that many people are destined for eternal life in hell.

1. There is analysis of a wide range of issues raised, showing extensive understanding of the implications of the question.

2. The paragraph focuses on the issues raised in the question throughout.

3. In this paragraph, the writer provides some examples to support a point of view, and the reasoning is sound.

4. There is some reference to scholarly views. The writer may be going on to include some more in future paragraphs.

5. This part of the answer does not make any reference to other areas of study. Perhaps the writer will go on to make links in future paragraphs.

6. There is confident use of specialist language and vocabulary.

AO2 practice question 1

Try answering the following question. There are some points to remember to help you write a developed response.

> *'Irenaean type theodicies are not compatible with a 21st Century world view.' Evaluate this view.*
>
> (Eduqas AS Level Religious Studies, Summer 2017, Component 2: An Introduction to the Philosophy of Religion, Question 4b)

Points to remember

- Begin by thinking about the statement and deciding whether or not you agree with it. You are trying to write a persuasive argument in which you give reasons to support your point of view, so begin by having a point of view.
- The question asks about Irenaean-type theodicies, so you can include the views of people like Hick and Swinburne, as well as those of Irenaeus.
- Concentrate on whether or not these theodicies are appropriate for the way modern people think, rather than just critiquing them more generally.

AO2 practice question 2

Now try answering this question on your own.

> *'Epicurus' form of the problem of evil is not a problem.' Evaluate this view.*
>
> (Eduqas AS Level Religious Studies, Summer 2019, Component 2: An Introduction to the Philosophy of Religion, Question 2b)

Mark schemes for all exam questions can be found at www.eduqas.co.uk and www.wjec.co.uk.

4 Challenges to religious belief: religious belief as a product of the human mind

One of the most significant challenges to religious belief is the idea that religion comes from the human mind, rather than from God. To believers, religion might feel as though it is a response to an invisible and transcendent supernatural being; but some critics argue that it is nothing more than a human invention. The mind creates the idea of a powerful and loving being as a way of coping with the harsh realities of adult life. The mind gives believers a reason to think that, despite the chaotic appearance of the world, everything is under control. The mind likes to imagine that death is not the end and that suffering is not random or pointless, and so it creates the idea of an afterlife, a goal for morality, and a comfort for those who wish they could see loved ones again after death; but it is all an illusion.

Religious believers have to find ways of answering this challenge. This chapter explores the ideas of some of those who have presented these challenges, and some of the ways in which believers have responded to them.

New Atheism is a movement that presents challenges to religious belief. New Atheists do not just opt out of religious belief in favour of other interests, but actively campaign against it, arguing that religion is damaging for individuals and for society. This chapter considers the arguments they put forward, and the responses from religious believers.

- Is religious belief really nothing more than wishful thinking?
- Can the challenge that religion is a construct of the human mind be supported with evidence?
- Is religion beneficial for people, or damaging?
- Does religious belief hold back scientific progress?
- How seriously should religious believers take such challenges?

Some critics of religious belief argue that religion is based on wishful thinking, rather than on reality.

AO1

This section of the chapter will enhance your **knowledge** and **understanding** of the topic and help you develop your AO1 skills.

Religious belief as a product of the human mind: Sigmund Freud

The psychoanalyst Sigmund Freud had a significant influence on modern atheism. Freud put forward the view that religion is a human invention, formed by our own subconscious minds, and it is something that damages human wellbeing. He thought religious belief should be recognised as a **neurosis**, a form of mental illness.

Who was Sigmund Freud?

Sigmund Freud was born in 1856, the eldest of eight children. Both his parents were of Jewish descent, but they brought up their children in a predominantly Catholic town called Freiburg, in what is now Czechia. Freud's father, Jacob, had been married before, and was much older than his wife Amalia. Sigmund grew up having a particularly close relationship with his mother, but found his father to be rather distant and austere.

Jacob Freud took his Jewish heritage seriously and studied the Torah and the Talmud, and Amalia's father came from a family of well-regarded Jewish scholars and rabbis. However, the household largely ignored Jewish festivals and instead celebrated Christmas along with the rest of the town. When Sigmund was a very small child, he had a Catholic nanny who used to take him to church, and taught him about heaven and hell. She was diligent about praying with her rosary beads. The nanny left the family when Sigmund was very small, but he always remembered her. The family then moved and settled in Vienna, Austria, where they spent most of their lives until the Nazis occupied Austria and forced people of Jewish descent to leave.

Sigmund Freud claimed that, in spite of the religious influences in his early life, he never held any kind of personal belief in God. He trained for a career in medicine and while he was a student, Freud became involved with the work of a neurologist called Jean-Martin Charcot who was studying paralysis. Charcot was interested in the differences between paralysis that had clear physical causes and paralysis that seemed to be brought about because of psychological disorder, with no obvious physical explanation. This fascinated Freud, who from then on wanted to know more about human psychology and the power of the human mind. He developed the belief that the human mind exerts incredibly strong influences on us in ways we do not always immediately recognise and, importantly, that experiences early in childhood can have a profound effect on people throughout their lives and shape the ways in which they interpret the world.

> ### Key term
>
> **neurosis:** a mental illness which results in high levels of anxiety, unreasonable fears and behaviour and, often, a need to repeat actions unnecessarily

Although he would have liked to spend his life in research, Freud wanted to get married to Martha, the daughter of a rabbi, and so had to earn a more reliable living than research could offer him. He opened a private practice in Vienna specialising in so-called 'nervous disorders', which gave him the opportunity to experiment with his theories. Wealthy Viennese women came to him in the hope of being cured of what was then called 'hysteria'. Hysteria was a term used to cover a wide range of mental health problems, particularly in women, such as anxiety and depression, bipolar disorder, epilepsy, and even some choices – such as the decision not to get married and have children – which were also considered signs of mental illness at the time. Through his encounters with his patients, and also through reports of mental health problems he received second hand, Freud developed the idea that the mind is not just a single, straightforward thing, where we are in control of our decisions and where we always know what we are thinking about. Instead, Freud thought that the mind, or **psyche**, is much more complex than that.

Freud thought that the psyche was made up of layers, rather like the layers in rock formations. Some of these layers are near the surface, so we are aware of them, but others are buried more deeply. Painful experiences that happen to people in childhood, such as the loss of a parent, neglect or abuse, or witnessing a traumatic incident, can be buried or 'repressed' in people's minds as a way of coping with trauma; and sometimes these repressed feelings emerge in later life and can cause distress. Freud thought that it was important to encourage people to uncover their repressed painful memories and work through them, so that they can recover. At first, Freud used hypnosis to help people uncover early painful memories, but later he realised that allowing his patients to talk freely, with some careful questioning, was therapeutic on its own without any need for hypnosis.

In Freud's view, the mind can be understood as having three layers:

1. The ego: this is the part of the mind closest to the surface. It is the conscious self and we are aware of it; we know our own likes and dislikes, opinions and moods, desires and fears.
2. The id: this is the unconscious self, and the part of our personalities that is not immediately obvious to us. It is made up of memories and feelings that we do not admit to ourselves, or have buried and repressed just by refusing to think about them for a long time. These memories can sometimes be brought to the surface when someone is under hypnosis.
3. The super-ego: this can be seen as similar to the conscience, as Freud understood it to be a driving moral force. As we grow up, we learn from parents, siblings, and peers about the kinds of behaviour that are acceptable and unacceptable in society. We internalise these social rules until they become a part of our personalities, shaping our values, and making us feel proud when we do something right and guilty when we feel we have fallen short.

Freud became a professor at the University of Vienna, and he and Martha brought up their six children in the city. Opinion about his work

> **Key term**
>
> **psyche:** the name given to the human mind, and sometimes to the idea of a human soul

in psychoanalysis was sharply divided. Some were excited about the opportunities Freud offered for treating mental illness; others found Freud's uncompromising and blunt exploration of areas such as human sexuality repellent and unsuitable for discussion in polite academic circles. Freud had a small group of loyal followers, among whom psychoanalysis as a science originated. Many others ridiculed his ideas, both for their content and more generally because Freud was Jewish, and antisemitism was on the rise again in Europe. Once Austria was under Nazi rule, Freud's books were burned and his daughter Anna was arrested by the Gestapo, forcing Freud to leave the country.

One of Freud's friends, Marie Bonaparte, was a very wealthy princess, and a descendant of Napoleon Bonaparte. She provided the money for Freud's escape from Austria to London in 1938, when he was 82. His four elderly sisters stayed in Austria and subsequently died in concentration camps. Freud himself was very ill with mouth cancer at the time of his escape, and although he settled comfortably in the London house that was to become the Freud Museum, he died in September 1939, just as the Second World War began.

Freud leaving his home in Vienna for London, on the Orient Express in 1938.

Freud's understanding of religion

Freud's study of religion started with the assumption that there is nothing in reality corresponding to what people think of as God. He thought instead that religion was a human construct, and so he set out to look at the reasons why people invent God, from a psychological point of view.

Religion as an illusion

One of the most important influences on Freud's thought was German philosopher and anthropologist Ludwig Feuerbach. Feuerbach wrote a controversial book called *Essence of Christianity* in 1841, in which he argued that belief in God comes from the human mind and not from any external, existent supernatural being. Feuerbach claimed, therefore, that religion is a human construction. It does not come from God, and when people feel they are being given some kind of divine revelation, they are in fact just listening to their own inner voices. Religion tells us about ourselves, showing us the sorts of people we wish we could be, how we wish we could have power over natural processes, and how we wish our lives had a purpose, as well as showing us our wish that we could be immortal. According to Feuerbach, these ideas are so powerful within the human mind that people project them into the universe, imagining a supernatural, invisible being that actually has and does all the things humanity wishes for. This imagined being seems very real.

Feuerbach's book was seen as very radical but it was also very popular, putting into words ideas that other people might have thought but felt they were not allowed to say. The writer George Eliot was a great admirer of Feuerbach, and translated his works into English. Karl Marx used Feuerbach's ideas in his own rejection of religion, and Freud too read Feuerbach when he was at university, finding the ideas very persuasive.

AO1 activity 1
Explain in your own words the three layers of the psyche that Freud identified.

> *What is characteristic of illusions is that they are derived from human wishes.*
>
> Sigmund Freud, *The Future of an Illusion*

Freud did not use the word '**illusion**' to refer to things like visions of God or hearing the voice of God in a dream. Instead, he thought that the *whole* of religion is an illusion, in the sense of being a wish based on no evidence, such as gamblers living under the illusion that they are about to win a great deal of money, or lazy students being under the illusion that they can get top grades without doing any work. Illusions, Freud said, are not necessarily false; what makes them illusions is the fact that they are based on wishes rather than on any kind of hard evidence.

> *Thus we call a belief an illusion when a wish-fulfilment is a prominent factor in its motivation, and in doing so we disregard its relations to reality, just as the illusion itself sets no store by verification.*
>
> Sigmund Freud, *The Future of an Illusion*

Religion as a collective neurosis

Freud thought that there must be reasons why some people still cling to unscientific beliefs in God even though there is no evidence to support them. They still follow rituals, and feel guilty if they neglect them, and think that serious consequences will follow if they stop religious behaviours. Freud thought that religious rituals, in particular, showed close similarities to what were then called obsessional neuroses.

Many people with an **obsessional neurosis** (today known as obsessive compulsive disorder, or OCD) feel compelled to perform certain actions repeatedly, such as touching every door handle twelve times, or washing their hands far more often than is usual. Freud studied these behaviours, and noticed what he thought were similarities with religious rituals, such as counting rosary beads while repeating prayers (as his Catholic nanny had done) or saying ritual prayers before eating (as in Judaism). He wrote *'Obsessive actions and religious practices'* in 1907, a paper that marked the beginning of his interest in religion as a mental health disorder, and introduced themes that he was to develop in later writings.

Freud thought that in both religion and obsessional mental illness, the repetitive behaviour patterns were associated with fear and guilt. In the case of mental illness, he thought, people performed the rituals from motives they did not entirely understand themselves, but it was often because they felt something dreadful would happen if they did not do them, and they thought that they would be to blame for possible misfortunes to others if they failed to perform them. He gave the example of someone having rituals before they go to bed, where a chair has to be in an exact position, and clothes folded in a particular way and laid out in a particular order, before the person can go to sleep.

Key terms

illusion: for Freud, an illusion involves seeing reality as you wish it to be

obsessional neurosis: a term once used in psychiatry to refer to obsessive compulsive disorder (OCD)

AO1 activity 2

In your own words, explain what Freud meant by 'illusion', and why he thought religion is an illusion.

This obsessional mental illness, argued Freud, derived from repressed desires: the patient has sexual urges or other desires that society requires them to keep under control, such as the desire to be selfish or greedy, and the act of repressing the desires and leaving them unfulfilled drives the patient to anxiety-driven obsessional rituals. **Repression** is a mechanism used by the mind to protect itself, keeping traumatic experiences safely buried in the unconscious and preventing them from surfacing to the consciousness. However, when the emotions are repressed, they build up and force their way out through other channels if the more obvious routes are blocked.

Freud saw similarities with ritual religious practices, which might include behaviours such as crossing oneself, repeating the words of a prayer, saying grace before meals, or attending church every Sunday. He called religion a 'universal obsessional neurosis', or a collective neurosis, as it is not just something that one individual does, but has rituals that are practised by large groups.

Because Freud thought of religion in terms of mental illness, he also thought that it was something people would be better off without. If people could learn to see religion for the illusion that it is, and find better ways of coping with anxiety and with the realities of life, they would have better mental health.

> **Key term**
>
> **repression:** the act of inhibiting or suppressing

AO1 activity 3

a) List religious rituals that believers might do repeatedly, such as crossing oneself in Christianity, or the rituals associated with prayer in Islam.

b) Explain why Freud thought that such rituals were similar to neurotic behaviour.

Religion and the Oedipus complex

When he was investigating the idea of repressed feelings, including looking back at his own childhood experiences, Freud came to the conclusion that neurosis has its roots in sexuality. He thought that sexual experiences and impulses in infancy have great importance, and that every child goes through a phase of having sexual feelings towards their parents. They develop a strong emotional attachment to the parent of the opposite sex, and feel a sense of jealousy and rivalry towards the other parent. Concentrating his attentions mainly on boys, Freud explained that when boys become aware of their gender, at the age of about two to five, they want to have a sexual relationship with their mothers and would like to get rid of their fathers. This feeling becomes even stronger if the little boy is allowed to share his mother's bed when his father goes away, but has to go back to his own bed when his father is at home. The son sees his father as competition for his mother's love, something that started when he stopped being breast-fed. Freud added to this the idea that little boys explore their own bodies and enjoy playing with their penises, but their parents tell them not to. This, he thought, gives them a fear of losing their penises, especially when they notice that not everyone has a penis. This frightens them, as they think females must have lost their penises as a punishment.

Freud thought that this is a universal stage of childhood development. He called it the **Oedipus complex**, based on the Greek legend of King Oedipus who unwittingly killed his father and married his mother, a story that was made into a play by Sophocles. In the play, Oedipus discovers what he has done, and feels so guilty that he gouges out his own eyes. Freud thought that the play had stood the test of time because people watching it recognised unconscious, repressed feelings of their own in it and found it both interesting and relatable.

The Oedipus complex relates to religion because, Freud thought, men feel guilty about secretly wanting to kill their fathers, and over-compensate by inventing a great father figure, God (using the ideas of Feuerbach). People create this father figure, attribute all kinds of powers to it, and submit to what they imagine is its authority, as a way of making amends for their secret murderous desires. They give the father-God all the characteristics they wish they had themselves – the ability to do everything and control everything – and then they worship it, so that they no longer need to feel guilty about wanting to get rid of their earthly fathers.

> *Psycho-analysis has made us familiar with the intimate connection between the father-complex and belief in God; it has shown us that a personal God is, psychologically, nothing other than an exalted father, and it brings us evidence every day of how young people lose their religious beliefs as soon as their father's authority breaks down. Thus we recognise that the roots of the need for religion are in the parental complex.*
>
> Sigmund Freud, *Leonardo da Vinci and a Memory of His Childhood*

Freud also wrote about the Electra complex, in which girls want to get rid of their mothers and have a sexual relationship with their fathers. This is not given very much attention in his writings however, perhaps because he based the Oedipus complex idea on his own childhood and had no personal experience of girlhood.

> ## Key term
>
> **Oedipus complex:** a term used by Sigmund Freud to mean that men secretly want to kill their fathers and have sexual relations with their mothers

AO1 activity 4

a) Look up and read the story of Oedipus from Greek mythology.

b) Explain how Freud interpreted this myth in relation to religious belief.

The primal horde

Freud worked at a time when Charles Darwin's ideas were still quite new. Darwin's ideas about the evolution of different species caught the public imagination, and people began to apply ideas about progress through evolution to areas of academic thought beyond biology. The science of anthropology, which looks at human cultures, took up the theme of evolution in its interpretations of cultural beliefs and practices. It was popular at the time to think of some cultures as 'primitive', and to study them to understand how Western society had developed its social systems. This was based on the assumption that Western society must once have operated in similar ways to these 'primitive' cultures, and had gradually evolved to become more sophisticated; at the time Freud was writing, most Europeans assumed that their own culture and customs were superior to those of people in other parts of the world. Darwinian approaches to anthropology included the idea that as societies became more developed and mature, people would learn that it was important they should get along with each other as a coherent group, and so they would learn to repress some of their individual instincts for the benefit of keeping the peace.

Darwin had suggested the possibility that in the early stages of the development of humanity as a species, hominids may have lived together in a simple society, or '**primal horde**', where they cooperated with each other for the purposes of hunting and safety. Using his observations of the indigenous people he encountered on his travels, Darwin thought that religion may have originated when early people tried to find explanations for natural occurrences, and attributed supernatural spirit powers to some animals or plants. Early people may also have experienced dreams of family members who had died, and thought that these ancestors had an existence after death and needed to be kept happy so that they would not bring bad luck. Darwin described his suggestions in a book called *The Descent of Man* in 1871, in which he explored the similarities between people and other animals.

The writer William Robertson Smith also had ideas that attracted Freud. Robertson Smith was a scholar who specialised in the Old Testament, and in his 1889 book *Lectures on the Religion of the Semites*, he made some guesses about what religion in the Ancient Near East might have been like in the days before Judaism. He thought that perhaps prehistoric hunter gatherers had a special animal that was their **totem**, and that they sacrificed and ate it once a year to gain whatever powers the animal has, such as strength and speed.

Using these ideas from Darwin and Robertson Smith, Freud wrote one of his best-known books, *Totem and Taboo*, in 1913. Moving from guesswork to assertion, he described how primal hordes had a totem which they regarded as their guardian spirit, and the members of the group had to protect that animal and never kill it. The totem defined who they were as a group, and there were taboos associated with the totem; for example, there were taboos against sexual relationships with people from the same totem clan. Anyone breaking the taboos became themselves taboo, and was shunned by the rest of the group. On special occasions, however, the totem was killed and eaten in a ceremony. Freud used his own imaginative descriptions of primal hordes and totems as a basis from which to explain the emergence and development of religion. Religion, he implied, did not have any basis in a real God, but instead grew out of primitive superstition.

Freud also developed the idea of the primal horde as a social structure, saying that the horde would have been ruled by a single dominant male who had control over all of the females in the group. Other males in the group would respect his authority but at the same time, resent him and his power. Male children would be seen as threats and be expelled from the horde, but they would return and kill their father, taking control of the horde for themselves. The totem animal then came to represent the father

Key terms

primal horde: a term used in the nineteenth century to refer to a very simple form of society, where prehistoric people gathered in groups to hunt together and protect each other

totem: a sacred object or symbol that serves as an emblem of a group of people

who had been killed, and it would be worshipped as a way of getting rid of the guilt of murdering the father. The idea of the Oedipus complex, then, is interwoven with this theory of the origin of religion, because it is based on the notion of tensions in father–son relationships.

Freud thought that the sense of guilt that comes from the original murder must somehow have the power to persist from one generation to the next. He did not give specific details of how this inheritance might happen, but hinted at the idea that there could be some way in which people inherit ideas that are shared with the rest of the community, using the kind of ideas suggested by Lamarck's theory of evolution through acquired characteristics. This part of Freud's analysis of religion was to be taken up and developed further by Carl Gustav Jung.

Freud thought that the Christian service of the Eucharist (Holy Communion) provided a clear demonstration of how these primitive practices had become embedded in religious thought. There were obvious similarities, with the sacrifice of Christ, and the sharing of bread and wine as the body and blood of Christ taking away sin and guilt. Freud thought that when Christians gather to celebrate the Eucharist and share bread and wine as representative of the body and blood of Christ, they are doing the same thing as their primitive ancestors who shared a totemic meal.

Religion, for Freud, corresponds to the stage in a child's development when their sexual instincts are directed towards a parent, and these instincts are repressed before finding expression in worship of an illusory God. Freud thought that for healthy individuals, there was a further developmental stage when the child realises that they can be independent and can function in the adult world without their parents. For Freud, adulthood corresponds in religion to the stage when people understand that the truth is to be found through science. The adult does not need religion, but can cope with the chaos and injustices of life independently with no childish dependence on an imaginary father. Religion, for Freud, is therefore an infantile illusion.

AO1 activity 5
Explain Freud's ideas about how religion originated, using the terms 'primal horde' and 'totem' in your writing.

Religion as wish fulfilment and a reaction against helplessness

Freud was not the first to suggest that religion is an illusion. David Hume's work *The Natural History of Religion*, published in 1757, had already made the case that religion developed from the superstitions of primitive humanity. Hume said that people looked to the supernatural to try and ensure that their lives were happy, ensure that they avoided suffering, and ensure that death would not be the end of their existence. Feuerbach had also published his idea that God is no more than a projection of human hopes. The idea of religion as nothing more than wishful thinking was not new; Freud's contribution was to add a psychological basis to this line of argument, by attempting to show how the Oedipus complex provided a motivation for religion.

Along with his predecessors, Freud agreed that religion exists because of people's need to live with an illusion rather than face life's realities. People make up religious beliefs, he thought, as a way of comforting themselves.

They wish they could be in more control of their lives, and so they invent a system in which everything makes sense, where they are looked after, and justice is done.

> *We shall tell ourselves that it would be very nice if there were a moral order in the universe and an after-life; but it is a very striking fact that all this is exactly as we are bound to wish to be* "
>
> Sigmund Freud, *The Future of Illusion*

People feel helpless. There are things they can control in their lives: they can work hard, they can make what they hope will be sensible choices, they can bring up their children to the best of their abilities, and they can contribute to their communities in the hope of getting the benefits of security in a group. However, there are many things that people cannot control, such as their health, the weather and its effect on crops, the success of their ventures, the safety of those they love, and the length of their own lives. Freud argued, as have others, that religion exists to help people feel that someone is in control of all the aspects of life that are, in reality, random and frightening; but, in fact, religion is nothing more than **wish fulfilment**, a way to satisfy the desire for certainty, and a reaction against hopelessness.

Evidence supporting Freud's analysis of religious belief as a product of the human mind

Freud was a scientist by training, and wanted his work to be accepted by the scientific community. But psychology is a notoriously difficult subject for scientific research, as there are limited ways of discovering what is really going on in someone's inner life, and scientific experimentation with human minds is very problematic. It is impossible to take identical people who have had identical experiences and introduce a single variable to test a theory, and therefore theories in psychology are very difficult to support with firm evidence.

Freud did try, nevertheless, to support his theories with evidence. He referred to case studies he wrote after treating patients, to case notes written by other doctors, and also to second-hand accounts written by the patients themselves or their family members, from which he argued that the neuroses they experienced were the result of repressed sexual feelings and redirected guilt complexes. When he wrote about the redirection of guilt complexes, Freud was referring to the human habit of avoiding facing feelings of guilt, and instead directing emotions towards a different target instead (known as 'displacement'). This is not a deliberate, conscious decision, but something that people do subconsciously: it occurs when someone is irritable with their partner because they are hungry, or when someone interprets another person's comments as an insult because they are feeling stressed about a completely different thing. Repression of feelings of guilt can, Freud argued, be manifested in other ways, such as by repeating religious rituals.

Key term

wish fulfilment: the satisfaction of desires and fantasies

AO1 activity 6

Explain, using examples, the idea that religion is nothing more than wish fulfilment.

It is often difficult for us to know exactly what causes our own emotions. Freud thought that people's repressed feelings of guilt related to the Oedipus complex are often redirected towards a different object entirely, without the individual understanding what they are doing. He noticed this in some of his patients:

- Little Hans: Little Hans was a pseudonym for the son of a well-known music critic. When he was a child, Little Hans developed an intense fear of horses, which meant he refused to go out into the street. Freud diagnosed this as a result of the Oedipus complex, where the child was displacing his fears of his father onto horses. Freud successfully treated the child, and considered that this success supported his diagnosis.
- Wolf Man: Freud used this pseudonym for a patient who suffered with depression and had a dream about being eaten by wolves. He diagnosed this as repressed trauma from Wolf Man witnessing his parents having sex.
- Daniel Schreber: Schreber was a judge who developed mental health problems explicitly connected with religion. He thought that God was trying to enter his body and turn him into a woman. Freud did not actually meet Schreber but, from reading the case notes, again diagnosed that his problems stemmed from the Oedipus complex, where the tensions of Schreber's relationship with his father in childhood were being displaced onto the idea of God.

More recent developments in psychology and psychotherapy support the idea that anxiety and other disorders can relate to unconscious childhood memories and trauma. People who develop addictions to alcohol or drugs often have a deep-rooted problem in their personal history that they have not come to terms with, and the drugs and alcohol are used as a means of forgetting and repressing. 'Talking therapies' are popular, where someone with anxiety or depression talks to a therapist or a counsellor on a regular basis, confronting feelings from the past in order to move forward; these therapies are often successful. In these ways, some of Freud's theories seem to be supported by evidence, and the work in psychoanalysis that Freud began to help people recover from mental health problems, should not be underestimated even if some of his ideas might seem far-fetched.

Freud also used the observations made by Charles Darwin as evidence to support his views. Darwin observed the behaviour and social structures of the Australian indigenous peoples he encountered on his travels, and Freud used Darwin's accounts to construct his theories about how early people must have lived, embellishing them with his own ideas about the Oedipus complex.

There is evidence to support the idea that modern people have some instincts that can be traced back to the fears and concerns of their ancestors. We still have very strong survival instincts when we are in danger, a powerful instinct to protect our young, and we still fear those who look or speak differently from ourselves without properly understanding why. People are still subconsciously on the lookout for predators; this is probably why we see faces in clouds and in the embers of fires, because we have a strong instinct to detect when we are being watched. And we still have strong sexual instincts, even though people living in the developed world do not need to have as many children as they did in the past because most of our offspring can be expected to reach adulthood. Although the details of Freud's analysis might be speculative, there is certainly some evidence to support the idea that dispositions and emotions, as well as physical characteristics, can be genetically inherited.

Before Darwin had developed his theory of evolution through natural selection, another scientist called Jean-Baptiste Lamarck had put forward a different idea, involving the inheritance of acquired characteristics. The idea was that in their lifetimes, animals (including human beings) gain or lose characteristics according to their usefulness, and then these characteristics can be inherited by their offspring. Lamarck's most famous example was that of the giraffe, where he suggested that stretching into the trees to reach the higher leaves might elongate the neck, and this characteristic would then be inherited by the giraffe's offspring, so that over time, giraffes developed the characteristic of long necks. He also suggested that a blacksmith would develop strong muscles in his arms, and that his sons would then be born with stronger arm muscles (Lamarck was writing at the beginning of the nineteenth century, when sons usually earned their livings in the same manner as their fathers). Lamarck's theories have been generally discarded in favour of Darwinism, especially since the development of an understanding of genetics. However, there are those who think that Lamarck may have been right in some respects, and Freud was one of them. If there is truth in Lamarck's understanding of inherited characteristics, then this adds evidential support to Freud's thinking.

AO1 activity 7

Explain how each of the following thinkers had an influence on Freud's thought:
a) Feuerbach
b) Lamarck
c) Robertson Smith
d) Hume
e) Darwin

Challenges to Freud's understanding of religion

Freud's thinking has met with many challenges, in his own lifetime and ever since. His views were seen as improper because of their emphasis on sexual urges, and his assessment of religion was unpopular. Many ridiculed him without making much effort to understand what he was saying. Some, however, presented more reasoned challenges to Freud's thinking.

A lack of anthropological evidence

One criticism that has been made of Freud's thought came from the field of anthropology. Freud seems to have taken other scholars' imaginative guesses about how early people might have lived, and asserted them as if they are true history. E.E. Evans-Pritchard, one of the key figures in twentieth-century anthropology, said of William Robertson Smith's ideas of totemism in 1965:

> *Bluntly, all Robertson Smith really does is to guess about a period of Semitic history about which we know almost nothing ... The evidence for these suppositions is exiguous [tiny].*
>
> E.E. Evans-Pritchard, *Theories of Primitive Religion*

When Darwin and Robertson Smith wrote their imaginative accounts of how early people might have lived, there was no reliable data for them to use, and so it was all conjecture. More modern research has not found evidence of primal hordes living under the authority of a single alpha male. There are some similarities between Freud's hypothesis and the social patterns of gorillas, but little to support the idea that people ever lived in the way Freud described. There does not appear to be evidence, either in human society or in the societies of primates, of a general characteristic of murderous aggression towards a leading male. Furthermore, Robertson Smith's ideas about the totemic sacrificial meal have negligible evidence to support them; it could have happened, but no one has found any evidence yet that it actually did.

Bronislaw Malinowski was an anthropologist who studied the Trobriand Islanders of New Guinea. He wrote a book in 1927 detailing his research and also challenging Freud. The Trobriand Islanders provided evidence against the idea that the Oedipus complex is universal, because their society was matrilineal. Sons did not develop close bonds with their mothers because they were detached from their mothers at an early age, and were allowed to engage in sexual activity with everyone's approval. Fathers were not authoritarian figures. Malinowski concluded that there could not be universal repressed desires for young men to overthrow their fathers, as in some societies there was no need for it. With no universal 'primal crime' of patricide, there could be no universal, inherited guilt. Malinowski did not say that the Oedipus complex did not exist at all, but he challenged the idea that it was innate and came from inherited instincts. He thought instead that the Oedipus complex, where it is found, arises from cultural practices. The culture causes the complex, rather than the complex causing the culture.

No firm psychological evidence for a universal Oedipus complex

In addition to the lack of anthropological evidence for the primal horde and the totemic sacrificial meal, there is also a lack of psychological evidence for Freud's theories. Freud diagnosed the Oedipus complex as the cause of a wide variety of mental health conditions, including phobias, depression, schizophrenia, and OCD. However, there is little evidence to support the view that these conditions all have the same cause, and it does appear that Freud was looking for support for his theories rather than assessing his patient's cases with an open mind. Cause and effect is always very difficult to assert with any kind of certainty.

Synoptic link

Link to *Chapter 1: Arguments for the existence of God: inductive*. Hume argued, in relation to the cosmological argument, that cause and effect do not operate as simply as we tend to assume.

The Oedipus complex focuses on the male, and his desire for his mother and his feelings towards his father. This makes it difficult to see how it can be considered universal because half of the world's population is female. Freud was very much a man of his times, with nineteenth-century views about the relative importance of men and women, and he focused much of his theorising on men. He did introduce a counterpart to the Oedipus complex, for women, called the Electra complex, but this is given far less attention or corroboration in his writings.

Evidence base is too narrow

Freud has often been criticised for using a small number of cases as evidence from which to generalise, which is not a method approved by scientists. His patients were mostly female, white and from wealthy Viennese backgrounds. He did not seem to have any evidence from people from ethnic minorities or lower income backgrounds, for example, and yet he described the Oedipus complex as 'universal' and claimed that 'all' neuroses had their roots in unresolved issues of sexuality. Because the case studies Freud used were so limited in number and in range, many have dismissed his findings as unscientific, arguing that he should have looked at a much higher number of people, and from a much wider range of backgrounds, before drawing his conclusions. Freud himself was not bothered by such criticisms, however, and was convinced that science would prove him right.

Freud wrote about the ways in which religion encourages people to have an over-developed sense of guilt, which can be damaging for them, particularly with regard to sexuality. However, he used his own experiences with his father and mother as evidence, and the experiences of his patients, who had come to him because of mental health problems, and so the range of people from whom he drew his evidence was not typical of the population as a whole. He started with people who had mental health problems and looked at religious belief only from their perspective, concluding that all religious people have neurosis; he should have concluded that some people with neurosis have religious belief. Critics of Freud have accused him of confirmation bias, where a researcher starts out with a hypothesis that they want to prove true, and only considers evidence that supports their idea, ignoring any evidence that might undermine it.

There could be plenty of religious people who do not have mental health problems and also do not have unhealthy, disproportionate feelings of guilt. Many religious people say they find their beliefs liberate them from guilt, and claim that their faith has set them free from the burdens of sin.

Freud concentrates his attentions entirely on religions that have a God who is understood in male terms, as a father. All of his patients came from cultural backgrounds where that was the way in which God was understood. A wider evidence base might have encouraged Freud to look at religions where there are female deities or where there is a pantheon of gods and not a single God. His analysis of religion, if appropriate at all, seems appropriate only for a particular kind of religious belief.

AO1 activity 8

Find out more about the problem of confirmation bias. Explain why some people might accuse Freud of confirmation bias in the way he conducted his research.

Not available to empirical testing

One of the difficulties of psychology as a science is that the usual scientific methods of experimentation are difficult to follow. When investigating the properties of something like copper sulphate, the scientist can ensure that the same amount of copper sulphate is measured into the same-sized test tubes every time, that the test tubes are kept at identical temperatures, and the experiment is conducted in exactly the same way repeatedly, so that whatever characteristic is being examined can be isolated and other variables can be controlled. But investigating what goes on inside people's minds cannot be explored in the same way. No two people have identical upbringings and life experiences, and no two interviews will be exactly the same. An experience cannot be re-lived for the first time more than once. The relationship between the patient and the psychiatrist will not be identical in every case. The fact that psychiatrists are dealing with human people, rather than with inanimate objects, makes it impossible for the psychologist to say with any certainty that a particular behaviour must have been caused by a single particular thing, and could only have been caused by that thing. In addition, psychological experiences are private to the individual. Unlike a rash or a broken limb, doctors cannot see psychological symptoms for themselves; they have to trust that what the patient is telling them is true and accurate. The patient could be led by a line of questioning into making statements that are what the researcher wants to hear.

A further, related problem is that science is open to **falsification**. This means that it should be possible to test the original hypothesis and know what counter-evidence looks like, so if counter-evidence is found then the researcher can rethink their original idea. For example, acid turns litmus paper red, so we know we can test a hypothesis that a substance is acidic. If the litmus paper does not turn red, we have counter-evidence and our hypothesis needs modification. We might hypothesise that all swans are white, but if we find a black swan, we have counter-evidence and have to revise our initial hypothesis.

However, it is not possible to falsify Freud's theories. Because he is arguing that all religious belief is founded on secret, repressed Oedipus complexes, any apparent counter-evidence can be dismissed by saying that the surface appearance does not match the secret reality. There are no tests that can be done to find out if Freud was right or not. This problem, for many people, makes Freud's conclusions unscientific.

However, although Freud's critics accuse him of not being properly scientific, the same could be said of other disciplines such as sociology, economics, anthropology, and even history: any academic study of human behaviour has the same kinds of problems as psychology because of the impossibility of isolating variables, and because of the ethical issues that arise in conducting any kind of experiment on human beings.

Freud's research is often accused of being unscientific because he started out firm in the belief that Feuerbach was right, and that religion

> **Key term**
>
> **falsification:** the action of proving a statement to be false

> **AO1 activity 9**
>
> Explain, in your own words, why psychology is difficult to conduct using the scientific methods used by physicists and chemists.

is nothing more than a product of the human mind. Freud conducted his research in order to support that view, rather than treating his original views only as a hypothesis and allowing the possibility that he might need to change his mind.

Freud's contribution to modern thought

Freud's writings, methods, and conclusions brought him a great deal of criticism and public ridicule, just as the theories of Darwin were criticised and ridiculed. Even today, casual mention of Freud is likely to be in the context of jokes. However, his importance as a thinker should not be overlooked.

- Before Freud, people with mental health problems were often written off, especially if they were women. They were dismissed as 'hysterical'. Freud opened up the way for therapies and even cures for some disorders, and saw how inner conflicts and repressed unresolved traumas were common, even universal.
- Even though Freud was rather cavalier with the scientific method, and possibly overstated the importance of sexuality in individual psychology, he made it possible for people to be a great deal more open about sexuality. In Victorian society, sex was something that was simply never mentioned. Young women were meant to know nothing about it, and young men often secretly resorted to visiting sex workers, sometimes contracting syphilis which was left untreated because they were too embarrassed to seek medical help for it. Things did not change overnight, but today people in many countries can talk to others about sexual abuse, sexual preferences, and gender identity with much more freedom.
- In relation to religion, Freud presents a serious challenge because he offers an alternative explanation for religious belief. Rather than reaching the conclusion that the best explanation for human religious feeling is God, Freud offered the alternative view that the best explanation for human religious feeling is found within human psychology. This is a challenge that religious believers need to address.

Religious belief as a product of the human mind: Carl Jung

Who was Carl Jung?

Carl Gustav Jung was a Swiss psychiatrist who came from a Christian family; his father and uncles were clergymen, and his grandfather had studied medicine. As a child, Carl Jung was close to his father but rather more distant from his mother, who suffered from depression and spent some of Carl's childhood in hospital. As he grew up, Jung considered a career as a clergyman, but changed his mind in his teenage years and decided instead that he would study medicine, where he became particularly interested in the new field of psychology. When Jung was a student, he researched the psychology of 'occult phenomena' (alleged ghostly appearances and communications from people who had died). Jung was particularly interested in this because his cousin Hélène believed herself to be a medium, with special abilities to contact the spirits of the dead.

After some time working in a psychiatric hospital, Jung set up his own private practice and began to correspond with Sigmund Freud. Jung was very interested in the idea of psychoanalysis, and Freud welcomed supporters. The pair developed a friendship and worked collaboratively for a while, going to conferences together and discussing their work with each other. However, after about six years, the relationship began to break down. Freud had seen Jung very much in terms of a pupil and a successor, someone who would carry on the work that he had started. Jung, however, did not want to spend his life working under the shadow of Freud. He wanted to develop his own ideas, and he did not always agree with the conclusions that Freud had drawn. Notably, he thought Freud had over-emphasised the importance of sexual urges in the formation of the unconscious.

Jung's understanding of religion

Jung's understanding of religion was markedly different from Freud's. Instead of seeing religion as an infantile illusion, Jung saw it as a response to deep psychological layers common to all of humanity.

The collective unconscious

Jung agreed with Freud that the psyche has different levels, but he had different ideas about what these levels are:

1. The consciousness (the ego): this is the part of the mind that is directly accessible to us because we are aware of it.
2. The personal unconscious: this is the unconscious layer of the mind that is personal to the individual. It contains repressed and forgotten memories and trauma, and social conditioning.
3. The **collective unconscious**: this is the deepest and the most extensive layer of the psyche. Jung argued that even deeper than our own personal subconscious inner world, there is a layer which is shared by all humanity irrespective of time or place. It is like a reservoir, containing a series of images or forms that Jung called 'archetypes', which we use to shape our understanding of the world.

> **Key term**
>
> **collective unconscious:** a subconscious layer of the mind that Jung identified and believed was shared among humanity rather than being personal to the individual

The idea of the collective unconscious is distinctive to Jung. Jung thought that this deepest layer of our inner worlds is not something we gradually develop, adding to it as we gain more experience. Instead, it is impersonal and is something we inherit, rather as birds inherit the instinct for hatching from an egg or migrating south for the winter. The collective unconscious is older than we are as individuals, dating back to the first evolutionary stages of humanity.

When he developed the idea of the collective unconscious, Jung used some of the ideas that Immanuel Kant had put forward in *Critique of Pure Reason* in 1781. Kant argued that the objects of our experience, called phenomena, are only understandable to us because our minds impose meaning on them. We like to classify things in terms of shape, colour, position in time, pattern, and sequence so that we know how they fit into our world. These classifications are mental processes that we do without knowing that we are doing them. It is impossible, thought Kant, for us to see things as they really are, because all of our experience is shaped by interpretation.

Jung thought that the collective unconscious has a similar function. It provides us with forms, or archetypes, that enable us to recognise and make sense of our experiences. We are not born with a 'blank slate' (sometimes known as the *tabula rasa*) but begin life with archetypal images already in our collective unconscious. Jung came to this conclusion because he was struck by how similar different people's dreams can be, how similar hallucinations are in patients with mental health problems such as schizophrenia, and how different myths from around the world have common themes.

Archetypes

Jung called the contents of the collective unconscious **archetypes**. Some of his writing about archetypes is rather obscure. For Jung, archetypes are the forms or images that we use to understand the world; they help us to recognise and to classify, and to construct a narrative so that we can understand the world around us and our place within it.

Jung was fascinated by myths, legends, folk tales, and fairy tales from around the world. What particularly captured his imagination was the way in which these traditional stories contain common elements and recognisable characters who reappear in different stories, even in cultures which have had little contact with each other; these characters are, for Jung, archetypes. Although it is not always clear exactly how Jung understood the meaning of 'archetypes', he gave many examples of them in these recurring characters. There is, for example, the archetype of the Mother, who is found in ancient fertility figurines, in Hindu deities, in fairy tales, and as the Virgin Mary. There is the Child-god, whose birth is surrounded with miracle and symbol, and this archetype can be found in stories of the boy Krishna, the birth of the Buddha, the birth and early childhood of Hercules in Roman mythology, the nativity of Jesus, the story of baby Moses, and in the poetry of William Blake. There is the archetype of the Hero, who is a small and seemingly insignificant figure who slays the monster, which can be found in the tales of Theseus and the Minotaur, David and Goliath, and Jack and the Beanstalk.

Key term

archetypes: typical examples of something; the original form of something, from which all versions are copied; for Jung, archetypes are forms or images we share in our collective unconscious, that help us to understand our experiences in the world

AO1 activity 10

List examples of myths, fiction, and folk tales from your own culture that contain one or more of Jung's Mother, Child-god, or Hero archetypes, so you can use them as examples in your essays.

Jung noticed that the motif of the Child-god is common in many different cultures.

In some respects, Jung's archetypes are similar to the Forms in the philosophy of the Greek thinker Plato. Plato believed that beyond the reality of this world, there is also a world of Forms, which are concepts or ideals. Plato thought that we know what justice is, or truth or beauty, because they have an ideal Form which people are aware of before birth. Jung's archetypes are similar to Platonic Forms in that they are not ideas that we have developed ourselves as individuals, but are universal, enabling us to shape our understanding of the world.

In theory, there are no limits to the number of archetypes in the collective unconscious. Jung thought that archetypes need not just be characters but could also be objects and animals, and even events that we all share, such as birth. In practice, however, some archetypes are more important than others. Jung gave special attention to five, and went into some detail explaining their characteristics:

- The Persona: this is the archetype of a pretend personality, where someone conceals who they really are and plays a role that they imagine society wants them to play. Jung thought that everyone does this, and it causes anxieties which are revealed in dreams; for example of being at an event in the wrong clothes.
- The Shadow: this is the archetype of the side of our personalities that we would rather keep hidden. It can be seen in literature in works such as Robert Louis Stevenson's *Dr Jekyll and Mr Hyde*, and Oscar Wilde's *The Picture of Dorian Gray*, where the lead characters have a sinister side they keep hidden from public view. Jung thought that we experience our own shadow sides when we project them onto other people, such as an ex-partner, and attribute our own worst flaws to them.
- The Anima and the Animus: these are archetypes of the aspect of the psyche that has characteristics of the opposite sex, so it is the feminine side of men and the masculine side of women. Jung thought that people are attracted to those who reflect their own anima or animus, so for example a man will be attracted to a woman who resembles his own feminine side.
- The Self: this is an archetype that Jung wrote about in quite an obscure manner. He saw symbols of the Self represented in images of royalty

and leading religious figures, and in geometric figures such as the mandala, and in plants such as the lotus and the rose. The Self balances the conscious and unconscious, and is close to what religious people refer to as the 'soul', or the 'atman' in Eastern thought.

In Jung's view, the archetypes present the potential for mental health problems if one becomes too dominant. For example, a person could have problems with their mental health if they allow their Shadow to be repressed to such an extent that it causes neurotic guilt, or if they become too concerned with their Persona and obsessed with how others see them to the extent that it causes social anxiety.

The God within

Jung's understanding of God is that God is an archetype. This means that in Jung's view:

- God is a manifestation of the deepest levels of our collective unconscious
- God is an image that we all share within the human psyche, whether we recognise it or not
- God predates us as individuals
- God exists within the human consciousness, but not necessarily 'out there' as an external reality.

Jung was not clear about whether God exists beyond the human mind. Michael Palmer, in his 1997 book *Freud and Jung on Religion*, compares Jung's position with that of Immanuel Kant. Kant argued that we have to postulate God (assume that God exists) to account for our moral nature, so for Kant, God is a conclusion that needs to be drawn to explain human psychology. Jung took a similar position, saying that God needs to be understood as an archetype to account for the ways in which people of all different cultures are predisposed to the idea of God. He said that the psyche could not 'leap beyond itself' to establish whether there was any objective truth to God outside the human mind; whether or not God exists, in the way that is traditionally understood, is a question that is outside the boundaries of psychology.

Jung argued that the ways in which the archetype of God is manifested vary according to different cultures, but the different ways are all symbols of the same thing. In some cultures, God is depicted as male and in others as female, and God is given different names. Different world religions offer different ways of accessing this part of the collective unconscious, for example through private and public worship, through meditation, and through sacred texts that provide powerful symbols. Jung thought the practice of meditation was particularly beneficial for people, encouraging them to set aside conscious distractions and allow the unconscious levels of the mind to be developed with the positive aims of calmness and kindness to the rest of the world.

Jung referred to the Self as 'God within us'. The Self is the centre of the psyche, like the nucleus of an atom, and is an unchanging part of ourselves. Jung did not say that the Self is the same as God, but that the Self is a

> **AO1 activity 11**
> Explain, using examples, how Jung understood archetypes.

139

representation of God. When we encounter the Self in the unconscious, it feels like a religious experience, and we come away feeling revitalised and enriched, as well as ready to re-evaluate our egos. We realise that our egos are not as important as we thought, and we are better able to manage our Personas and our Shadows, because we understand that the 'God within us' is more objective and universally shared than our own personal egos. Encounters with the Self as the God within us calm our inward psychological struggles, giving us the freedom to accept ourselves and be more generous and accepting of others.

AO1 activity 12

a) In your own words, explain what Jung meant when he wrote about 'the God within'.
b) Explain what Jung thought were the benefits of prayer and meditation.
c) How do Jung's ideas about God and prayer differ from those of traditional Christianity?

Individuation

Jung argued that every person has the potential for what he described as 'wholeness'. In many people's psyches, different aspects of their personalities, both conscious and unconscious, conflict with each other and cause problems. People feel that they are being pulled in different directions, or are impeded from being the kinds of people they want to be; they have feelings they cannot understand, or they get into relationships that make them restless and unable to be themselves.

Jung thought that everyone has an instinct which seeks to unify the different elements of their inner world and reconcile them, bringing all of the personal and collective unconscious together into a coherent whole, and coming to terms with them in the consciousness. Jung terms this process '**individuation**'. Archetypes help us to make sense of the world and should be acknowledged, including the archetype that is God. Religious belief, for Jung, could be helpful in the process of individuation, providing a channel through which people can access the collective unconscious and come to terms with the Self as the God within us.

In Jung's view, religious belief and religious experiences are an important part of individuation. People who experience God-images from the collective unconscious deepen and broaden their access to this important part of the psyche and gain insights into their own personalities. Religion gives them a means by which to recognise such archetypes as the Mother, represented by the goddess Kali perhaps, or Eve or the Virgin Mary, and the Shadow, represented by the Devil or by evil spirits. The Persona could be represented in religious vestments, and the Self in imagery such as Christ, or the lotus flower as it gradually leaves the muddy depths of a pond to become the symmetrical flower it always had the potential to become.

When people have religious experiences, they feel that they are connecting with something greater than themselves, something that is timeless and powerful, and that cannot readily be expressed in words. Jung thought that

Key term

individuation: in Carl Jung's thought, a process in which people bring together and reconcile different elements of their inner world

Synoptic link

Link to *Chapter 5: Religious experience (part one)*. Jung understood religious experience solely in psychological terms, unlike some other thinkers such as William James.

this was because the collective unconscious is beyond the control of the individual, and goes back in time for all of human history. Religious people come to understand their shared humanity through religion. The images and symbols connected with religious faith help them to recognise the Self and to understand what it can become. Practices such as meditation, silence, reflecting on the imagery in sacred texts, and prayer work in the same way as psychotherapy, allowing people to explore the unconscious and aid the process of individuation.

Supportive evidence

Supportive evidence for psychological theories is very difficult to find, as is evidence against them. Good evidence can be found when repeatable tests can be done easily. It is easy, for example, to find evidence that a hen's egg breaks when dropped onto a hard floor from a height; we can all try it and see the evidence for ourselves. However, it is much harder to find evidence to support interpretations, especially when the interpretations are based on invisible phenomena such as private thoughts and dreams.

Religion as a source of comfort

Jung did not think of religious belief in terms of a response to an objective God who exists beyond the human mind. He did not think of God as the creator of the universe or as a being with the power to perform miracles or answer prayer, although he also did not reject this; Jung thought it was impossible to know whether God exists outside the human mind. However, he was of the view that religion is beneficial.

Through his observation of patients, Jung concluded that religion could be a source of comfort for people. Religion offers the sense that there is a purpose to life and that people are part of a collective whole, whereas a lack of religion can make people feel that life has no meaning, and that we are each lonely individuals trying to find our own way in a purposeless existence.

Religion can offer a comforting way to interpret troubling dreams. According to Jung, dreams are a way in which we access the unconscious levels of our minds, and they present us with images and archetypes that we can process and understand from the viewpoint of religion. As the 'God within us' is recognised and the sense of individual ego is moved aside, the images in dreams can be seen for what they are instead of as a threat; they are reflections of the archetypes held in the collective unconscious, coming to the surface while we are asleep.

Religion can be a comfort in that religious leaders can act in similar ways to psychotherapists. Jung observed that religious leaders offer people a symbol of wisdom and of the individuated self. They offer people the chance to talk through problems in a similar way to the psychotherapist. They organise services of worship where people can come together and emphasise their shared humanity, and they teach meditative practices such as prayer, as well as giving uplifting sermons promoting a positive mindset, and meeting people's perceived need to access God.

AO1 activity 13
Explain, in your own words, how Jung understood religious experience.

Jung's view that religion promotes positive personal and social mindsets

Jung also observed that religion encouraged well-being in his patients, both on a personal level and on a social level. Most of his patients had lived through the First World War; some had experienced fighting first hand. Everyone had lost family members or friends. It was a time when people began to question the values of the pre-war years. After the war, people felt confused and disillusioned at the waste of young lives. Unemployment and economic depression, as well as rapid changes in science and technology, made it hard for people to feel that they understood the world any more. Jung found that those of his patients who had religious belief were better equipped to cope with post-war life. Religion gave them a reason to live morally and to try to make a better future; it also gave them some comfort that those who had died in the war had moved on to the afterlife. Jung found that depression and anxiety disorders were much more common among those who had no religious belief and those who had abandoned it.

Modern psychology tends to support the view that mind-sets such as those offered by religion are positive, as they provide a reality and a consistent narrative for people to understand their place in the world, both as individuals and as groups.

Evidence for Jung's analysis of religion could also be seen by looking at the ethical systems of different world religions. There is a strong tendency for religion to promote values of kindness, honesty, fairness, and concern for the weak, and this could be seen to support Jung's view that accessing the collective unconscious and understanding the Self as the God within encourages people to be less egocentric, and gives them a motivation for ethical behaviour.

AO1 activity 14

a) Explain how Jung's views on religion contrast with those of Freud.
b) Make a bullet-point list showing how Jung thought religion was beneficial for mental health.

Challenges to Jung's understanding of religious belief

Although Jung's analysis of religion has been influential, it has also been criticised on a number of grounds.

Lack of empirical evidence for Jungian concepts

Jung has been criticised for the lack of firm empirical evidence to support his theories. Although he collected data from studying his patients, there are many aspects of psychology which make it a difficult subject to test using empirical methods. Therefore, like Freud, Jung had to depend on theorising, and was unable to present the kinds of data that are available to scientists in other fields. The human mind is not accessible to external observation; although behaviour can be observed, the inner thought processes that lead to those behaviours cannot. Jung based his theories on interpretations of dreams and on observations of folk tales and symbolism, but dreams are private, subjective, and not capable of being repeated for testing, and stories are similarly not suited to scientific experimentation.

The American psychologist Gardner Murphy criticised Jung's methods, saying that Jung was far too quick to rush to conclusions. His criticism was that Jung saw that one mental phenomenon was somewhat like another, or shared a few characteristics with something else, and leapt straight to the conclusion that they were equivalent. In particular, Jung did this with myths that shared some common characteristics, jumping to the conclusion of the existence of unconscious universal archetypes.

Jung's argument in favour of understanding the unconscious in terms of archetypes is an inductive argument: he puts forward the view that this is the best explanation for the mental phenomena that can be observed. The recurrence of familiar characters in folk tales and myths could be explained using the idea of archetypes, but there could also be other explanations. Even though people live in different parts of the world and have different cultural upbringings, they still all have mothers, so the recurrence of a mother in stories is unsurprising, and does not inevitably lead to the conclusion that we must all share archetypal imagery. People all have to modify their behaviour and control their animal instincts if they want to live in any kind of society, so the Persona archetype may just be a reference to the practicalities of social life. It could simply be the case that, wherever in the world people live, the human experience has many similarities. There is no need to attribute these similarities to a collective unconscious. Jung, however, discounted any possibility that there could be a different cause for the similarities between cultural images.

Jung drew attention to the similarities in myths and folk tales, but there are also significant differences between them, which he ignored. For example, societies that have historically survived on fishing have mythical imagery of the sea and sea monsters, whereas people who live in landlocked countries have myths about crops and harvests. It could, therefore, be argued that the stories are not similar enough to support a theory of shared archetypes, even if they do have common elements.

Jung claimed that religious belief is important for human well-being. However, there are plenty of people who have good mental health and lead positive, active lives without religion. If Jung is right, we should expect a noticeable difference, with religious believers having better mental health than atheists, but this has not been identified in studies. Jung responded to this criticism by claiming that atheism is a form of religion. However, this claim undermines his assertion that religion leads to better mental health, as it begs the question, better than what? If every kind of attitude towards God is classified as 'religion' then there is nothing left for religious believers to be healthier than.

Synoptic link

Link to *Chapter 1: Arguments for the existence of God: inductive*. Jung, like Freud, used inductive argument to conclude that a psychological explanation for religion is the best explanation.

AO1 activity 15

a) Explain how Jung uses inductive reasoning in his theory about religion.

b) Why can inductive reasoning never give conclusive proof?

Reductionist views regarding religious belief arising from acceptance of Jung's ideas

People who accept the views of Jung (and/or Freud) can be considered to have a reductionist view. 'Reductionist' has a range of meanings, but in this context it means saying that religion is 'no more than' a product of the human mind. In a similar way, some sociologists look at the functions that religion has in society, and take a reductionist view by saying that religion is 'no more than' a way in which people come together to share an ethical code and help society cohere.

The challenge to Jungian thinking here is to question whether Jung successfully showed that religion is no more than a human construct. Jung himself did not make this claim, saying that questions of the objective existence of God cannot be resolved by psychology. However, many people who have accepted Jung's thinking have reached the conclusion that religion can be explained solely in terms of psychology. If God is no more than part of the human collective unconscious, then it follows that God did not exist before there were any people, and if Christ is to be understood as no more than a symbol for the Self, then it follows that the historical Jesus of Nazareth is not particularly important.

Many religious believers challenge this reductionist approach, and argue that God is the cause of all that exists. They claim that God can control nature, perform miracles, and answer prayers, none of which would be possible for a God who was a mental construct only. Christians argue that the historical Jesus was God incarnate, living and dying in the world as an atonement for human sin, and that the Christ of faith is the same person as the Jesus of history.

Of course, challenging the beliefs of Jung's followers with a different set of beliefs is unlikely to resolve the issue; there seems to be little prospect of moving forward with the debate, except for resorting to John Hick's idea of eschatological justification: the idea that at the end of time, the truth will be revealed.

> **AO1 activity 16**
> Explain what it means to take a reductionist view of religion.

> **Synoptic link**
>
> Link to *Chapter 3: Challenges to religious belief: the problem of evil and suffering*. John Hick's view that everything will become clear at the end of time is also found in debates about the problem of evil and religious language.

Atheism

Rejection of belief in deities

The word 'atheism' comes from the Greek *a* meaning 'not', and *theos* meaning 'God'. An **atheist** is someone who rejects the idea that there is a God, and says instead that there is no God.

Atheism, agnosticism, and theism are often put forward as the three options people have with regard to religious belief. However, belief is actually a spectrum, with a lot of different shades of opinion. Some people are theists most of the time but have moments of doubt, for example, or find belief in God their default position except for one issue that they struggle to accept. Some people have no belief, but occasionally have experiences that lead

> **Key term**
>
> **atheist:** someone who does not believe in any God or gods

them to wonder whether there is something in religious belief after all. Some feel strongly about their beliefs and try to persuade others to share their perspective, while others find religious questions less important or interesting. Atheism, like theism and agnosticism, is not one single position, and not all atheists think alike.

Antony Flew, in his 1976 book *The Presumption of Atheism*, makes a distinction between what he calls 'positive' and 'negative' atheism:

- A 'positive atheist' is someone who positively asserts the non-existence of God. This is sometimes called 'strong atheism'. Strong atheists might be hostile to religion.
- A 'negative atheist' is someone who is not a theist. This is sometimes called 'weak atheism'. Weak atheists might be indifferent to religion.

Flew argued, in his book, that discussions about the existence or non-existence of God should start from a negative atheist position. He said it is up to the theist to demonstrate the existence of God, but that judgement should be made from a position of someone waiting to see if they can be convinced, rather than someone who positively asserts that there is no God. Flew made a comparison with people applying for welfare benefits. The applicant has the burden of proof, in the sense that the person wanting to claim the benefit is the one who has to make their case. But the person making the judgement should not assume that all applicants are frauds and cheats unless they are persuaded otherwise; they should be prepared to listen.

Atheists are very often **materialists**, which means they believe the physical world constitutes all of reality. They believe that the chemistry, physics, and biology of the natural world constitute all that exists. Physical 'stuff' gives rise to emotions such as love, and to beauty and creativity, as well as to moral values; atheists do not generally deny that these exist, but they do not attribute them to anything other than physical causes. People have minds, and materialists view the mind as a function of the brain rather than as evidence of some kind of non-physical self or soul that exists independently of the physical body.

> **Key term**
>
> **materialist:** someone who believes that the physical world constitutes all of reality

The view that this physical world is all that exists dates back to pre-Socratic philosophers such as Thales, who rejected mythological and supernatural explanations in favour of scientific ones. Historically, atheism was often seen in a negative light. 'Atheist' was originally a pejorative term, used to describe godless people who supposedly rejected moral values and were on the side of the Devil. It was not something that people wanted to admit to openly, as it could mean that they were shunned by polite society and not allowed to take up positions of importance such as serving as Members of Parliament. It was not until the Enlightenment in the eighteenth century that people were willing to declare themselves atheists, when the popularity of reasoning meant they felt able to say that reason was more important than faith.

Atheism is now much more acceptable in many countries around the world, but even today, people still debate questions such as, 'Can an atheist be a moral person?' when they would never ask the same about a Christian.

Atheism contrasts with theism, and also with agnosticism.

The difference between agnosticism and atheism

Thomas Huxley, who was a friend of Charles Darwin, introduced the term 'agnostic' to mean 'without knowledge'. He used it to refer to people who have thought about the possibility of there being a God, and have come to the conclusion that it is a question that simply cannot be answered. We cannot know whether or not God exists, or whether or not there is an afterlife, so the rational position to take is a neutral one. Huxley saw agnosticism as similar to scepticism, arguing that a person should not claim to know certain things about which there is a significant degree of doubt.

Bertrand Russell gave a similar definition in 1953:

> *An agnostic thinks it impossible to know the truth in matters such as God and the future life with which Christianity and other religions are concerned. Or, if not impossible, at least impossible at the present time.*
>
> Bertrand Russell, 'What Is An Agnostic?'

Russell argued that the difference between agnostics and atheists is that both atheists and religious believers think that we can know the answer to the question of whether or not there is a God. Agnostics, on the other hand, think that the answer cannot be known. They can, however, hold views that are very close to atheism, if they think that the existence of God is so improbable that it is not worth considering. Russell said that he would not personally be able to demonstrate a clear proof that Zeus, Poseidon, and Hera do not exist, so he would have to be agnostic about their existence too, but it would, for practical purposes, mean the same as atheism.

Like atheism and theism, agnosticism has many shades of opinion. Some claim, like Huxley and Russell, that the question of the existence of God is one that cannot be answered with any kind of certainty. This is sometimes called 'strong agnosticism'. Others take a more personal and subjective view, saying that they have not made their own minds up on the question: this is sometimes called 'weak agnosticism'.

The rise of New Atheism (antitheism)

'**New Atheism**' is a name given to a modern movement that is deliberately and publicly hostile to religion; it is sometimes called 'militant atheism' or 'antitheism'. It is usually associated with four main thinkers: Sam Harris, Richard Dawkins, Daniel Dennett, and Christopher Hitchens. Other people, such as A.C. Grayling, Ricky Gervais, Stephen Fry, and Philip Pullman, have also aligned themselves with New Atheist thinking. It is primarily a British and American movement, mainly attacking Protestant Christianity, although Sam Harris is Jewish and Dawkins devotes considerable attention

Key terms

agnostic: someone who does not know whether or not there is a God, or thinks it is impossible to know

New Atheism: a philosophical movement from the late-twentieth/ early-twenty-first century which views the concept of God as a totalitarian belief that destroys individual freedom, and sees religion as a threat to the survival of the human race; sometimes referred to as antitheism because of its aggressive countering of all forms of theism

AO1 activity 17

Explain, in your own words, the key differences between atheism and agnosticism.

to attacking Islam. One of the main reasons for the rise of New Atheism has been the increase in religiously-motivated terrorist attacks. These have led atheists to the view that 'tolerating' different belief systems, in a relativist way, is not enough. People should not be expected to tolerate those who are themselves intolerant, and should speak out.

The views put forward by the New Atheism movement are not in themselves particularly new. They argue that religion is out of date, irrational, damaging to human wellbeing, and anti-scientific, just as other thinkers before them have argued, such as Hume and Russell. What is new is that these modern thinkers have the benefit of modern methods of communication, giving them much wider platforms from which to publicise their views; and each of the four main thinkers has written a book which has caught the public imagination and become a best-seller. In 2008, the four 'leaders' of the movement discussed their views about religion in a recording known as the 'Four Horsemen', referring to the four horsemen of the apocalypse in the Book of Revelation in the Bible. In the Bible, the four horsemen herald the end of the world, whereas the New Atheist movement considers itself to mark the beginning of the end of religion.

Sam Harris' book *The End of Faith* (2004) started as a response to the New York terrorist attacks on 11 September 2001. Harris concentrates on the dangers posed by religious extremist groups, whose belief in martyrdom and the afterlife makes them particularly dangerous. He makes a case that the idea of tolerance for different religious beliefs and opinions has gone too far and should stop: there are some beliefs that should not be tolerated, and a culture of moderation leaves people unable to oppose those who promote violence. Like Freud, Harris compares religious belief to mental illness, where people believe in a creator God who can hear their prayers just as those with mental disorders have hallucinations or paranoia. Religious belief has no empirical foundation to support it, and has been the cause of conflict, terrorism, and torture throughout history, because the people who hold the beliefs are completely blind to the idea that they could be wrong and insist that others either share their views or die. Harris suggests that faith is aligned with ignorance and subsequently hatred, whereas reason and honesty lead to a loving society.

Sam Harris

Richard Dawkins, a British biologist, began writing arguments against religion in his book *The Selfish Gene*, first published in 1976. In this book, he promotes Darwinian ideas of evolution, and uses genetics to argue that human altruism is the result of how genes reproduce, rather than anything to do with God. Other works by Dawkins include *The Blind Watchmaker* (1986), in which he directly attacks Christian design arguments for the existence of God, saying that all apparent evidence of design in the world can be attributed to natural processes. Dawkins' main argument is that in the light of modern science and in particular Darwin's theory of evolution, it is no longer rational to cling on to belief in God. His most scathing and direct attack on organised religion and personal religious belief was *The God Delusion*, which went straight to the top of the best-seller lists in the UK and the US when it was released in 2006. In this book, Dawkins explains

Richard Dawkins

147

why he believes there is no God, basing his atheism on a lack of evidence, the ineffectiveness of prayer, and the failure of arguments for God's existence. He also argues that religion is damaging: religion is at the root of wars and terrorism, and is detrimental to scientific enquiry; it encourages a warped morality of violence, tribalism, and blind following of authority; and encouraging children in religion, by sending them to faith schools and indoctrinating them about heaven and hell, is a form of child abuse.

Daniel Dennett's book *Breaking the Spell* (2006) challenges the view that science should not study religion, which is, according to Dennett, a view held by religious believers. Writing from an American perspective, he says:

> *[Religion has a] traditional exemption from certain sorts of analysis and criticism.*
>
> Daniel Dennett, *Breaking the Spell*

In his book, Dennett argues that religion should be analysed according to scientific principles, and that it should be studied as a human phenomenon. Using the tools of evolutionary biology to look at how an idea can grow and take hold, Dennett (like Freud) suggests that modern religion grew out of folk beliefs, and he traces what he understands to be the history of religion. His book is called *Breaking the Spell* because he intends to break through the hold that religion has on people's minds by showing it for what it really is: a human construction. Dennett argues that there is no problem in people holding false beliefs as long as they do not harm anyone else, but religion affects politics, economics, and conflicts, and is, therefore, a matter of concern for everyone.

Daniel Dennett

Christopher Hitchens' book *God is not Great* (2007) makes the case that religion, especially organised religion, is damaging to society. The subtitle of his book when it was first published in the US was 'How Religion Poisons Everything'. In this wide-ranging book, Hitchens takes issue with a number of different facets of religion. He argues that religion comes from a human tendency to want to have faith in something beyond ourselves because of our fears about our own mortality, but that it encourages behaviours and attitudes that are harmful to society. Religious people insist on interfering in the lives of atheists, instead of keeping their beliefs to themselves, and try to impose a morality and an outlook on others in an arrogant way. Religion, argues Hitchens, relies on an understanding of the world which is grossly out of date, looking back to a time when people needed God to explain features of the world that are now perfectly well explained by science. He argues that the Bible is nothing more than a collection of oral traditions, many of which have no basis in fact, crudely put together long after the supposed events they report, and is full of contradictions. In Hitchens' view, religion is intolerant, encouraging bigotry and often racism. It encourages ignorance, oppresses women, and is hostile to scientific enquiry.

Christopher Hitchens

AO1 activity 18
If possible, read extracts from the books written by the New Atheists to gain a deeper understanding of the arguments they are making.

The criticism that religion is non-thinking

One of the common criticisms atheists make of religion is that it is non-thinking. They often use the term 'blind' to describe religious faith, claiming that religious believers simply accept whatever their religion tells them to accept, without thinking it through. Richard Dawkins sums up this claim when he criticises **fundamentalists** (those who hold that their sacred text is literally true).

> *Fundamentalists know they are right because they have read the truth in a holy book and they know, in advance, that nothing will budge them from their belief. The truth of the holy book is an axiom [self-evidently true], not the end product of a process of reasoning.*
>
> Richard Dawkins, *The God Delusion*

Key term

fundamentalist: a religious believer or group who follow a strict adherence to the fundamental principles of any set of beliefs, including the belief that their sacred texts are literally true

The New Atheists argue that religious truth claims should be open to being tested, just like the claims made by scientists, and the evidence in support of them should be assessed. But instead, religion encourages acceptance of all kinds of bizarre claims without any testing, and applauds such acceptance as virtuous faith. The Bible is alleged to need no further support because it is the word of God and, therefore, cannot be challenged. Religious believers, claim New Atheists, say that the Bible is true because it says so in the Bible, and they will not accept any evidence that the Bible could be mistaken, outdated or even immoral, no matter how well substantiated such evidence might be. Dawkins argues that in the light of modern science, and particularly since Darwin proposed the theory of evolution through natural selection, it is impossible to maintain belief in God with any kind of rationality. People have to be wilfully ignorant and ignore all the evidence in front of them if they intend to persist in religious faith.

Dawkins accuses religion of discouraging people from looking for answers to scientific questions, and discouraging people from pointing out the contradictions in their belief systems. Instead, they are told to embrace the concept of mystery, acknowledge that there are things humanity should not question, and be satisfied with their own ignorance.

The writer John Loftus presents a more gentle but related argument, giving the view that religious believers have a blind spot for their own faith. In *The Outsider Test for Faith*, which published in 2013, he argues that believers in a particular religion, such as Christianity, reject other world religions and other belief systems as untrue or unsupported, but do not subject their own faith systems to the same tests. Members of one religion are ready to explain what is wrong with other people's religions, but refuse to turn the same spotlight on their own.

Religion is also criticised as non-thinking in the sense of being incoherent. Atheists point out that God cannot possibly allow people to have free will and yet be in control of everything they do at the same time. God cannot be said to be all-loving if there is also evil in the world. Jesus could not have been God in human form if he prayed to God in heaven while he was on Earth. God should not have needed to sacrifice Jesus to atone for the sin of humanity because God could just have waved a magic wand and undone the sin, given that God is meant to be omnipotent. People should not have to pray to God for help if God already knows their every thought and already

AO1 activity 19

Write a series of bullet pointed notes to summarise the key reasons why New Atheists consider religious believers to be unthinking.

knows exactly what is going to happen for all of time. Religious people, it is argued, are forced into a position of trying to believe contradictory, nonsensical, and impossible things, without thinking about them very closely at all.

The criticism that religion presents an infantile worldview

Sigmund Freud wrote of religion in 1929:

> *The whole thing is so patently infantile, so foreign to reality, that to anyone with a friendly attitude to humanity it is painful to think that the majority of mortals will never be able to rise above this view of life.*
>
> Sigmund Freud, *Civilization and its Discontents*

New Atheists take the same view, arguing that religion encourages people to believe in an imaginary father-figure in the same way that children are encouraged to believe in Father Christmas. God is presented as an invisible source of love and care, who will give meaning to people's lives and tell them what to do, reward them if they are good and punish them if they are naughty, just as if they are small children who are incapable of leading independent lives of their own or making their own decisions.

Dawkins and others criticise the world-view held by some Christians that the world began with a garden, with a talking snake in it, as in a fairy tale; that millions of animal species of every kind floated in an Ark without killing each other; that the Red Sea parted so that people could walk across its dry bed to escape danger; and so on. The alternatives that science presents, such as the theory of evolution, are dismissed, and some Christians have campaigned to prevent evolution being taught in schools, instead wanting their children to learn Bible stories as if they were science. Rational people, argue the atheists, grow out of these kinds of beliefs by the time they reach the age of about ten.

Atheists argue that religion can be used as a form of social control. It teaches ordinary working people to be meek and humble, not to argue back but to accept what they are given and, in this way, the people in power can keep themselves in power. Karl Marx argued that those in control of a country's money, land, and means of production use the influence of religion to keep the workers in their place. They are told there will be rewards for them after death if they accept the role God has given them, and so they are controlled in the way that children are controlled by adults in authority.

The criticism that religion impedes scientific progress

Atheists argue that religion is not just an alternative to science but is actually an impediment to it. The mindset of religion encourages people to give up enquiries at an early stage and declare the problems to be miracles or mysteries, or to say that 'God did it', rather than pursuing their research. There are also religious beliefs that put up barriers to some scientific endeavours. The most famous example is Galileo Galilei, who got into trouble with the Catholic Church in the seventeenth century for saying that the Earth was not the centre of the universe but revolved around the Sun. Charles Darwin also found it difficult to get his ideas accepted because his theory of evolution through natural selection contrasted sharply with Bible teaching about the origins of humanity. In the US, there have been legal disputes about the teaching of evolution and creationism in schools, where scientists have argued that evolution should be taught and some people have argued that the teaching of the Bible about creation should be presented to children as scientific fact.

Today, religious people often object to scientific research involving human embryos, because of the belief that human life is sacred. Stem cell research, used to develop therapies and cures for many illnesses such as AIDS and multiple sclerosis, requires cells from fertilised human eggs, but some Christians object to this because they believe it means a potential human life is being sacrificed for the benefits of research. Religious people are involved in ethics committees making decisions about healthcare, for example deciding whether the use of condoms is acceptable to help slow the transmission of HIV. The Catholic Church opposes the use of artificial contraception, which has caused problems for scientists wanting to promote safe sex and family planning, especially in developing countries.

Dennett, in *Breaking the Spell*, makes the point that people assert their beliefs vigorously, but sometimes so vigorously that it gets in the way of good science. He gives the example of the belief in the equality of all people regardless of their ethnicity, which he thinks is a position that reflective people of good will should hold. However, some people hold the belief so firmly that they will not allow scientific enquiry into possible biological differences between ethnic groups, for fear that this will lead to racism. What this inhibition of scientific enquiry actually means is that things that would be useful to know, such as how people of different ethnicities respond differently to some medications or whether people of some ethnicities are more prone to some kinds of illness, are left unexplored, to the detriment of some ethnic groups. It is an example of how a firmly held belief, even a right one, can mistakenly be allowed to hold back science.

AO1 activity 20

Make a list of some examples that New Atheists use, or could use, to support the view that religion is:

a) unthinking
b) infantile
c) a hindrance to scientific thought.

Religious responses to the challenge of New Atheism

Just as New Atheists have access to a wide audience through social media, so too do those who want to respond to their arguments. Religious believers, in particular, want to reply to the challenges put before them.

Increase in religious apologists in the media

The prominence of New Atheism has brought responses from a wide range of people in the media, from people in popular culture, such as Russell Brand, to academics and philosophers. These people are known as **apologists**: they speak in defence of a belief system, in this case religion. They have put forward several different responses:

> ## Key term
>
> **apologist:** someone who speaks in defence of a cause, a point of view, or a belief system such as Christianity

- In response to the books published by Harris, Dawkins, Dennett, and Hitchens, many religious commentators have argued that the New Atheists concentrate on anecdotal evidence of the misuse of religion, rather than on the content of religion itself. Of course, there are people who misuse religion, and cultures in which religion is a tool of oppression, but this should not be the main focus of discussion. Desmond Tutu, in 2006, gave the analogy that religion is like a knife. In the wrong hands, it can be a murderous weapon, used in hatred and to threaten; but when it is used properly, it can cut bread to feed the hungry. The problem is not religion itself but its employment, and the New Atheists are wrong to focus only on the misuse of religion while ignoring all the good it has done. They ignore all that religious believers have contributed to civil rights and to charity work and overseas aid, looking only at examples that support their case and being manipulative in their presentation of what religion is.

- Critics of the books argue that the New Atheists are ill-informed and that none is an expert on religion. They overlook centuries of scholarly study and philosophical thought, and cultural and social reform, to concentrate only on those who blindly believe in a God who arbitrarily blesses and curses and demands unthinking obedience. They criticise religious extremists as though they are typical of all religious believers, and so commit the logical fallacy of the 'straw man'. A 'straw man' argument is when the position one wishes to attack is caricatured and, consequently, does not accurately represent a point of view. (The expression comes from soldiers doing bayonet practice, when they attack scarecrows made out of straw who are easy targets but not very representative of an actual human enemy.) The New Atheists have a tendency to criticise Christian believers as if they all reject evolution and have a literal view of the Bible, and they criticise Islam as if all Muslims are terrorist extremists.

- The Oxford theologian Keith Ward's book *Is Religion Dangerous?* (2006) responds to some of the criticisms made by Dawkins and others. Ward points out the good that religion has done over the centuries, and argues that human society would be considerably worse off without it.

- Richard Swinburne, also a professor at Oxford University, brought out a second edition of his 1977 book *The Coherence of Theism* in 2016, in which he argued that religious belief is not in fact contradictory, but can be held by rational thinking human beings.

- Tina Beattie, the feminist theologian, examines the debate in her book *The New Atheists: the Twilight of Reason and the War on Religion* (2007).

> *Dawkins demands proof of God's existence, for only that which we can prove beyond reasonable doubt is worthy of belief. But the word 'God' does not denote a 'thing' whose existence we can prove, any more than we can prove the 'existence' of love, beauty, compassion or hope.*
>
> Tina Beattie, *The New Atheists: the Twilight of Reason and the War on Religion*

Beattie criticises the New Atheists for their uncritical engagement with an outmoded model of religion, and also draws attention to the dominance of white men on both sides of the discussion.

In addition to religious apologists, some atheists have also objected to militant atheism, and have wanted to dissociate themselves from it. The left-wing journalist Owen Jones wrote a scathing article against Richard Dawkins in the *Independent* in 2013, claiming that Dawkins used atheism as a platform for bigotry, particularly anti-Muslim bigotry, and should not be allowed to represent most atheists.

Rejection by religious groups of New Atheist claims regarding incompatibility of science and religion

Many religious believers reject the claim made by New Atheists that science and religion are incompatible. They often draw attention to the ways in which religion has been supportive of scientific endeavour, as well as the many people who have successfully combined religious faith with a career in science.

Although there are many scientists who hold the materialist view that the physical world is all that exists, there are also many scientists with firm religious beliefs. Robert Boyle, who developed our understanding of elements and of gases, was a devout Christian, as was Michael Faraday, who worked in the field of electromagnetics. Gregor Mendel, who developed the science of genetics, was a monk, and his research was funded by the Catholic Church. Georges Lemaître, who discovered that the universe is expanding, was a Roman Catholic priest. Jewish scientists Karl Landsteiner and Gerty Cori won Nobel Prizes in Medicine for their discovery of human blood types and work on glycogen respectively. Muslims dominated mathematics and science in the Middle Ages, and in 2006, Anousheh Ansari became the first Muslim woman in space. The Sikh academic Sir Harpal Kumar was knighted in recognition of his pioneering work in the detection of early signs of cancer.

The theologian Alister McGrath converted from atheism to Christianity as a result of his involvement in science. After completing a doctorate in molecular biophysics, he went on to write a book called *The Dawkins Delusion* in 2007 in which he presented reasoned arguments in response to the accusations made by Dawkins. In his book, McGrath argues that there are many people who convert to religious faith as adults and cannot be said to be clinging on to beliefs from their childhood. He points out that science and religion can coexist, each looking at the world through different lenses;

and he also draws attention to Dawkins' lack of expertise in either religion or psychology. McGrath claims that the petty, vicious God the New Atheists describe bears no relation to the God of Christianity, and that Dawkins is as dogmatic as the people he criticises by failing to recognise any evidence that does not support his atheism.

Francis Collins, the American director of the Human Genome Project, is another scientist who has spoken and written in defence of Christianity. As a scientist, Collins has discovered the genes responsible for conditions such as cystic fibrosis and neurofibromatosis. Collins was an atheist until he went to college, where a conversation with a hospital patient led him to explore religious belief and eventually convert to Christianity. He does not accept the belief of some Christians in intelligent design, but considers himself a serious Christian, and wrote a book called *The Language of God* in 2007 in which he explained how he found that the scientific discoveries he was making confirmed his faith and showed how science and religion work together.

John Polkinghorne, a physicist at Cambridge University and an Anglican clergyman, wrote many books and gave many talks arguing along the same lines: that the more he learned about the way the physical world works, the deeper his faith became. Science offers one way of looking at the world and religion offers another, not as conflicting views but as different lenses that reveal different and complementary aspects of the truth.

Religious believers, then, argue that it is mistaken to think that rational, scientific people cannot be religious, as there are plenty of well-respected and innovative scientists who successfully manage to reconcile their faith with their scientific endeavours.

Increase in fundamentalist religious activity relating to morality and community

One of the effects of the challenges to religious belief raised by the New Atheist movement is an increase in fundamentalist religious activity. The term 'fundamentalism' usually refers to people who have a strictly literalist approach to sacred texts and belief systems. Fundamentalist Christians believe that the world was created exactly as described in Genesis, and that the teachings of the Bible should be taken at face value rather than interpreted as myth. The New Atheist movement particularly targeted this kind of religious belief and, consequently, people with fundamentalist views have responded by reaffirming the literal truth of the Bible. They argue that the truth of the Bible is always going to stand and, where scientists disagree, it is the scientists who must be wrong because the Bible comes from God and science comes from fallible human minds.

Islam has also seen a growth in fundamentalism, with some Muslims seeing the Western media as the greatest threat to their faith, and some sticking even more closely to the teachings and cultural practices of their faith as a result.

This section of the chapter will enhance your ability to **analyse** and **evaluate** the topic and help you develop your AO2 skills. For each question, think about the different positions you might take, and decide which you find most persuasive and why. It is not enough to memorise a list of 'for and against' points; you need to develop an argument.

How far can religious belief be considered a neurosis?

This question is asking for an evaluation of whether Freud is right to classify religious belief and religious behaviour as a kind of neurosis. Are there similarities between religious rituals and neurotic behaviour, and if so, are such similarities significant?

The view that religious belief can be considered a neurosis

Some hold the view that religious belief can be considered a neurosis.

- There are similarities between some religious rituals and obsessive compulsive disorder (OCD), particularly when it comes to ideas about cleanliness and the repetition of symbolic actions. For example, parallels could be drawn between obsessive-compulsive handwashing and the Muslim practice of washing before prayer, or the Jewish practice of a ritual bath (mikveh) after menstruation.
- Darwin's theory of evolution through natural selection supported the idea of early human beings living in primal hordes. Perhaps Freud is right in his claims that religious belief and behaviour originated in inherited feelings of guilt about wanting to destroy a patriarch.
- People often feel guilty if they have not been to Mass or have broken a religious rule, which could be equated with neurosis.
- Increased religiosity is a well-recognised symptom of some mental health conditions.
- People often turn to religion, sometimes as a last resort, when they are feeling particularly stressed or helpless, which could be seen to support Freud's idea that religion is no more than an expression of repressed trauma.

The view that religious belief is not necessarily linked with neurosis

Others hold the view that religious belief is not necessarily linked with neurosis.

- Recent research, such as that conducted by Raphael Bonelli in 2013 using data collected systematically over twenty years, has found that there is good evidence to support the view that religion and spirituality have positive benefits for mental health. Involvement with religion correlated with better mental health in many people, especially in connection with substance abuse, depression, dementia, and stress-related illness. Those with religious belief suffered less severely than those without.

- Although there may be similarities between religious rituals and some obsessive-compulsive behaviours, Freud over-emphasised the importance of ritual in religion. His own experience of religion was from Judaism and Catholicism, where there are many rules and rituals, but other religious belief systems, such as non-conformist Protestant traditions like Quakerism, have significantly fewer rituals. Religious belief should not be seen as little more than repetitive ritual behaviour, as religions are much wider-ranging and more complex than this.

- There are significant differences between religious rituals and behaviours resulting from OCD. OCD behaviours are often done unwillingly and furtively; they are typically accompanied by feelings of shame and anxiety. Religious rituals are usually done willingly and openly with others, and help the believer to feel affirmed in their faith and at peace. Concentrating on the behaviours of people with OCD rather than on their mental health trivialises a serious and distressing disorder.

- Ritual does not have to be seen as a symptom of neurosis. People celebrate birthdays with ritual songs and candles, and have rituals when they leave school, or get married. These help to create a sense of community and belonging, and have little to do with neurosis.

- Religious rituals can help to alleviate anxiety, but this does not preclude them from relating to a real, existent God. Freud takes a reductionist view of religion, seeing it as 'no more than' a symptom of neurosis; but it would be quite reasonable to argue that a real God would want people to feel comforted when they go through the rituals of worship. The rituals do not demonstrate God's non-existence, even if they do relieve anxiety.

AO2 activity 1

To what extent, in your view, can religion be considered a neurosis? Give reasons to support your view, and reasons to explain why you think the opposite opinion is weaker.

How adequate is Freud's explanation of religious belief?

This question asks for a consideration of whether Freud's understanding of religion gives a thorough and plausible account of religious belief. For some people, Freud has successfully shown that religion is no more than an illusion, whereas for others, Freud has missed the point of religion completely, and given an explanation that has no basis.

The view that Freud presents an adequate explanation of religious belief

- Freud could be right that religious rituals are expressions of neurosis.
- Freud was not the first to point out the elements of wish fulfilment in religious belief. There is a strong similarity between the characteristics

that religious believers attribute to God and the imaginary characteristics that children give to their imaginary friends. People want to be looked after, to have purpose in their lives, and to believe that death is not the end for themselves and their loved ones. The idea of religion as wish fulfilment is persuasive.

- Some people do rely on religion to help them when they are feeling helpless. Those who find social interactions difficult sometimes take comfort in a church community, for example. And some elderly people return to religion to help them face the ends of their lives with more optimism.
- Religion can be psychologically damaging for some people, giving them feelings of guilt and unworthiness, and increasing their anxieties.
- Freud was proved right when he said that people would come to discard religion and recognise it for what it was. Fewer people today go to church than ever before, and many are much more willing to proclaim themselves atheists than in the past.

The view that Freud does not present an adequate explanation of religious belief

It can also be argued that Freud does not present an adequate explanation of religious belief.

- Freud is often accused of faulty reasoning because his argument relies on what is known as the '**genetic fallacy**'. This is where someone attacks a belief or an argument based on its origins, rather than on its merits. An example that uses the genetic fallacy is: 'This argument in favour of saving Prisoner X from the death penalty comes from someone who has a criminal record themselves; therefore, the argument can be ignored.' It is fallacious because the argument for saving Prisoner X might be very strong, and the background of the person making the argument is irrelevant. In the case of Freud, the genetic fallacy occurs when he attempts to trace the origins of religion and uses this to reach the conclusion that religious beliefs are not true. Religious beliefs should be judged on their own merits; how they may or may not have begun is irrelevant.

- Not all religious belief centres around a father God. Some traditions, such as Hinduism, have both male and female deities, and many religions do not have a clearly gendered concept of God. Many Buddhists do not have a belief in God at all. Freud's assessment of religion can only be applied to some religious beliefs and practices, not all of them.

- Not all societies view fatherhood in the same way, as demonstrated by Malinowski. The Oedipus complex cannot be universal if the role of the father is markedly different in some parts of the world.

- Freud is criticised for setting out to find a theory to support his atheism, rather than formulating a theory on the basis of the evidence he had collected. He accepted only the evidence that supported the views with which he started.

> **Key term**
>
> **genetic fallacy:** the use of faulty logic in which a proposition is attacked on the basis of where it comes from rather than evaluated on its merits

- Freud's primal horde theory, with the ritual of the totemic sacrifice, is unsubstantiated. It has a prominent place in Freud's argument but there is no evidence for it. Freud jumps from an imaginative 'what-if' to an assertion of historical truth, without justification.
- Freud's assertion that religion is an infantile neurosis does not take into account the very many people who have shown remarkable bravery because of their religious beliefs. Freud suggests that religion is a crutch, something for the weak to lean on if they cannot cope with adult life; but it is not difficult to think of many examples of people who have been strengthened by their faith and put themselves in danger in order to help others. The Quakers, for example, ran an 'underground railroad' in the US to help African Americans escape enslavement, at great risk to their own lives. Christians have been burnt at the stake rather than give up their beliefs, and Jews and Muslims have risked and sometimes lost their lives for religious reasons. Freud ignores this side of religious belief, and concentrates only on those who have mental health issues.
- Belief in God can be very much influenced by a child's relationship with their father, but this does not demonstrate that it always is, or that God therefore does not exist. It could be the case that the parent–child relationship is a reflection of the relationship God has with creation.
- Even if it could be shown more conclusively that religion is based on wishful thinking, this does not mean that it always is. Humanity's profound desire for God and for an afterlife does not prove that God and an afterlife exist, but it does not prove that they are non-existent either. It could be the case that we are created by God with a sense and desire for God (the *sensus divinitas*, a term popularised by the theologian John Calvin). If there is a God, it is probable that God would meet our needs, and so the correspondence between human wishes and God could be used as evidence for, rather than against, God's reality.
- Freud's assertion that religion provides a comfort for those unable to cope with the harsh realities of life ignores the fact that many religious people find that when they are faced with evil and suffering, their religious beliefs add to their difficulties. Not only do they have to cope with the practical problems of suffering, but they also have to face difficult questions about why God allows suffering in the world. It could be argued that the harsh realities of life are easier for the non-religious, who do not have such questions to answer but can, instead, simply blame bad luck for their misfortunes.

AO2 activity 2

How far would you agree with Freud's assessment of religion? Give his views a star rating out of five, and write a brief review explaining why you have given the number of stars you have chosen.

To what extent was Jung more positive than Freud about the idea of God?

Freud dismissed religion as an infantile neurosis, while for Jung, God is an archetype. It could appear that Jung is therefore more positive than Freud about religion; however, it can also be argued that they are equally negative. This question invites an evaluation and comparison of Freud and Jung in their discussion of the idea of God.

The view that Jung was more positive than Freud about the idea of God

There are several ways in which Jung appears to be more positive than Freud about the idea of God:

- Jung saw religious experience and religious practices as beneficial to mental health, whereas Freud dismissed them as symptoms of neurosis.
- Jung thought that religion helped people to come to terms with themselves and progress towards individuation, whereas Freud thought religion was infantile and held back personal development.
- Freud saw religion in terms of a neurosis with a basis in repressed sexuality, whereas Jung rejected this view.
- Freud thought that religious practices were symptoms of neurosis which needed curing, whereas Jung thought that they were beneficial in helping people access the unconscious levels of the psyche.
- Freud thought that religious belief was nothing more than wish fulfilment, whereas Jung thought it was part of psychological development and progress in mental well-being.
- Freud thought that religion was an illusion, preventing people from seeing things as they really are, whereas Jung thought that recognising the God within us is a part of seeing things as they really are, moving us closer to the truth.

The view that Jung was not more positive than Freud about the idea of God

It can also be argued that Jung was not more positive than Freud about the idea of God:

- Jung appears more positive than Freud but, like Freud, never claimed that God exists outside the human mind. Both Freud and Jung reduce the idea of God to a human construct, and do not engage with the possibility of a God who can create the universe and perform miracles.
- Jung can be seen to have reduced religion to little more than psychological self-help.
- Jung's ideas about symbols and myths come close to saying that stories in sacred texts are not true in any literal or historical sense.
- Some see, in Jung's views, the beginning of new 'spiritual but not religious' ways of thinking, where people seek spiritual meaning for their lives without reference to traditional beliefs such as Christianity. This can be seen as undermining religion, as it tries to offer the benefits of religious belief and practice without actual belief in God, possibly diluting religion and dismissing its centuries of wisdom and cultural influence.
- Although Freud appears completely negative about religion, he did occasionally admit that religious belief might not be damaging to mental health, and that in some cases it could lead to people being more confident and well-balanced. Freud allowed that there could be a link between religious belief and creativity; so, he was not completely negative about every aspect of religion. It could, therefore, be argued that both Freud and Jung were similar in their assessments of the idea of God.

AO2 activity 3

To what extent, if at all, do you think Jung was more positive than Freud about religion? Give reasons to support your answer.

How effective are empirical approaches as critiques of Jung's views on religion?

Some people have criticised Jung's views on religion on the grounds that they are not scientific, because they are not about phenomena that can be observed with the senses. These empirical approaches are critiques of Jung's view, and this question invites consideration of whether the critiques achieve their aims.

The view that empirical approaches are effective as critiques of Jung's view on religion

It is possible to argue that empirical approaches to establishing the truth or otherwise of a hypothesis provide effective criticism of Jung's view of religion.

- Jung's evidence was based on people's reports of their dreams and private mental experiences, so it was inevitably second hand and impossible to repeat or test.
- Science should be capable of being falsified. It should be possible to know what kind of evidence would necessitate a review of the original hypothesis. However, Jung's analysis of religion is not falsifiable because if people reject the idea of the collective unconscious, the rejection is dismissed and regarded as a failure of individuation.
- The collective unconscious is not something that can be conclusively verified with empirical evidence. Shared experiences and similarities of symbolism and myth could be given other equally plausible explanations.

The view that empirical approaches are not very effective as critiques of Jung's view on religion

It is possible to argue that empirical approaches to establishing the truth or otherwise of a hypothesis do not provide effective criticism of Jung's view of religion.

- Jung insisted that his methods were scientific and empirical. He collected data about common imagery, dreams that were similar in different patients, and ethics that are common to different religions and different cultures.
- The idea of archetypes is, in some ways, akin to the instincts found in animals, and therefore has some empirical support. Konrad Lorenz, a Nobel Prize-winning Austrian zoologist, studied instinctive behaviour, particularly in birds, and developed the theory of imprinting. He argued that animals can be observed carrying out instinctive behaviours according to an inner drive, and he supported Jung's theory of archetypes, seeing no reason why human beings should not have a similar kind of imprinting related to the collective unconscious.

- No scientific experiment or data-collection methodology can be completely free from subjectivity. The scientist chooses what to study and has an idea of what the outcome will be; results require interpretation, and results can be presented in different ways to support particular points of view. It is unfair to criticise Jung for conducting his science in the way that he did, as if other scientists have complete objectivity. In psychology, the researcher has little choice but to base theories on subjective experiences. The alternative is not to do psychological research at all, but people need help with mental health problems.
- Jung achieved good results with his patients, helping to improve their mental health, which suggests that his theories have a basis in truth and were not just speculation.

AO2 activity 4

Do you think that Jung should be disregarded on the grounds that his research was not scientific enough? Give reasons to support your answer.

How successful are atheistic arguments against religious belief?

Atheists put up a range of arguments against religious belief. This question invites an evaluation of whether these arguments are persuasive in demonstrating that religious beliefs are false.

The view that atheist arguments against religious belief are successful

It can be argued that atheist arguments against religious belief are successful.

- Atheists offers arguments based on evidence. They are right to say that there is no solid evidence to support belief in the existence of God, and also right to say that people should not believe in things without sufficient evidence.

> *A wise man proportions his belief to the evidence.* "
>
> David Hume, 'Of Miracles', from *An Enquiry Concerning Human Understanding*

With no evidence, there should also be no belief.
- The argument that religious belief is infantile is a successful argument. There are clear similarities between a parent–child relationship and the idea of God as a father figure. Religious belief encourages people to feel dependent and helpless when there is no need, and discourages them from taking responsibility for their own decisions and their own actions.
- Atheists are right to say that religious belief is incoherent. Many religious beliefs, such as the idea that God is both omnipotent and incapable of doing evil, simply do not make sense. Resorting to saying that God is a mystery that the human mind cannot understand is unsatisfactory as a response. People should not be expected to believe nonsense.

- Religion has been the cause of many conflicts. These conflicts are particularly prolonged because there is no way for religious believers to compromise if they think that they are fighting with God on their side. Atheists are right to say that the world would be a better and more peaceful place without religion.
- Children have the right to grow up learning the truth, including scientific truth. It is wrong to indoctrinate them into outdated religious beliefs and frighten them by making them believe that God is watching them and waiting to punish them. Atheists are right to want to protect children from being misled.
- Some people are atheists because they do not want anything to do with a God who allows the innocent to suffer. Even if there is a God, if God has created a world in which children get cancer and some animals survive by inflicting great pain on others, God is not worthy of worship and should be rejected. Atheists are right to reject God, given that there is evil and suffering in the world.

The view that atheist arguments against religious belief are not successful

It can also be argued that atheist arguments against religious belief are not successful.

- Tina Beattie argues that:

> *to suggest that religion can be universally defined and condemned by referring to various forms of extremism which have flourished in late modernity is to give a distorted and reductive account of a much more complex and diverse human phenomenon.*
>
> Tina Beattie, *The New Atheists: the Twilight of Reason and the War on Religion*

  Atheist arguments against religious belief are not successful because they make a straw man of religion, criticising beliefs that most religious people do not actually hold. Many of the most outspoken atheists have little or no expertise in the subject of religion, and rely instead on anecdotal evidence that distorts the true nature and richness of religious faith.
- Religious belief is not infantile. There have been numerous courageous and innovative religious believers, whose faith has inspired their strength and motivated them to work for the benefit of society. Atheists ignore the long history of religious social reformers and activists, which undermines their position.
- Atheist ideologies have also been the cause of many conflicts. The so-called cultural revolution in China, the tyranny of Stalin and the fanaticism of Nazism are all examples of harm done by atheism. It is wrong to say that most conflicts are caused by religion, because many are political. Religions nearly always teach peace, and there is a strong strain of non-violence in religion that is absent from much of atheism.

- Children benefit from growing up in religious families and being a part of a religious community. It gives them a sense of belonging and security. Religious belief encourages children to cultivate strong characters, to be generous to others, and to be self-disciplined. It instils values in them that enable them to become active in their communities and positive, responsible contributors to society.
- Religious belief is not incoherent. It is arrogant to assume that the human mind is capable of understanding everything about God. Atheism encourages arrogance and self-importance.

AO2 activity 5

How persuasive do you find the arguments of atheists? Do you find some of their arguments stronger than others? Give reasons to support your answer.

To what extent have religious responses to New Atheism been successful?

New Atheists have made scathing criticisms of religious belief, and religious people have responded to these criticisms in a range of ways. This question asks for a consideration of whether these religious responses provide convincing rebuttals of the criticisms made, or whether the criticisms still have force despite the religious responses to them.

The view that religious responses to New Atheism have been successful

It can be argued that religious responses have successfully countered the arguments put forward by New Atheism.

- Religious responses to New Atheism have been successful where they have provided reasoned and thoughtful counter-arguments. Theologians and scientists have shown that New Atheism makes a straw man of religious belief, caricaturing it in order to make it easier to attack. The New Atheists lack expertise and knowledge of religion, and base their arguments on a few extreme examples and a lot of emotional rhetoric rather than on sound reasoning. Well-respected theologians, such as Keith Ward and Richard Swinburne, have successfully made the case for religious faith.
- Religious responses have been successful in demonstrating that there is nothing incoherent about religious faith. A rational person can hold sincere religious beliefs without contradiction.
- It is unreasonable to expect religious believers to produce empirical evidence to support their faith, as religious belief is about non-empirical things. It is not as if atheists can provide empirical evidence to prove the non-existence of God.
- There are plenty of successful and intelligent scientists who are experts in their field and also have religious faith. It is not true that science and religion are incompatible. They do not provide different and conflicting answers to the same questions, but instead ask different questions and shed light on reality in different and complementary ways.

- It is misleading and historically inaccurate to suggest that religion is the major cause of world conflict. Conflicts have many causes, and are often to do with territory, resources, and clashes in political ideology. Religion should not be made a scapegoat for human aggression.
- By delivering calm and well-reasoned responses to New Atheism, religious believers have presented themselves in a more favourable light, showing New Atheists to be aggressively militant and ill-informed.

The view that religious responses to New Atheism have not been successful

It can also be argued that religious responses to New Atheism have not successfully countered the arguments New Atheism puts forward.

- New Atheism has made itself a powerful voice on social media, in books, podcasts, and on other platforms. Religious responses to New Atheism have not been successful in preventing its popularity and growth.
- Fundamentalist religious responses have not been successful in undermining atheism, as they reinforce the idea that religious believers hold unscientific and out-dated views.
- Some religious views continue to hold back the progress of science by, for example, arguing against the use of Covid-19 vaccinations on the grounds that their production may have involved experimentation on human tissue. This gives New Atheism an opportunity to attack religion for being detrimental to scientific progress.
- Religious belief involves a wide spectrum of views, whereas New Atheists present very similar arguments. This means that religious responses are diluted, as not everyone is saying the same thing in response to the challenges presented by New Atheists.
- New Atheists present themselves as taking a radical and fresh look at religion, uncovering it for what it 'really is', whereas religious believers seem to have nothing new to say.

AO2 activity 6

On balance, how successful do you think the religious responses to the challenges presented by New Atheism have been? Do you think there are better arguments they could have made? Give reasons to support your answer.

Exam support

Practising AO1 questions

AO1 questions begin with one of a range of possible command words (see pages 8–9 for more detail.) The following question begins with the word 'Explain'. 'Explain' questions require you to demonstrate knowledge and understanding of the key features of the topic in the question by writing a systematic and comprehensive account. You do not need to consider the quality of an argument, nor offer any views about it.

Read the past paper question and the example paragraph taken from a longer answer written in response, before completing the activity on page 166.

> *Explain Freud's view of religious belief.*
>
> (WJEC A Level Religious Studies, Summer 2018, A2 Unit 5: Philosophy of Religion, Question 2)

Example

Freud's[6] view of religious belief was that it is[2] an infantile illusion[7]. By 'infantile', he meant that the origins of religion in a person's life can be traced back to their childhood relationship with their parents; and by 'illusion' he meant that religion encourages people to see the world as they would wish it to be, rather than as it really is.[1] Freud[6] did not believe that religion has any basis in a real and existent God. He thought, instead, that religion is part of the psychology of people who suffer from[1] neuroses[7]. A neurosis is an anxiety disorder, such as OCD[3], and Freud[6] thought that anxiety disorders were the result of repression[7], which is when people bury memories of painful events and traumas, such as bereavements or abuse, in layers of their[3] subconscious[7] so that they do not have to think about them[3]. But these repressed memories then appear in later life and cause mental health problems.[1] Freud[6] thought that the[1] Oedipus complex[7], where a boy wants to kill his father and have a sexual relationship with his mother, but represses those feelings, is universal and he thought that the Oedipus complex was at the root of religion[1].

1. This paragraph shows thorough, accurate, and relevant knowledge and understanding throughout, with the student explaining what Freud meant by some of the vocabulary he used.

2. The paragraph focuses on the specific question set, and does not introduce any irrelevant material.

3. The answer is detailed, and the writer gives some examples to clarify the meaning of some terms.

4. There are no references to sacred texts or sources of wisdom and authority in this section of the essay, as they are not necessary here.

5. This section of the essay does not make links with other areas of study, but they are not necessary here.

6. Scholarly views other than Freud's own are not mentioned in this section.

7. There is extensive and confident use of specialist vocabulary here.

Activity

Read the example paragraph on page 165. It is taken from a longer answer. The writer has made a good start by focusing on the requirements of the question, and giving an accurate and detailed response.

Continue with the explanation of Freud's understanding of religious belief, giving further details about the Oedipus complex, before moving on to explain Freud's thinking about the primal horde.

AO1 practice question 1

Try answering this question, using the points to remember to help you write a developed response.

> *Examine the main criticisms of religion made by New Atheism.*
>
> (Eduqas A Level Religious Studies, Summer 2019, Component 2: Philosophy of Religion, Question 3a)

Points to remember

- Note that the question refers to New Atheism specifically, so your answer should concentrate on the arguments put forward by militant atheists in the twentieth and twenty-first centuries, rather than on atheism more generally.
- The question asks for an examination of the main criticisms, so avoid spending much of your essay giving a history of atheism.
- Try to cover a range of different criticisms, rather than concentrating too heavily on just one or two.
- You might be able to refer to criticisms made by particular thinkers, such as Harris, Dawkins, Dennett, and Hitchens. If possible, make specific reference to their books, as well as their writing in more general terms.

Activity

Read the guidance about Assessment Objective 1 in 'Understanding the Assessment Objectives' on pages 6–7. Then go through your response to AO1 practice question 1 and see if you have demonstrated all the skills you need to demonstrate. Make revisions to your response if necessary.

AO1 practice question 2

Now try this question by yourself.

> *Examine Jung's explanation of religious belief.*
>
> (Eduqas A Level Religious Studies, Summer 2018, Component 2: Philosophy of Religion, Question 4a)

Practising AO2 questions

AO2 questions are designed to assess your ability to evaluate and analyse critically. You therefore need to concentrate on weighing up different possible views, and identifying their strengths and weaknesses. You should avoid spending too much of your answer presenting your knowledge in a descriptive way.

Activity

Here is an example of a past paper question, and the first paragraph of an answer to it. The writer has made a good start, focusing on the question, confidently demonstrating their knowledge and understanding, and making excellent use of examples.

Continue the answer. The writer has said that religious responses are only successful to a limited extent, so continue that line of argument, giving reasons and examples to support it.

'Religious responses have overcome the challenges from New Atheism.' Evaluate this view.

(Eduqas A Level Religious Studies, Summer 2019, Component 2: Philosophy of Religion, Question 3b)

Example

Religious responses have only overcome the challenges presented by New Atheism to a limited extent.[1] New Atheism continues to have a wide audience, with people listening to the arguments New Atheists present. Well-known figures, such as Ricky Gervais and Stephen Fry, use social media platforms such as Twitter to reach a wide audience[3], and religious believers have not been successful in stopping their influence from spreading[2]. New Atheists often time their criticism of religion to coincide with acts of terrorism, reinforcing the idea that religion is a source of violence and conflict in people's minds. Religious believers, however, have been quite successful[2] in showing that New Atheists are unnecessarily militant and aggressive. Thinkers such as Alister McGrath, Richard Swinburne and Keith Ward[4] respond to New Atheism in a scholarly and calm way which shows up New Atheists as people who make wild unsubstantiated claims.

1 The essay starts confidently, with a clear sense of what the writer intends to argue. The student then goes on to analyse a good number of points supporting their argument.

2 The paragraph focuses on the precise demands of the question throughout.

3 The paragraph contains good use of examples to support the points being made.

4 There is reference to scholarly views, which should be discussed in detail in future paragraphs.

5 This section of the essay does not make links with other areas of study, but these links should not be forced and should only be included where appropriate.

6 While there are no examples of specialist language in this short paragraph, the student is using a good academic style, and there should be opportunities to demonstrate specialist vocabulary in context in future paragraphs.

AO1 practice question 1

Try answering this question. There are some points to remember to help you write a developed response.

> *'Jung was more positive than Freud about the idea of God.'*
> *Evaluate this view.*
>
> (Eduqas A Level Religious Studies, Summer 2018, Component 2:
> Philosophy of Religion, Question 4b)

Points to remember

- Try to present a balanced argument, showing that you understand that some people may agree with the statement while others may disagree, even if you have strong views on one side.
- Make sure your own line of argument is clear throughout your answer, and not just tacked on at the end.
- Try to use specialist vocabulary in your answer, to demonstrate that you have a detailed and confident understanding of the views of Freud and Jung.

AO2 practice question 2

Now try this question by yourself.

> *'Empirical approaches prove that Jung's views on religion are*
> *wrong.' Evaluate this view.*
>
> (WJEC A Level Religious Studies, Summer 2019, A2 Unit 5:
> Philosophy of Religion, Question 3)

Mark schemes for all exam questions can be found at www.eduqas.co.uk and www.wjec.co.uk.

5 Religious experience (part one)

One of the puzzles raised by the whole notion of experience is that different people can experience the same objects and events entirely differently. School sports days, for example, are very different experiences for those with sporting talent than they are for those without. If you go to a music event with friends, a band starts playing a song and immediately some people in the audience are swept away by the music, singing along and obviously knowing all the words – while others have never heard the song before, or are left unmoved. Even experiences such as sharing a plate of food will be different for each participant, depending on their tastes and how hungry they might be. If you have siblings, you will each have different experiences of being in the same family; you and your friends will have different experiences of your school days, even if you have always been in the same class.

All of our experiences are unique to us, and in many ways, private. Because we are different people, our experiences are shaped by our personalities, our pasts, our gender, our culture, our health, our tastes, and many other factors, including our beliefs. When we perceive things with our senses, we interpret them, and those interpretations are subjective.

Some people have experiences that they interpret as 'religious'. Religious experiences can take a range of forms, and they are considered religious because the person having the experience interprets them as such, believing that they have in some way encountered God, or ultimate truth, or whatever they consider the divine to be. They may claim to have had a dramatic experience in which they have seen a vision, or to have heard the voice of God. It may be that a religious experience converted them to religious belief. They may claim that because they have a religious outlook, all of their daily experiences have a religious element, as they feel the presence of God within them, guiding them in their lives. They may claim to speak with God, and say that God has answered their prayers.

In the Bible, Mary has a religious experience in which she is told that she is going to have a son by the power of the Holy Spirit.

- How are such claims to be judged, given that all of our experiences have a strong element of subjectivity?
- Is there any way of knowing whether a religious experience is genuinely an experience of God?
- Can religious experience give people valuable insights into reality?
- Is religious experience nothing more than people putting a religious interpretation onto something more ordinary? Can religious experiences be 'explained away' by science?
- Should we accept reports of religious experience at face value, or should we treat them with scepticism?

AO1

This section of the chapter will enhance your **knowledge** and **understanding** of the topic and help you develop your AO1 skills.

The nature of religious experience

People have different understandings of what the term 'religious experience' means. Some think of a religious experience as a very rare and dramatic occurrence, in which a person has a direct encounter with God, perhaps seeing God in a vision or hearing the voice of God speaking to them clearly. Others consider religious experience to be much more common, and part of the lives of religious believers.

Religious experience is a complex subject to study. It is private and subjective; people have experiences that they interpret to be from God, and report their experiences to others, but these experiences are not repeatable and in many ways are not possible to test. The experiences are difficult for people to describe in ordinary, everyday language, with the result that they are often puzzling and obscure to those learning about them; but at the same time, they are extremely important to the people having the experiences, whose lives are often given a completely new sense of direction because of them. Sometimes the experiences are so powerful for the individuals that they speak with authority about the things they believe they have learned, giving rise to new religious movements as others also become convinced that the religious experience was genuinely from God. For example, the religion of the Sikhs originated with the religious experiences of Guru Nanak; the Franciscan order of monks in the Catholic Church began as a result of the religious experiences of Francis of Assisi; and the Religious Society of Friends (commonly known as the Quakers) started with the religious experiences of George Fox and others.

But, alongside these powerful experiences that many believe to be genuine encounters with God, there are also those who report religious experiences who are clearly suffering from mental illness, and those whose reports raise suspicions that they are attention-seeking rather than reporting the truth. In addition, there are people who are sceptical about the whole idea of religious experience, saying that a natural explanation for heightened emotion is a much more probable explanation than the view that the experiences are really from God.

Religious experiences are unique to each individual, like other kinds of experience, and yet there are some characteristics that they appear to have in common. Many religious people have reported seeing visions of God, or of Jesus or Mary, for example. There are also reports of people hearing the voice of God speaking to them, or having a powerful awareness of God that inspired them to convert to a religious belief when previously they had none. Because religious experience is not uncommon, and many of the reports have striking similarities, some argue that this provides evidence for the existence of God and good reasons for believing that the experiences are genuine encounters with the divine. After all, if several people experienced an art exhibition, and many of them came away saying that they had seen similar things in the exhibition and felt similar emotions, we would not question that the exhibition really exists and genuinely contains those pieces of art. Others, however, take the view that reports of the supernatural should always be treated with scepticism, and say that there will always be a natural explanation for alleged religious experience, such as hallucination or illness.

Visions

When people have **visions** in the context of religious experience, they feel as if they can see something supernatural and otherworldly; other people may not be able to see what they are seeing, and yet they feel as if they can see it clearly. When they are describing their vision to others, they talk in terms of what something looked like to them; they might describe it in terms of size, shape, and colour. One of the best known and most vivid examples in the Bible comes from the prophet Isaiah. He describes his vision of God, in a dramatic religious experience when he felt that God was calling him to be a prophet:

> **Key term**
>
> **vision:** in a religious context, seeing something either with ordinary sight or in a spiritual way, and understanding it to have deep religious significance

'In the year that King Uzziah died, I saw the Lord, high and exalted, seated on a throne; and the train of his robe filled the temple. Above him were seraphim, each with six wings: With two wings they covered their faces, with two they covered their feet, and with two they were flying.

And they were calling to one another: 'Holy, holy, holy is the Lord Almighty; the whole earth is full of his glory.'

At the sound of their voices the doorposts and thresholds shook and the temple was filled with smoke.

Isaiah 6:1–4, *Holy Bible (NIV)*

Isaiah does not say 'it was as if I saw the Lord …', or 'it felt as though …'; the vision is described as something wonderful that he saw with his eyes. In Isaiah's account, God tells Isaiah that he must work as a prophet: in other words, Isaiah has a commission to be a messenger between God and the people, passing on to them the words that God will give him to say. His religious experience gave him a new focus for his life, and was clearly, in his opinion, not just a subjective feeling but a convincing confirmation of the existence and will of God.

The Bible has a great variety of records of religious experiences. Some are presented with clarity and others are more difficult to understand. God appears to Moses in Exodus 3 in the form of a burning bush, and Moses hears God's voice speaking to him. The prophet Ezekiel had a vision of the chariot of God with strange creatures, which Ezekiel described in terms of bright colours and precious stones (Ezekiel 1). In the Gospels, people have religious experiences where they witness miracles, or suddenly come to understand

Jesus as the Son of God; in Acts 10 there is an account of a vision in which Peter realises that Christians do not need to keep the food laws of Judaism. The book of Revelation is full of visions about the end of time.

Religious visions are not exclusive to Judaism and Christianity. In Islam, for example, the story of the Night of Power details the visions of the prophet Muhammad when the Qur'an was revealed to him (Qur'an, Surah 96–98). In Hinduism, the god Krishna reveals himself in his universal form to Arjuna (Bhagavad Gita 11). Visions are characteristic of religious experience, and are also puzzling.

One of the issues raised by reports of visions is that it is not always clear how to understand them. We use the verb 'to see' in a variety of ways, some of them literal and others metaphorical; for example, we say 'I see trouble ahead', 'I see what you mean', 'I see they have decided to close that restaurant', 'I see there is no butter in the fridge', 'I see myself running my own company in ten years' time', and 'I'll see what I can do', using the word with related but different meanings: to predict, to understand, to infer, to visualise aspirations, to consider. The metaphors of sight and of vision are used not only to denote physical things that are there objectively in front of our eyes, but also to denote coming to an inner clarity of understanding.

In the context of religious visions, when people report what they saw, there is often a combination of meanings. People who report religious visions believe that they had a genuine encounter with an objective reality. There really was something there; they encountered God, and God initiated the encounter. In a religious vision, the person having the experience feels sure that it relates to an objective reality, in just the same way as they feel sure that they can see the ground beneath their feet. They come away from the experience with pictures in their minds of what they saw in the vision.

There is a difficulty, however, because religious experiences are private. If you go shopping with someone else to choose a piece of furniture, you can both see the same items and can exchange views on which to buy. But if someone has a religious vision, they cannot say to anyone else, 'Come and have a look at this'. Some people argue, therefore, that religious visions should not be taken seriously. They cannot be tested or repeated, and so they cannot be used as evidence for the existence of God or for anything else. They could, perhaps, be a sign of mental illness and a cause for concern. Others, however, believe that they are genuine encounters with God, and should be studied as ways of learning more about God.

Sensory visions

Sensory religious experiences are the kind where somebody is awake and conscious, and it seems that there is an encounter with an external reality that can be experienced using the senses. For example, hearing a voice would be a sensory religious experience, as would feeling the presence of a rushing wind on a still day. A sensory vision is where something seems to be before someone's eyes and can be described visually. For example, in France in 1858, a young girl named Bernadette Soubirous reported seeing

AO1 activity 1
Read the story of the Transfiguration of Jesus in Matthew 17. Do you think the reader is meant to understand this as a personal, subjective inner experience of the disciples, or would someone who happened to have been walking past at the time been able to see the Transfiguration too?

visions of 'a small young lady' by a stream in Lourdes. The figure told her to drink the stream water, which miraculously ran clear. In a later vision at the same place, the young lady told Bernadette that a chapel should be built on the site where she stood. When Bernadette told others of her visions, they identified the figure as Mary the mother of Jesus. Bernadette could describe clearly what the lady was wearing, what she said, and where she had appeared. Sensory visions can also involve other senses, such as smell and touch, and sometimes even taste.

In rare cases, sensory visions can be corporate, which means that several people report being able to see or hear the same thing. In the Bible, the story of the coming of the Holy Spirit at Pentecost in Acts 2 describes how a group of people all heard the same sound of a rushing wind, and all saw what seemed to be tongues of fire, in a corporate sensory experience that gave them the courage to go out into the world as Christian missionaries. In 1981, a group of six young people in Medjugorje (in Bosnia and Herzegovina) all reported seeing the same visions of Mary and hearing her give them messages to the world.

Teresa of Avila and intellectual visions

Teresa of Avila was a sixteenth-century Catholic nun; she was a very intelligent, influential, and sensitive woman who lived in Spain at the time of the Inquisition, when officials from the Catholic Church policed religious writers and teachers to make sure that they kept within the orthodox traditions of Catholic belief. Unusually for a woman in a convent, Teresa was a prolific writer, and under the instruction of monastic authorities, she kept a record of her religious life, practices, and religious experiences, giving people today a remarkable insight into her spiritual life in its historical context.

Because Teresa often had religious experiences and saw visions (and may have been epileptic), she was keen to understand whether she should trust them as genuinely coming from God, or whether she should be suspicious that they were from the Devil, trying to tempt her away from the true faith. In her writings she identified three types of visions:

1. The corporeal vision: Teresa gave this name to sensory visions that people see with their eyes, where the object of the vision seems physically very real. Teresa and her spiritual mentor John of the Cross did not always trust corporeal visions, thinking that they were the most likely kind of vision to be presented by the Devil. Teresa was writing at a time when little was understood about mental illness; it was often attributed to possession by evil spirits.
2. The imaginative vision: this is where the vision is seen in someone's mind's eye, or with the 'eyes of the soul' as Teresa put it.
3. The intellectual vision: in Teresa's view, this was not where people actually 'see' something, but has to do with gaining a deeper understanding of God within the soul, as an inner revelation of the presence of God. This type of vision, Teresa thought, was spiritually the

AO1 activity 2
Find out more about the reported visions in Medjugorje. What did the young people report seeing and hearing, and how did the Church respond to their reports? Why were some people sceptical about these visions? Do those who reported the visions still keep to the same version of events now that they have grown up?

most important. Intellectual visions might give the recipient a deep understanding of the nature of Christ or of the Trinity, for example, and are understandings that the recipient could not have worked out for themselves with their reason alone.

> *So far down in the depths of the soul does this contact take place, so clearly do the words spoken by the Lord seem to be heard with the soul's own faculty of hearing, and so secretly are they uttered, that the very way in which the soul understands them, together with the effects produced by the vision itself, convinces it and makes it certain that no part in the matter is being played by the Devil.*
>
> Teresa of Avila, 'Sixth Mansions', in *Interior Castle*

Teresa explained how to know when an intellectual vision is authentic:

1. It is clear and distinct.
2. It refers to things that the person has never thought of or imagined before.
3. It gives a level of understanding that is both very deep and very difficult to put into words.
4. Importantly, the genuine vision leaves the person with a sense of peace and light, whereas an inauthentic vision leaves someone restless and doubtful.

Examples of visions: *Julian of Norwich*

Julian of Norwich was a woman who lived in the fourteenth century as a religious recluse, in a cell in the wall of St Julian's Church in Norwich. Having witnessed the terrors of the Black Death when she was a child, Julian devoted her life to prayer, and in her writings, *Revelations of Divine Love*, she recorded her religious experiences and visions. This is the first book in English written by someone known to be a woman. This extract from Julian of Norwich's writings exemplifies Teresa of Avila's understanding of the imaginative and the intellectual vision:

Teresa of Avila was a prolific writer whose exploration of religious experience has been very influential in Christianity.

> *In this same time our Lord shewed me a spiritual sight of His homely loving.*
>
> *I saw that He is to us everything that is good and comfortable for us: He is our clothing that for love wrappeth us, claspeth us, and all encloseth us for tender love, that He may never leave us; being to us all-thing that is good, as to mine understanding.*
>
> *Also in this He shewed me a little thing, the quantity of an hazel-nut, in the palm of my hand; … I looked thereupon with eye of my understanding, and thought: What may this be? And it was answered generally thus: It is all that is made. I marvelled how it might last, for methought it might suddenly have fallen to naught for little[ness]. And I was answered in my understanding: It lasteth, and ever shall [last] for that God loveth it. And so All-thing hath the Being by the love of God.*
>
> Julian of Norwich, *Revelations of Divine Love*

Visions in dreams

Some accounts of religious visions are connected with dreams, where it seems that God appears to someone while they are sleeping, and leaves them with lasting mental images and a new understanding. There are several examples in the Bible: in Genesis 28, Jacob had a dream in which he saw a ladder going up to heaven, from which he learned that he had happened to go to sleep in a holy place where a temple should be built. Another example is in Matthew's gospel (Matthew 1:28) where Joseph is told in a dream that he should not be afraid to marry Mary even though she was pregnant with a child that was not his, and Joseph was reassured.

Religious visions in dreams seem to be different from ordinary dreams. In usual circumstances if, for example, Jane dreams about Bob, she does not wake up and expect Bob to know all about what happened to them both in the dream. But in a religious dream experience, the person does not feel simply that they dreamed about God, but instead that they encountered God in the dream. God deliberately chose to appear to them in reality, and not just in their imagination; and so the dream is understood as a significant event and not just the wanderings of the mind in semiconsciousness.

Visions as a form of religious experience often do not fall neatly into one category or another, but may have different elements: for example, a sensory vision could give a feeling of deep intellectual understanding as well, or an imaginative vision could be experienced when awake or asleep.

Conversion

Conversion refers to 'turning around' or 'changing'. In everyday life, we use the word 'conversion' to refer to things like changing the use of a building from a garage to a shop, or changing a substance from a solid to a liquid. The word 'conversion' is used about people in non-religious contexts as well as religious. For example, moral conversion refers to a change in belief about right and wrong (such as converting from meat-eating to vegetarianism). Political conversion refers to someone changing their political ideals and deciding to vote differently in the future.

In the context of religion, conversion refers to someone's decision to give up their former ways of looking at the world and start again with a new focus on God. Religious conversion experiences are common because everyone with active religious beliefs (rather than nominally belonging to one tradition or another) had a point where those beliefs began. In some religious traditions, such as evangelical Protestant Christianity, conversion is given great importance, and Christians are invited to 'give their testimony', where they talk about their conversion experiences in meetings to inspire others. They talk about their old way of life and the things they used to think were important, and then describe what happened to make them change direction and turn to Christianity.

> ## AO1 activity 3
> Look up these examples of Biblical dreams so that you could use them as examples in your own writing:
> - Genesis 37:5–10
> - Judges 7:13–15
> - Matthew 2:13

> ## Key term
>
> conversion: changing from one thing to another; in the context of religious experience, conversion refers to a radical change of belief

Some religions have ceremonies that mark a person's conversion, such as adult baptism, where water is used as a symbol of washing away sin and beginning again in a new life, or confirmation, where people choose to reaffirm for themselves the promises that were made on their behalf when they were infants.

In some Christian traditions, adult baptism is a ceremony that marks a personal decision to convert to Christianity.

In other religious traditions, conversion is not given as much prominence, and is seen as a private experience. Some people take the view that a conversion experience, while important, is not an essential part of faith, arguing that too much emphasis on conversion experiences can make people feel excluded from a religious community if they have not had such an experience themselves. The German theologian Karl Barth was keen to point out that religious experiences come from God, and should not be boasted about as if they are the individual's own achievement, or sought after as if people can choose when and whether God is revealed to them.

Some religions, such as Christianity and Islam, actively seek converts while others (such as Judaism and Hinduism) do not.

AO1 activity 4

Look up some examples of conversion experiences told by people in their own words. You could research well-known people, or anyone who has reported their conversion on the internet, or a mixture. William James has some examples in his book *The Varieties of Religious Experience*.

Do the experiences have much in common with each other? In the experiences you researched, what was the person doing just before they had their religious experience? Were they hoping to have an experience of God, or did it come out of nowhere?

Individual conversion experiences

Conversion experiences can be dramatic, where the individual can pinpoint the date on which it happened and where they were at the time; or they can be slower to develop, where someone gradually makes a decision to change after wrestling with the idea for a while.

Charles Wesley recorded in his diary, in April 1738, a discussion he had with his brother John. Both were clergyman in the Church of England, and their discussion was about whether conversions could happen gradually or whether they were always instantaneous. John thought conversion happened suddenly, and a person could change from being an unbeliever to a believer in a moment. Charles thought the process was more gradual; someone could slowly come around to developing a deeper faith, and there did not have to be a distinct moment of conversion. The discussion turned into a heated argument, and Charles stormed out of the room.

However, a month later, Charles had a conversion experience that made him change his mind. On 24 May 1738, he went to hear someone preaching from the letter to the Romans in the Bible, and he wrote:

> *I felt my heart strangely warmed. I felt I did trust in Christ, Christ alone, for salvation; and an assurance was given me that he had taken away my sins, even mine, and saved me from the law of sin and death.*
>
> John Wesley, *The Journal of John Wesley*

As an ordained clergyman, Charles believed himself to be a Christian already, but his religious experience marked the beginning of a new enthusiasm for Christian teaching and ministry. It marked the point at which he moved from agreeing with Christian teaching to living a life inspired by it, with a strong sense of the presence of God.

John Wesley, whose position as the fifteenth child in the Wesley family made him the older brother, had a similar experience three days later. John founded the Methodist Church, and Charles (child number eighteen) became a leading figure in the Methodist movement, well-known for his writing of hymns such as 'Christ the Lord is risen today', 'Hark the herald angels sing' and more than 6,000 others.

Sometimes, conversion experiences are classified as 'active' and 'passive':

- Active conversion: the person takes the initiative to look for answers, for example by reading the Bible or Qur'an, going to an evangelical event, visiting a religious leader with questions, going to a country such as India to explore spirituality. Their conversion arises from these efforts to seek the truth.
- Passive conversion: the person does not know they are looking for God, but is taken by surprise by an experience in which God is suddenly revealed to them.

These experiences can mark a total change in a person's belief system, such as when someone converts from atheism to Islam; or they can mark a point where someone moves from doing no more than identifying as a member of a particular religious tradition, to having a deep personal faith in its teachings. Although conversion experiences vary quite significantly, they also have some common features that have been identified by psychologists and philosophers of religion. Conversions tend to follow a pattern:

1. The individual is dissatisfied with their current outlook on life. People do not usually have conversion experiences if they are quite satisfied and content as they are.
2. They search at an intellectual and emotional level for something that will help them make a decision. For example, they may spend time

reading a holy book, ask religious friends lots of questions, go and stay in a quiet place for a retreat, or attend religious services.

3. There is a turning point, which is often a time of intense emotion, and difficult to describe. It may be accompanied by physical symptoms such as shaking or a feeling of warmth. Often, people describe their conversion experiences in terms of a strong sense of the presence of God, accompanied by a sense of their own sinfulness. Sometimes they describe seeing bright lights, seeing visions or hearing voices.

4. The turning point is followed by emotions of peace and relief, as well as a desire to share the new faith with others and talk about the experience.

5. The convert has a long-lasting new sense of direction, which is 'God-centred' rather than self-centred.

Because individual conversions usually include a keenness to tell others about the experience, there are many well-documented accounts.

In Christianity, the most famous is probably that of Paul in the Bible, who had a sudden and dramatic conversion experience on the road to Damascus. He was formerly known as Saul of Tarsus, and had never personally met Jesus, although there were many people still alive who had. Saul was actively engaged in the first-century persecution of Christians, and was on his way to Damascus to seek out and arrest some, when a blinding light flashed from heaven and he heard a voice from God. The experience convinced him to become a Christian himself, and he changed his name from Saul to Paul to mark the new direction of his life. After his conversion, Paul devoted himself to teaching about Christianity through missionary work and writing. In his letters to new Christian churches, Paul wrote frequently of his conversion, and how it had convinced him that Jesus was the Son of God and had risen from the dead.

> **AO1 activity 5**
> Familiarise yourself with the story of the conversion of Paul. The conversion is described in Acts 9:3–19, and Paul refers to it in his own words in his letters, for example in Galatians 1:11–16. Make some notes to remind yourself of the key features of this story.

Francis of Assisi had a conversion experience in 1206 CE when he was 24 years old, recorded by his friend and contemporary Thomas of Celano. Thomas explained that Francis was a high-spirited boy, full of vitality and artistic, but that he 'miserably squandered and wasted his time'. Francis felt 'divided'. He was especially dissatisfied by his own repulsion at ugliness and the way his instincts drew him back from beggars and people with leprosy, and wanted to be different. Francis was walking in the countryside in Assisi when he came across a dilapidated little church. Thomas of Celano, writing in the thirteenth century, described what happened:

> *Led by the Spirit, he went in to pray. He fell down before the crucifix* *in devout supplication, and, having been smitten by unwonted visitation found himself another man than he who had gone in.*
>
> Thomas of Celano, *The Memorial of the Desire of a Soul Concerning the Deeds and Words of Our Most Holy Father Francis*

George Fox, one of the founders of the Religious Society of Friends (the Quakers), described his conversion experience in his journal of 1647:

> *Though my exercises and troubles were very great, yet were they not so continual but that I had some intermissions, and I was sometimes brought into such an heavenly joy that I thought I had been in Abraham's bosom. … One day, when I had been walking solitarily abroad, and was come home, I was taken up in the love of God, so that I could not but admire the greatness of His love; and while I was in that condition, it was opened unto me by the eternal light and power, and I therein clearly saw … But O! then did I see my troubles, trials, and temptations more clearly than ever I had done.*
>
> George Fox, *Journal of George Fox*

Communal conversion experiences

Communal conversion experiences happen when a group of people have religious experiences simultaneously, which change their lives and belief systems. They are much rarer than individual experiences, but there are references to them in the Bible and elsewhere. The story of the coming the Holy Spirit in Acts 2 could be considered a conversion experience. Those attending a service for the Jewish festival of Pentecost arrived feeling afraid and despondent because Jesus had been crucified and they had no leader or sense of direction, but after the religious experience, they had a new courage to talk about their faith.

References are made in the Bible to the communal responses of crowds when they witnessed Jesus' miracles or heard Christian preaching:

> *And when they climbed into the boat, the wind died down. Then those who were in the boat worshipped him, saying, "Truly you are the Son of God."*
>
> Matthew 14:32–33, *Holy Bible (NIV)*

In this story, Jesus performed a miracle to calm a storm. Those in the boat, who had been afraid they were going to drown, communally recognised Jesus as the Son of God.

> *While Peter was still speaking these words, the Holy Spirit came on all who heard the message.*
>
> Acts 10:44, *Holy Bible (NIV)*

This verse is part of a description of a communal conversion experience for those who heard Jesus' disciple Peter preaching about Christianity.

Some Christian denominations have a tradition of 'revival meetings', where visiting speakers hold a series of meetings in different locations with the aim of rekindling interest in Christianity and encouraging conversion. These were popular in the nineteenth century, and again for several decades beginning in the 1940s. Billy Graham, an American evangelist, held mass rallies called 'crusades' in the US and also in the UK at places like Harringay Arena and Wembley Stadium. He would speak about his own Christian faith, and encourage people in the crowd to come forward for prayer and to make a commitment of conversion alongside others. Thousands of people claim to have had conversion experiences at these events, and at similar crusades led by other speakers.

Communal conversion experiences are sometimes met with scepticism. Those who witnessed the followers of Jesus on the day of Pentecost were not all convinced: some were 'amazed and perplexed' while others made fun of them, saying they had had 'too much wine' (Acts 2:13). A frequent criticism made of communal conversion experiences is that people are easily led by the emotions of a crowd; they can be stirred up to the extent that they become very suggestible. Talented motivational speakers make use of this human tendency, using repeated phrases and the power of their voices to sweep people along into agreeing with their message, possibly making them believe that they have experienced God when it was nothing more than the hyper-emotion of a crowd. A similar effect can be seen at political rallies, where speakers stir up crowds. However, others argue that many people who have attended evangelical crusades and had conversion experiences there have retained their faith for the rest of their lives, demonstrating that their conversion was more than just emotion in the heat of the moment. John Habgood, for example, was converted from atheism to Christianity at an evangelical crusade in Cambridge in the 1940s, and went on to become Bishop of Durham and then Archbishop of York, exercising considerable influence in the Church of England.

The American evangelist Billy Graham held Christian rallies which effected communal conversion experiences.

Mysticism

Mysticism is a form of religious experience that is very difficult to define, and one that has been given different definitions by different thinkers. Some use the term 'mysticism' to encompass every type of religious experience, including visions and conversion experiences. Mysticism does not necessarily have to be seen in contrast with other forms of religious experience, as it is often a part of them. Writers often use the term 'mysticism' to describe a particular element of religious experience in which people feel that they have in some way left behind worldly concerns for a while and accessed spiritual truths, where the experience has brought them closer to whatever they understand ultimate reality to be.

The difficulty of defining mystical experience is seen to be one of its characteristics. Other kinds of religious experience, such as seeing a vision, hearing a voice or converting to a new focus in life have parallels in the everyday world: we know what it means to see, and to hear, and to have a change of heart. But mystical experience is something that does not have any everyday parallel, making it difficult to find words to describe it to people who have not had such an experience.

The term 'mystical experience' started to be used in the nineteenth and twentieth centuries as part of a movement towards finding common ground between the different world religions. The Victorian practice of sending out missionaries to foreign countries to convert the 'heathen' to Christianity was coming to an end, as people were less certain than before

> **Key term**
>
> **mysticism:** religious experience in which the sense of self is lost, in an encounter with God or ultimate reality

that Christianity was the only true religion, and many were beginning to find spiritual wisdom in other world faiths. Some people were of the belief that all religions are essentially involved in the same quest, looking for the divine or ultimate truth in different cultural contexts. They looked for examples of 'mystical experience' to demonstrate that this was something all religious believers had in common: all religious traditions contained reports of people having some kind of deep inner sense of communion with God or with ultimate truth, a 'mystical experience'.

In the Christian tradition, there have been various people who have been regarded as mystics. Many lived in the Middle Ages when religious experience was highly respected, and so their reports of religious experience were taken seriously, preserved, and circulated. Julian of Norwich, Teresa of Avila, John of the Cross, Meister Eckhart, and Hildegard von Bingen are all examples of such people, although they would not have seen themselves as mystics but simply as Christians.

Although mystical experience is difficult to define, most people who have written about it have identified some common features:

1. Mystical experience is described as **transcendent**: this means that the experience feels as if it is beyond space and time, as an encounter with something that is not of this world.
2. It is described as **ecstatic**: this means that the person having the experience is transported beyond the normal range of emotions to a state of complete bliss, and may appear to go into a trance in which they are unaware of what is going on in the world around them until the experience is over.
3. It is also described as a **unitive religious experience:** this means that the person having the experience loses the consciousness of being an individual self, and feels a sense of unity with the divine or with the rest of creation. The mediaeval mystics sometimes referred to this unitive quality in terms of 'spiritual marriage', where they felt they had entered into a relationship with God in which their own will had become united with the will of God. After the experience was over, they were not so interested in worldly achievements as they had been, but instead were focused on deepening their relationship with God and encouraging others to do the same.

The mystical experience of Manikka-Vacchagar

Manikka-Vacchagar was a poet and saint in the Hindu tradition of Shaivism (where the god Shiva is the focus of worship). Manikka-Vacchagar's poetry about his own mystical experience was collected by a scholar called Nicol MacNicol, whose aim in writing his book *Indian Theism* in 1915 was explicitly to draw parallels between Christian mystical experience and the mystical experience of those who practised Indian religions. MacNicol hoped that his book would be read by Christian missionaries, who he thought would be better equipped to convert others to Christianity if they could see the close relationship between Indian and Christian religious experiences.

> **Key terms**
>
> **transcendent:** having existence outside the material universe
>
> **ecstatic:** when a person feels like they are transported beyond the normal range of emotions to a state of complete bliss
>
> **unitive religious experience:** when a person feels their identity is overwhelmed and they become part of God or the universe

Manikka-Vacchagar wrote about the way in which God transcends all description and all human knowledge, and yet can be met in unitive and ecstatic religious experience:

> *When it seemed I ne'er could be with Thee made one, – when nought of Thine was mine, –*
>
> *And nought of mine was Thine, – me to Thy feet Thy love*
>
> *In mystic union joined, Lord of the heavenly land, – 'tis height of blessedness.*
>
> Manikka-Vacchagar, *Tiruvãcakam*

The mystical experience of Abraham Abulafia

Abraham Abulafia was a Jewish mystic of the thirteenth century, whose main aim was to open the way for people to experience divine reality. As a young man, he was a great traveller, working his way through the Near East, Greece, and Italy. During his travels, he was attracted by the practice of yoga, and the ways in which it offered methods of attaining peace and wisdom through discipline of the mind and body. Abulafia combined his Jewish beliefs with yogic practices and took up meditation, believing it to be a way of freeing the soul from distractions, from the confines of religious orthodoxy, and from the limitations of the five senses. As a focus for meditation, Abulafia chose the letters of the Hebrew alphabet, and in particular the name of God; he taught that concentrated meditation on the name of God would, with sufficient training and practice, lead to spiritual ecstasy. In his writings, Abulafia refers to his 'Master', which may have been a reference to a spiritual teacher such as a guru, or may have been a reference to God.

Abulafia wrote of his mystical experience:

> *the man who has felt the divine touch and perceived its nature is no longer separated from his Master, and behold, he is his Master, and his Master is he, for he is so intimately united to Him that he cannot by any means be separated from Him.*
>
> Abraham Abulafia, 'The Knowledge of the Messiah and the Meaning of the Redeemer'

AO1 activity 6

Research and make some notes about the teachings of the mediaeval mystic Meister Eckhart, who thought that the unity of the soul with God should be the primary focus of human existence.

Prayer

Prayer is a form of religious experience in which people seek a union with God. It does not happen to people when they are least expecting it, but is something they choose to do, in the hope of having an encounter with God and gaining a greater understanding of what God wants them to do. People might hope to have an encounter with God at times when they are feeling especially grateful for something; when they have an important decision to make and are unsure of what to do; when they feel helpless in the face of suffering, and want to ask for help to alleviate someone's situation; or when they know that they have done something wrong, feel guilty, and want to be forgiven. Some religious people pray every day as part of their daily routine, and others pray only occasionally.

Types of prayer

Prayer is often classified into different kinds according to its purpose:

- Prayers of worship and thanksgiving, praising God, and showing recognition of God's power, and thanking God for specific things.
- Prayers of petition, where people ask God for help, or perhaps for some kind of sign to indicate the right choices to make. They might pray for healing for the sick, peace in times of conflict, or comfort for people who are in difficult situations.
- Prayers of confession and repentance, where people contemplate the wrong they have done and seek God's forgiveness.

Prayer can be communal, where people gather together and say or listen to the same words of prayer, or are silent together; or it can be individual, where someone says a quick prayer as they go about their everyday life, or retreats to somewhere quiet and private, away from others to pray. Prayer is used in services of religious worship; different religions and different denominations within those traditions have different practices. Some follow the words of a prayer book, some are led by a minister or reader, and some use spontaneous prayer where anyone in the congregation can speak. Some use techniques of quiet contemplation and meditation. Many religious traditions use a combination of these. Although practices vary significantly, the purpose is the same: to initiate a religious experience, from which the individual hopes to learn and be strengthened in their faith.

Teresa of Avila on prayer

The philosopher William James described Teresa of Avila as 'one of the ablest women, in many respects, of whose life we have the record'. Although Teresa came from a wealthy family, she chose to devote her life to study and prayer in a Carmelite convent. Born in 1515, Teresa was a keen reader, and an admirer of the writings of Augustine as well as of the work of the mediaeval mystics; she studied their experiences of contemplative prayer, and decided to follow the spiritual path they suggested. Augustine had written an autobiography detailing his religious life, the questions he struggled with, and the answers he found, and Teresa's own writings followed his example. A period of serious illness left her with paralysis for several years, after which she began to experience visions of Jesus. She was embarrassed at first to tell other people about them, in case they thought she fancied herself as the new Saint Paul or Saint Jerome, but some of the authorities in her religious order were encouraging, and asked her to write about her prayer life and her religious experiences in the hope of inspiring others. When she wrote, Teresa scribbled at breakneck speed, never going back to rewrite anything, and saying that she wished she could write with both hands simultaneously so that she could get everything down onto paper as quickly as it came into her head.

When she wrote about prayer in her autobiography, Teresa said that her aim in setting out different stages of prayer was to help people to realise that there was much more to be gained from prayer than just a few moments each day of repeated words. She wrote:

> *And anyone who has not begun to pray, I beg, for love of the Lord, not to miss so great a blessing.*
>
> Teresa of Avila, 'Life of St Teresa', from
> *Complete Works St Teresa of Avila*

Teresa saw prayer in terms of a spiritual exercise, where, if taken seriously, it is possible to progress through different levels. At the beginning, prayer takes a lot of effort, but it is worth it because the aim is to work towards a point in which the soul achieves a spiritual union with God. Each stage takes a considerable time to develop and cannot be rushed. In her autobiography, Teresa used the analogy of someone watering a garden in the hope that everything will eventually grow and flower – some methods of getting the water to the garden are harder than others.

1. Meditation: this is first stage of prayer, for beginners, and the only one of the four stages that can be achieved at least in part by someone's own efforts. People should set aside distractions and anxieties, and concentrate their thoughts on the life of Jesus. Teresa recommended that people might look at a field, or water, or flowers, to help them get rid of distractions. They will eventually be filled with love for God. Teresa compared this stage of prayer to watering a garden using a bucket to draw up water from a well. It is hard work, and sometimes the well is dry, and sometimes the gardener feels like giving up, but it is important to continue.

2. The Prayer of Quiet: this is the second stage, which cannot be achieved by the individual but comes upon them. They no longer have to make an effort in prayer, but are able to rest in it, feeling the grace of God, and a deep inner sense of contentment. It can feel as if it is the final stage of prayer, because it provides such an overwhelming sense of bliss that the person feels as if there could be nothing better. Teresa compares this stage of prayer to being able to draw up water from a well using a windlass, which is a notched wheel or pulley that holds a rope, enabling the person using it to raise a bucket from a well much more easily than by their own muscle-power:

> *By using a device of windlass and buckets the gardener draws more water with less labour and is able to take some rest instead of being continually at work.*
>
> Teresa of Avila, 'Life of St Teresa', from
> *Complete Works St Teresa of Avila*

3. Union: in this stage where the soul becomes unified with God. The person praying has to make the effort to pray, but finding a connection with God is now much easier. All the senses go into a kind of sleep or trance, with no focus other than God. Teresa compares this stage of

prayer to watering a garden by siphoning off water from a river or a spring:

> *This irrigates the garden with much less trouble, although a certain amount is caused by the directing of it.*
>
> Teresa of Avila, 'Life of St Teresa', from
> *Complete Works St Teresa of Avila*

4. Rapture: Teresa struggles to find words to describe the final stage of prayer, saying 'The persons who must speak of it are those who know it, for it cannot be understood, still less described.' The soul is gathered up into God and soars away from the created world. According to legend, Teresa's experiences of prayer of rapture were so powerful that her body levitated completely off the ground, and other nuns had to hold her down to stop her from floating away. Using her garden analogy, she writes of this final stage of prayer in terms of a garden being watered by the rain, sent down from heaven without the gardener needing to make any effort at all – but also being something that gardeners cannot choose or summon to suit themselves.

> *Speaking now of this rain which comes from Heaven to fill and saturate the whole of this garden with an abundance of water, we can see how much rest the gardener would be able to have if the Lord never ceased to send it … This rain from Heaven often comes when the gardener is least expecting it.*
>
> Teresa of Avila, 'Life of St Teresa', from
> *Complete Works St Teresa of Avila*

Synoptic link

Link to *Chapter 7: Religious language (part one)*. Teresa uses analogies to help clarify her meaning. Chapter 7 looks at the use of analogy in religious language in more detail.

Teresa wrote other works in addition to her autobiography. The best-known is *The Interior Castle*, sometimes translated as *The Mansions*, in which Teresa gave further details about the stages of prayer. She wrote the book as a response to a vision of a crystal globe in the shape of a castle, with seven interior courts or mansions. The court in the centre was filled with light, but outside the castle everything was dark and filled with poisonous creatures. Teresa interpreted this vision of a castle to form an analogy of the soul in its relationship with God. Moving from the outside of the castle to the innermost chamber represents the soul's journey through prayer to the highest and best state of union with God that is possible to achieve in this world.

1. The first mansion – this is the point of entry into the 'interior castle', where the soul is easily distracted by poisons from outside, and learns to be humble.
2. The second mansion – this is warmer than the first mansion, and gives the soul knowledge of the importance of moving through the stages of prayer.
3. The third mansion – the soul is learning self-discipline, but still makes mistakes, and there are still temptations to give up.
4. The fourth mansion – this corresponds to Teresa's ideas about the 'Prayer of Quiet', where the soul can rest in prayer.

5. The fifth mansion – this is where the soul is taken over by God in spiritual union, and corresponds to the analogy of the river irrigating the garden.

6. The sixth mansion – Teresa's description of this stage is often difficult to understand. It involves ecstasy but also pain. The soul wants to spend every moment in a 'spiritual marriage' with God, and does not want to be distracted by worldly concerns.

7. The seventh mansion – this is the ultimate state of prayer, where the soul transcends reason and is in complete unity with God.

AO1 activity 7

a) Makes some notes to remind yourself of the two analogies that Teresa of Avila used to describe the path of prayer: the garden analogy, and the castle analogy.

b) Teresa's imagery of a garden and a castle would have been familiar to her contemporaries in sixteenth-century Spain. What analogies could be used in the twenty-first century to convey a similar understanding of the stages of prayer? (For example, apps that chart progress from being a couch potato to running 5k could make a good analogy.) Think of some examples of your own.

Mystical experience

In the study of religious experience, two writers are particularly important. William James, at the beginning of the twentieth century, and Rudolf Otto, soon after the First World War, each gave a detailed consideration of religious experience, giving it attention that it had not been given before. William James wrote as someone with a scientific background but no particular religious convictions, aiming to collect accounts of religious experiences as a scientist would collect data, and to examine these accounts to see what could be learned. Rudolph Otto wrote as a Christian, wanting to explore and distil the essence of religious experience and find words to describe it, as well as discussing the place of religious experience in Christian belief.

William James (right) came from a talented family of thinkers; William was a philosopher who studied religious experience, while his brother Henry was a novelist.

William James

Who was William James?

William James came from a wealthy family that lived in Boston, Massachusetts. He was brought up at the end of the nineteenth century in a very talented family which was well-connected to interesting thinkers, and not afraid to talk about ideas and to challenge popular beliefs and opinions. William's brother was the novelist Henry James; the two seem to have had a rather uneasy relationship, as Henry was gay in an era when this was considered unacceptable, and William had a serious sense of traditional morality while Henry was more artistic and mischievous. They wrote to each other in adult life in a friendly way, but neither had much praise for the other's work.

William James chose a career in medicine and qualified as a doctor at Harvard, where he was interested in philosophy and the newly-developing science of psychology. He was very interested in religious experience, and decided to try to study it as objectively as possible. Rather than trying to demonstrate that God did or did not exist, James wanted to apply scientific method to religious experience, looking at a wide range of accounts to see if there were any common threads or characteristics that could add to human understanding.

His book, *The Varieties of Religious Experience*, which began as a series of lectures, was published in 1901 and immediately became popular. It continues to be considered one of the most important books on religion. James collected first-hand reports of religious experience in people's own words, to make them as authentic as possible, and to avoid misrepresenting others by giving their accounts his own interpretations. He classified these accounts into different categories, including 'conversion' and 'saintliness', and also included in his book two lectures on mysticism in which he set out four key characteristics that he thought formed a common thread in mystical experience.

William James' four characteristics of mystical experience

In *The Varieties of Religious Experience*, James set out four characteristics that he thought distinguished mystical experience.

1. The first quality James identified was that of **ineffability**. By this, he meant that the experience is impossible to express adequately in normal language. It 'defies expression', he wrote, and to be properly understood it has to be experienced, as it is impossible for those who have had mystical experiences to be able to make clear what has happened so that others can fully understand them. James gave the analogies of a musician who knows the value of a symphony but cannot explain it to someone without a musical ear, and of someone in love who will find it impossible to explain how they feel:

> one must have been in love one's self to understand a lover's state of mind
>
> William James, *The Varieties of Religious Experience*

James quoted the poet Tennyson, who wrote about the ineffability and unitive quality of religious experience in a letter:

> I have never had any revelations through anæsthetics, but a kind of waking trance—this for lack of a better word—I have frequently had, quite up from boyhood, when I have been all alone. This has come upon me through repeating my own name to myself silently, till all at once, as it were out of the intensity of the consciousness of individuality, individuality itself seemed to dissolve and fade away into boundless being, and this not a confused state but the clearest, the surest of the surest, utterly beyond words—where death was an almost laughable impossibility—the loss of personality (if so it were) seeming no extinction, but the only true life. I am ashamed of my feeble description. Have I not said the state is utterly beyond words?
>
> Alfred Tennyson, in a letter to Mr B.P. Bland, 7 May 1874

Key term

ineffability: the quality of being difficult to express in normal vocabulary

Synoptic link

Link to *Chapters 7 and 8: Religious language*. William James talked about religious experience as ineffable, which is an issue discussed in religious language. How can people communicate ideas about religious belief, if they are impossible to put into words?

2. **Noetic** quality: the experience makes the person feel as though they have been given an understanding of important truths, which could not have been reached through the use of reason alone. People who have had religious experiences often speak in terms of having had the truth revealed to them. James gives the example of someone who converted suddenly from Judaism to Catholicism, and wrote about the knowledge this person suddenly gained of sin and salvation:

> *… at the bottom of that gulf I saw the extreme of misery from which I had been saved by an infinite mercy; and I shuddered at the sight of my iniquities, stupefied, melted, overwhelmed with wonder and with gratitude. You may ask me how I came to this new insight, for truly I had never opened a book of religion nor even read a single page of the Bible.*
>
> William James, *The Varieties of Religious Experience*

3. **Transiency:** the experience is over quite soon, lasting no more than a couple of hours, even though the effect of the experience could last a lifetime; as James writes, 'Mystical states cannot be sustained for long' (*The Varieties of Religious Experience*). James quotes, for example, the account of a Swiss man who had a religious experience while hiking:

> *The state of ecstasy may have lasted four or five minutes, although it seemed at the time to last much longer.*
>
> William James, *The Varieties of Religious Experience*

Once the experience is over, the memory can only reproduce the experience imperfectly, but if the person has another mystical experience, they recognise it as a continuation of the previous experience.

4. **Passivity:** the person having the experience feels as if the experience is being controlled from outside themselves; they are the recipients of the experience, rather than the instigators of it. Although they might make efforts to have a mystical experience, for example by fasting, meditating, or isolating themselves from the rest of the world, when a mystical experience starts, the person feels as if they no longer have a will of their own but are being held by an immense superior power. James writes of how, in some cases, the person having a mystical experience reports phenomena such as 'prophetic speech, automatic writing, or the mediumistic trance'. After the mystical experience, the person may have no memory of what happened, although the effects of the experience will have a lasting influence. One of James' examples is a man of 27, who wrote:

> *I have on a number of occasions felt that I had enjoyed a period of intimate communion with the divine. These meetings came unasked and unexpected, and seemed to consist merely in the temporary obliteration of the conventionalities which usually surround and cover my life.*
>
> William James, *The Varieties of Religious Experience*

Key terms

noetic: gaining special knowledge or insights that are unobtainable by the intellect alone

transiency: lasting only for a short time

passivity: being acted upon, rather than taking the initiative

Rudolf Otto

Who was Rudolf Otto?

Rudolf Otto was a German theologian who wrote the influential book *Das Heilige*; it was first translated into English in 1923, called 'The Idea of the Holy'. In this book, Otto aimed to show that a meeting with what he called 'natural forces' at a personal level is fundamental to religion. He followed and developed the thinking of Friedrich Schleiermacher in the eighteenth century, who claimed that the essence of religion was in personal experience of the divine. It was not enough, Schleiermacher thought, for people to agree to doctrines and ethical principles in order to call themselves religious believers. As well, they needed to be aware of a sense of God, and try to find ways to develop this sense. Schleiermacher thought that religion should go beyond reasoned acceptance of arguments, and be led by personal conviction based on personal experiences.

Having studied the scientific outlook that developed during the nineteenth century, including Darwinism, Otto argued forcibly that science is not capable of explaining or understanding human spirituality. A long journey around the world before the First World War brought Otto into contact with the great religions of the East, which made him think that although each religion has special and unique qualities, they share a common basis in religious experience, even if their beliefs and practices are very different. Otto lectured in London in 1927 on mysticism, where he was very popular, partly because of his natural friendliness, and more importantly because his ideas struck a chord with those who were disillusioned with traditional religion after the war but who had retained their interest in spirituality. In Germany, Otto was for a time a Member of Parliament, and he wanted to set up a museum of comparative religion in his home town of Marburg, but the rise of Hitler's Third Reich stood in his way. He died in 1937 as the result of a tragic accident.

The concept of the numinous

Otto wrote his book because, like Schleiermacher, he thought that in discussion of God and of religion, there was too much emphasis on the rational. Religious people wrote about the attributes of God in terms that could be understood by human reason, such as in terms of good will and of purposes; these sorts of attributes can be understood rationally, as we recognise them as being similar to our own attributes. (Those who wanted to 'explain away' religion, on the other hand, wrote in terms of mythology, primitive humanity, and evolution, finding alternative explanations to account for religion.) But, argued Otto, putting reason in a position of such high regard has led to a dismissal of an essential aspect of religious belief, and that is the non-rational sense of the 'holy' or 'sacred', which has more to do with feeling than with reason.

'Holiness', Otto thought, is not quite the right word for what he was trying to express because 'holy' had become very closely associated with ethics, so that people understood it to be a word for moral perfection. The element of religion Otto wanted to explore is related to moral goodness, but goes beyond it, and is something people feel. He decided we needed a special term for it:

> *For this purpose I adopt a word coined from the Latin* numen. Omen *has given us 'ominous', and there is no reason why from* numen *we should not similarly form a word* numinous.
>
> Rudolf Otto, *The Idea of the Holy*

Otto said that this cannot be strictly defined in any other way, and so people will only really understand what it means to have a feeling of the **numinous** when they experience it for themselves. It is in a category of its own, a '*sui generis*' (of its own kind). Those who have experienced the numinous can only say what it resembles or contrasts with, and often cannot do even that. The numinous cannot be taught, Otto said, but only awakened in the mind, as it goes beyond reason.

At the start of his book, Otto went as far as advising that the person who has never had any kind of religious experience should not read any further, as they would not be able to relate to what was being said.

In his exploration of the numinous, Otto identified several characteristics:

- 'Creature-consciousness' – Otto explained how in a numinous experience, people become very aware that they have been created and that they are not independent. He refers to the writing of Schleiermacher, who also wrote about the feeling of absolute dependence on God, and who argued that religious experience should be at the heart of all religion, not doctrines. When people have numinous experiences, they become aware of their own smallness in contrast with the infinite presence of God. Otto writes:

> *All that this new term, 'creature-feeling', can express, is the note of submergence into nothingness before an overpowering, absolute might of some kind.*
>
> Rudolf Otto, *The Idea of the Holy*

- The 'wholly other' – numinous experiences are totally different from anything else, and cannot be mistaken for other kinds of experience. They are also experiences of something that is different from ourselves. Although there are many attempts to describe such experiences, they cannot be completely captured in words. Otto thought that in a numinous experience, people are very aware of being in the presence of something 'Other'; they know that they are encountering an objective reality and not, for example, delving into deep layers of their own psyches.
- The numinous experience, thought Otto, evokes an emotional response that is a mixture of dread and love, or fear and attraction. Many reports of numinous experiences say that the person fell to their knees or to the ground, feeling overwhelmed by terror but unable to tear themselves away. The awareness of the holiness of God produces a deep sense

Key term

numinous: a word coined by Rudolf Otto to refer to the feelings evoked by a non-rational sense of being in the presence of God

Synoptic link

Link to *Chapter 7: Religious language (part one)*. Otto explains that understanding the non-rational aspects of religion raise issues of language, where believers are trying to communicate things that cannot be put into words.

of fear and moral guilt, but also a longing for God on a level that goes beyond expression. The feelings are profound, with the result that a conversion experience is much more radical and long-lasting than a rational decision to have a change of lifestyle.

AO1 activity 8

Many Biblical examples of religious experience show the reactions of Biblical characters when they realise that they are in the presence of God. Otto uses as an example Abraham's reaction, in Genesis 18:27. Look up the following passages, and make a note of how the people in the narratives respond to being in God's presence:

- Genesis 18:27
- Job 40:3–4
- Isaiah 6:5

Examples of numinous experiences

In the *Bhagavad Gita*, the warrior Arjuna sees a vision of the god Krishna in his full divinity. Arjuna's response to this vision and numinous experience is a mixture of fear and astonishment, and an immediate need to worship God:

> The Supreme Lord of all mystic power, the Personality of Godhead, displayed His universal form to Arjuna.
> Arjuna saw in that universal form unlimited mouths, unlimited eyes, unlimited wonderful visions. The form was decorated with many celestial ornaments and bore many divine upraised weapons. He wore celestial garlands and garments, and many divine scents were smeared over His body. All was wondrous, brilliant, unlimited, all-expanding.
>
> If hundreds of thousands of suns were to rise at once into the sky, their radiance might resemble the effulgence of the Supreme Person in that universal form. At that time Arjuna could see in the universal form of the Lord the unlimited expansions of the universe situated in one place although divided into many, many thousands. Then, bewildered and astonished, his hair standing on end, Arjuna bowed his head to offer obeisances and with folded hands began to pray to the Supreme Lord.
>
> *Bhagavad Gita* 11:10–14

Kenneth Grahame's book *The Wind in the Willows*, published in 1908, has a strange chapter in it where Rat and Mole have a numinous experience while out on the river. The chapter is interesting for the way in which Grahame depicts a numinous experience in fiction. It also illustrates the popularity of religious experience as a topic of discussion at the beginning of the twentieth century. In the story, Rat and Mole are out looking for the baby otter Portly who has gone missing, when Rat hears some strange pipe-music (in a sensory religious experience), but all Mole can hear is the wind in the reeds. As they get nearer to the place Rat thinks the music is coming from, Mole too is overcome with a numinous experience:

> 'This is the place of my song-dream, the place the music played to me,' whispered the Rat, as if in a trance. 'Here, in this holy place, here if anywhere, surely we shall find Him!'
>
> Then suddenly the Mole felt a great Awe fall upon him, an awe that turned his muscles to water, bowed his head, and rooted his feet to the ground. It was no panic terror—indeed he felt wonderfully at peace and happy—but it was an awe that smote and held him and, without seeing, he knew it could only mean that some august Presence was very, very near.
>
> Kenneth Grahame, *The Wind in the Willows*

AO1 activity 9

Read the whole of chapter 7 of *The Wind in the Willows*, called 'The Piper at the Gates of Dawn'. How does Grahame convey a sense of the numinous?

Mysterium tremendum

Otto tried to find words to express the awe-inspiring feelings of being in the presence of God in a religious experience. He came up with a cluster of Latin words that he hoped would capture the essence of numinous experience: *mysterium tremendum et fascinans*.

- By *mysterium*, Otto meant to convey the sense of strangeness or otherness of God. Someone having a religious experience knows that they are in the presence of something beyond their comprehension, something that goes beyond the everyday.
- By *tremendum,* Otto wanted to capture the sense of the magnitude of God, and the feeling of being overwhelmed by a presence much greater than oneself.
- By *fascinans*, Otto described the mixture of dread, awe, and fascination felt by the recipient of a numinous experience. They are at the same time terrified and filled with wonder, unable to tear themselves away.

The human predisposition for religious experience

As was fashionable at the time Otto was writing, he turned his attention to the idea that human religious belief and behaviour has evolved from simple origins to the present day. Like many of his contemporaries, Otto argued that early religion started with ideas about what was clean and unclean; with worship of the dead, especially ancestors; with belief in souls, spirits, and magic; and with fairy tale, myth, and totemism. He claimed that human feeling for the numinous is a part of our nature that dates back to the earliest stages of human development. As humanity evolves, so does the human need for numinous experience and for a sense of the divine. Otto illustrates this predisposition by referring, for example, to feelings that a place is eerie or haunted, where we have the vague idea that it may be the place of evil supernatural beings; and in the same way, we may have feelings of 'primal numinous awe' when we have a mental impression of being in a holy place. Otto discusses the 'faculty of divination', or human ability to sense the presence of the supernatural. He argues that the sense of the holy is an '*a priori* category of the mind'. Not everyone experiences this sense, but everyone has the capability of experiencing it, and it can be awakened in anybody.

Synoptic link

Link to *Chapter 4: Challenges to religious belief: religious belief as a product of the human mind*. Otto's ideas about the human disposition for religious experience are similar in many ways to the ideas of Carl Gustav Jung.

Challenges to the objectivity and authenticity of religious experience

Objectivity

The word 'objectivity' is used as a contrast to 'subjectivity'. Something is viewed objectively if it is viewed without any bias, and if the viewer has no personal vested interest in it. In science, objectivity involves trying to look at something with the aim that any scientist looking at the same data might be able to draw the same conclusions. It is an important part of fair testing: at a country show, the judge would not be allowed to enter any of their own cattle into a competition they were judging, because it would cloud their objectivity. Examiners are not allowed to mark the work of their own classes or their own relatives for the same reason. Scientists have to be careful to be objective if they are working on something that could potentially make them a lot of money; drug trials for new medicines, for example, have to be capable of being objectively tested by other scientists with no vested interest before the medicines are released for sale.

Religious experience is very difficult, if not impossible, to consider objectively. People have a view on whether or not God exists. An agnostic view, where someone thinks that God may or may not exist but is not convinced either way, is still a view. This means that when anyone looks at other people's reports of religious experience, they will already have a bias in one direction or another, inclining them to believe it or treat it with scepticism.

Because religious experience is a private, personal experience, some people have claimed that it has no evidential worth at all. It is not available to be tested by anyone other than the person who had the experience. It cannot be replicated. One person may have had a religious experience after reading a passage from the Bible, or going on a pilgrimage, but this is no guarantee that someone else reading the same passage or making the same journey will have the same experience.

Those who have religious experiences are usually completely convinced that what they experienced was real and coming from outside themselves, rather than just their mind playing tricks on them. A conversion experience may change the direction of someone's life completely; a near-death experience, where someone is convinced that they had a glimpse of the afterlife, can change someone's whole attitude to the way they live the remainder of their life and their approach to death. However, the certainty of people that they have experienced something real is a certainty that is only available to them, as individuals. Others cannot see the evidence or recreate the experience for themselves.

A group of philosophers known as logical positivists argue that if a claim cannot be tested, using empirical data (in other words, using any of the five senses) to see whether it is true or false, it has no value as a claim at all. Thinkers such as A.J. Ayer and Antony Flew argue that for a claim to be meaningful, it must be possible to know what kind of test would prove the claim one way or the other. If someone says they saw the Eiffel Tower, we can test this claim by checking that the Eiffel Tower really exists, that the person was in Paris when they said they were, and that their eyesight is good enough. But there is no way of checking someone's claim that they saw an angel or heard the voice of God. If the claim cannot be tested, logical positivists would rule it out as having any meaningful worth.

Religious believers, however, might respond to this challenge by saying that all of our experiences are subjective. Immanuel Kant argued that when we experience something, we interpret it; interpretation is an inseparable part of experience, and it is impossible for us to perceive anything truly objectively. Kant made a distinction between 'phenomena' and 'noumena', where phenomena are things as they appear to observers, and noumena are things 'in themselves' (using the word 'noumena' rather differently to the way Otto used the term 'numinous'). We can experience phenomena, but not noumena. Therefore, even when people are conducting scientific experiments using empirical methods, they are recording their observations as they appear to the scientists, and not the 'things in themselves'.

When we hear music, for example, the vibrations making the notes hit our eardrums, but we interpret these vibrations subjectively. We understand it as music, rather than just sequences of sounds. We interpret it as 'sad music', or 'music that reminds me of last summer', or 'not my kind of music'. Those claims cannot be tested empirically, any more than religious claims can be tested, but they are usually regarded as meaningful statements to make. It can be said to be unfair to treat religious experience as something that can be easily dismissed purely on the grounds of subjectivity, when we give much more respect to other kinds of subjective experience.

People might also respond to the challenge of objectivity by pointing out that many people have reported religious experiences of some kind. Even if the experiences are personal and private, a lot of people have had them, which must give them at least some evidential force. They may not demonstrate the existence of God in a clear and provable way, but they do at least demonstrate that religious experience, as it seems to the individual, is a significant part of being human.

Authenticity

'Authenticity' is the quality of being real, genuine, or true. Religious experiences are sometimes challenged on the grounds that we have no way of knowing whether the claim of an encounter with God is genuine.

Critics object that we can have no way of knowing whether the object of someone's religious experience is actually God, or whether it just seemed like God to that person. The fact that a lot of people report similar experiences does not necessarily mean that those experiences are authentic. A lot of people dream about flying through the air, but the

Synoptic link

Link to *Chapter 7: Religious language (part one)*. Chapter 7 contains a more detailed exploration of the views of the logical positivists.

frequency of this kind of dream does not add authenticity to the claim that human beings can really fly.

How, after all, would anyone recognise God well enough to know for certain that it really was God, given that God is usually believed to be unavailable to sense experience? Challenges to the authenticity of a religious experience consider whether the person is telling the truth: did they really have such an experience at all, or are they making up the whole thing? They also consider whether they have interpreted the experience correctly: was it really an encounter with God, or is it more likely that the person was deluded, ill, or overly influenced by religious beliefs and so interpreted normal emotions in an unwarranted religious way?

Sigmund Freud's challenge to religious experience was a challenge on the basis of authenticity. He argued that sexual urges and repression account for the feelings of a religious experience, rather than God. The person might think that they are experiencing God, but they are mistaken.

When people report religious experiences, the challenge of authenticity may come from non-believers, or may come from within the religious tradition. When Bernadette Soubirous first reported visions of the Virgin Mary at Lourdes, the local priests and religious officials did not believe that her claim was authentic. She was a fourteen-year-old peasant girl, and the authorities thought her an unlikely candidate for an important vision. They only began to take her more seriously when she repeated her claims insistently, and said that Mary had revealed herself as 'the Immaculate Conception', a term unlikely to be familiar to an illiterate young girl.

Natural explanations of religious experience

Sometimes people use religious experience as an inductive argument for the existence of God, saying that if a person believes they have experienced God, the best explanation is that there is a God, who therefore must exist. If many people report religious experiences, this adds weight to the argument that there really is a God who wants and has encounters with humanity, especially if these experiences have common features. Others, however, argue that religious experience is more plausibly explained in naturalistic terms; that is, without any reference to the supernatural.

Claims of religious experience are sometimes rejected on grounds of misunderstanding: someone thinks they have had a religious experience, but in reality, their experience is attributable to other causes. They have misunderstood their own perceptions; they think they saw a bright light that others could not see, but were in fact experiencing visual disturbances through dehydration, perhaps. They think they heard the voice of God, but actually their memories were vividly recreating the voice of their parents, or they were dreaming.

Sometimes, those who read about the religious experiences of people who lived at times when medicine was less well-understood look at the details of reports of religious experience and suggest that there may have been a physical cause. They point out that the experiences of the so-called mystics of the Middle Ages often seem to have occurred when the person had been fasting, held in solitary confinement or had a high fever, so the more reasonable explanation for the experience would be hallucination, with natural causes. Some reports of religious experiences, such as the bright light experienced by Paul on the road to Damascus, could be attributed to conditions such as epilepsy, rather than to a real experience of God. Francis of Assisi was very ill before he had his religious experience, so perhaps he was hallucinating as the result of a fever. Hildegard von Bingen, a German nun and composer from the Middle Ages who experienced visions, may have suffered from migraines. People at the time did not understand illness very well, and may have mistakenly interpreted their mental disturbances as experiences coming from God.

Claims are sometimes rejected on the grounds that they are delusional. The person is not experiencing God but instead has a mental health issue. The voices they think they hear and the strong emotions they feel are a symptom of illness, rather than evidence of anything objective. Sometimes so-called religious experiences are the result of substance abuse, where visual and auditory hallucinations and 'out of body' sensations are caused by drugs or alcohol. Feuerbach, and Freud after him, put forward the view that religious experience is not an experience of any external reality, but instead is an illusion, caused by people 'projecting' their own hopes and unresolved conflicts onto a made-up God, and imagining that the experiences relate to some kind of objective reality, when in fact they are nothing more than symptomatic of psychological illness.

Some argue that the fantastical accounts that some people give of their alleged religious experiences are so contrary to ordinary, everyday experience that they cannot be taken seriously. Although reports of feelings of peace or comfort could be considered believable, some reports may stretch credibility too far. For example, Teresa of Avila claimed that her prayer life was so profound that her body was literally lifted off the ground, and other nuns had to hold her down to prevent her from floating away.

Within the field of medicine, neurophysiologists study the brain and nervous system, and some have turned their attention to what goes on in the brain when someone feels as if they are having a religious experience. One such study took place in the 1980s, led by Michael Persinger, who wanted to know if the sensations of religious experience could be recreated artificially. Using a specially designed helmet that transmitted weak magnetic signals through the brain, Persinger reported that a significant number of volunteers experienced feelings that matched the descriptions of those who claimed to have had religious experiences. This led Persinger to the conclusion that when people report religious experiences, they give accurate reports of their feelings and emotions, but they wrongly attribute these experiences to the existence of God when in fact they are caused by magnetism.

Persinger's challenge to religious experience has been criticised. His scientific method has been questioned: the participants knew in advance what it was expected that they might feel, and this may have encouraged them to confirm what they thought the scientists wanted to hear. Attempts to repeat his experiment have been unsuccessful, leading to inconclusive results, rather than any firm evidence that magnetism induces feelings similar to religious experience. In addition, demonstrating that feelings similar to religious experience can be created artificially does not, in itself, demonstrate that religious experiences always have natural causes and cannot have been caused by God. It is possible, after all, to induce feelings similar to those of flying in an aircraft artificially, using a flight simulator, but this does not demonstrate that real air travel is a fiction.

In their book *Phantoms in the Brain*, V.S. Ramachandran and Sandra Blakeslee also describe experiments carried out on the temporal lobes of the brain which made patients feel a strong sense of divine presence. This sort of experiment has led some critics to argue that religious experience is not, therefore, evidence of a real God, but instead shows that something is happening within the brain, which people misinterpret to be God. Others might answer this challenge by saying that there is no reason why God should not appear to people when they have been taking drugs, or are undergoing experiments, or have been fasting. Also, even if the artificially created 'religious experiences' are not caused by God, this does not demonstrate that no religious experience can have come from God.

Swinburne's defence of religious experience

Richard Swinburne argues that religious experience should be taken seriously, and can be taken as evidence for the existence of God. In his 1979 book, *Is there a God?*, he puts forward the argument that religious experience should be given the same kind of treatment as other, non-religious forms of experience. If we think we heard our phone ringing, then it probably did ring. We could have been mistaken; it might have been a phone on the television, or the phone of someone walking past, but usually we can and should trust the evidence of our senses. We would not be able to get through life if we constantly doubt what we think our senses are telling us. Swinburne thought that if we have religious experiences, we should treat them in the same way as we treat other, more ordinary sense experiences. We should not dismiss them as nonsense straight away. No one has proved beyond doubt that there is no God; and if there is a God, then it is likely that God would want to communicate with people.

Swinburne proposes that people should use two principles when they are considering religious experience: the **principle of credulity**, and the **principle of testimony**.

1. The principle of credulity: this principle says that we should believe the evidence of our senses, unless we have good reason to think we might be mistaken. Experience is normally reliable. We know that sometimes our senses deceive us and we make mistakes, but usually

Key terms

principle of credulity: the principle that we should, in general, believe the evidence of our senses

principle of testimony: the principle that we should, in general, believe what other people tell us we should trust them. In a religious experience, if it seems to us that we are experiencing God, then we should trust that experience as genuinely coming from God, unless we have a good reason to think we could be wrong, for example if we had taken drugs that are known to cause hallucinations. It is not unreasonable to think that God will want relationships with humanity, so the experience should not be dismissed.

2. The principle of testimony: the second principle relates to other people's reports of religious experience. Swinburne argues that if other people tell us of their religious experiences, we should be prepared to believe that they genuinely experienced God. Of course, they may be lying, mistaken, or joking, but if they are usually trustworthy people, and under other circumstances we believe what they say, we should be prepared to believe that their experiences did genuinely come from God.

Swinburne argues that if someone has an experience that appears to be an experience of God, then the probability is that they really did experience God, and that there really is a God. We should only doubt them if there is a strong probability that God does not exist, and there is no such strong probability.

> **AO1 activity 11**
> Explain in your own words what Swinburne meant by his principles of credulity and testimony.

Caroline Franks Davis' exploration of challenges to the authenticity of religious experience

The Canadian scholar Caroline Franks Davis studied under the supervision of Swinburne, and decided to explore further the question of the extent to which religious experience should be taken seriously. In her 1989 book, *The Evidential Force of Religious Experience*, she looks in detail at the questions of whether religious experience can be counted as evidence for God's existence, and under what circumstances people who report religious experiences should be believed.

In order to explore these questions, Franks Davis looks at how we normally react when others tell us of their experiences. She largely agrees with Swinburne, saying:

> *In both the religious and the secular spheres, we should consider a person's auto-description more probably than not to be sincere and accurate description of the experience, as it seemed to them at the time, unless there are grounds for suspicion.*
>
> Caroline Franks Davis, *The Evidential Force of Religious Experience*

She argues that when the reports are not about anything religious, we usually believe people, unless we have good grounds not to take what they say at face value. There are circumstances, however, when we should doubt what people are telling us; she looks at what those circumstances might be, and how they could relate to religious experience.

Franks Davis identifies three kinds of challenges that we might reasonably make when someone reports an experience: description-related challenges, subject-related challenges, and object-related challenges. She then looks to see if those challenges undermine the authenticity of reports of religious experiences.

Description-related challenges

Description-related challenges are challenges we might make to the content of whatever it is that someone has told us. There is something in their description of events that does not add up, making us less inclined to believe them. For example, if there are obvious logical inconsistences in the report, we would not accept it straight away. Franks Davis gives the example of someone claiming to have seen a square circle. We would want to ask questions to see if the person could explain away the inconsistency, for example, to see if they were speaking metaphorically.

Another example of a description-related challenge is when the report does not fit with things we already know. Franks Davis gives the example of someone claiming to have seen a dodo. As we already know that dodos are extinct, we have good reason to doubt their claims, and we would be acting reasonably if we thought that it must have been a dodo-like creature but not actually a dodo, or that the person was joking or telling lies. We might also reasonably doubt an account if a person's behaviour is not consistent with what they tell us they experienced, for example if they said they could see a cobra in the corner of the room but did not seem worried or frightened by this. When looking at religious experiences, people need to ask themselves whether the story makes sense. Is the story consistent? Does it contradict other things we already know?

Franks Davis looks at description-related challenges in relation to religious experience. She argues that religious experiences do not normally need to be doubted on these grounds. It is not often that reports of religious experience are logically inconsistent. Sometimes, however, we should doubt the content of the reports, for example if somebody claimed to have heard the voice of God telling them to do something evil and cruel, and it was something that they wanted to do anyway. This would conflict with what people already understand about God, and so this kind of report should be rejected. We would also have reason to doubt the report if it seemed to be highly interpreted rather than just presented at face value. For example, if someone said they experienced the Trinity as Father, Son, and Holy Spirit, or if they said that they experienced the suffering of Jesus in the Garden of Gethsemane, then this might suggest that they had read a lot into their experience, based on their knowledge of Christianity, and they were not giving a plain version of the experience, but had embellished it.

Subject-related challenges

Subject-related challenges are challenges we might make about the person giving the report (the 'subject'). For example, we might challenge a report that someone had seen some red roses if we know that the person is colour blind; or we might challenge a report that they had seen a celebrity in the distance if we know that their eyesight is weak and they never

> **Key terms**
>
> **description-related challenges:** challenges to reports of experience based on the idea that the account (description) of the experience is illogical or implausible
>
> **subject-related challenges:** challenges to reports of experience based on the idea that the person who said they had the experience (the subject) is unreliable

recognise anyone until they are close by. Another example of a subject-related challenge is if the report is given by someone who does not have the training or education to know what they are talking about. Franks Davis gives the example of someone reporting to recognise a voice on the telephone, which we would reasonably doubt if they had never before heard that person speak. When looking at religious experience, we should ask if the person giving the report is reliable and likely to have accurate perceptions of whatever they say they experienced.

In the category of subject-related challenges, Franks Davis also raises the issue of when a large number of people claim to have perceived something but give conflicting accounts of it. This casts doubt on all of the accounts, even though some of the people may be right and others might have misperceived or have poor memories. Franks Davis gives the examples of where there are many witnesses to an accident with all saying different things about what happened, different accounts of an argument, or different descriptions of a city. If a corporate religious experience has many conflicting reports, it would have to be considered as generally unreliable.

The most common subject-related challenge is that there were some other factors involved, relating to the subject, which could make their report of the experience unreliable as a source of knowledge. If they were asleep or under hypnosis, this could affect their ability to perceive accurately. If they were under the influence of alcohol or other drugs, it would be reasonable to doubt that their perceptions were accurate, as it would be if they were suffering from an illness such as a high fever or dementia, or if they had some kind of damage to their eyes or ears. We might doubt their experience was really from God if it coincided with a time of fasting or with an epileptic episode, or even if they were extremely tired. It would be reasonable to doubt their reports if they were gullible or suggestible characters.

Franks Davis says that this is the challenge most often cited by 'reductionists', in other words those who claim that religion is 'no more than' superstition, or 'no more than' psychological illusion. She summarises a reductionist approach as one which claims that in the modern world, science can explain religious experience away. These challenges attempt to explain reports of religious experience in terms of mental illness, sexual frustration, psychological immaturity, or physiological factors such as migraine. Her own assessment is that such challenges are unlikely to succeed on their own; if they are to work, the people making the challenge also need to show that it is highly improbable that God exists. Some reports of religious experience may be best explained as no more than illusions, but this does not mean that they are all best explained in this way.

Object-related challenges

The third kind of challenge that Franks Davis identifies is the **object-related challenge**. In other words, whatever it is that is meant to have been perceived is called into question. When looking at religious experience, we need to ask if the thing people said they experienced is likely or unlikely to exist.

> **Key term**
>
> **object-related challenge:** challenges to reports of experience on the basis that the thing that was allegedly experienced (the object) is beyond credibility, does not exist, or cannot have been present

It could be that it is impossible for the object of the experience to exist, for example, or it could be improbable that the object was present at the time of the experience. If I claimed to have seen Henry VIII this morning walking around the market buying vegetables, you would doubt my report, not because my description of Henry VIII was logically inconsistent, or because you suspected that I had been drinking alcohol beforehand, but primarily because Henry VIII has been dead for some time. You would assume I had mistaken someone in costume for the real king, perhaps, but you would be unlikely to accept my claim at face value. To give another example, if someone claimed to have been hit by a snowball, but they were outdoors in Dubai at the time in the middle of summer, there would be reasonable grounds to doubt their report because it does not snow in Dubai.

In the case of religious experience, people challenge reports on the grounds that they think it is highly improbable that God exists. They reject the idea that someone has had an encounter with God, in the same way that they would reject a report of an encounter with a unicorn or a leprechaun. For this challenge to be successful, that challenger needs to be able to demonstrate that God does not exist, and Franks Davis argues that the non-existence of God cannot be successfully demonstrated.

AO1 activity 12

Test your understanding of Franks Davis' list of challenges by thinking of your own examples. For example:

- Description-related challenges: A claim can be reasonably challenged if the description is incoherent, *for example a claim to have seen a pure white rainbow.*

- Subject-related challenges: A claim can be reasonably challenged if the person giving the report is unreliable, *for example …*
- Object-related challenges: A claim can be reasonably challenged if the thing people said they experienced is beyond credibility, *for example …*

Caroline Franks Davis' conclusions

In her book, having explored a wide range of challenges to religious experience, Franks Davis concludes that although some reports of religious experience may be doubtful, on balance the challenges against it fail. There are clearly some reports of alleged religious experience where mental illness, misperception, or suggestibility have played a part, and these should be treated with scepticism. However, there have been a great many people whose religious experiences have had profound and positive effects on them, and these experiences should not be dismissed solely on the grounds that the person hearing about them does not believe in God.

Other responses to challenges to religious experience

Religious experiences do not present overwhelming evidence for the existence of God, but many believe they do provide substantial evidence that human beings have a 'true self' which is related to the divine, and that there is a holy power beyond this world.

Individual experience could be valid, even if not verifiable

Some people challenge religious experience on the grounds that it is difficult, if not impossible, to test whether someone who reports it is telling the truth. We have no way to verify what they are saying – there can be no independent witnesses to an inner experience, and it cannot be reproduced. Some thinkers, such as logical positivists, argue that if a claim cannot be tested using the five senses, it can be dismissed as meaningless.

Franks Davis argues, however, that religious belief is not the kind of thing that can be proved true or false with testing, yet it is still meaningful. In ordinary, secular life, we have many subjective experiences that we cannot verify, but they are still valid because of their importance to us. We make all kinds of decisions based on internal intuitions and emotions, even though these internal feelings cannot be verified. We might buy a house because it just feels right, or marry someone because we know they are the right person for us to spend the rest of our lives with; and these subjective feelings cannot be tested and verified, or repeated by others, but are nevertheless important.

Franks Davis argues that occasionally but significantly, intuitions that appear to give us knowledge can later be shown to be correct intuitions. She uses the example of the scientist August Kekule, who was struggling to understand the structure of carbon atoms in benzene. He fell asleep in front of the fire, and began to dream of atoms whirling around like snakes. One of the snakes caught its tail in its mouth, and Kekule woke up with the insight that the six carbon atoms in benzene form a circular chain. The example shows that intuition is not confined to religion, but is a part of our psychology that can subconsciously find short-cuts to solutions; we should not dismiss intuitions about God just because they are intuitions. Scientists and historians have intuitions too, which surprisingly often can lead to significant new knowledge.

William James argues that although religious experience cannot be tested in the sense that people cannot reproduce someone else's experience under controlled conditions, it is still possible to judge whether or not a religious experience is valid. James was a philosophical pragmatist, which means that he believed the truth of something could be found in its practical results. If the behaviour of the person, after the experience, is consistent with what we would expect if God really does exist, then this adds weight to the validity of the experience. If the experience gives long-lasting and positive results, then the experience is valid. James gives examples of people who gave up drinking alcohol or who stopped smoking after their religious experience, or who devoted their lives to helping other people after their religious experience, and for James, this provided supporting evidence for its genuineness.

The Bible, too, suggests that religious belief can be demonstrated by its outcomes. In Paul's letter to the Galatians, Paul contrasts the kinds of immoral behaviour people might have indulged in before experiencing the Holy Spirit, and then lists the 'fruits of the Spirit'. Those who have had religious experiences of the Holy Spirit will have lasting effects in their lives:

> *But the fruit of the Spirit is love, joy, peace, forbearance, kindness,*
> *goodness, faithfulness, gentleness and self-control.*
>
> Galatians 5:22–23, *Holy Bible (NIV)*

This could be considered a kind of 'test' of religious experience; the qualities are not the kind that could be tested empirically by scientists, but their presence in people's characters and outlooks could be taken as evidence that an individual experience is valid, even if not verifiable.

Another response to the challenge that religious experience cannot be tested would be to question the assumptions behind the challenge. We do not have to accept the rule that for something to be valid or meaningful, it must be capable of being tested. It might be a rule that works for science, but not everything has to be considered scientifically; there are other ways of gaining meaning and understanding of the world as well. Rather than trying to find ways in which, up to a point, religious experience might be testable, religious believers could reject the idea that it needs to be open to empirical testing at all. Schleiermacher argued that religious experience is 'self-authenticating'. It does not require any extra, empirical evidence to back it up.

Claims could be genuine

Franks Davis agrees with Swinburne's principles of credulity and testimony, saying that we should trust other people's integrity and believe that they are giving accurate accounts of what happened, as it appeared to them at the time, unless we have good grounds for disbelieving them. It is impractical to mistrust others as a default position. We should be prepared to accept that others are telling the truth, or at least could be telling the truth. The person who reports religious experience should be considered 'innocent until proven guilty'. Franks Davis does, however, note that the existence of God is not some kind of trivial matter where we should be happy to take someone else's word for it without any further investigation at all.

One-off experiences could still be valid even if never repeated

Some people have a single religious experience that affects them profoundly. They might try to recreate that experience, through prayer and study and going to places of worship, but never again experience the close encounter with God that they once felt. This does not invalidate the one-off experience. In science, experiments should be repeatable so that others can test them and see the results, but in other areas of life, this does not happen and is impractical. We have lots of non-religious experiences that evoke strong emotions and are unrepeatable, and yet are still valid: it is impossible to repeat seeing Venice for the first time, or having your last day at secondary school, or discovering a new taste, but these experiences and the emotions that go with them are not made less important or even meaningless just because they are not repeatable. In the same way, a religious experience that happens only once can still be valid. Religious experiences are not the same as physical objects, and should not be expected to conform to some kind of standard in order to make them testable by science. Science should recognise its own limitations.

AO1 activity 13

Make a list to summarise the different responses people have given to challenges to the validity of religious experience.

This section of the chapter will enhance your ability to **analyse** and **evaluate** the topic and help you develop your AO2 skills. For each question, think about the different positions you might take, and decide which you find most persuasive and why. It is not enough to memorise a list of 'for and against' points; you need to develop an argument.

How far do religious experiences have an impact upon religious belief and practice?

The question of the extent to which religious experiences have an impact on religious belief and practice depends on how religious experience is defined. If religious experience is considered in its wider sense, including experiences such as attending a service of worship or regular daily prayer, then religious experience has a great deal of impact on belief and practice. However, if religious experience is taken to mean rare and dramatic occurrences, then the impact could be considered to be less.

The view that religious experiences have a major impact upon religious belief and practice

The answer depends on how religious experience is to be defined. If religious experience is seen to include things like daily prayer, services of worship, and doing things for religious reasons such as avoiding some kinds of foods, then religious experience will have a great deal of impact on religious belief and practice, because they are the same thing. If people believe that they are guided by God in everything they do and are surrounded by their faith in God, then all of their practices will be, in a sense, religious.

Even if we consider a religious experience to be a unique and rare event, it is still something that has had a major impact on religious belief and practice. Religious beliefs and practices are often started because of someone's reported religious experience. Founders of religious movements recount conversion experiences or revelations from God or enlightenment to the truth, telling them that the established religion around them is going in the wrong direction, and commissioning them to begin a new faith group. William Booth's religious experiences and personal convictions led him away from the Methodist Church and into the foundation of the Salvation Army. Guru Nanak's religious experiences led him to reject some of the teachings of Hinduism and Islam, and inspired him to begin the Sikh religion. The experiences therefore have a profound effect because the whole belief system, with its practices, would not exist without the experience of the founder.

Religious experience is often cited in sacred texts, when there are stories of God speaking to prophets, or the witnessing of miracles, or accounts of dramatic conversion. Sacred texts form the basis of some religious traditions, and are studied often and used as a model. The sacred texts themselves are often said to have originated from religious experience, where the writer of the text did not use their own words but instead wrote the words that were given or revealed in the religious experience.

People who have dramatic religious experiences are held up as examples for religious believers to follow. Prophets, saints, gurus, and martyrs are people who claim that they have received some kind of direct revelation from God. These people are highly respected within religious traditions; their stories are told to inspire children, and their lives are presented as goals to emulate.

The view that religious experiences have a minor impact upon religious belief and practice

If religious experience is understood in the narrower sense of referring to unusual and dramatic events, then it may not have so much impact on people's ordinary everyday lives. Religious experiences have little effect on the daily rituals and practices that believers follow.

Not everyone who is religious has a dramatic experience of God. Some people who have been brought up in a religious tradition, or who find themselves drawn to its teachings in adult life and sincerely want to deepen their own faith, never have the kind of overwhelming religious experience that others describe, even though they may desperately want one. They find it quite possible to continue with religious beliefs and practices even without a clearly defined religious experience, demonstrating that unusual and powerful religious experiences are not essential for faith.

Some religious experiences have more impact on beliefs and practices than others. There are some reported religious experiences that many people, including religious believers, treat with scepticism, such as alleged experiences where someone claims that they have been called by God to be a leader and then they ask people to give them money, or alleged experiences where the subject of the experience clearly has mental health problems, or claims that God told them to harm others. Reports of religious experiences are not always trusted, even by religious believers; instead, followers of a faith are likely to investigate a report to see whether or not it fits with the beliefs they already hold. They are likely to reject reports that contradict their belief system as being illusions or fictions. In this way, it could be argued that religious experiences have an impact when they confirm faith and teachings, but have much less impact, if any, when they contradict central elements of an established faith.

Many religious practices perform a function of holding the community together and giving people shared, common goals. The practices do not have to initiate religious experiences in order to be worth having, and people will join in with corporate religious practices for the social benefits, whether or not they induce religious experience. Religious practices and beliefs can be more about reinforcing a shared morality than about religious experience. Doing things together such as celebrating festivals and rites of passage helps a community to be cohesive, which increases people's desire to behave in a way that everyone else finds acceptable.

AO2 activity 1

To what extent does religious experience have an impact on religious belief and practice, in your view? Write two or three paragraphs to support your opinion, giving examples where appropriate.

Can different types of religious experience be accepted as equally valid in communicating religious teachings and beliefs?

One of the recurring questions in discussions of religious experience is whether or not it is possible to distinguish between an experience that genuinely comes from God, and an experience that could have other, natural, causes. Some mental health conditions can cause visual or auditory hallucinations, such as schizophrenia, dementia, and psychoses related to substance abuse. Some conditions, such as epilepsy and migraine, can cause sensations such as seeing bright flashing lights. It is difficult, and perhaps impossible, to know for certain whether a report of religious experience should be understood as a genuine and valid encounter with God, teaching important truths, or whether a natural explanation should be found. It could be argued that some types of religious experience are generally more valid than others. Perhaps experiences of feeling surrounded by the love of God could be seen as more likely to be valid than dramatic visions of God on a throne with angels, as everyone experiences feelings of love, whereas few of us see angels.

The view that some types of religious experience are more valid than others

Caroline Franks Davis argues that some types of religious experience could be less reliable than others and are therefore less likely to be valid. Dreams, 'hunches,' and 'intuitions' are, she says, not considered to be solidly reliable sources of knowledge in everyday, secular life. Although sometimes a person will have a dream which is later borne out by the facts, this is rare. Intuitions can sometimes be proved to be correct, and sometimes not. If this source of knowledge is not always reliable in secular life, the chances are that it will also be unreliable in a religious context.

It could be argued that religious experiences that fit well with established religious teaching are more likely to be valid. For example, if someone has a religious experience in which they see a vision of Jesus and believe themselves to be saved from sin as a result, this fits well with the Christian message that Jesus saves people from sin. On the other hand, it could be argued that these experiences are less likely to be valid, as the person having the experience has a prior knowledge of what such experiences 'ought' to be like, and may interpret their feelings in accordance with an existing framework, rather than understanding them for what they really are. By this reasoning, the most valid types of religious experience would be the most unusual, as they are least likely to have been copied from others.

It could be argued that the most common types of religious experience (such as conversion) are the most valid, simply because they have more data to support them, in terms of the quantity and similarity of reports, and the evidence of long-lasting effects. This could make them seem more valid than, for example, mystical experiences, which vary more. However, it could also be argued that people know what to expect of a conversion experience, and so interpret their experiences in accordance with their previously held understanding, rather than taking them at face value.

Individual, private religious experiences could be considered to be more valid than corporate experiences, as there is no crowd or peer pressure on the individual at the time of the experience. On the other hand, corporate religious experiences could be considered more valid than individual ones as there are, to some degree, witnesses to corroborate what happened.

The view that it is the 'fruits' (outcome) rather than the type of religious experience that makes it valid

It could be argued that a religious experience should be judged by its 'fruits' or its outcome, rather than by the way in which it happened. It does not matter whether the subject heard a voice or saw a vision, had a dream, or had an emotional sense of the numinous. The important criterion is whether or not the experience had a long-lasting and positive effect. This is the point of view put forward by William James. Religious experience can be considered valid if it produces positive effects. If the subject behaves in a way that is consistent with what we would expect if they had genuinely had the experience they describe, then we can consider the experience to be valid.

On the other hand, some people argue that the effects of an alleged religious experience have no bearing on its validity. The sincerity of someone's belief in something does not necessarily make it true, as many people have sincerely believed many false things. Bertrand Russell gave the example of a child's belief in Father Christmas. The child's behaviour may be much improved by the belief that Father Christmas brings presents to good children on Christmas Eve, but the improvement in the behaviour of the child, even if it has lasting effects, has no bearing on the existence or non-existence of Father Christmas.

The view that it is the trustworthiness of the subject, rather than the type of experience, that makes it valid

Some might argue that the main criterion for judging the validity of religious experience should be whether or not the person giving the report is generally reliable and trustworthy. If someone is known to be an attention seeker, and in everyday life often makes claims that are later shown to be untrue, their claim to having had a vision of God is also less likely to be valid. If, however, someone whose opinion we respect and who has a reputation for integrity reports a religious experience, we are likely at least to accept that the report is a valid account of the experience as it seemed to them, even if we do not accept that it is likely to have come from God. Others might argue that anyone can have an experience of God, whether they are a person of integrity or any other kind of person; it is up to God when and to whom religious experience can happen.

The view that it is the way the experience is interpreted, rather than the type of experience, that makes it valid

It could be argued that the main criterion by which an experience should be judged is the way it appears to the subject. If two people have identical inner experiences, and one of them believes they have had a religious experience while the other believes they might have a neurological disorder, then the experience is valid as a religious experience for the first person, but not for the second. Perhaps the existence of God could be 'true' for some people, but not for others. Perhaps interpreting the experience as a religious experience can be valid and true for one person, but not for another.

Those who understand religious belief in terms of a subjective framework for understanding the world, rather than relating to any objective truth, might argue that a religious experience does not have intrinsic validity or invalidity, but instead has value within a belief system. It makes sense and is valid for those who operate with a religious way of understanding things, and does not make sense and is not valid for those who do not operate in that way. Religious believers might disagree with this way of looking at faith, and argue that God is true whether people are theists or not; God is more than just a way of describing an attitude towards life.

> ### Synoptic link
>
> Link to *Chapter 8: Religious language (part two)*. This chapter considers religious language and ideas about language games, as understood in the thinking of Wittgenstein. Religious experience could be seen as valid within one kind of community, and invalid within another.

The view that no type of religious experience is valid

Many people argue that religious experience cannot be ranked according to which types are more valid than others, because none of them are valid. People such as Freud, Dawkins, Dennett, and other atheists would argue that there are naturalistic explanations for religious experience, which demonstrate it does not come from God. Those who believe that they have experienced God are mistaken or deluded. Religious believers would argue in response that it is unreasonable to dismiss all religious experience as false, from the outset; atheists have made up their minds about the verdict before they have considered any evidence.

AO2 activity 2

a) How far, if at all, do you agree with Swinburne's principles of credulity and testimony (pages 197–198)? Do you think people should be prepared to believe religious experience to the same extent that they believe other forms of experience? Write one or two paragraphs either supporting or challenging Swinburne's views.

b) In your view, are some forms of religious experience more valid than others? For example, do you think that a dramatic religious experience is more likely to be valid than a gradual one? Give reasons to support your answer.

c) 'A religious experience is valid if the subject interprets it as being religious.' How far, if at all, do you agree with this claim? What arguments might be offered for and against it?

To what extent are James' four characteristics adequate in defining mystical experience?

James gave four characteristics that he felt to be typical of mystical experience. This question invites consideration of whether these four characteristics provide a good definition of mystical experience, or whether perhaps James could have found a better way to describe it.

The view that James' characteristics are inadequate in defining mystical experience

It could be argued that James' four characteristics are inadequate in defining mystical experience. Although they capture some of the elements of a mystical experience, the characteristics he chooses as defining may be seen as too broad. For a definition to work well, it should lead the reader to the identification of one specific thing, but James' characteristics cover such a wide range of experience that they would work equally well as descriptors of other, non-religious emotional experiences, such as the experience of giving birth. Caroline Franks Davis notes that the term 'ineffable' could be used to describe many kinds of experience; we cannot put into words the taste of an orange, for example. A tighter set of descriptors would work better than James' characteristics, to capture the essentially religious nature of mystical experience, and to distinguish it more clearly from other kinds of experience.

James' characteristics do not describe all kinds of mystical experience. For example, in his book, James cites a religious experience in which the subject talks about living constantly in the presence of God:

> *God surrounds me like the physical atmosphere. He is closer to me than my own breath. In him literally I live and move and have my being.* "
>
> William James, *The Varieties of Religious Experience*

The descriptor 'transient' does not match the kind of religious experience in which someone feels that their whole life is an encounter with God.

James' characteristics do not include the ideas of ecstasy and unitive experience that others have identified as being central characteristics of mystical experience. He also concentrates on how a religious experience feels to the subject, without commenting on what it is that is being experienced; some would say that he is missing the point of what makes a religious experience explicitly 'religious', rather than just 'an experience', by failing to mention God or ultimate truth. He also does not raise the possibility that for a religious experience to be 'religious', it is important that the subject identifies it as such.

James defined mystical experience more than a hundred years ago, and there have been many other reports of mystical experience since. Our definitions should be open to being updated in the light of new understanding of religious experience and of a wide range of belief systems; we should not consider the definition to be fixed and set in stone for ever.

The view that James' characteristics are adequate in defining mystical experience

It could be argued that James' four characteristics successfully capture the essence of what it is to have a religious experience. He identifies the main characteristics described by all different kinds of people, from a range of types of religious experience, showing their common elements. At the same time, his book illustrates ways in which religious experiences differ. James therefore succeeds in distilling the core elements of religious experience without over-simplifying.

His characteristics are chosen as the result of a scientific-style method. James collects data in the form of anecdotal evidence in the subjects' own words, and uses this data to draw his conclusions, rather than simply imposing his own interpretation of how a religious experience might feel. His definitions are based on observation, rather than just detailing his own views.

James' four characteristics work successfully in different faith contexts. James does not assume that the only kind of genuine religious experience has to be a Christian experience. By avoiding describing the object of the experience and calling it 'God' or 'Truth' or similar, James leaves open the possibility of mystical experience occurring in different world religions, or for people who do not identify with any particular religious tradition.

James successfully provides a foundation from which other scholars have developed their views. His characteristics help to initiate discussion of the nature of mystical experience, and also help in distinguishing a genuine religious experience from an episode of mental illness or hallucination.

> **AO2 activity 3**
>
> On balance, how helpful do you find James' characteristics in defining mystical experience? Give reasons to support your answer.

To what extent does Otto present an adequate definition of the 'numinous'?

Otto coined the term 'numinous' to describe an overwhelming religious experience, and wrote about it in terms of '*mysterium tremendum et fascinans*'. This question asks for a consideration of whether this description is successful in conveying the nature of religious experience.

The view that Otto does not present an adequate definition of the 'numinous'

Some could argue that Otto's definition of the numinous does not say enough about the nature of God, beyond a sense of awareness of something 'other'. This might be adequate at explaining the feelings associated with religious experience, but it is inadequate as an explanation of the object of the experience. The definition could equally be applied to experiencing something ominous and evil. With such a vague description of what this something 'other' might be, it could be difficult for anyone who has had a similar experience to know whether they were experiencing God or something different.

Otto concentrates on the feelings of someone having a numinous experience, rather than on any external reality that might be the object of these experiences. This emphasis on the inner emotions could appear to reduce religious experience to feelings or sensations which could have other causes, such as the weak magnetism Persinger used in his experiments. Otto does not define the numinous itself, only the feelings someone might have when encountering it.

Otto defines one particular kind of religious experience, but does not adequately address other kinds. For example, he does not include the sort of religious experience in which someone comes to a gradual understanding of the existence of God, or where people change their beliefs on the basis of the evidence presented to them rather than because of an overwhelming feeling. The writer C.S. Lewis, who wrote the Chronicles of Narnia series, described in his 1955 autobiography his own conversion experience in Oxford, where after many years and conversations, he finally and reluctantly admitted the existence of God:

> *You must picture me alone in that room at Magdalen, night after night, feeling, whenever my mind lifted even for a second from my work, the steady, unrelenting approach of Him whom I so earnestly desired not to meet … In the Trinity Term of 1929 I gave in, and admitted that God was God, and knelt and prayed: perhaps, that night, the most dejected and reluctant convert in all England.*
>
> C.S. Lewis, *Surprised by Joy*

This kind of experience seems to be at odds with Otto's description, which concentrates solely on the 'numinous', and does not seem to take other kinds of religious experience as being quite so important.

Otto himself admits that his writings will not make sense to people who have not had a numinous experience.

The view that Otto presents an adequate definition of the 'numinous'

Otto is successful in presenting a definition that is compatible with many religions, rather than just Christianity. His definition may not match the experiences described by Buddhists in their practice of meditation, but otherwise he leaves open the description of God or ultimate truth, and does not confine it to the God of Christianity.

In choosing a cluster of words rather than a single descriptor, Otto's '*mysterium tremendum et fascinans*' is both successful in capturing the feelings associated with a numinous experience, and successful in giving some idea of the object of the experience. Unlike James, who concentrates solely on the feelings of the subject, Otto treads a fine line by suggesting the nature of what is being experienced while retaining the sense of ineffability.

Otto's description of the numinous matches descriptions given by people who have had such experiences. His use of examples in his book *The Idea of the Holy* helps to support his definition by exemplifying it, while being careful to avoid pinning God down in a way that would make God seem too small. In accepting that human language is inadequate to define numinous experience, Otto helps to avoid misunderstanding.

> **AO2 activity 4**
> If you were to give Otto's definition of numinous experience a star rating out of five, how many stars would you give it? Write a few sentences to explain why you gave it the rating you chose.

To what extent can the challenges to religious experience be considered valid?

This question asks for an evaluation of the challenges critics have made to religious experience. Some have considered it to be meaningless, or to be attributable to natural causes rather than to God. How successful are these challenges?

The view that the challenges to religious experience cannot be tested and are therefore meaningless

The logical positivists and Antony Flew put forward the view that it has to be possible to verify or falsify claims in order for them to be meaningful. In other words, we have to know what tests we could apply, and what evidence would show them to be true or false. 'The Post Office is closed on Wednesdays' is the kind of statement that is meaningful, because we know that we could test it by going to the Post office on a Wednesday to see if it is open, or we could look up its opening and closing times; the claim might be true, or it might be false, but the important thing is that we know what we would need to do in order to find out. Religious experience, however, does not give us the same opportunities for testing. All we can do if someone reports a religious experience is to decide whether or not to believe them, but we have no way of administering any kind of test. Even if we have religious experiences ourselves, we cannot test whether or not they are from God, or whether perhaps we are ill or imagining things. The report or the experience is unverifiable and unfalsifiable: we do not know what tests we could apply to establish its truth.

> **Synoptic link**
> Link to *Chapters 7 and 8: Religious language*. These chapters include a fuller discussion of Logical Positivism in the context of religious language.

Some argue that this inability to be tested makes religious experience meaningless. It is not worth discussing, and similarly questions about life after death, or whether there is a God, are also meaningless. For some, talking about religious experience is like arguing with a child about an imaginary friend's likes and dislikes. It is impossible to get anywhere significant or reach any worthwhile conclusions, and so this challenge is valid.

Others, however, have different views. Some argue that religious experience is capable of being tested. Paul's letter to the Galatians talks about the 'fruits of the Spirit' as qualities we should expect to see if someone is genuinely led by God. Teresa of Avila distinguished between authentic and inauthentic visions by the feelings of peace that an authentic experience gives. William James argued that a religious experience can be tested by its long-lasting, positive effects, in the same way that we can test whether a medicine works. Those who argue that religious experience can be tested would argue that this challenge is not valid.

There are also those who argue that religious experience does not need to be testable. Schleiermacher said that religious experience is 'self-authenticating'. For many religious believers, once they have had a powerful religious experience, they are convinced of the existence of God. The experience is enough on its own to convince them, and they do not feel they have to go on and look for further supporting evidence. Swinburne argued, with his *Principles of Credulity and Testimony*, that it is impractical and unnecessary to be sceptical of sense perceptions and of the reports of others. We should not feel the need to test everything but should be prepared to take things at face value, as they seem to us. In everyday life, if we meet a person face-to-face and communicate with them, we do not then feel the need to investigate further to discover whether the person really exists or whether we really did meet them. We just trust our senses, and we should do the same if we feel we have encountered God. This point of view disputes the validity of this challenge by saying that religious experience is meaningful without being capable of being tested.

The view that the challenges to religious experience are better explained naturalistically than with reference to God

Those who think this challenge is valid argue that a natural explanation is always going to be more likely than a supernatural one. Visions, voices, and misunderstandings occur in some mental illness, and this should always be a concern if someone reports a religious experience. Conditions such as migraine and epilepsy can account for some historical reports of religious experience. Often the report says that the subject fell down or saw a bright light, and these characteristics would be consistent with some neurological disorders. So-called religious experiences can also be people simply telling lies or exaggerating for attention. These explanations are always more likely to be true than explanations involving supernatural beings.

Others, however, argue that atheists are ignoring the evidence without being prepared for a moment to take it seriously, and that people who report experiences should be trusted. They were the ones who were there at the time, not the sceptics.

AO2 activity 5

Do you think that religious experience needs to be capable of being tested in order to be considered meaningful? Give reasons to support your answer.

Evelyn Underhill, in her 1911 book *Mysticism*, writes:

> *We have the strangely named rationalists, who feel that they have settled the matter once for all by calling attention to the obvious parallels which exist between the bodily symptoms of acute spiritual stress and the bodily symptoms of certain forms of disease … Yet it may well be doubted whether that flame of living love which could, for one dazzling instant, weld body and soul in one, was really a point of weakness in a saint: whether Blake was quite as mad as some of his interpreters, or the powers of St Paul and St Teresa are fully explained on a basis of epilepsy or hysteria: whether, finally, it is as scientific as it looks to lump together all visions and voices – from Wandering Willy to the Apocalypse of St John – as examples of unhealthy cerebral activity.*
>
> Evelyn Underhill, *Mysticism*

In other words, Underhill is arguing that it is not at all reasonable to treat all reports of religious experience the same way. 'Wandering Willy', an old-fashioned name for the kind of homeless person who might suffer from hallucinations and wander around making strange claims, should not be put in the same category as those whose religious experiences have inspired and motivated generations. Science, when done properly, should be open to the suggestion that its conclusions could be wrong. Dismissing religious experience in favour of naturalistic explanations simply because they are religious is not good science.

> **AO2 activity 6**
> Do you think that naturalistic explanations for religious experience are better than supernatural ones? Give reasons to support your answer.

How persuasive are Franks Davis' different challenges?

Caroline Franks Davis suggests three categories of challenges to reports of all kinds of experience, which might make people doubt that the reports are accurate or relate to anything real. This question asks for an assessment of whether the different challenges are successful in undermining the idea that religious experience comes from God.

The persuasiveness of description-related challenges

Description-related challenges could be seen as persuasive in relation to religious experience. People describe what they experienced in terms that are sometimes contradictory, or inconsistent with other beliefs, or over-interpreted in order to conform to previously-held beliefs. For example, Isaiah said that he saw God seated on a throne, but this is inconsistent with the belief that God is invisible and has no body. Otto wrote of numinous feelings as a mixture of dread and fascination, but these could be seen as contradictory; if we dread something, we do not want to get closer to it. Bernadette Soubirous reported seeing the figure of Mary at Lourdes, but her description was of the kind of statue of Mary that can be seen in any European Catholic church; her description could be seen as over-interpreting whatever she experienced, because she lived in a Catholic country and already had expectations of what Mary ought to look like.

Description-related challenges could, alternatively, be seen as unpersuasive in relation to religious experience. God is described using symbols and metaphors, and these do not have to be consistent with each other. In everyday life we might compare love with a rose or with a flowing river; it does not matter that a rose is nothing like a flowing river, they are just two different metaphors. In the same way it could simply be the case that people use different and contrasting metaphors of God. Perhaps people over-interpret their experiences, or perhaps God appears to people in different forms so that they can recognise God. God might choose to appear as Krishna to Hindus and through Mary to Catholics. God is not bound to appear in the same way to everyone. This could account for inconsistent descriptions.

The persuasiveness of subject-related challenges

Subject-related challenges could be seen as persuasive in relation to religious experience. The subjects of religious experience are fallible human beings like everyone else. They could be mistaken, or deluded. They could be unreliable witnesses, led by wishful thinking. They could be suffering from some kind of disorder that affects the accuracy of their perception. They could simply be telling lies. Anyone could claim that their own opinions have the authority of God, but we do not have to believe them.

Subject-related challenges could also be seen as unpersuasive in relation to religious experience. We do not normally question everyone else's integrity when they tell us things. It is unreasonable to explain religious experiences as signs of mental illness if the person has no other symptoms of mental illness apart from the religious experience. We have good reason to doubt people we know to be untrustworthy, but we should not doubt them solely on the basis of reports of religious experience, if they are in other ways reliable.

The persuasiveness of object-related challenges

Object-related challenges could be seen as persuasive in relation to religious experience. The existence of God is by no means certain. People do not see God, angels, or saints in everyday life, just as they do not see fairies and unicorns. There is no successful argument to prove the existence of God, and no tests that can be done to verify God's existence. The problem of evil provides evidence against the existence of God. Therefore, the challenge that people cannot have experienced the object they claim to have experienced is valid.

Object-related challenges could also be seen as unpersuasive in relation to religious experience. Many people report encounters with God, adding weight to the evidence that God exists, and there are many similarities between the reports and common characteristics. There are good reasons to support belief in God, such as the fact that the universe exists at all. Reports of encounters with God should not be dismissed just because the person hearing the report has unsubstantiated beliefs that there is no God. When European people first saw a duck-billed platypus, their reports were not believed, and even when travelling naturalists produced examples of the animal, other scientists were still sceptical and tried to see how the trick had been done to produce such an unlikely creature; but their scepticism was misplaced. Reports of perceptions of an object that is outside normal experience should not be automatically dismissed.

AO2 activity 7
How persuasive do you find the challenges presented by Caroline Franks Davis, in the context of religious experience? Write two or three paragraphs to explain your view.

Practising AO1 questions

AO1 questions begin with one of a range of possible command words (see pages 8–9 for more detail). The following question begins with the word 'Examine'. 'Examine' questions require you to write a systematic and comprehensive account of a topic, exploring underlying reasons, focusing upon the aspect highlighted in the question. You do not need to consider the quality of an argument or offer any views about it.

> *Examine challenges to the objectivity and authenticity of religious experience.*
>
> (Eduqas A Level Religious Studies, Summer 2019, Component 2: Philosophy of Religion, Question 1a)

Example

Reports of religious experience have been challenged on the grounds of their objectivity.[2] This means that they are said to be entirely[1] subjective[7], as internal experiences in the mind of the individual and so not available for testing or repeating.[1] The reports have also been challenged on the basis on their authenticity.[2] No one can test whether the subject is telling the truth, that they really did have the experience, and no-one can test whether what they say they felt relates to anything real, outside their own minds.[1] Caroline Franks Davis, in her book *The Evidential Force of Religious Experience*[6], looked at three kinds of challenges people might make when they hear a report from someone else about an experience: description-related challenges, subject-related challenges and object-related challenges. By[3] description-related challenges[7], she means challenges that question whether the report is coherent, it is not contradictory and it fits with what else we know. By[3] subject-related challenges[7], she means challenges that question whether the person making the report is reliable. By[3] object-related challenges[7], she means challenges that question the credibility of the thing that was being experienced, asking whether it really exists.[3]

1 The paragraph shows accurate and relevant knowledge and understanding.

2 The response answers the question set specifically, rather than just addressing the general topic of religious experience.

3 The paragraph contains evidence but it would be much improved if it contained specific examples to clarify what is meant.

4 Sacred texts and sources or wisdom and authority are not relevant in this part of the answer, and so it is appropriate that none appear in this paragraph.

5 This paragraph does not make links with other areas of study. These should not be forced and so their absence is appropriate here.

6 Well-chosen scholarly views are used in this paragraph.

7 There is accurate use of specialist language throughout.

Activity

1. Look at the example of a past paper question and an example paragraph taken from a longer answer written in response on page 216. The paragraph is accurate and relevant to the question, but it lacks examples to clarify meaning and show engagement with the topic. Rewrite it, adding in examples as often as you can.
2. As well as referring to the challenges explored by Caroline Franks Davis, what other challenges might the answer include? Read 'Structuring your responses' and 'Making essay plans' on pages 9–10. Then, plan the rest of the answer; try to include scholarly views, examples and, if possible, references to sacred texts in your plan.

AO1 practice question 1

Try answering the following question. There are some points to remember to help you write a developed response.

> *Examine the nature of religious experience with reference to visions and mysticism.*
>
> (Eduqas AS Level Religious Studies, Summer 2017, Component 2: An Introduction to the Philosophy of Religion, question 5a)

Points to remember

- Try to demonstrate that 'religious experience' is not always understood in exactly the same way, and that there is a range of possible definitions.
- In this part of the course, examples are particularly useful to clarify meaning and to illustrate. You could use examples from one or more religious traditions.
- Note that the question asks you to 'examine', so you need to give a detailed account of the topic, but you are not required to give an opinion of your own or weigh up different points of view.
- Note that the question asks for two different forms of religious experience, so make sure you allow roughly equal time for each. You should acknowledge that these are not the only two forms of religious experience, but should concentrate your answer on these two rather than writing at length about, for example, conversion experience.

AO1 practice question 2

Now try this question on your own.

> *Examine the four characteristics of mystical experience as presented by William James.*
>
> (Eduqas A Level Religious Studies, Autumn 2020, Component 2: Philosophy of Religion, question 3a)

Practising AO2 questions

AO2 questions are designed to assess your ability to evaluate and critically analyse. Concentrate on weighing up different views, and identifying the strengths and weaknesses of each view. Avoid spending too much of your response presenting your knowledge in a descriptive way.

> *'Religious experience has a major impact on religious belief and practice.' Evaluate this view.*
>
> (Eduqas AS Level Religious Studies, Summer 2019, Component 2: An Introduction to the Philosophy of Religion, Question 5b)

Example

Religious experience has a major impact on religious belief and practice, for a wide range of reasons.[1] It is often religious experience that inspires individuals to teach new religious ideas that begin new religious movements.[2] For example, the religious experiences of Abraham, during which God promised Abraham that he would be the father of many people, could be understood to mark the origin of Judaism. In Islam, the prophet Muhammad's religious experience where the words of the Qur'an were revealed to him is at the heart of Muslim belief. Guru Nanak's experiences bathing in a river led him to lead the religion of Sikhism.[3] Religious beliefs are sometimes influenced by religious experiences[1] because the experience gives the subject new knowledge[2] (a noetic experience[6]); for example the Christian belief in the resurrection came about because of the experiences of the followers of Jesus, who experienced Jesus walking around three days after his crucifixion[3]. Some religious festivals are inspired by religious experience[2], such as the Christian festival of Whitsun, which commemorates in Christianity the giving of the Holy Spirit in a[3] corporate religious experience[6]. Religious experience can affect the practice of individual believers[1]; for example a[3] conversion experience[6] can inspire someone who was not religious before to start attending church[3].

1 This paragraph shows some confident analysis and evaluation; the writer makes their position clear.

2 The writer concentrates on the question throughout the answer.

3 There is excellent use of examples to illustrate meaning.

4 There is no reference to scholarly views or schools of thought in this paragraph.

5 This paragraph does not make explicit connections with other areas of study, but these links should only be made where they come naturally.

6 There is some use of specialist language; the writer clearly understands the vocabulary of this topic.

Activity

Look at the example of a past paper question and a paragraph taken from an answer written in response on page 218. The paragraph demonstrates a lot of knowledge, and examples are given in support of the writer's argument, but the work is rather muddled and unplanned. It reads as though the writer is thinking of ideas as they write, rather than organising their material to form a coherent line of argument.

Read 'Structuring your response' and 'Making essay plans' on pages 9–10. Then, plan an answer to the AO2 question.

AO2 practice question 1

Try answering this question. There are some points to remember to help you write a developed response.

> *'Mystical experiences are not adequately defined by James' four characteristics.' Evaluate this view.*
>
> (Eduqas A Level Religious Studies, Autumn 2020, Component 2: Philosophy of Religion, Question 3b)

Points to remember

- If you have worked your way through the AO1 practice questions above, you will already have given a thorough examination of James' four characteristics. You do not need to repeat a lengthy description of them in this response.
- You need to think about what constitutes an adequate definition, and how an adequate definition should capture the essence of whatever it is trying to define, while at the same time not being so broad as to also apply to inappropriate examples.
- You could compare James' four characteristics with, for example, the descriptions given by Otto, although this is not explicitly required by the question.

AO2 practice question 2

Now try this question on your own.

> *'Visions and mysticism are valid means of communicating religious teaching and belief.' Evaluate this view.*
>
> (Eduqas AS Level Religious Studies, Summer 2017, Component 2: An Introduction to the Philosophy of Religion, Question 5b)

Mark schemes for all exam questions can be found at www.eduqas.co.uk and www.wjec.co.uk.

6 Religious experience (part two)

This section explores two areas: the ways in which religious experience relates to religious life for individuals and for communities; and the concept of miracle.

The first area looks at the importance of religious experience in religious practices and faith. Religious experiences are private, subjective events, but they have an effect on the ways that religious believers deal with all kinds of aspects of their lives.

- How are religious practices, such as following the rules of kashrut or going to religious services, related to religious experience?
- How far do the religious experiences of key figures influence the way that a religion is practiced in everyday life?
- How far are elements of religion such as festivals and sacred writings dependent on religious experience?

The second area looks at the idea of miracle, and considers different ways in which miracles have been defined. It also looks at whether the usual laws of nature have to be broken in order for an event to be properly described as a miracle, and whether reports of miracles should be believed.

- Does a miracle have to be some kind of impossible event that science cannot ever explain?
- Is something a miracle as long as the people who experience it define it as such?
- Does belief in miracles belong to a superstitious past, or could reasonable modern people believe that miracles happen?

Many religious festivals, such as Hanukkah, have their origins in religious experiences and miracles.

The influence of religious experience on religious practice and faith

Some people would argue that religious experience is identical with religious belief and practice. Those who have religious faith interpret their lives in terms of God, or whatever they consider the divine to be. They may understand the unfolding everyday patterns of their lives in terms of God's plan for them, so that whatever happens, whether it is a chance meeting with an old friend or a rejection from a job application, they understand it as a planned event and part of God's revelation to them. A Sikh or a Hindu may understand good or bad luck in terms of karma, where eternal processes of cause and effect influence an individual's fortunes; so even something as basic as hitting one's head could be considered a 'religious experience' in the broadest sense, if it is understood as the effects of karma, within a religious framework. If every aspect of someone's life, however trivial, is understood within a religious framework, then religious experience, faith, and practice are all inextricably linked.

The value of religious experience for a religious community

Religious experience at the foundation of faith systems

Religious experience is cited as a key factor in the beginning of most religious movements, and so in this sense, it can be considered essential for belief and practice in a religious community, as the community would not have started without the religious experience to initiate it.

For example, in Jewish belief, Abraham had a religious experience in which God appeared to him. In this experience, Abraham learned that he was to be the patriarch of the Jewish people, and that God was going to make a covenant with him, where God made promises to the people (including giving them a Promised Land), and the people in return would be expected to follow God's commandments. These concepts are central in Judaism, and were initiated by Abraham's religious experience:

> When Abram was ninety-nine years old, the Lord appeared to Abram and said to him, 'I am El Shaddai. Walk in My ways and be blameless. I will establish My covenant between Me and you I will make you exceedingly numerous.'
>
> Abram threw himself on his face; and God spoke to him further, 'As for Me, this is My covenant with you: You will be the father of a multitude of nations. And you shall no longer be called Abram, but your name shall be Abraham, for I make you the father of a multitude of nations.'
>
> Genesis 17:1–5, JPS Tanakh: *The Holy Scriptures*

In Christianity, it was Mary's vision of the angel Gabriel that gave Christians the central beliefs that Jesus was born of a virgin and that Jesus was the Messiah promised by the prophets:

> *God sent the angel Gabriel to Nazareth, a town in Galilee, to a virgin pledged to be married to a man named Joseph, a descendant of David. The virgin's name was Mary. The angel went to her and said, 'Greetings, you who are highly favoured! The Lord is with you.'*
> *Mary was greatly troubled at his words and wondered what kind of greeting this might be.*
>
> *But the angel said to her, 'Do not be afraid, Mary; you have found favour with God. You will conceive and give birth to a son, and you are to call him Jesus. He will be great and will be called the Son of the Most High. The Lord God will give him the throne of his father David, and he will reign over Jacob's descendants forever; his kingdom will never end.'*
>
> Luke 1:26–33, *Holy Bible (NIV)*

Bernadette Soubirous' visions of the Virgin Mary in the nineteenth century give authority and affirmation to the Catholic belief that Mary ascended into heaven, and that praying to Mary is important as she will intercede between the worshipper and God. The beliefs were already held, but the religious experience confirms them.

The religious experiences cited in the Bible in which Jesus' disciples realise that Jesus has risen from the dead after his crucifixion are also essential for Christian belief. Jesus' resurrection appearances affirm for Christians their belief that Jesus was the Son of God, and affirm their belief that there is life after death. In his first letter to the Corinthians, Paul writes of his own religious experience in which he became certain that Jesus had risen from the dead, and also refers to the experiences of those who saw Jesus after his death:

> *For what I received I passed on to you as of first importance: that Christ died for our sins according to the Scriptures, that he was buried, that he was raised on the third day according to the Scriptures, and that he appeared to Cephas, and then to the Twelve.*
>
> 1 Corinthians 15:3–6, *Holy Bible (NIV)*

Reports of **near-death experiences** from Christians affirm these beliefs. For example, people who have experienced a cardiac arrest or come close to dying in hospital have reported religious experiences in which they felt as if they had left their bodies behind. They report being able to look down from above and see medical staff trying to resuscitate them, while they experienced a bright light and being surrounded with feelings of peace and love.

In Buddhism, the story of the Buddha's Enlightenment forms the foundation of the faith. After trying different practices in an attempt to understand suffering, the Middle Way led the Buddha to recognise the Three Noble Truths and the way to escape from the endless cycle of samsara, birth and death, which form the basis of Buddhist doctrine. Although Buddhists do not believe that there is an ultimate God, the stages of meditation and enlightenment could be considered to be equivalent to prayer and religious experience, in that they give the individual a sense of detachment from worldly concerns and a focus on ultimate truth.

Key term

near-death experiences (NDEs): subjective experiences commonly reported when someone is close to death; these can include levitation, bright lights, and feelings of peace

In Islam, the prophet Muhammad's religious experiences gave him the authority to teach Muslims the 'straight path' of belief and practice, and in Sikhism, Guru Nanak's religious experiences formed the basis of the Sikh faith. Hinduism, with its wide variety of beliefs and no central orthodoxy, contrasts with other major faiths, as its origins cannot be traced back to the religious experiences of a single individual.

Individual religious experiences very often correspond to people's cultural and religious backgrounds. Hindu religious experience involves visions of the deities Kali, Shiva, or Krishna, whereas a Christian sees Jesus. This suggests that people interpret their experiences according to their previously held beliefs or the beliefs in their surrounding culture; or it could be the case that God chooses different forms in which to encounter individuals, so that they will recognise what they see as God. The experiences help to affirm the belief system.

Religious experience and the origin of sacred texts

Sacred texts are at the heart of some world religions, in particular Judaism, Christianity, and Islam. The texts are believed to have authority as the word of God, and are not just the opinions of ordinary people. They are believed to have been revealed to the writers through religious experience, so that their writing was inspired by God and can therefore be trusted as having eternal truth.

For example, in Judaism, the Ten Commandments, detailing rules for religious and moral behaviour, were given to Moses by God at Mount Sinai. Moses' followers were afraid when they saw signs of the presence of God, and so they sent Moses alone to hear the commandments and relay God's messages.

> *When the people saw the thunder and lightning and heard the trumpet and saw the mountain in smoke, they trembled with fear. They stayed at a distance and said to Moses, 'Speak to us yourself and we will listen. But do not have God speak to us or we will die.' Moses said to the people, 'Do not be afraid. God has come to test you, so that the fear of God will be with you to keep you from sinning.'*
>
> *The people remained at a distance, while Moses approached the thick darkness where God was.*
>
> *Then the Lord said to Moses, 'Tell the Israelites this: "You have seen for yourselves that I have spoken to you from heaven"'*
>
> Exodus 20:18–22, *Holy Bible (NIV)*

These commandments are at the heart of the Jewish faith, displayed on the walls in synagogues as being the authoritative word of God as revealed to Moses. The words revealed to Moses in his religious experience shape everyday Jewish life, giving guidelines for moral behaviour, and for practices such as observation of the Sabbath.

AO1 activity 1

Do some research into the religious experiences of the prophet Muhammad. What did he experience during the Night of Power, and how did this experience help to shape Muslim beliefs and practices?

This painting from the beginning of the sixteenth century illustrates reports of near-death experiences of being in a tunnel with a bright light.

The prophets, too, spoke with authority because they believed their religious experiences gave them words to speak that were God's, rather than their own:

> *The Lord put out His hand and touched my mouth, and the Lord said to me: Herewith I put My words into your mouth.*
>
> Jeremiah 1:9, JPS Tanakh: *The Holy Scriptures*

Christianity gives a similar authority to the words of the Bible, as inspired by religious experience:

> *Above all, you must understand that no prophecy of Scripture came about by the prophet's own interpretation of things. For prophecy never had its origin in the human will, but prophets, though human, spoke from God as they were carried along by the Holy Spirit.*
>
> 2 Peter 1:20–21, *Holy Bible (NIV)*

These religious experiences give the sacred texts their authority and their place in religious life. Leaders in the religious community, such as rabbis, ministers, and vicars, study the sacred texts and teach them to others. Reading the sacred texts forms an important part of communal worship.

In Islam, the religious experiences of the prophet Muhammad included the revelation of the words of the Qur'an. The prophet was in a mountainside cave when the angel Jibril appeared to him and gave him the words of God to remember and recite. The Qur'an was revealed in religious experiences to Muhammad over a period of 23 years. Muslims learn Arabic so that they can read the text in its original language rather than just in translation, which could slightly alter the meanings of the words given by God.

More recently, the Church of the Latter Day Saints (known as the Mormons) was founded as a result of a religious experience that Joseph Smith had in 1823, when he was in his teens. He said that an angel appeared to him and the Book of Mormon was revealed, written on golden plates. His religious experience gave him the ability to translate the words into English, and this marked the beginning of a new religious movement in the USA.

It is religious experience, then, that gives sacred texts their authority. The texts inform beliefs and practices, such as setting out the details for **kashrut** (kosher) laws in Judaism, and the reason why religious believers follow these texts is because they are believed to have been revealed by God in religious visions and mystical encounters.

Religious experience shaping communal rituals and practices

Many religious practices are closely related to religious experience, because the aim of the practice is to put the believer into circumstances that could lead to an encounter with God. Reports of religious experiences often include details of what the subject of the experience was doing at the time; for example, the Buddha was sitting under a bodhi tree in meditation at the time of his enlightenment, and so Buddhists will sit in quiet meditation in

Key term

kashrut (kosher): 'fit' or 'proper' in accordance with Jewish law, often used in relation to food laws

AO1 activity 2
Find out more about the sacred texts of world religions. In your research, look at beliefs about how the sacred texts came into being. Make some notes so that you can use them as examples in your writing.

Synoptic link

Link to *A Level Religious Studies for Eduqas: Religion and Ethics, Chapter 1: Ethical thought (part one)*. The idea that the moral rules of sacred texts come directly from God links with Divine Command theories of normative ethics.

the hope of gaining some insights into eternal truth. Sometimes religious experiences are reported as a result of reading a sacred text, fasting, hearing a sermon, through prayer, or sitting in silence; and therefore, such practices are used by believers, who are hoping that by recreating a similar situation, they may experience God in a similar way. Evangelical rallies such as those held by Billy Graham have been cited as the catalyst for conversion experiences, and so some churches put efforts into holding such rallies, and people who are looking for meaning and truth attend them.

Other religious practices also have religious experience at their origins. For example:

- The Muslim practice of praying five times a day comes from Muhammad's religious experience on the Night Journey, when God revealed the number of times Muslims should pray.
- In Judaism, the rules of kashrut (kosher), setting out what is fit and proper for Jews to eat or wear or use, come from the books of Deuteronomy and Leviticus in the Hebrew Bible, believed to be holy texts revealed to the writers through religious experience.
- Christians do not practise the kashrut food laws of Judaism because of the religious experience of Peter, who reported a vision from God (Acts 10) in which he learned that all food is considered clean for Christians to eat.
- Sikhs bathe in the Pool of Nectar at the Golden Temple in Amritsar, echoing the story that Guru Nanak was bathing in the river when he received his religious experiences.

Religious believers often report a sense of being in the presence of God when they attend a religious service. The religious belief, that there is a God who should be worshipped, comes from religious experience. It then encourages the believer to go to the temple or synagogue or church, and while they are there, they may feel that they experience God. These experiences may happen during the prayers, or when they are hearing teachings, or taking part in singing or chanting, or in times of silent meditation. The sense of being somewhere 'holy', and taking part in **rituals** with others can trigger feelings of religious experience, which then underpin religious belief, affirming it and making it stronger.

Even the architecture of places of worship can be shaped by religious experience. Unitive mystical experiences, in which the individual loses a sense of self and feels at one with God and with the rest of humanity, could inspire a place of worship to be built with a design that enables a lot of people to gather together as equals. Religious experience of God as transcendent can inspire places of worship with vast domes or towering spires.

Pilgrimage to sites of religious experience

The practice of pilgrimage is usually inspired by religious experience. Many sites that are considered holy by religious believers have a special significance because they are places where a well-known figure from religious history had a profound religious experience.

Key term

ritual: a series of actions done in a prescribed order, often for religious reasons

AO1 activity 3

Choose a place of worship, such as Lincoln Cathedral, the Blue Mosque, or the Golden Temple, or any other that appeals to you. Make some notes about aspects of the architecture that could inspire or be inspired by religious experience.

The city of Makkah, for example, is important to Muslims because of the religious experiences of Ibrahim (Abraham) and Muhammad when they were in Makkah. It is not only believed to be the birthplace of Muhammad, but is also the nearest city to the cave where the Qur'an was revealed to Muhammad in a religious experience. Muslims aim to make a pilgrimage (Hajj) once in their lifetime to Makkah, where there are many traditional rituals, including running between two small hills, Safa and Marwa, to remember Ibrahim's wife Hagar's miraculous religious experience of receiving water from a spring given by God.

The sites of religious experiences can become holy places of pilgrimage for religious communities, such as Bodh Gaya in India.

The site of Bodh Gaya in the Indian state of Bihar is the holiest place of pilgrimage for Buddhists. It is a place of pilgrimage for both Hindus and Buddhists, marking the place where Gautama Buddha sat meditating under a tree and attained Enlightenment. The Buddha's experience produced the Noble Eightfold Path, which is the guide for Buddhist life.

In Christianity, Lourdes in France is a place of pilgrimage because it is the site of the visions of Bernadette Soubirous, who had religious experiences of Mary the mother of Jesus beside a stream. In Knock, Ireland, in 1879, fifteen witnesses shared a vision of Mary, Joseph, and John the gospel writer, with the result that the church there has become a site of pilgrimage. People visit these sites where religious experiences are said to have happened partly as a way of concentrating their minds on their faith in the company of other believers, and also partly in the hope of receiving a religious experience themselves.

Schleiermacher on the importance of religious experience for shaping beliefs and practices

The theologian Friedrich Schleiermacher argued that all religious beliefs and practices should be led and shaped by religious experience. Schleiermacher, who was a great influence on Rudolf Otto, claimed that religious experience is the essence of all religion. It is not enough, he argued, simply to agree to a set of beliefs and moral values. Religious people should develop their personal consciousness of the divine. Schleiermacher thought that religious experience is 'self-authenticating'. It does not need to be tested to see whether or not it is genuine. Others had argued that religious experience should be measured against the teachings of the Church to see whether or not it is true and valid, but Schleiermacher's view was that things should work the other way around. The experiences should take priority, and the doctrines, beliefs, and practices should be formulated to fit them.

Some criticised Schleiermacher's view, saying that he put too much emphasis on the subjective. It reduces religion to emotion and undermines the argument that religious claims are based on fact and have a truth-value. Some critics argued that Schleiermacher did not give enough attention to the authority of scripture in formulating doctrines. They argued that

AO1 activity 4
Choose a place of pilgrimage associated with the religion you are studying, and research the reasons why pilgrims go there, so that you can use it as an example in your essays.

religious experience has to be tested against other authority, such as the Bible and the teachings of the Church, because otherwise there is no way of knowing whether experiences caused by substance abuse or mental illness should be accepted or rejected.

The influence of religious experience in the promotion of faith value systems

Religious experience is inextricably linked with faith value systems in many ways.

The value system originates in religious experience

Religious experiences can be part of the origin of value systems. For example, a unitive mystical experience could give the subject the firm conviction that everyone is equal, regardless of race, gender, or wealth. If this is the experience of someone who is held in high regard in a religious tradition, it can influence and shape values and practices. The values of equality that originated with the religious experiences of the Sikh gurus influence the practice of offering free food at langars; anyone who visits a gurdwara (a Sikh place of worship) will be offered a free meal, and everyone sits on the floor together to eat.

The value system is affirmed by religious experience

Religious experiences can affirm value systems that are already in existence. For example, Francis of Assisi's religious experience affirmed the Christian belief in caring for the poor and living a simple life, free from material goals of wealth and status. This was already a Christian teaching, but not one that Francis had found easy to accept. His religious experience gave him the confidence and authority to affirm and model these values in his own life, setting up the order of Franciscan monks, which is still in existence today.

Religious experience is judged by the value system

When people claim to have had religious experiences, they may have had a valid experience that is genuinely from God or they may be deluded (among other possibilities), and those hearing about the experience need to judge it against other criteria. Within a community of believers, reports of religious experiences will often be judged according to how well they fit with the existing value system. An experience that coheres with the faith values of the community is more likely to be considered authoritative.

The value system is given authority by religious experience

Religious values are sometimes challenged by secular society, as society changes. For example, secular society in the West challenges some religious values about sexuality and gender. Religious experience gives authority to religious values as coming from God and set down in sacred texts. This can give religious people strength in the face of opposition as they feel that they are keeping to the values of God; but it can also cause difficulties if it

AO1 activity 5
Summarise Schleiermacher's views about the relationship between religious experience and religious doctrines.

sets religious communities at odds with the values of the general secular population. This has given rise to conflicts over some issues, where religious believers may feel unable to change their values because they are believed to have been revealed by God, but these values do not sit well with the rest of society.

The importance of religious experience in strengthening the cohesion of a religious community

Émile Durkheim, one of the founders of the academic discipline of sociology, believed that religion was fundamental in helping societies to function successfully. Religious experience can work to affirm common beliefs and faith values in a religious community, and by doing so, can help the community to be cohesive. In other words, it helps the community to share common beliefs and moral codes, rather than being divided up into little groups who disagree with each other. In Durkheim's view, religion was no more than this; it has a function in society, which is why people do it, but it does not relate to anything real.

For religious believers, religious experience is important to the community because it underpins and affirms many of the social aspects of religious life.

Collective worship

Religious experience is important for collective worship. Religious buildings provide a setting in which people can feel separated from everyday life and religious experience may be triggered. For example, the building may have a high dome or elaborate ceiling to create feelings of being small in the presence of something great; it may be dimly lit or lit by candles to create an atmosphere of mystery; and there may be scents such as incense which stir the memory. During services of collective worship, there may be readings from texts inspired by or originating from the religious experiences of others. There may be chanting or collective silence, providing an environment conducive for prayer. Prayer can be considered to be a communal religious experience: people pray together, for common concerns.

Coming together in a religious building for communal prayer can work as a trigger for religious experience.

Festivals

Many religious festivals have their origins in religious experiences. For example, the Jewish festival of Hanukkah commemorates a time when the oil for lamps in the Temple in Jerusalem burned miraculously for eight days even though there was only enough oil for one day. This experience is celebrated communally by Jews by lighting menorah candles in their own homes. They also come together to eat fried foods such as doughnuts and potato latkes, play a traditional game and exchange gifts. The Christian festival of Christmas recalls the religious experiences of Jesus' mother Mary, the religious experiences of the shepherds at the Nativity, and the miraculous events surrounding Jesus' birth. Communities gather to sing carols, share special foods, exchange cards and gifts, and spend time together. Festivals are important in community life, giving people the opportunity to gather, deepen their relationships, and enjoy themselves. Traditions give a sense of communal history and shared goals.

Leaders

Leaders are important for community cohesion. They set an example, initiate communal events, encourage people to work together, and try to resolve disputes before they escalate. Religious experience has a role in religious leadership. Many founders of religions reported personal religious experiences that gave them the confidence and authority to take up positions of leadership. Those who lead religious communities are those whose personal beliefs are underpinned and affirmed by their own experiences of God, or whatever they understand ultimate truth to be.

Solidarity in times of persecution

Because religious experiences underpin and affirm faith, they help a community to come together at times when they face opposition. Religious experiences help people to believe that God is on their side; communities are more likely to stick to their principles in the face of opposition if they believe that the principles have been revealed to them by God. The more orthodox branches of Judaism, for example, have grown during and after times of persecution, as people have felt it to be especially important to keep to their ways and nurture them when under threat.

The value of religious experience for the individual

Religious experience is important for individuals as well as for the community.

Religious experience as faith restoring

An individual's religious experience may be life-changing. It could mark the start of a person's faith as a conversion experience, giving them a long-lasting change of direction that others could observe. Religious experience could restore a faith that was waning; for example, if a person began to have doubts about the existence of God, a religious experience could confirm to them personally that God does exist and is interested in them. The conversion of Charles Wesley could be seen as faith-restoring: although Wesley was already a Christian, his religious experience when hearing teaching from the book of Romans gave his faith a new vigour and urgency.

Strengthening faith in the face of opposition

Religious experience can give an individual courage when faced with opposition. Some people have found that following their religious experiences, they have been disbelieved, or there have been objections to the new direction they wish to take. Bernadette Soubirous, for example, was doubted when she first said she had seen visions of Mary at Lourdes, but her experiences remained very real to her, and she continued to insist that she genuinely had been visited by Mary. Francis of Assisi faced objections from

AO1 activity 6

Make a large spider diagram or mind map to show different ways in which religious experience can affect and be affected by a religious community. Add as many examples as you can, concentrating especially on the religion you are studying.

Synoptic link

Link to *Chapter 5: Religious experience (part one)*. Charles Wesley's religious experience led to the foundation of the Methodist movement.

his wealthy father when he wanted to give up his inheritance and devote his life to the poor, but his religious experience gave him a sense of conviction. William James noted that mystical experiences have the characteristic of being noetic: they give the subject the sense of having learned something they did not know before, and this quality can give people a feeling of certainty that enables them to have a strong faith.

Renewal of commitment to religious ideals and doctrines

Religious experience can give individuals a different relationship with religion, even if they have grown up within that tradition. Sometimes this new commitment is marked with ritual or ceremonies. For example, in Sikhism, someone might decide to confirm their faith by taking part in the Amrit ceremony, a ritual that originated with Guru Gobind Singh in 1699. Sikhs who are old enough to make their own decisions and who want to start a new life of purity within the Sikh faith are initiated with holy water, and take on new names to indicate their renewal of commitment. In Christianity, some denominations offer confirmation ceremonies in which people can reaffirm the promises that were made on their behalf at their baptism. Decisions to renew commitment to a faith are often initiated by a religious experience of some kind.

The theologian Martin Buber wrote about two different kinds of relationships: I-It, and I-Thou. In an I-It relationship, the individual relates to someone else only in relation to the service or role they provide, for example as the person behind the till, or the person who cleans the school. In an I-Thou relationship, there is emotional involvement and the relationship works two ways, with each caring about the other as a person. It could be understood as the difference between knowing about someone, and getting to know them. If you know about someone, you might know their name and what they do, and you might have seen pictures of them. If you get to know them, you will understand a lot more about them and develop a relationship with them.

Religious experience moves someone from an I-It relationship with God, perhaps where God is understood to be the impersonal creator of the world, to an I-Thou relationship, where the individual feels that they are in a deeper relationship with God, and have an emotional commitment and sense of dialogue.

Defining miracles

Before any discussion is possible of whether miracles occur, it is important to consider what exactly people mean when they call an event a 'miracle'. In everyday use, the term 'miracle' is used to refer to a wide range of events, such as an achievement that was much greater than expected, a disaster narrowly missed, or a product that produces remarkable results. People might say things like 'the fact that he gained a degree in engineering, despite having recently come to this country as a refugee, is nothing short

Synoptic link

Link to *Chapter 5: Religious experience (part one)*. William James explained four characteristics of mystical experience.

AO1 activity 7

Write a paragraph summarising the value of religious experience for the individual. If possible, find your own examples of people whose religious experience has given value to their life in some way.

of miraculous'; or 'it was a miracle that our baby survived, given that she was so premature'; or 'this stain remover works miracles, it got the red wine stain out of my white carpet'. In everyday life, the word 'miracle' is used metaphorically to mean something that has welcome results against unlikely odds, overcoming obstacles that appeared to be difficult if not impossible.

There are also differences of opinion where some use the term 'miracle' to refer to all kinds of wonderful or happy events, while others restrict its use only to those events where it is impossible to see how the incident could have occurred within the normal operations of the laws of nature.

In theological terms, however, the word '**miracle**' is used to mean more than just outperforming everyone's expectations. Usually, when religious believers use the term 'miracle', they mean to imply that the special event was brought about by God, and could not have happened without God's intervention.

The question of whether miracles actually happen depends a great deal on the definition being used. Few people would dispute that there are occasionally wonderful events that exceed all expectations; but not everyone would accept that there is a God, and that sometimes God performs miracles of a kind that science cannot explain. Amongst others, Thomas Aquinas, David Hume, R.F. Holland, and Richard Swinburne have given different definitions of what properly constitutes a miracle.

> ### Key term
>
> **miracle:** an act of wonder; variously defined, for example, as a violation of the laws of nature (Hume) and an unusual and striking event that evokes and mediates a vivid awareness of God (Hick)

Thomas Aquinas

Thomas Aquinas attempted, in his book *Summa Contra Gentiles*, to define different events that could be called 'miracles'. He understood that calling an event a 'miracle' involves making an interpretation of it and expressing an opinion about it, just as calling an event a 'tragedy' also interprets the event and expresses an opinion. In trying to define miracles, he realises that something might appear miraculous to those who do not understand it, whereas others who have more expertise might not call it a miracle. To make this point, he uses the example of astronomy: an eclipse might seem to an uneducated person to be miraculous, but the astronomer will understand how and why it happens, and so will not interpret it in the same way.

> *Things that are done occasionally by divine power outside of the usual established order of events are commonly called miracles (wonders). We wonder when we see an effect and do not know the cause. And because one and the same cause is sometimes known to some and unknown to others, it happens that of the witnesses of the effect some wonder and some do not wonder: thus an astronomer does not wonder at seeing an eclipse of the sun, at which a person that is ignorant of astronomy cannot help wondering.*
>
> Thomas Aquinas, *Summa Contra Gentiles*

For an event to be strictly a 'miracle', Aquinas argues, it has to be something that is intrinsically wonderful, and not just wonderful to one person but not to another. It must have a cause which is 'absolutely hidden'. A magic trick, then, however clever, would not be a miracle by Aquinas' criteria, because the audience might think it wonderful and be unable to understand how the magician did the trick, but the magician will know, and so it is not 'absolutely hidden'.

Aquinas thought that miracles were not all of the same degree of wonderfulness, but could be placed in a rank order. The highest in the order of miracles were described by Aquinas as:

> *Miracles of the highest rank are those in which something is done by God that nature can never do.*
>
> Thomas Aquinas, *Summa Contra Gentiles*

Aquinas gave some examples of this highest order of miracles from the Bible. One was from Isaiah 38:7–8, where God made a shadow move backwards, as a sign to Hezekiah; another was from Joshua 10:12–14, where the Sun and Moon were made to stand still. Joshua and his army were trying to defeat their enemies the Amorites, but the daylight was fading, so God paused the Sun to give Joshua time to win the battle before returning to their camp. Miracles such as these fall into the highest rank because they are things that could never be done in nature without the guiding hand of God. The normal, natural order of things is suspended by God for the miracle to occur.

For the second rank, Aquinas wrote:

> *Miracles of the second rank are those in which God does something that nature can do, but not in that sequence and connexion.*
>
> Thomas Aquinas, *Summa Contra Gentiles*

These kinds of miracles are when something happens that can also happen naturally, but God intervenes to change the natural sequence of events. Aquinas gave the example of people being able to see after being blind, where in the natural order of things, people start out with good eyesight but then become blind. He also gave the examples of people coming to life after being dead, and people walking after being lame or paralysed. In Aquinas' thirteenth-century world, before modern medicine, such things did not happen this way.

The third rank of miracles, according to Aquinas, is:

> *. . . something done by God, which is usually done by the operation of nature, but is done in this case without the working of natural principles, as when one is cured by divine power of a fever, in itself naturally curable, or when it rains without any working of the elements.*
>
> Thomas Aquinas, *Summa Contra Gentiles*

AO1 activity 8
Look up in the Bible the miracles that Aquinas chooses as examples of the first rank, to familiarise yourself with the stories.

The things that happen are things that normally happen, but in a miracle, they happen without any of the usual natural causes.

Aquinas did not think that the laws of nature have to be broken before an event can be called a miracle. Instead, he emphasised that God is in control of the laws of nature, so God can occasionally make them work differently in order to fulfil a particular purpose. The laws of nature only behave the way they do because of the guiding hand of God.

AO1 activity 9

How would Aquinas rank the following – first order, second order, or third order miracles?

- A field of wheat suddenly springing up from the ground.
- Someone old regaining their youth.
- The Moon shining as brightly as the Sun.
- A broken arm healing in a moment.
- Someone walking on water.

David Hume

David Hume's definition of what constitutes a miracle is part of his argument that reports of miracles should be rejected. Hume's view was that in order for an event to be termed a 'miracle', it has to be something that never happens in the normal order of things. He gives examples of things that always happen according to the laws of nature. All people die; lead cannot float around in the air without support; fire consumes wood, and is extinguished by water. It would require a miracle to prevent these things from happening.

> *A miracle is a violation of the laws of nature ... Nothing is esteemed a miracle, if it ever happens in the common course of nature ... There must therefore be a uniform experience against every miraculous event, otherwise that event would not merit that appellation.*
>
> David Hume, *An Enquiry Concerning Human Understanding*

Even if something occurs only rarely, it should not be considered a miracle, thinks Hume. It can only justifiably be called a miracle if it never happens at all. Hume gives the example of someone who is apparently healthy and dies suddenly. Fortunately, this does not happen very often, but it does happen rarely and occasionally. If, however, a dead person came back to life, then that would be a miracle, Hume says, because that has never been observed. (It seems that Hume is being deliberately provocative here, as his Christian readers will immediately think of the Biblical accounts of the resurrection of Jesus, and of miracle stories in the gospels, where Jesus brings back to life Lazarus and Jairus' daughter after they had died. Without referring to these Biblical stories directly, Hume is saying that they never happened.)

For Hume, then, a miracle has to break the laws of nature if it is to be called a miracle at all. It cannot be something that happens only rarely, or is wonderful but does not break any physical laws. It must be something that never happens, and that breaks physical laws.

Hume defines a miracle in this way:

> *A miracle may be accurately defined, a transgression of a law of nature by a particular volition of the Deity, or by the interposition of some invisible agent.* "
>
> David Hume, *An Enquiry Concering Human Understanding*

To be a miracle, an event must break the laws of nature, and must have happened because of the will of God or some other supernatural being, such as an angel, a demon, or a fairy. If the event broke the laws of nature but it was a pure accident, then it would not be a miracle, because no supernatural being had willed it.

R.F. Holland

R.F. Holland was a twentieth-century British philosopher who was influenced by the thinking of Wittgenstein. Holland thought that the definitions of miracle given by Aquinas and Hume were too narrow, ruling out some events that could justifiably be called miracles.

In an article called 'The Miraculous', published in *American Philosophical Quarterly* in 1965, Holland put forward the view that miracles could happen without there necessarily being any violation of the laws of nature. For Holland, the most important and defining feature of a miracle is that it is interpreted as such; it should include events that are contradictory to our usual experience. Holland said that a miracle can be defined as:

> *A remarkable and beneficial coincidence that is interpreted in a religious fashion … an event that in certain circumstances has a human significance.* "
>
> R.F. Holland, 'The Miraculous'

Holland's understanding of miracle is sometimes referred to as a '**contingency miracle**' or a 'coincidence miracle'. He suggests the example of a child playing with a toy car on a railway track, just around a bend. The driver of the oncoming train has no idea that the child is there, and the child does not see the train coming. The child's mother, positioned on a hillside where she can see both her child and the fast-approaching train, is frantic but unable to do anything to help. Suddenly she sees the train slow down and stop, just a few feet from her unharmed child, and she thanks God for the miracle. There was a natural explanation for this: the driver had fainted, and the brakes had automatically applied. So there was nothing supernatural about the narrow escape, as there were plausible scientific explanations for the stopping of the train. Even so, the mother, and perhaps the child too, would always understand what had happened to be a miracle.

Holland thought that this hypothetical situation illustrated the possibility that an event could be described as a miracle even if there is no suspension

---

AO1 activity 10

Explain what Hume means by a 'violation of the laws of nature'.

Key term

contingency miracle: term used by R.F. Holland to define extraordinary and beneficial coincidences that do not break the laws of nature but appear miraculous to witnesses; also known as 'coincidence miracle'

of the laws of nature. The coincidence of events, the disaster that is narrowly averted against the odds, and the beneficial outcome could cause someone to believe in the power of God. Holland, then, argued that a miracle could be defined as something that can happen within the laws of nature, and which is understood by believers to be performed by God. This would not prove the existence of God, but the sceptic could not straight away deny God's involvement (except on the grounds that the sceptic did not believe in God, which would be an unprovable assumption).

Holland's view of miracle is different from Hume's because it does not necessarily involve a breaking of the laws of nature, which for Hume was the main part of his definition. It is different from Aquinas' understanding because Holland emphasises that in order to be a miracle, the event must be 'beneficial', which Aquinas did not include in his definition.

Holland's example of the child on the train track is hypothetical. A real-life example that is often used to illustrate Holland's view of 'coincidence miracle' was reported in *Life* magazine in 1950. Fifteen members of the West Side Baptist Church choir in Beatrice, Nebraska, were meant to arrive at church by 7.20pm for their weekly choir practice. Usually everyone was there by 7.15pm. On 1 March 1950, the practice was scheduled to happen as usual, and at 7.25pm there was a huge explosion caused by a gas leak that destroyed the church building and blew the windows out of nearby buildings. None of the fifteen members of the choir was killed or even injured in the blast, because every single one was running late that evening, for separate trivial reasons. The minister was about to set off with his wife and daughter when one had discovered a stain on her dress and had gone back inside to change it; the pianist had overslept from a nap; two had been listening to a radio programme and wanted to hear the end before setting off; two had found their car would not start, and had to wait for a lift from a third who needed to finish her homework; one had simply started out late because it was a cold evening and she had stayed indoors until the last minute; these and other similar small reasons meant that nobody was in the building when the blast happened.

Nothing, then, violated the laws of nature on the evening of the explosion. But the fact that all fifteen people, who were never usually late, had avoided being killed, seemed to them and to others to be a miracle.

Richard Swinburne

Richard Swinburne, a Christian and a professor of philosophy at Oxford University, produced another definition of miracle that qualifies the definition given by Hume. In his article 'Miracles', published in *Philosophical Quarterly* in 1968, Swinburne offers a definition very similar to that of Hume:

> *I understand by a miracle a violation of a law of nature by a god, that is, a very powerful rational being who is not a material object (viz., is invisible and intangible).* 99
>
> Richard Swinburne, 'Miracles'

AO1 activity 11

Here is another example of a hypothetical event that could fit Holland's understanding of a miracle: Nina's business is failing; she is in a lot of debt and does not know where to turn for help. She is a single parent and is struggling to feed her children. She is about to be evicted from her accommodation, when she gets a letter telling her that she is inheriting a lot of money from an aunt she did not know existed. The money is enough to solve all of her financial problems and get her business back on track.

Now think of your own example of a 'coincidence miracle'.

However, Swinburne adds to Hume's definition by going on to argue that a 'violation of a law of nature' is not just something that has not been observed before. It has to be something that is not repeatable and could not be recreated. He gives as an example a holy person levitating in a way that contravenes established laws of physics, or the resurrection back to full health of someone who had been clinically dead for more than 24 hours.

Swinburne also argues that in order for an event to be a miracle, it must have been caused by God. In this respect, his definition is similar to those of Aquinas and Hume, and differs from Holland. Swinburne adds that for an event to be a miracle, there should be some point to it; it should indicate something about the nature of God, for example, or show people what God wants them to do. This could rule out unexplained events such as statues that allegedly produce milk or blood.

Consideration of reasons why religious believers accept that miracles occur

There are many reasons why religious believers accept the idea that God acts in the world through the performance of miracles.

Evidence from sacred texts

The sacred writings and traditions in many religions contain stories of miracles. Some believe that the miracle stories literally happened as described, and others believe that the stories may be poetic ways of giving important truths, but the fact that they appear in the sacred texts mean that religious believers take them seriously.

Miracles are a significant feature of the sacred writings of Judaism. Miracles are seen to be examples of the power of God, and of God's interest in the Jews as the chosen people. At festivals throughout the year, in homes and synagogues, Jews recall miracle stories from scripture as a way of keeping their history alive. For example, Exodus includes the story of the parting of the Red Sea, where God enables the Jewish people to escape from slavery under the Egyptians by making a dry path for them across the sea:

> *Then Moses held out his arm over the sea and the Lord drove back* *the sea with a strong east wind all that night, and turned the sea into dry ground. The waters were split, and the Israelites went into the sea on dry ground, the waters forming a wall for them on their right and on their left.*
>
> Exodus 14:21–2, JPS Tanakh: *The Holy Scriptures*

In Buddhism, although texts point out that the Buddha himself refused to use miraculous powers to impress his audience, there are nevertheless accounts in sacred texts of the Buddha's ability to transcend the laws of nature:

AO1 activity 12

Make a list of three or four hypothetical events that would fit Swinburne's definition of a miracle.

> *He dives in and out of the earth as if it were water. Without sinking he walks on water as if on earth. Seated cross-legged he travels through the sky like a winged bird. With his hand he touches and strokes the sun and the moon.*
>
> *Aṅguttara Nikāya 5:28*

In Christianity, miracles are used by the gospel writers as evidence to show that Jesus really was the Son of God, for example to show that Jesus had power over nature and was the fulfilment of prophecy:

> *The people were amazed when they saw the mute speaking, the crippled made well, the lame walking and the blind seeing. And they praised the God of Israel.*
>
> *Matthew 15:31, Holy Bible (NIV)*

Many believe that the essence of the Christian message depends upon the concept of miracle: the miracle of God becoming human in the form of Jesus; the miracle of his taking on the sin of the world; and the miracle of his resurrection. They might argue that to reject the view that God performs miracles is to reject the whole of Christianity.

In Islam, the entirety of the Qur'an is understood to be miraculous, as it was revealed to the prophet Muhammad rather than having any human source.

Affirmation of faith traditions

Religious believers accept that miracles occur if this belief in miracles coheres with their other beliefs:

- The belief that God is omnipotent: Many religions, including Christianity, hold the belief that God is omnipotent. God can do anything at all, and therefore God can perform miracles, just as God can create the universe and govern the laws of nature. God organised creation to work in the way that it does, and has the power to suspend the normal workings of the universe from time to time. To suggest that it is impossible for God to perform miracles is to say that God is not omnipotent after all. If Anselm is right in defining God as 'that than which no greater can be conceived', then God must be able to perform miracles; otherwise we would be able to conceive of another, greater God who could.
- The belief that God is loving: Many religions have the belief that God is loving and answers prayers. When situations seem impossible, people pray for a miracle, and sometimes it seems to them that the prayer has been answered. Someone who has been longing for a baby for a long time finally conceives, or someone who was seriously ill makes a better recovery than doctors expected. Occurrences such as these affirm people's faith that God is loving, compassionate, and can act in the world in answer to prayer even against the odds.
- The belief that God can intervene in human history: Most religions believe that God is not an impersonal being outside of time and detached from humanity, but instead that God can and does intervene in human affairs.

Synoptic link

Link to *Chapter 2: Arguments for the existence of God: deductive.* Anselm's definition of God implies that God is capable of doing anything.

- The belief that God wants to communicate: Many religions hold the belief that God is personal, and takes an interest in humanity and in the affairs of individual lives. Miracle events affirm this belief, demonstrating a God who is responsive to human needs and who wants to be revealed to people.

In Christianity, the Apostles' creed is a statement of belief that is recited together in the services of some denominations. Worshippers confirm their belief that Jesus was miraculously conceived by the Holy Spirit, and that he miraculously rose from the dead. In saying the words of the creed together, Christians emphasise their shared acceptance of miracles.

Some, but not all, Christians believe that miracles have occurred at sites of pilgrimage such as Lourdes in France. The Catholic Church accepts 67 confirmed cases of miraculous healing at the shrine at Lourdes; this coheres with Catholic beliefs that Mary will intercede for them if they pray to her. Reports of miracles at Lourdes are problematic, because in order for a cure to be classified as a miracle by the Vatican, the cure has to be instantaneous, complete, and without any subsequent relapse. The person seeking healing must be cured without any medical intervention; but this requirement causes difficulties, as in the developed world, people with serious illnesses will be encouraged to have them treated by doctors. As a result, there have been very few miracles at Lourdes confirmed by the Church since the nineteenth century.

Personal experience

Some religious people accept that miracles occur because of their own experiences, where something happened to them or they witnessed something that they understand to be a miracle. It could be a remarkable coincidence where disaster was narrowly avoided, or where something beneficial happened against the odds. It could be an event that seemed to be an answer to prayer, such as the recovery of someone who was very ill or badly injured. Different people will have different ideas about whether such events are properly called 'miracles'. The ordinary birth of an ordinary baby may seem miraculous to the parents, even though this is a common occurrence and in keeping with the laws of nature.

Personal experience of miracles, like other kinds of personal religious experience, can be treated with scepticism by others, who might argue that statistically some people are going to be lucky, and coincidences occur all the time. But for the person who believes they have experienced a miracle, the event will convince them of the existence of a personal God, and will make them more likely to believe in others' reports of miraculous events.

Reasons why some religious believers reject the idea that miracles occur

Bultmann and demythologising

In his 1941 essay 'New Testament and Mythology', the Christian scholar Rudolf Bultmann called into question the idea that miracle stories should

> **AO1 activity 13**
>
> Make a list of reasons why some people might believe in miracles, using the ideas here and any other reasons you can think of.

be taken literally. Bultmann was an existentialist, which meant that he believed the most important aspect of religious faith was the personal choice of the individual to accept or reject God. He argued that modern intelligent people, brought up in a scientific age, struggle to believe stories such as Jesus walking on water or miraculously feeding 5,000 people with just a small amount of food. Bultmann argued that the gospel writers were never trying to make an accurate record of historical facts, in the way that news reporters are supposed to do. Instead, he argued, people understood history and myth differently in the first century. They expressed themselves in figurative terms, using myth rather than literal accounts of what happened. They wanted to show their belief that Jesus was the Son of God, so they presented Jesus as having miraculous power over nature; but this was always a mythological way of expressing belief.

Bultmann thought that modern Christians should not be put off the essential messages of Christianity by being expected to believe the impossible. Miracle stories, visitations by angels, and other supernatural events are not credible to modern people, he thought. The important thing is for individuals to reach their own personal decision about God. They can reject miracle stories as true accounts and need not try hard to believe things that they find impossible to take literally, but instead should understand stories of miracle as myth. The miracles did not really happen just as described, but should be understood as vivid poetic ways of expressing belief about Jesus.

Bultmann, then, although he was a Christian himself, saw miracle stories as an obstacle to faith. He thought that people were likely to reject the whole Christian message if they were expected to take reports of miracles literally. They could still continue with their Christian faith if they understood the stories mythologically, and instead focused on the main point, which in his view was the personal choice to commit to a life of faith.

Maurice Wiles and 'God's Action in the World'

Maurice Wiles was a twentieth-century philosopher of religion who argued against traditional Christian belief in miracles. Like Bultmann, Wiles believed that miracle stories were difficult for modern people to take literally. In his book *God's Action in the World*, Wiles says that the early Christians might not have found it too difficult to accept the occurrence of miracles because they lived in an age where the workings of natural laws were all seen as entirely dependent on the will of God. There was nothing difficult for people of the first century in accepting that sometimes God might make the world work differently from usual.

Wiles did not rule out the possibility of miracles on scientific grounds. Like Swinburne, Wiles thought that the laws of physics are not closed and final, but are open to the possibilities of change and of new discovery. Wiles thought that there was no reason to claim that some things are impossible, even for God. God could, for example, choose to dry up the sea, because after all, God made the sea in the first place. Wiles nevertheless rejected the idea that God performs miracles, but on moral rather than scientific grounds.

> **Synoptic link**
>
> Link to *Chapter 8: Religious language (part two)*. Bultmann suggested that the Bible should be 'demythologised' to make it more accessible to modern people and enable them to make a personal decision about faith in God.

Wiles argued that if we take the view that God performs miracles of the kind that break existing laws of nature, then this raises acute problems for theodicy. It is difficult, if not impossible, to understand why a God who is capable of performing miracles at any moment has not intervened in the world more often. Wiles asks why a God who can and does perform miracles apparently did nothing miraculous to help the Jews when they were in Nazi concentration camps. God apparently did nothing miraculous to prevent the Japanese city of Hiroshima being devastated by a nuclear bomb. Wiles says that the miracles reported in the Bible 'seem trivial by comparison'; Jesus turned water into wine to save wedding hosts from embarrassment, and fed 5,000 people with a small amount of bread and fish because otherwise they would have had no lunch. Christians are expected to believe that it was important enough for God to do those things by performing miracles; and yet God does not seem to intervene to prevent suffering on a large scale.

Wiles rejected the traditional idea of miracles, therefore, on the grounds that they suggest God is arbitrary and unfair, helping the occasional blind person to see but leaving countless other people blind, or feeding 5,000 people through a miracle but leaving millions of others to starve. Wiles thought that it must be the case that God works in other ways. God does not do occasional miracles like magic tricks, suspending the laws of nature and then reintroducing them. Instead, God works through people, by inspiring them to cure others or to feed each other.

Hume and Swinburne on miracles: a comparison of two key thinkers

David Hume's scepticism about miracles

David Hume, writing in the eighteenth century, presented what is generally understood to be the most comprehensive rejection of the idea that people should believe in miracles. As an empiricist, Hume thought that, by their definition, miracles were events that no sensible person could believe really happened. He did not say that miracles were completely impossible, but instead said that for any event that some people call a miracle, there will always be a natural explanation for the occurrence; sensible people should believe the natural explanation rather than the supernatural one.

Hume worked hard on his arguments against belief in miracles, and was very pleased with the results:

> *I flatter myself, that I have discovered an argument of a like nature, which, if just, will, with the wise and learned, be an everlasting check to all kinds of superstitious delusion, and consequently, will be useful as long as the world endures.*
>
> David Hume, *An Enquiry Concerning Human Understanding*

AO1 activity 14

Explain in your own words:
a) why Bultmann rejected belief in miracles
b) why Wiles rejected belief in miracles.

Wiles asks why God would perform trivial miracles such as turning water into wine, but not do anything miraculous to save large numbers of people from suffering.

According to Hume, wise and sensible people base their beliefs on solid evidence. The extent to which a person believes something should be in proportion to the evidence, so they should only be certain of things where there is plenty of evidence. It should be more likely that something is true rather than false, before we believe it. Hume argued that when there are reports of miracles, we need to weigh up the likelihood that there really was a miracle. We need to think about whether it is likely that the laws of nature, such as gravity, will have carried on working as normal, or whether it is more likely that they were suspended and a miracle happened. We know that, for example, people cannot usually walk on water, so if we hear a report of a miraculous event in which someone did walk on water, we should pause and weigh it up. We need to decide whether we believe that on this occasion, the properties of water behaved differently; or whether we believe that water behaved just as it always does, and the report is therefore false.

Hume argued that for a miracle to be called a miracle at all, it must be something that never happens in the normal world: and therefore, miracles do not happen, by their own definition. In his own words:

> *There must therefore be a uniform experience against every miraculous event, otherwise that event would not merit that appellation. And as a uniform experience amounts to a proof, there is here a direct and full proof, from the nature of the fact, against the existence of any miracle.*
>
> David Hume, *An Enquiry Concerning Human Understanding*

Hume developed his argument by considering whether or not reports of miracles should be believed. He looked at the likelihood of what was being said; the chances that the witnesses were reliable; the human tendency to look for evidence of the supernatural; and also the fact that different religions use different miracle stories to support their contrasting faith claims.

Testimony-based belief

Hume considers how wise and sensible people should respond, if someone says that they have witnessed a miracle. The reporter could be telling the truth, or they could be lying, or mistaken. He argues that the reasonable person will opt for the most likely of the options. Even if the person reporting the miracle is usually honest, does not normally make jokes, and usually gets things right, the option that the miracle actually occurred is always going to be the least likely explanation. The balance of probability shows that it would be unwise to believe that a miracle had actually happened.

Credibility of witnesses

Hume claims that stories of miracles tend to come from 'ignorant and barbarous places and nations'; in his view, the reports usually come from less educated people who are not familiar with scientific ways of looking at the world. He says that there are no very well-supported reports of cases where the miracle had been witnessed by a number of reliable people. No miraculous occurrences had been reported by people who were known to be consistently reliable, sensible, and well educated. Credible witnesses need to be people who have nothing to gain from their story, and they need to be people who have a good reputation in society, so that they would have something to lose if others found out they were lying. They need to be well educated people who are known to be trustworthy.

Susceptibility of belief

Another objection Hume raises to belief in miracles is that, in his view, people like to believe in the supernatural and the paranormal. Because they want to believe in such things, they tend to look for it, even when the evidence does not support a supernatural interpretation. People enjoy surprise and wonder, and a report of a miracle gets other people's attention and perhaps their admiration. A person who is already religious may make up a story in order to gain converts to their own faith; those who believe it are, in Hume's view, always ignorant people who do not know any better.

Contradictory nature of faith claims

Finally, Hume argues that different miracle stories from different faiths tend to cancel each other out. A miracle story from one tradition is meant to show that its founder is sent by God; another tradition believes the first one to be false, and has different miracle stories supporting the authority of its own leaders instead. Hume thought that these conflicting reports of miracles weakened the evidential force of all of them.

> **AO1 activity 15**
> Make a bullet-pointed list summarising Hume's arguments against miracles. It is worth reading Hume in his own words to add to your knowledge.

Richard Swinburne's defence of miracles

Swinburne gives a critique of Hume's argument against miracles, going through each of the points Hume makes. According to Swinburne, it can be reasonable to believe that miracles have occurred, as he argues in his article 'Miracles' (published in *Philosophical Quarterly* in 1968) and in his book *The Concept of Miracle* (1970).

Hume argued that a miracle transgresses laws of nature that have been firmly established by our experience. We have what Hume calls 'uniform' experiences of the laws of nature, which work in the same way each time without exceptions. Our uniform experience gives us very solid reasons for knowing what is possible and what is not possible.

Swinburne argues that Hume is missing the statistical nature of natural laws. We reach our understanding of a law of nature based on data, from which we then make predictions about what could happen in the future. In *The Concept of Miracle*, Swinburne compares finding laws of nature with making sense of the points on a graph. There will always be a number of possible formulae for explaining the data, and the scientist chooses the simplest and best to be regarded as provisionally correct. If, as more data comes in, the formula seems to work, then this increases its credibility as a law. He gives the example of two different theories used to suggest how the universe may have originated: 'big bang' theories and 'steady state' theories. The same data led different scientists to different potential 'laws of nature', and subsequent data provided more support for one and less for the other. His point is that any proposed law of nature will be 'corrigible'; in other words, it will be open to the possibility of being corrected. If we get new data that contradicts what we thought was a law, and these contradictions are repeated, then we need to find a new law.

> *If the laws of nature are statistical and not deterministic ... it is not in all cases so clear what counts as a counter-instance to them.* 99
>
> Richard Swinburne, 'Miracles'

Swinburne says that a miraculous event does not fit in with the laws of nature as we understand them, but this does not make it impossible. An event is a miracle if it is contrary to the laws of nature, and also if it is not repeatable. If an event is not repeatable, then there would be no point in modifying a law of nature to accommodate it, because the law remains correct except for this one anomalous instance.

In Swinburne's view, the extraordinary event would only be a miracle if it is brought about by God and has some kind of religious significance. This begs the question of how we would know that the event has been brought about by God and is not just an accident. Swinburne answers this by saying it would be reasonable to assume that the event had been brought about by God if:

- it was impossible to know otherwise what the cause could be, or impossible to witness the cause happening
- the event happened after a request, for example in answer to a prayer
- the event included some kind of affirmation, such as a voice agreeing to the request
- the event fits in with other miracles, such as bringing about justice or helping someone who was suffering.

According to Swinburne, God could make laws of nature and also suspend them, as God is omnipotent. It would not make sense for God to suspend the laws of nature on a regular basis, as then they would not be laws at all; we would not be able to go about our daily lives if we never knew whether gravity would work in the afternoon in the same way that it did in the morning. Nevertheless, there is nothing unreasonable in the suggestion that God could very occasionally intervene in the laws of nature, just as a parent might have rules for their children but once in a while allow the rules to be suspended (so that their children could stay up until midnight on New Year's Eve, perhaps, or have the biscuit Grandma made, even though it was nearly lunchtime). God is benevolent and wants to interact with creation; but miracles have to remain rare. Swinburne claims that if God did miracles more often, then people would have less incentive to work through difficulties on their own; for example, they would not strive to find cures for cancer if God usually miraculously healed cancer sufferers.

Credibility of witnesses

Hume argued that there had never been reports of miracles that were reliably reported by a sufficient number of well-educated, honest people. Swinburne questions this. He challenges the idea that a number of reliable first-hand witnesses to an event would be the only possible evidence that the event happened. There could be other valid evidence, such as physical traces. Swinburne refers to Sherlock Holmes, who used evidence such as the layout of furniture or the mud on someone's boot as evidence in cases where there were no witnesses. In the context of a miracle, there could be physical traces, such as people seeing the person who was once paralysed walking about in their home town after they had been miraculously cured.

Hume does not specify how many witnesses would be enough witnesses for a miracle to be evidenced, but he seems to be excessively stringent in his demands for their quality and reliability. In other contexts, such as historical accounts or scientific observations during experiments, we do not demand that there must be hundreds of witnesses and that they must be of totally irreproachable character before we accept the balance of evidence. Swinburne suggests that perhaps if Hume witnessed a miracle for himself, he might think differently.

Where Hume says that people like to believe in the paranormal and so are likely to be gullible with regard to reports of miracles, Swinburne argues that this could be applied to all kinds of personal reports. We could question people's claims when they describe their dreams or their emotions, but the principle of testimony should be applied: we should be prepared to believe what people tell us, unless we have a good reason to doubt them.

Contradictory nature of faith claims

In response to Hume's claim that reports of miracles from different traditions cancel each other out, Swinburne says that Hume is wrong. Evidence for a miracle in one religion would only cancel out a miracle in another religion if the two religions taught contradictory things. Swinburne gives the example of a hypothetical Catholic miracle that provided evidence for the doctrine of transubstantiation, which is a doctrine accepted by Catholics but not by Protestants. If there were also a Protestant miracle that provided evidence against the doctrine of transubstantiation, then these events would be contradictory and Hume would have a fair point. However, there are not miracle stories in existence that contradict each other in this way.

> **Synoptic link**
>
> Link to *Chapter 5: Religious experience (part one)*. Swinburne's principles of credulity and testimony are relevant to his discussion of miracle.

> **AO1 activity 16**
>
> In your own words, explain why Swinburne thinks that reports of miracles should not be immediately dismissed.

This section of the chapter will enhance your ability to **analyse** and **evaluate** the topic and help you develop your AO2 skills. For each question, think about the different positions you might take, and decide which you find most persuasive and why. It is not enough to memorise a list of 'for and against' points; you need to develop an argument.

How far do religious experiences have an impact upon religious belief and practice?

For this discussion, see the previous chapter pages 204–205.

Are religious communities entirely dependent on religious experiences?

This question asks for consideration of the extent to which religious communities (such as a Jewish community, a church, or a religious order of monks) depend on religious experience. It includes ideas such as whether the community would have come into existence without religious experience, or whether religious experience is significant but perhaps not the main motivation for a religious community.

The view that religious communities are entirely dependent on religious experience

- Religious experience is very often the reason why the religious community began; it would not exist without the religious experiences of its founders.
- Without religious experience, the community would just be a social group of people who agreed to the same way of looking at the world. It is only properly called religious if there is a sense of the presence of God among the people in the community.
- Sacred texts, which are at the heart of many religious communities, depend on religious experience, both for their origins and for their content. Many religions are dependent on their sacred texts for their history, traditions, and moral guidance.
- Without religious experience, people would have to depend on reasoned arguments in order to sustain belief. Advances in science and naturalistic explanations of religion would put this in danger unless believers had religious experience to affirm their faith.
- Religious experience gives the community of believers its cohesion. Even though the community may consist of very different personalities, they share common experiences of God, which unifies them in their beliefs and enables them to work together in cooperation.

The view that religious communities are not entirely dependent on religious experience

- Religious experiences are very varied in nature, and people have different views on what constitutes a religious experience. Some religious believers would say that they have never had the kind of dramatic experience that others describe; they have never seen a vision of God or heard God speaking to them directly. Nevertheless, they find that belonging to a religious community supports their faith, gives them a sense of tradition and belonging, and helps them to learn important truths.
- The religious experiences described in sacred texts, and by people such as mediaeval mystics, could be seen to belong to a different era. Today people are more sceptical about the supernatural, and some of the stories of religious experiences have become heavily mythologised in a way that modern people could struggle to relate to. Although religious believers may find the stories inspiring, they do not always form an important part of their everyday religious lives.
- Ninian Smart, a professor of Religious Studies when it was still a new discipline in the mid-twentieth century, identified seven different features of religion:
    - narrative stories, such as creation narratives and stories of leaders
    - experiential feelings and emotions, such as those described in reports of religious experiences
    - rituals, such as rites of passage
    - material things and places, such as artefacts and religious buildings
    - social and institutional features, such as communal worship and groups
    - ethical laws that govern moral behaviour and social behaviour for the religious community
    - doctrine and philosophy, including the features of a belief system such as beliefs about life after death or about the place of suffering in the world.

    These different features show that religious experience is an important part of what it means to be religious and to belong to a religious community, but it is not everything. There are many other facets to religious life, and some will be more important than others to different believers.

- The relationship between religious experience and sacred texts can present some difficulties for religious communities, as they may have different views about whether a text is meant to be the direct and infallible word of God, or instead the thoughts of someone who was inspired by religious experience to express ideas in their own human way. The view that religious texts give once-and-for-all moral teaching has been rejected by some religious believers, who want to adapt the religious teachings of their communities to align them more closely with modern views about issues such as gender and sexuality, or with scientific views about the origins of species. It is sometimes argued that the religious texts were inspired by religious experiences, but interpreted by the writers in their cultures; the original religious experience does not have to be taken as everlastingly binding in every respect.

How adequate are the different definitions of miracles?

For a definition to be a good definition, it should communicate clearly in order to avoid misunderstanding. It should be precise enough to make it clear how this one thing differs from everything else. Defining a cat as a 'fluffy pet' is an inadequate definition, as there are some fluffy pets that are not cats, some cats that are not pets, and some cats that are not fluffy. The definition fails to make it clear exactly what distinguishes cats from other things. Different definitions of 'miracle' have been suggested that may or may not carefully distinguish miracles from other kinds of events.

Aquinas' definition

Aquinas defined miracles as 'things that are done occasionally by divine power outside of the usual established order of events'. He wrote about miracles belonging to higher and lower ranks, and also explained that calling an event a 'miracle' involves interpreting it.

The view that Aquinas' definition could be considered adequate

Aquinas' definition has several strengths. When writing about miracles more generally, he noted that calling an event miraculous involves making an interpretation of it, which is a useful consideration. It is quite possible that an event could be seen as miraculous by one person but not by another. He also noted that miracles can be ranked in order of importance, which is something other thinkers disregard. Aquinas' definition allows for the possibility of miracles happening within the laws of nature, such as an unusually quick healing; miracles can be, but do not have to be, totally extraordinary.

The view that Aquinas' definition could be considered inadequate

Aquinas does not allow the possibility that an ordinary event could justifiably be called a miracle. People who have been longing for a child and who have a lot of IVF treatment over several years, and eventually produce a healthy baby, might consider the birth miraculous, even though successful IVF happens fairly frequently. However, Aquinas would not have regarded IVF as miraculous, because the people performing the necessary medical procedures for IVF would know how it was done and would not be awestruck at a resulting pregnancy. He does not consider the kind of 'coincidence miracle' Holland describes, as these are not outside the usual order of events. It could be argued, then, that Aquinas' definition is inadequate, because he does not include the idea that an ordinary event could be a miracle for those involved. Aquinas also does not elaborate on

AO2 activity 1

In your view, how important are religious experiences for religious communities? Give reasons to support your answer.

the idea that a miracle should have a point to it, in revealing something about God or God's purposes; and he does not offer the idea that a miracle should have beneficial effects. Other scholars think that the idea that miracles reveal something of God is essential to any definition of miracle.

Hume's definition

Hume defined a miracle as 'a violation of the laws of nature'.

The view that Hume's definition could be considered adequate

Hume's definition neatly sums up the key feature of a miracle as something which contradicts everyday experience. If something happens rarely, it is not a miracle; the rare occurrence shows us that we need to modify what we used to think were laws of nature, but it does not show that a miracle has happened. Hume therefore says that for an event to be a miracle, there must be uniform experience against it. His definition is useful for his own refutation of miracles that follows. Modern liberal theologians such as Bultmann might agree with Hume where he says that reasonable people will not accept that miracles have occurred, because there will be a more probable explanation.

The view that Hume's definition could be considered inadequate

Many, including Swinburne, argue that Hume's definition of miracle fails to recognise that the so-called 'laws of nature' are descriptive rather than prescriptive. In other words, the laws of science describe what has been observed so far, but they do not tell nature what it may or may not do. If something goes against the laws of nature, then it is no more than something different from what has previously been observed. A 'transgression' of the laws of nature is something we have not seen before, but this does not make it an impossibility. Scientific discoveries happen all the time, and scientists often come across anomalies and counter-examples that make them rethink their conclusions.

Hume does not consider the idea that calling an event a 'miracle' is to give the event an interpretation. He does not consider that an event could be a miracle for one person but not for another. This could seem unnecessarily narrow. He also does not include the idea that a miracle should be beneficial. A sudden unexplainable violation of the laws of nature that caused almost everyone to die would not meet most people's ideas of a miracle.

Hume also could be considered to miss the point of a miracle, which is its revelatory function. Miracles are not just exceptions to the laws of nature, but are events with special religious significance, done by God for a purpose, such as to reveal God's nature or to encourage people. An event that was merely extraordinary but had no point to it, such as all the black umbrellas in the world suddenly turning yellow, would not generally be regarded as a miracle even though it would fit Hume's definition.

Holland's definition

Holland defined a miracle as 'a remarkable and beneficial coincidence that is interpreted in a religious fashion,' and also 'an event that in certain circumstances has a human significance'.

The view that Holland's definition could be considered adequate

Holland does not insist that miracles have to violate laws of nature. His definition allows for narrow escapes and fortunate coincidences, which are often seen as miraculous events in the modern world. Miracles should not have to be confined to extraordinary violations of the laws of nature. Holland is right to stress the interpretation given to the event by those who experienced it; those affected by the event are in the best position to judge the impact on their lives. Calling something a miracle is a subjective judgement, and Holland recognises this. It is not like calling something a mammal, where the object has to fit predetermined criteria.

An event that violated the laws of nature, but which was not witnessed by anyone and had no effect on anyone, would be considered miraculous by some other thinkers, but Holland is wise to avoid including such events in his definition.

Holland recognises that a miracle needs to be understood within its context, so an event could be seen as a miracle within a community of believers and just a happy coincidence to non-believers.

The view that Holland's definition could be considered inadequate

Holland could be accused of 'Humpty Dumptyism'. This is an expression sometimes used by philosophers to indicate the practice of giving words entirely new meanings in an effort to win an argument. It comes from a passage in Lewis Carroll's 1871 *Alice Through the Looking Glass*, where Alice is in conversation with Humpty Dumpty, who has just said 'There's glory for you!':

Holland could be accused of 'Humpty-Dumptyism' – redefining a word to mean something very different from the way it is normally used.

> 'I don't know what you mean by "glory,"' Alice said.
>
> Humpty Dumpty smiled contemptuously. 'Of course you don't – till I tell you. I meant "there's a nice knock-down argument for you!"'
>
> 'But "glory" doesn't mean "a nice knock-down argument,"' Alice objected.
>
> 'When I use a word,' Humpty Dumpty said in rather a scornful tone, 'it means just what I choose it to mean – neither more nor less.'
>
> 'The question is,' said Alice, 'whether you CAN make words mean so many different things.'
>
> Lewis Carroll, *Through the Looking Glass*

Holland uses the word 'miracle' in a way that it is not normally used; by removing the idea of a violation of the laws of nature from his definition, he could be said to have changed the meaning of the word to such a great extent that it is no longer recognisable.

Holland's definition could be argued to be inadequate on the grounds that it is too broad. It reduces the extraordinary nature of miracles to the more ordinary. The emphasis on subjective interpretation means that it is difficult to argue for the truth of miracles in any objective sense; they just become 'true for me' rather than universally true.

Swinburne's definition

Swinburne defined a miracle as 'a violation of a law of nature by a god, that is, a very powerful rational being who is not a material object (viz., is invisible and intangible)'.

The view that Swinburne's definition could be considered adequate

Swinburne uses a definition very similar to that of Hume, which is helpful because it means that they are both talking about the same thing when Swinburne critiques Hume. Swinburne, however, concentrates on the ways in which science operates, rejecting Hume's view that the laws of nature are 'fixed', and instead referring to them as 'corrigible' or capable of change. Swinburne's definition can therefore be seen as adequate as it is a development and refinement of Hume's. He includes the involvement of God, which is helpful in clarifying how miracles are usually understood. A miracle should be understood as a theological concept, and not just as a happy coincidence or stroke of luck. Swinburne's definition captures the unique, remarkable nature of miracles. In his further explanation of miracles, Swinburne highlights the element of subjectivity in their interpretation, which is an important point also noted by Aquinas.

The view that Swinburne's definition could be considered inadequate

Swinburne does not consider how we might define a violation of the laws of nature that was not done by God, if such an event were ever to happen. He also does not allow the possibility of miracles happening to non-religious people; if a miraculous act has to be done by God in order to qualify, then this rules out any secular claims. It could be seen as a kind of arrogance to insist that miracles are only miracles if they are done by God, as if religious people have a monopoly on miracles. If non-religious people want to claim that the event they experienced was a miracle, they should be able to make that claim.

> **AO2 activity 2**
> a) Which definition of miracle, if any, do you think best captures the essence of what a miracle is? Give reasons for your choice.
> b) How would you define a 'miracle'?

How far can different definitions of miracles be considered as contradictory?

This question is asking for a consideration of whether the different definitions of miracle contradict each other, or whether perhaps they simply emphasise different aspects of miracle.

The view that the different definitions of miracles are contradictory

There are significant differences in definitions of miracle, and these contradict each other.

- The most striking contradiction is that Hume's definition is at odds with that of Holland. Hume insists that a miracle has to be a violation of the laws of nature, whereas Holland says that the laws of nature do not have to be broken for an event to be considered a miracle. An extraordinary coincidence could still be a miracle without any breaking of natural laws.
- Hume writes about natural laws being 'violated', whereas Aquinas, in contrast, writes about God doing things that nature can never do, not in terms of breaking natural laws but of going beyond them.
- Aquinas and Swinburne assume that God created natural laws, and can use them and suspend them at will as this is part of God's omnipotent nature; Hume does not make this assumption.
- Hume's understanding of miracle refers only to reports of miracles. Other thinkers consider the possibility that someone might experience a miracle first-hand.
- Swinburne does not understand 'laws of nature' in the same way that Hume does. Hume appears to think that these laws are unbreakable, whereas Swinburne argues that the laws of nature are 'corrigible'; we can change them if we make new discoveries or have new experiences.
- Different thinkers have defined miracles differently because they disagreed with the definitions of others, so their definitions are bound to contradict.

The view that the different definitions are not contradictory

The definitions have different emphases, but the apparent contradictions are only superficial. They all see miracles as extraordinary events that are unexpected, and that give people the sense that God has intervened in the world. They all make the assumption that a miracle has to have witnesses in order to be called a miracle, and that the interpretation given to the event is intrinsic to the definition, even if this is implicit in some definitions. They look at different facets of miracle, rather than contradicting each other.

> **AO2 activity 3**
>
> In your view, are the different definitions of miracle just emphasising different things, or do they contradict each other?

How far can the challenges to belief in miracles be considered effective?

Some thinkers have challenged the idea that miracles happen. This question asks you to consider those challenges, and decide whether they are persuasive.

The view that challenges to miracles are effective

Hume's challenges to miracles can be seen as effective. He is right to point out that there is a reason why laws of nature are called laws: they always behave in the same way, and therefore there are no violations of them. In a scientific age, we should look for natural explanations of events, however unusual they might be, as the balance of evidence will always be in favour of a natural rather than a supernatural explanation. It is lazy thinking to ascribe unusual events to God as being miraculous. If someone suddenly recovers from what was thought to be a terminal illness, we should use tried and tested, repeatable scientific experiments to find out why they recovered, so that we can improve our medical knowledge, rather than calling it a miracle as if we are stuck in a superstitious past. Hume gives a comprehensive set of reasons against belief in miracle, which together make a strong case.

Bultmann's challenges to miracles can be seen as effective. People in the twenty-first century have a much more empirical way of understanding the world than people of the past. Stories of miracles and wonders do not fit with modern life, and can be obstacles to faith. Those who want to have a deeper religious belief could find it impossible to believe miracle stories at face value. Bultmann is right to argue that miracle stories are better understood as myth than as literal historical truth.

Wiles' challenge to miracles is powerful. It is impossible to understand why God would perform trivial miracles such as turning water into wine or moving a shadow on a wall, but not help people who are being massacred in genocide or dying in thousands because of a pandemic. If God can miraculously give sight to the blind, there is no explanation of why there are so many blind people in the world. The idea of God occasionally intervening in the world to perform miracles for a random few people makes God seem to have favourites, and not to care about others at all. Wiles' idea that God works in the world by inspiring people to do good is much more palatable.

The view that challenges to miracles are ineffective

Hume's challenges to miracles can be seen as ineffective:

- Hume's choice of definition is too narrow; by defining miracles only as violations of the laws of nature, he is ruling out other possibilities, such as Holland's coincidence miracles.
- Hume does not recognise that God is omnipotent, and that therefore God can do anything. A God who creates all life is quite capable of restoring it to someone who has died. God created the laws of nature, so the laws of nature cannot tell God what is and is not possible.
- Hume only discusses reports of miracles, and does not consider the possibility that he might experience a miracle himself.
- Hume's commitment to empiricism blinds him to other kinds of knowledge, such as the knowledge gained through religious experience.

- Hume makes unfair attacks on religious people as being ignorant and untrustworthy, attacking their character rather than what they are saying (an '*ad hominem*' attack).
- Hume understands the laws of nature in a way that is too deterministic. In other words, he sees them as closed and final, where they could not work in any other way from the ways that have been observed, whereas there is the possibility that they may be more flexible.

Bultmann's challenges to miracles can be seen as ineffective. He assumes that miracle stories cannot be literally true, and ignores the fact that God can do anything. Understanding miracle stories as myth dilutes them to such an extent that the whole message of Christianity is undermined. Christianity teaches that Jesus was miraculously born of a virgin, and was resurrected after his death on the cross. If these stories are understood only as myth, there is not much left of Christianity.

Wiles' challenges to miracles can be seen as ineffective. He has missed the point that we cannot expect to understand the mind of God, and is instead thinking in terms of 'what I would do if I were God', which is arrogant. Wiles has not taken into account the idea that miracles have a revelatory function. They are meant to reveal something about the nature of God, and are not just about helping particular individuals. For example, giving sight to a blind man reveals the enlightening power of God; the miracle is not meant to be simply giving help to one individual.

> **AO2 activity 4**
>
> Do you find the challenges made to the idea of miracle effective, or ineffective? Take each of the challenges and write three or four sentences for each, explaining whether you think it is a strong or a weak challenge.

To what extent can Swinburne's responses to Hume be accepted as valid?

In the twentieth century, Richard Swinburne replied to the critique of miracle that Hume had made 200 years previously. Taking Hume's criticisms one by one, Swinburne offered counter-arguments. This question requires a consideration of whether Swinburne's counter-arguments are effective.

The view that Swinburne gives a valid response to Hume

- Swinburne correctly identifies how scientific laws of nature operate, in terms of statistics; he recognises that laws of nature are 'corrigible' rather than fixed for ever.
- Swinburne calls Hume 'bigoted' for refusing to accept any report of a miracle from a religious person, and this is a fair accusation. Swinburne's principles of credulity and testimony are good general rules: we should not doubt the evidence of our senses, or the evidence given by other people, unless we have good reasons to be sceptical about them. Hume dismisses the evidence because the people giving it are religious, and not because of a fault in the evidence.
- Swinburne is right to say that other kinds of evidence could be offered to support miracles, apart from testimony. Physical evidence is

important, and is taken seriously in courts of law. If there is physical evidence that a miracle has taken place, this should be recognised.

- Swinburne is right to say that Hume's standard for reliable witnesses is unreasonably high. Events are witnessed by anyone who happens to be there; very few events of any kind are witnessed by large numbers of people who are impeccably reliable and well-educated. The bar should not be raised just because the event is a miracle.

- Swinburne is right to point out that accounts of miracles in different religions do not cancel each other out in the way Hume describes. Perhaps they would cancel each other out if the stories actually did contradict each other, but they do not.

The view that Swinburne does not give a valid response to Hume

- Swinburne's view, that there can be occasional, unrepeatable violations of the laws of nature that do not change the laws of nature themselves, is incoherent. Anomalies do change the way laws of nature are understood by science. A scientific law that says something like 'All Xs do Y' is challenged even if there is only one X that does not do Y. Karl Popper's work on falsification in science makes this clear. If just one exceptional X does not do Y, then the law has to be changed to 'Most Xs do Y'; we cannot continue to insist that 'All Xs do Y'.

- Swinburne adds to the definition of a miracle that it has to be 'unrepeatable'. This does not work, as we have no way of knowing whether an event is repeatable or not. We do not and cannot know if something has happened for the one and only time, or if it has happened for the first time in a sequence.

- Swinburne's principles of credulity and testimony are good as general rules but, as Caroline Franks Davis notes, they work best when the experience is relatively trivial. If we have an experience or hear reports of an experience that is likely to have serious consequences, such a violent crime or a miracle, then we need more than just the evidence of our senses or the trustworthiness of the reporter. Further investigation needs to be done. If miracles do happen, this is important. 'God brought my daughter back from the dead' is a much more serious claim to make than 'Nina likes cheese'. We might accept the latter claim on fairly thin evidence as it would not matter a great deal if we turned out to be wrong, but the former claim requires much more solid evidence to be acceptable.

- Hume may be right in saying that religious people have a tendency to be gullible and want to believe in miracles; he says that they see acts of God because they want to see them, rather than because of the evidence. Swinburne argues that this is bigoted of Hume, but perhaps it is fair.

Synoptic link

Link to *Chapter 5: Religious experience (part one)*. Caroline Franks Davis offered a detailed discussion of the evidential force of religious experience, including experience of miracles.

Practising AO1 questions

AO1 questions begin with one of a range of possible command words (see pages 8–9 for more detail). The following question begins with the word 'Explain'. 'Explain' questions require you to give an account, exploring the reasons behind something and its key features. You do not need to consider the quality of an argument or offer any views about it.

Explain the different understandings of miracles given by Holland and Swinburne.

(Eduqas A Level Religious Studies, Autumn 2020, Component 2: Philosophy of Religion, Question 5a)

Example

Holland's[6] understanding of miracles is very different from that of[2] Swinburne[6]. Holland did not think that the[2] laws of nature[7] have to be broken in order for an event to be termed a 'miracle'[2]. He believed there can things called[1] 'contingency' or 'coincidence' miracles[7], where an extraordinary and unlikely coincidence of events happens that is beneficial and is understood to be a miracle by witnesses, even if it can be explained in[1] natural[7], scientific terms.[1] Holland gives the example of a child playing with a toy on a train track as a train approaches around a bend. The child's mother is on a hillside and can see both the child and the train coming towards them. The train stops suddenly and does not hit the child. The mother understands this to be a miracle, even if there is an explanation that does not break the laws of nature, such as the driver fainting and applying the brakes automatically.[3] Holland said this would be a miracle because the mother understands it as a miracle. Her interpretation is what makes it miraculous.[1]

1. The paragraph shows accurate and relevant knowledge, correctly identifying Holland's understanding of miracles.

2. The response answers the question set. Rather than generally addressing the topic of miracles, it clearly focuses on the two thinkers specified.

3. There is good use of an example in this paragraph.

4. Sacred texts are not relevant in this part of the response, and so it is appropriate that none appear.

5. Connections to other areas of study are not relevant in this part of the response, and so it is appropriate that none appear.

6. The scholarly views used in this answer fit the question's requirements.

7. There is accurate use of specialist language and vocabulary in context.

Activity

1. Look at the example of a past paper question and an example paragraph, about Holland, taken from a longer answer written in response on page 255. Write some feedback for the student who produced this paragraph, explaining what is good about it and where they could have provided more detail or greater clarity, or other improvements.

2. Read the guidance about Assessment Objective 1 in 'Understanding the Assessment Objectives' on pages 6–7. Then, write a similar paragraph detailing Swinburne's understanding of miracles. Include Swinburne's definition of a miracle, and explain what he means when he talks about unrepeatable breaking of natural laws. Use specialist vocabulary where possible.

AO1 practice question

Try answering the following question. There are some points to remember to help you write a developed response.

Examine the term 'miracle' with reference to three scholars.

(Eduqas A Level Religious Studies, Summer 2019, Component 2: Philosophy of Religion, Question 2a)

Points to remember

- Note that you have studied four scholars, and you are asked for three. You will not get more marks for writing about four, so choose just three to give yourself enough time to develop some detail in your response.
- The question asks you to 'Examine', so you need to give a detailed, thorough account of each scholar's definition of 'miracle'.
- Try to use specialist vocabulary in your answer.
- Make sure that you clearly demonstrate that you understand the scholars were writing at different times. They were not all answering each other because they were not all contemporaries.

Practising AO2 questions

AO2 questions are designed to assess your ability to evaluate and critically analyse. Concentrate on weighing up different views, and identifying the strengths and weaknesses of each view. Avoid spending too much of your response presenting your knowledge in a descriptive way.

Read the past paper question and the example paragraph taken from a longer answer written in response, before completing the activity on page 258.

> *'All definitions of miracles are inadequate.' Evaluate this view.*
>
> (Eduqas A Level Religious Studies, Summer 2019, Component 2: Philosophy of Religion, Question 2b)

Example

A definition is adequate if it successfully sums up the thing it is trying to define, while ruling out other things. Many people have tried to define what a miracle is.[2] Aquinas[4] said that miracles are things that are done occasionally by God that go against the laws of nature. He gave examples of three different levels of miracle, where the highest kind is something that is done by God that nature can never do, such as making a shadow move or making the Sun stand still in the sky, which are examples from the Bible. A lesser kind of miracle is where God changes the natural order of things (for example, making someone see when they used to be blind when, in nature, people tend to go blind after they have been able to see), or when God does things that happen in nature but on a different timescale (for example, healing someone instantly when in nature it would take some time).[3] In my view, Aquinas' definition is too rigid, because people should be able to define a miracle in any way they want.[1]

1. There is very little analysis and evaluation. There is an assertive statement of the writer's position at the paragraph end, but the writer has only described Aquinas' view and has not explored it or weighed it up.

2. The paragraph would be better if it focused more clearly on the issues in the question.

3. The paragraph contains examples but they are not used to support arguments because the writer has not developed an opinion of their own and justified it with reasoned arguments.

4. There is some reference to scholarly views, but this is done in a descriptive way rather than an evaluative way.

5. There are no links made with other areas of the course; this is acceptable because there are no appropriate links.

6. This paragraph does contain specialist language and vocabulary in context.

Activity

Read the example paragraph on page 257. It is taken from a longer answer. The paragraph is weak, because the writer has included a lot of factually-correct description, but has not used analysis and evaluation to construct an argument. There is an assertive statement, but it is not supported with reasoning or justification.

Write a better answer, making sure that you offer a clear point of view that you justify with reasoning, and that you show you understand opinions that are different from your own. You could take each of the definitions you have studied in turn and evaluate them one by one, or you could write a response in which you consider the definitions together.

AO2 practice question 1

Try answering this question. There are some points to remember to help you write a developed response.

> *'Religious experience has more value for an individual than for a religious community.' Evaluate this view.*
>
> (Eduqas A Level Religious Studies, Summer 2019, Component 2: Philosophy of Religion, Question 1b)

Points to remember

- The question is asking for an opinion, not just a list of descriptive points about religious experience for the individual and then a list of descriptive points about religious experience for the community.
- You need to weigh up different ideas and decide on a point of view: do religious experiences have more value for the individual, more value for the community, an equal amount of value for both, or no value at all?
- Give reasons to support your point of view, rather than just asserting it.
- Try to give examples to illustrate the points you make, and refer to scholarly views where possible. This is not a topic where there are firm views from different scholars on either side of a debate, but you could make reference to thinkers such as Ninian Smart and Émile Durkheim.

AO2 practice question 2

Now try this question on your own.

> *'It is impossible for miracles to happen'. Evaluate this view.*
>
> (WJEC A Level Religious Studies, Summer 2019, Unit 5: Philosophy of Religion, Question 4)

Mark schemes for all exam questions can be found at www.eduqas.co.uk and www.wjec.co.uk.

7 Religious language (part one)

This chapter and the next chapter look at some of the philosophical problems of communicating religious ideas, especially between people who do not share the same faith. 'Religious language' refers to the language that is used between believers and when talking about religious faith and religious ideas, just as 'the language of physics' or 'the language of cricket' refers to the ways in which people use words in those contexts. Religious language has its own issues, however.

If you have ever tried to explain to your grandparents how to use modern technology, or tried to explain the rules of chess to someone who has never played before, you will know that problems arise when people do not have the same experiences or the same vocabulary. In religion, there can be similar difficulties, when some people want to talk about God, sin, salvation, or heaven, but the people they want to talk to have no understanding of what these things mean, because they see reality entirely differently.

Ideas about meaning have occupied philosophers for centuries. Debates about religious language form part of this much larger philosophical discussion. The debate raises interesting questions:

- If people have very different religious beliefs, or no religious beliefs at all, how can they find ways of communicating so that they understand each other? Is it even possible?
- Are religious ideas worth discussing, or are they actually meaningless, or lacking in any real content?
- Is it worth discussing anything if you can't test it to prove who is right and who is wrong?
- Are religious statements about facts, or are they subjective expressions of personal feelings and preferences?
- Are there ways of helping people understand religious concepts successfully by, for example, using analogies?

It can be difficult for people to explain their religious beliefs to others who do not share their faith.

AO1

This section of the chapter will enhance your **knowledge** and **understanding** of the topic and help you develop your AO1 skills.

Inherent problems of religious language

In this section, we will explore some of the **inherent** problems of religious language: in other words, some of the problems that are characteristic of religious language and are embedded in its very nature.

We use language as one of our main means of communication, and often assume that other people know what we mean by our choice of words.

Languages develop and change as we need new words. If someone comes up with a new food or a new type of clothing, or a new scientific discovery is made, we need a new word for it so that we can talk about it with others. We also need language in order to think: language helps us organise our thoughts and memories, and understand our emotions, ideas, and experiences. Language is an essential part of living in a community; but it can have its limitations.

Difficulties in communication using language can arise when the same words have several different meanings, as, for example, in the saying 'Time flies like an arrow, but fruit flies like a banana'. In this sentence, the word 'flies' functions first as a verb and then as a noun, and the word 'like' functions first as a comparative and then as a verb. We are misled into thinking of flying fruit or of strange creatures called 'time flies' that enjoy arrows, because of the ambiguities inherent in our language.

Statements such as 'There is a mouse on my desk' or 'This plate has a chip on it' could be interpreted in different ways, and we need to know the context before the pictures created in our minds are accurate. Context can make a great deal of difference to the way we understand things, and so can our previously held assumptions. People with autism and young children often find the ambiguities of language very difficult. An example of this is a young boy who was terrified by a particular stretch of road on his way home from school, because there was a sign that said 'Road bears left' and he was scared of the road bears. Often, we assume that other people know what we mean when we say something, but misinterpretation is common.

There can also be difficulties when the subject matter under discussion has a vocabulary all of its own. Specialisms such as software engineering, theoretical physics, ballet, wine-tasting, gymnastics, horse-riding, and

> **Key term**
>
> **inherent:** being part of something as a characteristic attribute

Many specialisms have their own vocabularies that are difficult for non-specialists to understand.

many other fields of interest, have their own specialist words. Outsiders listening in to a conversation between people with a shared specialist interest might find themselves unable to understand many of the nouns and verbs.

All language, then, can carry potential communication problems. Religious language has its own particular inherent difficulties that are interesting to explore, as they raise questions about the limitations of language when talking about the non-physical, and also questions about the whole nature of meaning.

AO1 activity 1

Think of an activity you enjoy that has a specialist vocabulary, such as gaming, music, or a sport. Choose three of the words that have special meanings in your activity, and write a sentence for each to explain their special usage for someone who does not share your interest. These could be useful examples to use in your essays.

For example: *Coupé* means 'cut' in French, but in ballet it is a linking step where you put your weight on one leg and the other leg cuts in front or behind, with the toes of the lifted foot pointing at the level of the ankle bone of the other foot, before you transfer your weight.

The limitations of language for traditional conceptions of God

For religious believers, one of the problems inherent in religious language is that God cannot be completely understood by the human mind. The Bible talks of the mystery and otherness of God, and of how the ways of God are beyond human understanding.

> *How great is God – beyond our understanding!*
> *The number of his years is past finding out.* 99
>
> Job 36:26, *Holy Bible NIV*

> *Oh, the depth of the riches of the wisdom and knowledge of God!*
> *How unsearchable his judgments,*
> *and his paths beyond tracing out!*
> *'Who has known the mind of the Lord?*
> *Or who has been his counsellor?'* 99
>
> Romans 11:33–34, *Holy Bible NIV*

Religious believers talk about attributes of God that are difficult, if not impossible, for the human mind to comprehend. For example, they say that God is eternal; existing outside time; and able to see the past, present, and future all at once: a description that people struggle to conceptualise. As human beings, we live within time, and struggle to imagine anything that is timeless. Believers talk of God in terms of infinity: God is infinitely loving, infinitely powerful, infinitely wise, they say. We might have an idea of what great love looks like, or extreme power, but we have difficulty in comprehending these qualities on an infinite scale.

Synoptic link

Link to *Chapter 3: Challenges to religious belief: the problem of evil and suffering.* When he was struggling with the problem of why God allows evil and suffering, Job came to the conclusion that he should not expect to understand the ways of the Almighty.

If God cannot be completely understood even by those who believe in God, this creates a problem inherent to religious language: how can believers communicate their faith when its subject matter is beyond human comprehension? The problem is not just a question of how to talk to others of different faiths (or none); it is also a question of how believers of the same faith communicate successfully with each other.

Thomas Aquinas recognised this problem of religious language. He was celebrating Mass on the Feast of St Nicholas on 6 December 1273 when he had a religious experience so profound that he stopped writing his great work, *Summa Theologica*, and never finished it. Brother Reginald, his secretary, begged him to carry on writing, but Aquinas said that he could not do it. 'All I have written seems like straw,' he said. Aquinas did not mean that he had written rubbish, but he realised that he had not got any further than the basics, just as straw is a basic building material (or was, in the thirteenth century). The experience he had received of God made him recognise that God cannot be captured and pinned down by human language so that everyone can clearly understand. Aquinas realised that his great masterpiece had hardly got off the ground.

AO1 activity 2

a) Look up these passages in the Bible and make a note of them. They all express the idea that God is beyond human comprehension:
- Ecclesiastes 3:11
- Isaiah 55:8–9
- 1 Corinthians 2:16

b) Do you think that these verses communicate anything at all about God? If so, what?

The challenge to sacred texts and religious pronouncements as unintelligible

A second, related problem inherent in religious language is that religious texts, such as the Bible, perhaps cannot be easily understood except by someone who is already part of that faith community.

Metaphysical vocabulary

The Bible is full of language and ideas that need explanation, and many of these ideas are central to the whole Christian message. There is the idea, for example, that sin came into the world through the disobedience of Adam and Eve; 'sin' is a religious concept that might not be comprehensible to someone with no belief in God. There is the Christian belief that Jesus was the Messiah expected by the Jews and promised by the prophets; the concepts of Messiahship and prophethood may only make sense from within the community of Christian and Jewish believers, and these two faith communities are likely to understand the concepts in different ways.

These concepts and others are not about usual, everyday experiences; they are **metaphysical** concepts. 'Meta' literally means 'alongside' and therefore 'metaphysical' means going alongside the physical; metaphysical language

> **Key term**
>
> **metaphysical:** relating to existence or knowledge that are non-physical, supernatural and beyond purely sensory description, such as love, truth, and God

is not about the physical world, but accompanies it and is about a different aspect of reality. Talk of metaphysical ideas is inherently problematic because we are talking about things that cannot be experienced using our five senses; we are not talking about empirical experiences.

Who we are shapes our understanding

Whatever we experience, we experience it from our own individual point of view. We might experience something as a Chinese woman, or as a middle-aged man, or as a sixteenth-century peasant, or as a blind person. Who we are shapes how we interpret things, and perhaps it is impossible to understand the language of religious texts and pronouncements unless we are religious people with a religious way of understanding the world.

Although it was written over a time period of at least 400 years, the Bible is for the most part a continuous narrative. It starts with stories of how God, the Creator of the world, formed the universe and made everything in it, including the first people. It tells the story of how those people disobeyed God and distanced themselves from God; and then how their descendants, through many events and battles, times of hardship and exile, and times of plenty, developed an understanding of God. The narrative is called *Heilsgeschichte* in theology, a German word that means 'salvation history'. It is a history of how God interacts with his people through the prophets, and through religious experiences and miracles, until eventually, God's son Jesus Christ is sent into the world to save people from their sins through his sacrificial death and resurrection. The Bible then continues the story after Jesus' death, showing how the first Christians formed the first Christian communities in the face of persecution, led by the Holy Spirit.

It could be argued that those who do not have a Christian faith cannot readily understand this whole story. Perhaps only those with faith can truly understand language about miracles, or resurrection, or the power of the Holy Spirit; perhaps you have to be totally immersed in the whole worldview of Christianity to know what the language of the narrative really means. Still more difficult might be the problem of taking isolated pieces of text or individual stories, and trying to understand them out of their context as part of the Biblical narrative.

The special status of religious writings

Perhaps the status and authority of religious texts for a community of believers is also something that can only be understood from within. In many religious traditions, copies of sacred texts are treated with a special reverence to signify the role they play in the life and worship of believers. Followers of some traditions keep their holy books on the highest shelf, or have a special place set aside in the house for reading from them, or keep them wrapped in expensive cloths when not in use. Places of worship often have designated places for reading from holy books, to show that these texts are believed to be from God and are not just like any other book.

Religious writings have a special status in the lives of believers. Some believers might study them every day as a source of moral and spiritual

> **AO1 activity 3**
> Make a list of three or four metaphysical concepts used in religion, such as 'redemption from sin' or 'glorifying God'. You could use these as examples in essays.

guidance. They might use the religious texts to settle disputes, to answer questions, or to help them deal with a problem in their lives.

It could be argued that those outside the religious tradition cannot fully understand the sacred texts, even if they can understand what the words say, because they have not experienced their role, their sacredness, and their authority in the lives of people of faith.

The language of worship

The language used during worship could also be unintelligible to non-believers. Pronouncements such as 'I baptise you in the name of the Father, and of the Son, and of the Holy Spirit,' or 'When we eat this bread and drink this cup we proclaim your death, Lord Jesus, until you come in glory,' are packed with religious significance and symbolism which could be lost on people who are not part of a Christian tradition.

Ludwig Wittgenstein, whose ideas are explored in the next chapter, put forward the view that language, including religious language, can be understood using the analogy of a game. People who visit players of a game only briefly might have difficulty understanding what the different moves mean, and how the scoring works; just as a visitor to a place of worship might struggle to understand what is going on. But becoming involved in the worship would help the visitor make more sense of the language, just as joining in with a game helps a newcomer pick up the rules.

Some scholars, such as Ayer and Flew (whose ideas will be explored in detail later in the chapter), have taken the view that religious texts and pronouncements are not just difficult to understand, but are actually meaningless and empty of content. Because we cannot test with our senses whether or not God exists, or whether an action is a sin, or whether Jesus' death can bring about salvation, these ideas are meaningless.

Religious claims and literal truth

A further problem is that in some religious texts, there are ideas and statements that seem to be inconsistent. Using the Bible again as an example, there are potentially contradictory ideas: Jesus is seen as God incarnate (both God and human at the same time); God is all-loving, and yet God commands wars, allows people to suffer, and performs miracles for only a few; God is beyond time and all-knowing, and yet God has to wait and see how the people respond to commandments before deciding what to do next. The gospels record Jesus' last words, when he was dying on the cross, but they all have different last words; they cannot all be correct.

If the claims in the Bible are not meant to be literally true but need to be understood in some different, metaphorical way, the difficulties of comprehending religious language become even greater. However, if the claims should be understood as literally true, then there are difficulties in comprehending how seemingly contradictory statements can both be true.

Sacred texts hold a special status and authority in the lives of believers. Non-believers might struggle to understand this.

AO1 activity 4

Find some examples of ways in which copies of sacred texts are shown respect in religious life. For example, the Guru Granth Sahib in the Sikh religion is kept wrapped in silk cloths when not being read.

The challenge that religious language is not a common shared base and experience

One of the inherent problems of religious language is that a lot of our language is about things that can be experienced with the senses, in a shared way. In the UK, we know what other people mean when they say they have had a cheese sandwich or that they can see a seagull. If we live in a shared context with others, we understand what they are talking about. But if we go to a foreign country and people talk about foods or birds we have never heard of or experienced, we find it hard to understand them; even after they have spoken, we still do not know what they ate or what they can see, because the words mean nothing to us.

Some of the words and phrases we use today, such as 'social media', 'vegan', or 'windscreen wiper' would be completely incomprehensible to someone living 300 years ago; and, similarly, the language that Chaucer used when he wrote *The Canterbury Tales* in the fourteenth century can be difficult for us to understand today without the aid of a study guide. Shared bases and shared experiences are very important for successful communication through language.

Religious language, then, can be problematic because it uses words and phrases that do not match experiences shared with people of other faiths or of no faith. Many of the words make sense only within the religious context, such as 'Holy Spirit', 'sacrament', and 'incarnation' in Christianity, or 'mikveh', 'kosher', and 'shekinah' in Judaism.

It can be difficult to find words to describe and communicate things that are totally outside someone else's experience, such as childbirth, bereavement, or how it feels to live with a life-limiting illness – but perhaps it is not completely impossible. Perhaps there are ways in which religious language can be used to get around the problems inherent in it, so that believers can communicate at least something of their faith to others.

The insider/outsider problem

The 'insider/outsider problem' refers to the difficulties encountered whenever people set out to learn about societies, cultures, and belief systems that are different from their own; for example, when an anthropologist from the UK wants to learn about the urban poor in Mexico. It can be a problem because the way things look on the surface, to someone from a different culture, can be misinterpreted. It is easy for the outsider to let their own concerns and assumptions colour the way they see the lives of others.

In the study of religion, the insider/outside problem raises the question of whether significant understanding can be achieved only from within a religious tradition.

Professor Ninian Smart is an example of a scholar who did a lot of work on the problem of how 'outsiders' can understand religion and religious language. He was one of the first to shape the academic subject of Religious Studies as we know it today. In the past, students studied Theology, with

> **AO1 activity 5**
> Make a note of examples of experiences some people have that other people might not share, and yet they might still want to communicate about them. For example, what it is like to grow up knowing you were adopted, or what it is like to be colour blind.

the assumption that Christianity should be the focus and that the students were themselves Christian. Ninian Smart wanted to find ways in which religion could be studied by anyone, regardless of their personal beliefs. In the newly-founded University of Lancaster in the 1960s, he helped to develop an approach known as **phenomenology**, where people study the observable, external features of religious traditions, such as the places of worship, the festivals, and the sacred objects, and also try to understand religion from the perspective of the believer.

Smart wrote of the need to adopt what he called a 'methodical agnosticism', where you 'bracket out' or put to one side your own beliefs as far as possible, and look at different religious traditions in a genuine spirit of enquiry, trying not to let your own previously held views colour the way you interpret the religious life of others. He thought that the aim of Religious Studies should be to try to grasp the meaning and significance of religion for believers, trying to see it through their eyes in a way he called the 'eidetic vision'. Smart was of the opinion that it is possible to gain some understanding of religious belief, even as an 'outsider'.

The differences between cognitive and non-cognitive language

In philosophical discussion of language, a distinction is made between cognitive and non-cognitive language.

Cognitive language refers to statements that are about things that can be known. (Think of 'recognition', which means 'knowing again'.) Language is cognitive if a statement is made about facts, and we could know whether the statement is true or false using our reason and/or our senses. Philosophers sometimes refer to cognitive statements as being '**truth-apt**'; in other words it is apt, or relevant, to think of them in terms of truth and falsity. **Non-cognitive** language is not about things that can be known, true or false. It is about feelings, attitudes, preferences, and interpretations.

It might help to understand this distinction by thinking about the questions you would write if you were setting a quiz. You would want to include questions with cognitive answers: answers that you can mark right or wrong so that you can work out the score.

You might choose questions where the answers include things like: Tallinn is the capital of Estonia, the letter K is worth five points in Scrabble, and the Shannon is the longest river in Ireland. Even if the quiz contestants get the answers wrong, their answers are still cognitive statements, because we know that they are wrong. If they get an answer wrong and argue with the referee, someone can look up the facts and the matter can be settled.

But questions asking for non-cognitive answers would not work in a quiz: What are the most interesting animals in the zoo? Does pineapple belong on a pizza? Who is the greatest footballer of all time? These would not work in a quiz because the answers would be non-cognitive statements. Nobody

---

Key terms

phenomenology: an approach to study that concentrates on things that can be observed

cognitive: connected with thinking or mental processes relating to knowledge; a cognitive statement is a statement that can be known to be true or false

truth-apt: capable of being called 'true' or 'false'

non-cognitive: a proposition that is not concerned with facts about the world and cannot, therefore, be known as true or false

AO1 activity 6

Explain what Ninian Smart meant by 'phenomenology' in the study of religion.

could know for certain whether the answers were true or false, and so nobody would know how to mark them. Instead, the answers would reflect personal opinions, tastes, and attitudes.

AO1 activity 7

Which of these statements are cognitive, and which are non-cognitive?

a) The Battle of Hastings happened in 1066.
b) Jazz is better to listen to than rap.
c) In class, teachers should spend exactly the same amount of time with each student in the room.
d) *Summa Theologica* was written by J.K. Rowling.

Now write three cognitive statements and three non-cognitive statements of your own.

In A Level Religious Studies, you make cognitive statements for AO1, where you are asked to show your knowledge and understanding through accurate recall and explanation of facts. The examiner looks at your answer and thinks, 'Yes, that is what Aquinas said, true; no, that is not the cosmological argument, that part is wrong'. For AO2, you are asked to use non-cognitive language when you make personal judgements, assessments, and interpretations. The examiner cannot look at your answer and say, 'No, you disagree with Aquinas so you are wrong,' because there is no way of demonstrating whether your interpretation is true or false. For AO1, you are marked according to whether you got it right or wrong, and for AO2, you are marked on your skill in argument and reasoning; but for AO2, the examiner cannot know definitively whether your judgements are true or false.

Of course, in the real world of language usage, things are more complicated and blurred than this, and people do not always agree about whether a statement is cognitive or non-cognitive in its meaning. In ethics, there is much debate about whether moral statements are cognitive or non-cognitive. If I say 'Eating meat is wrong,' am I making a cognitive claim about a fact, or am I expressing my preference for vegetarianism or veganism as a personal lifestyle choice?

In religious language, there is much discussion about whether religious truth claims – statements that suggest something is true – are cognitive or non-cognitive. Are people making factual claims when they say, 'In the beginning, God created the heavens and the earth,' 'Jesus is alive today,' or 'God loves the world'? Or are they expressing their preferred attitude and way of interpreting reality? Different people have different views about this.

Synoptic link

Link to *A Level Religious Studies for Eduqas: Religion and Ethics, Chapter 2: Ethical thought (part two)*. There are strong links between the issues in religious language and meta-ethical language.

Religious language as cognitive (traditional religious view), but meaningless (logical positivists' view)

Traditionally, religious believers have taken the view that when they make truth claims, they are talking about facts. When they say that God exists or that God created the world, they mean others to understand that they are talking about an objective reality. They believe that there is a real God 'out there' who created and sustains the world.

In the Bible, the Psalmist writes:

> *The fool says in his heart,*
> *'There is no God.'*
>
> Psalms 14:1 and 53:1, *Holy Bible NIV*

It is clear that the writer of the Psalms thinks that those who disbelieve in God are factually wrong. The writer is making what they intend to be a cognitive claim. Religious believers usually understand the claims they make about God to be cognitive claims: matters of objective truth and facts.

However, a way of thinking, called Logical Positivism, claims that religious statements have no meaningful content. Religious statements are cognitive because they make claims that can be considered true or false, but they are meaningless because they cannot be tested.

Logical Positivism, A.J. Ayer and verification

The British philosopher A.J. Ayer (known as Freddie) presented an important challenge to religious language when he wrote a very influential book called *Language, Truth and Logic* in 1936.

In this book, Ayer took up some of the ideas of a group known as the Vienna Circle, as he had been studying in Vienna himself. The Vienna Circle was a group of philosophers who met regularly at the University of Vienna in the 1920s and 1930s to discuss philosophical issues arising in mathematics, the social sciences, and logic. They were very interested in questions raised by the philosopher Ludwig Wittgenstein, whose ideas are explored in more depth in the next chapter. Wittgenstein had been puzzling over the issues raised by the whole concept of 'meaning', and was looking at the limitations of the human mind in understanding, and the problems and possibilities of communicating meaning between different people.

After discussion, the Vienna Circle developed a position known as **Logical Positivism**. They came to the conclusion that statements (sometimes called 'propositions') can be divided into three categories:

1. **Analytic statements**: these are statements where reason can tell us whether they are true or false. Mathematical statements fall into this category, and so do definitions and tautologies. Reason tells us that the square root of 9 is 3, that bachelors are unmarried men, and big shoes are large (tautologies are where a sentence says the same thing twice).
2. **Synthetic statements**: these are statements where observation of the physical world can tell us if they are true or false. We can test them using our senses. An example of a synthetic statement might be 'the

Freddie Ayer wrote his profoundly influential book Language, Truth and Logic when he was only 26.

Key terms

Logical Positivism: a philosophical position that says statements have to be either analytic or capable of empirical testing if they are to be meaningful

analytic statements: these are statements where reason can tell us whether they are true or false

synthetic statements: these are statements where observation of the physical world can tell us if they are true or false

daffodils in my garden are in flower'. It is not an analytic statement, because 'in flower' is not part of the definition of a daffodil, and I could not tell using reason alone whether the statement is true. But I can test whether it is true by looking in my garden.

3. Meaningless statements: any statement that is neither analytic nor able to be tested with the senses is meaningless (according to logical positivists). This idea of being able to test statements with our senses is known as the **verification principle:** a principle that says synthetic statements are meaningless if there is no possibility of supporting them with physical evidence to verify them.

This way of thinking echoes the position of the Scottish philosopher David Hume. Hume thought that theological discussion was a waste of time.

> If we take into our hand any volume; of divinity or school metaphysics, for instance; let us ask, Does it contain any abstract reasoning concerning quantity or number? No. Does it contain any experimental reasoning concerning matter of fact or existence? No. Commit it then to the flames: for it can contain nothing but sophistry and illusion.
>
> David Hume, *An Enquiry Concerning Human Understanding*

In his book, Ayer put forward this logical positivist view, quoting Hume for support. He argued that in order for a statement to be meaningful, it has to be, in principle, verifiable using empirical methods. We do not necessarily have to go as far as doing the testing, to find out whether the daffodils in my garden really are in flower, but we have to know what kind of test could be applied to find out whether the statement is true or false. We know that we would need to look in my garden, and then we could see for ourselves, and this would be a good test.

The implications of Ayer's book included the idea that if synthetic statements are only meaningful if they can be tested empirically, then religious claims should be considered meaningless. According to the logical positivists, claims such as 'God created the world,' 'God has a plan for each of us,' or 'the Lord is my Shepherd' cannot be shown to be either true or false using the senses. Religious believers cannot state under what circumstances they would call these claims true or false, and they cannot suggest a test we could carry out, using our senses.

Key term

verification principle: a principle that says analytic statements are meaningful, but some synthetic statements are meaningless if there is no possibility of supporting them with physical evidence to verify them

Synoptic link

Link to *Chapter 2: Arguments for the existence of God: deductive*. Discussion of the ontological argument involves a debate about whether the claim 'God exists' is analytic or synthetic.

AO1 activity 8

a) Explain, using examples, what is meant by 'analytic statements' and 'synthetic statements'.

b) Explain the verification principle in your own words, using examples of your own to clarify your explanation.

Criticisms of verification

Not surprisingly, the verification principle of meaning was not universally welcomed.

The verification principle itself cannot be verified

The most significant criticism was that the statement of the theory itself does not pass the test as a meaningful statement. The verifiability theory cannot be verified by sense experience (we cannot tell, using our senses, if these are the only types of statement to have any meaning), and so is not a meaningful synthetic statement; and if it is analytic, it is giving a new sense to the word 'meaningful', a new definition which we do not necessarily have to accept. If the theory fails its own test, then it cannot be successful.

Some scientific claims cannot be verified

The idea that all meaningful synthetic statements have to be empirically verifiable rules out far more than the logical positivists intended. The logical positivists wanted to dismiss as meaningless all claims that were made about God and the supernatural, while still allowing that scientific statements are meaningful.

However, many of the claims made by advances in science, such as the existence and nature of black holes, cannot be verified by sense experience. The human senses are insufficient for many scientific experiments, and need to be extended using artificial 'senses' such as X-rays, telescopes, and ultrasonic equipment; but even with these aids, there are still claims in science that are accepted as meaningful without being capable of testing using the senses.

Universal claims made in science cannot be verified empirically, such as 'All water is colourless, tasteless, and odourless' (can we really test all water, past, present, and future?) or 'Action and reaction are equal and opposite' (can we observe and measure this every time anything moves?). Scientists work on the basis that if something is observed enough times, we can safely assume the theory is true, or at least is true until something comes along that disproves it. But the verification principle does not allow religious beliefs the same generosity as it allows science.

So-called 'soft' sciences have their own problems of verifiability. The science of psychology, for example, depends on people explaining and describing their feelings and symptoms, but the doctor cannot verify a claim such as 'I feel a terrible sense of imminent doom' using their senses of observation.

Only statements about the present can be verified

Historical statements, where claims are made about events that happened in the past, cannot be tested using the senses. We cannot use our eyes and ears to verify whether Henry VIII died in 1547. We can only use reports of historical events to know what happened, but these can be unreliable. Nevertheless, historical claims are still considered meaningful, and are important for our everyday lives; we could not claim wages for work we did last week, or prosecute somebody for a crime committed last month, for example, if all our claims about past events are judged as meaningless.

Statements about the future might have to be considered meaningless too, if we want to adopt the verification principle; 'The festival will take place on 11 July' cannot be tested empirically, or at least not until 11 July. The verification principle seems to be ruling out too much; we need to be able to make meaningful reference to the past and the future in all kinds of activities, including scientific investigations.

Ethical claims cannot be verified

Statements about ethics also present problems of meaning. For example, if someone claims that 'torture is wrong', this cannot be verified empirically. We can see the outcomes of torture, that it causes pain and trauma, but we cannot tell whether this is right or wrong. For the logical positivists, this meant that a new way of interpreting ethical claims had to be found, as such claims could not be classified as meaningful cognitive statements. Ayer went on to conclude that ethical statements must be expressions of emotion rather than references to moral facts.

> **Synoptic link**
>
> Link to *A Level Religious Studies for Eduqas: Religion and Ethics, Chapter 2: Ethical thought (part two)*. Ayer was central to the development of the meta-ethical approach of Emotivism.

AO1 activity 9

Explain why the verification principle makes it difficult to class the following as meaningful:

a) historical claims

b) universal scientific claims

c) ethical claims

d) the verification principle itself.

The possibility of 'eschatological verification'

Some philosophers, most notably John Hick, argued that even if we do accept that a claim must be verifiable in order to be meaningful, religious truth claims are verifiable, because they are 'eschatologically verifiable'.

Hick put forward an important challenge to the idea that religious language is meaningless. He said that although we cannot test and see at the moment, in this life and this world, whether the good will be rewarded, or whether God really does exist and love us, these claims will be verified after death, at the end of time. (They cannot be falsified, however, as no one will be able say, after death, that there is no life after death.) 'Eschatological' refers to the end of time.

In 1961, Hick wrote:

> *Two men are travelling together along a road. One of them believes that it leads to the Celestial City, the other that it leads nowhere. But since this is the only road there is, both must travel it. Neither has been this way before, therefore neither is able to say what they will find around each corner. During their journey they meet with moments of refreshment and delight, and with moments of hardship and danger. All the time one of them thinks of his journey as a pilgrimage to the Celestial City and interprets the pleasant parts as encouragements and the obstacles as trials ... prepared by the king of that city and designed to make of him a worthy citizen of the place when at last he arrives there. The other, however, believes none of this, and sees their journey as an unavoidable and aimless ramble ... Yet, when they turn the last corner, it will be apparent that one of them has been right all the time and the other wrong.*
>
> John Hick, *Faith and Knowledge*

In other words, people can have very different understandings of human existence, with some seeing it as purposeful, part of God's plan, and leading to a destination with God, while others see it as purposeless and simply to be enjoyed while it lasts. There is no way in this world of telling which, if either, viewpoint is the closer match to reality; but, Hick claims, after death the purpose of human life will be verified. Hick's parable is very much like John Wisdom's parable of the gardener (see page 273), which Flew uses to show that the world is 'religiously ambiguous'. There is no clear, conclusive evidence for the existence of God, or against God's existence. But each uses the parable to draw different conclusions.

In Hick's parable, one traveller believes the journey is purposeless, and the other believes it is leading to the Celestial City.

Ayer modifies the verification principle

Logical positivists accepted that there was a problem with the verification principle, and that they were disallowing too much as meaningless. As a result, Ayer modified the verification principle so that it allowed for more than just immediate verification using sense experience. He made two distinctions.

One distinction Ayer made was between verification in practice and verification in principle:

- Verification in practice: it is practically possible to check the truth or falsity of a claim. For example, we can test the claim that 'the temperature in this room is 18 degrees Celsius' using a thermometer.
- Verification in principle: we know what we need to do to check a statement, but it is not practically possible to do the test. For example, we know how to test the claim that 'the temperature of the Earth's core is 6,000 degrees Celsius' but it is not practically possible to carry out the test. This modification allows universal scientific claims to be considered meaningful.

Ayer also distinguished between strong verification and weak verification:

- Strong verification: we can demonstrate conclusively, using empirical evidence, that a statement is true or false. For example, 'Bill committed the murder' could be strongly verified by 'We all saw Bill commit the murder'.
- Weak verification: empirical evidence suggests that it is probable the statement is correct, but it cannot be demonstrated conclusively. For example, 'Bill committed the murder' could be weakly verified by 'Even though nobody saw him do it, Bill has no explanation for where he was at the time of the murder and the weapon belongs to Bill'. This modification allowed historical and other statements to be classified as meaningful.

Ayer was, nevertheless, adamant that metaphysical claims were meaningless. He thought there was nothing that could be offered as a test of their truth, either practically or in principle, and there was no empirical evidence that could be offered to support a metaphysical claim, either strongly or weakly.

AO1 activity 10
Explain what Hick meant when he used the term 'eschatological verification'.

AO1 activity 11
Explain in your own words, and using your own examples, the difference between:
a) verification in principle and verification in practice
b) strong verification and weak verification.

Antony Flew and falsification

Antony Flew's article 'Theology and Falsification' has become one of the best-known pieces of writing on the subject of religious language.

After the Second World War, philosophical discussion about language was one of the key interests at Oxford University. However, the debate between the logical positivists and those who wanted to defend religious language had reached something of a stalemate. The logical positivists said that religious language was meaningless, and that religious statements that sounded like assertions were no more than 'utterances' without any genuine content or significance. Defenders of religious belief and religious language, on the other hand, disagreed with this conclusion; and the discussion did not appear to be making any progress. Antony Flew wanted to turn the debate in a more fruitful direction by raising some fresh issues and questions.

In a symposium (an academic conference) of Oxford philosophers in 1971, Flew presented the article he had written, 'Theology and Falsification', which explains his **falsification principle**. He invited responses from his colleagues R.M. Hare and Basil Mitchell.

AO1 activity 12

There are reports that Ayer became less convinced about atheism in his later life. Do some research and find out more about this. What allegedly persuaded Ayer that there might be truth in religious claims after all?

Key term

falsification principle: a statement is only meaningful if it is known what would show it to be false

AO1 activity 13

Read Flew's article 'Theology and Falsification' carefully (you can find it online). Summarise the main points that Flew is making, and the question he leaves his listeners to think about and respond to.

Explain, in your own words, why an inductive argument can lead to probable conclusions but can never lead to a definite final proof.

In his article, Flew returned to the debate begun by the logical positivists, but he suggested that instead of insisting that a statement should be verifiable, the statement should instead be falsifiable. What he meant by this was that we need not necessarily have to be able to provide supporting evidence for what we are saying; but we should know, when we say something, what we are ruling out when we make our claims. The falsification principle says that a meaningful statement must rule out at least some states of affairs, otherwise it is 'empty'.

Flew began his article by referring to a parable from John Wisdom's paper 'Gods'. In this parable, two explorers come across a clearing in the jungle, and in the clearing there are both flowers and weeds. One of the explorers, who is called the Believer, is convinced that there must be a gardener who comes to the clearing and looks after it; but the other, the Sceptic, disagrees.

The two explorers decide to settle their argument by lying in wait for the gardener and watching for his arrival. However, the gardener never appears. The one who believes in the existence of the gardener suggests that perhaps he is an invisible gardener, so they set up all sorts of traps

Flew presents the Parable of the Gardener to illustrate his falsification principle.

that might detect his presence, but still no gardener is found. The Believer continues to qualify his assertion that there is a gardener, by saying that he is silent, intangible and so on, until eventually the sceptical explorer asks:

> *But what remains of your original assertion? Just how does what you call an invisible, intangible, eternally elusive gardener differ from an imaginary gardener or even from no gardener at all?*
>
> Antony Flew, 'Theology and Falsification', from *New Essays in Theological Theory*

One of Flew's points, then, is that if religious believers keep on saying that 'God is different from us', 'the usual characteristics of a being don't apply to God' and so on whenever they are challenged, then they end up with a description of God that has no content.

Flew moves on, in his article, to draw a parallel between the Believer and a religious person who makes claims such as 'God loves us as a father loves his children' and 'God has a plan'. According to Flew, when these beliefs are challenged, for example when evil and suffering are encountered, religious believers do not accept that they are wrong and that God does not love us after all, or that God has no plan. Instead, they qualify their claim by saying that God's love is not like human love, or that God's plans are a mystery to us. Every time something happens to challenge their belief, religious people meet it with further modifications, until eventually there is nothing left of the original assertion. Flew concludes that the claims religious believers make about the nature and activity of God die a 'death by a thousand qualifications'; in the end, the believers are saying nothing at all because their statements are empty. They are not meaningful but 'vacuous'.

For Flew, if a statement is to have any meaning, it has to assert something and at the same time, deny the opposite of that assertion. An assertion has to rule out some states of affairs. If I say 'Dan came top of the class' then I am ruling out a state of affairs in which Dan wrote the weakest essay. If I say 'My car won't start' then I am ruling out the possibility that the engine is running normally. If someone tells you their name, then you know by implication that they do not want you to call them something different entirely. Whenever we make an assertion, we are saying 'this thing is the case', and at the same time, without saying it, we are implying 'and therefore these other things are not the case'.

In 1982, C.S. Evans put Flew's point of view as follows:

> *An assertion which does not rule out anything, but rather is compatible with any conceivable state of affairs, does not appear to assert anything either.*
>
> C.S. Evans, *Philosophy of Religion*

So, to give another example, if I said I am spending the morning baking a fruit cake, that would rule out some states of affairs. I would not be in a coma, for example, on a transatlantic flight, or in a swimming pool. If you asked 'Under what circumstances would your claim to be baking a fruit cake be false?' I could answer with some examples. This is how alibis work in court. If the defendant can show that they were doing something else at the time of the crime, then participation in the crime can be ruled out.

But, Flew argues, when theists talk of God and his attributes, they refuse to rule out any states of affairs. If asked, 'Under what circumstances would your statement that God loves us be false?' they would not be able to think of any. Whatever happens, however cruel or frightening, they still cling to their original assertion, all the while qualifying it with claims that God's love is mysterious or does not operate in accordance with the normal ways we expect love to work. For Flew, a claim that cannot be falsified is not really saying anything at all. We need to know what the world would look like if God did not love us, for the claim 'God loves us' to have any meaningful content.

Flew was writing and speaking only a few years after the end of the Second World War, when the horrors of the fighting, the concentration camps and prisoner of war camps, and the effects of the atomic bomb were very much in living memory. Although he does not refer to the events of the war in his article, his listeners and readers must have thought perhaps he was right to question whether faith in the loving care of God really meant anything, if religious believers continued to assert that there is a loving God even in the face of such suffering.

Criticisms of falsification: responses from Hare, Mitchell, and Swinburne

Richard Hare and Basil Mitchell heard Flew's presentation of 'Theology and Falsification' at the symposium, and each presented a response to it. Richard Swinburne's reply came later.

Richard Hare: bliks

R.M. Hare gave the first and probably the most radical response to Flew's article. He suggested that when people use religious language, their statements need not be interpreted as truth claims in a cognitive sense, but as expressions of what he called a '**blik**'. (Hare made up the word 'blik' because no word existed that encapsulated what he wanted to say.) Hare responded to Flew in the journal *New Essays in Philosophical Theology* with a parable of his own. He asked us to imagine a 'lunatic' (he is using language that is not considered acceptable today) who is convinced that all university dons (lecturers) want to murder him. No matter how many kindly dons he meets, he is not shaken from his belief that they are only pretending to be kind as part of their plots to kill him. There is nothing that the dons could ever do to persuade him that he is wrong in his belief and Hare uses the word 'blik' to describe this man's unfalsifiable conviction.

Hare's argument is that we all have our own 'bliks' with which we approach the world and make judgements about it: we all have unfalsifiable ways of framing our understanding of our experiences, which help us to find meaning in the world. The belief that everything happens by chance is just as much a 'blik' as the belief that things happen according to the will of God

> **Key term**
>
> **blik:** a word R.M. Hare made up to describe a person's way of interpreting the world; it could be described as their 'lens' or their 'worldview'

or that everything is 'meant to be'. Religious people have 'bliks', but so do atheists, and each of us uses our 'blik' as a framework for understanding the world and finding meaning in it.

Hare did not go on to develop his ideas further in writing, but other thinkers, such as D.Z. Phillips, took up his approach as a way of defending religious language, claiming that religious statements are not cognitive truth claims at all but are non-cognitive expressions of a personal attitude or commitment to a particular way of life.

Basil Mitchell: the partisan and the stranger

Basil Mitchell also responded to Flew with his own story, known as the parable of the partisan. Hare had conceded that Flew was right and offered a different way of understanding religious language, but Mitchell was not as ready to give up the view that religious truth claims are cognitive.

In Mitchell's parable, he asks us to imagine a scenario where a country is occupied by the enemy during a war and the 'partisan' is a resistance fighter. The partisan meets a stranger who makes a strongly favourable impression on him. The stranger asks the partisan to trust him, even though the stranger will sometimes need to behave in ways that will make it seem as though he is on the enemy side. The partisan makes a commitment to trust the stranger.

Sometimes, the stranger is clearly helping the resistance, and the partisan reassures other resistance members that the stranger is on their side and can be trusted. However, sometimes the stranger can be seen working alongside the enemy and helping to capture resistance fighters. The partisan has made a commitment to trust the stranger, and continues with this commitment even when he is sometimes faced with counter-evidence. He admits that sometimes he doubts his decision to trust the stranger, but he tells himself that there is a reasonable explanation for the stranger's behaviour, even if he does not always know the details of it.

> *Sometimes he is seen in the uniform of the police handing over patriots to the occupying power. On these occasions his friends murmur against him: but the partisan still says 'he is on our side.' He still believes that, in spite of appearances, the stranger did not deceive him … Sometimes his friends, in exasperation, say 'Well, what would he have to do for you to admit you were wrong and that he is not on our side?' But the partisan refuses to answer. He will not consent to put the stranger to the test.*
>
> Basil Mitchell, 'The Falsification Debate', from *New Essays in Theological Theory*

Mitchell argued that religious language is cognitive, even if people need to make a commitment to religion based on trust rather than facts.

Mitchell's view was different from Hare's view, because Mitchell was arguing that religious beliefs, statements, and commitments do have a factual content (are cognitive), whereas Hare gave a non-cognitivist view. The partisan might find out, eventually and if he survives the war, whether or not he was right to trust the stranger, because there is truth and falsity to be found. However, while the war is going on, the partisan has to make a decision whether or not to trust on the basis of incomplete and ambiguous evidence.

Mitchell makes a parallel between his parable and belief in a loving God. While we are in the world, the evidence for a loving God can seem incomplete and can be ambiguous, but, according to Mitchell, there is still a factual content to religious assertions of the existence of a loving God. 'God loves us' is, in the end, either true or false, even if, at the moment, we cannot offer a definitive test of it and just have to choose whether or not to trust the claim. In this respect, Mitchell also differed from Hare, because Hare claimed that our 'bliks' were groundless whereas, for Mitchell, the partisan's trust in the stranger is not groundless. The partisan makes a deliberate choice to trust the stranger because of the impression he made on him when they first met; he has a good reason for his belief.

Richard Swinburne: the toys in the cupboard

Richard Swinburne's response to Flew came later. In his 1977 book, *The Coherence of Theism*, Swinburne discusses the verification and falsification principles, and disagrees with them. He argues that these principles are not useful in determining meaning, by giving examples of statements which could not be verified or falsified and yet have meaning and content. One example he gives is 'There is, was, or will be a man with two heads'. Swinburne writes:

> *No observation can falsify such statements. However many observations you make and fail to find a two-headed man, there may be one somewhere where you have not looked, or one may be born tomorrow.*
>
> Richard Swinburne, *The Coherence of Theism*

Swinburne's best-known example to illustrate his rejection of the falsification principle is of toys in a cupboard.

> *Some of the toys which to all appearances stay in the toy cupboard while people are asleep and no one else is watching, actually get up and dance in the middle of the night and then go back to the cupboard leaving no traces of their activity.*
>
> Richard Swinburne, *The Coherence of Theism*

This would be unconfirmable because if people were watching or trying to observe in some way, the toys would stay where they were. After all, they only move about when no one is looking. Yet the claim does have content, and is meaningful to us.

Swinburne, then, rejects the verification and falsification principles as effective measures of meaningfulness. He notes that those who support them make allowances for scientific and other statements, but are not prepared to make the same allowances for religious claims. In his view, it is quite possible for a claim to be meaningful without it being capable of verification or falsification.

Swinburne gave the example of toys in a cupboard, dancing around when nobody is looking, to illustrate his rejection of the falsification principle.

Developments in the science of quantum mechanics have given this debate an interesting twist. The observer effect suggests that particles behave differently when they are observed, and the very act of measuring them alters what they do. This could have interesting implications for the verification and falsification principles, where empirical observation does not certify the truth of some scientific claims, but actually alters the truth of them.

AO1 activity 14

Make four flashcards, one for each of the parables and examples listed. Place the name of the parable or example and the name of the scholar who used it on one side of the flashcard, and summarise what it was intended to illustrate about religious language on the other.

Religious language as non-cognitive and analogical

One possible way forward in the discussion of religious language is to understand it as non-cognitive. In other words, when religious believers make truth claims, perhaps these are better understood as expressions of attitudes, interpretations, and feelings, rather than as references to actual facts.

Discussions of religious language did not begin in the twentieth century. In the Middle Ages, thinkers such as Maimonides in the Jewish tradition and Aquinas in the Christian tradition were grappling with the difficulties of comprehending and expressing the nature of God in language. Both of these thinkers held the view that God is not comprehensible, and so any attempt to make claims about the nature of God is full of difficulties.

One possible approach to religious language is to treat it as analogical. An **analogy** is when one thing is compared with another, in the hope of aiding understanding. For example, Paley used the analogy of finding a watch on a heath and looking at its design when he was explaining his design argument for the existence of God.

Aquinas and analogy

Some thinkers have argued that we cannot say anything positive that is literally true of God, because the use of ordinary human language automatically limits God, placing his attributes only within our experience and understanding. They propose that we speak of God only in negative terms (the *via negativa*).

However, Aquinas suggested, in *Summa Theologica*, that there could be a way of making positive claims about God and conveying positive ideas, as long as we understand that the words we use have an analogical, rather than a literal, application. He explained the difference between univocal, equivocal, and analogical language.

Sometimes, we use the same word to describe two different things in a way that is univocal. This means that the word has the same meaning in both

Key term

analogy: a comparison between one thing and another for the purpose of clarification; saying one thing is like another in a particular respect, to aid understanding

Synoptic link

Link to *Chapter 1: Arguments for the existence of God: inductive*. Paley used a watch analogy to demonstrate his belief that the existence of God could be seen through observation of the natural world.

contexts. For example, when we talk about a 'glass vase' and a 'ceramic vase', the word 'vase' has the same meaning in both cases, as a vessel for displaying flowers.

And sometimes we use the same word to describe two different things in a way that is equivocal, when the same word means different things in both descriptions. For example, when we talk about 'a fruit punch' and 'a hole punch', or 'a dining table' and 'a periodic table', or 'a fountain pen' and 'a pig pen'.

Aquinas recognised that these two ways of using language, univocal and equivocal, were common and readily understood. But he realised that neither was appropriate for speaking about God. When people talk of the love of God, they are not using the word 'love' in the same, univocal way that they might speak of the love of a mother for her child, as God's love is on an entirely different, infinite scale. They are not using the words equivocally either; if words used about God meant something entirely different from their normal usage, they would communicate nothing.

When we speak of God, Aquinas wrote, we use words in a way that is analogical. This means that the same word is used, in not exactly the same sense, but in a similar or related sense. For example, we might talk about rough sandpaper and someone having a rough time. The word 'rough' is used analogically to describe the person having a rough time; their experiences are not literally rough to the touch, but we use the word 'rough' because it has connotations of being uncomfortable and hard work. Metaphors, such as 'emotional roller-coaster' or 'a storm of abuse', use analogies; we use them to help clarify what we mean when we communicate, and to make our communication more vivid.

Aquinas said people need to remember that whenever they speak of God, they are using analogy, whether they are aware of it or not. When they speak of the love of God, or the justice of God, the words 'love' and 'justice' are not being used univocally. We understand love and justice from our dealings with other people, but these concepts cannot be directly translated to apply to God. This is because the love of God and the justice of God are infinite, whereas the examples we know from experience are temporal and flawed.

Analogy is understood as a non-cognitive use of religious language because analogies are used to talk about God in a non-literal way. Expressions such as 'The Lord is my Shepherd' are analogical and non-cognitive. The speaker is using the analogy of a shepherd to convey God's protection, authority and care, and the phrase is non-cognitive because it cannot be tested true or false; analogy is not truth-apt.

Analogy of attribution and proportion

Aquinas wrote about two kinds of analogy:

1. Analogy of attribution, where there is a causal (cause-and-effect) relationship between the two things being described. For example,

> ## AO1 activity 15
> Make a list of five words that can be used in different contexts with completely different meanings, such as 'plane' or 'bat'. You could use these as examples of equivocal language in your essays.

> ## AO1 activity 16
> Summarise, in your own words, the reasons why Aquinas said we need to think of religious language in terms of analogy.

a seaside town might be called 'healthy' because it causes the people who live there to be healthy, while a sickly cake might be called 'sickly' because of the effect it has on the person eating it. In Aquinas' view, when we attribute characteristics to God, such as 'power', 'mercy', 'wisdom', and so on, we need to bear in mind this causal relationship, this analogy of attribution. God does not simply have these characteristics in the way that we might have them, but is the cause of them, both in God's own nature and in the whole of the rest of the universe. We need to remember, when we speak of the power of God, that all power comes from God; when we speak of the love of God, that all love comes from God. Aquinas believed God is the source of everything, and so we need to recognise that when we speak of God as 'wise', we are not acknowledging that God is an example of one of the many wise beings in the universe, but instead recognising that God is the source of all wisdom wherever it is found. And when we speak of God as 'living', it means that God is the cause of all life.

We think of clever dogs and clever scientists, and understand 'clever' in an appropriate proportion.

2. Analogy of proportionality, where the words relate to objects or qualities that are different in proportion. For example, we might speak of a clever dog and a clever scientist, and the words are used in proportion; the dog is clever as dogs go, and the scientist is clever in comparison with other scientists. We would not call a scientist 'clever' just because they could roll over or fetch the post, but for a dog, this is understood to be clever.

In religious terms, then, Aquinas thought that we can use terms such as 'loving' and 'faithful' when we speak of God, but when we do, we have to recognise that God's love, faithfulness, and so on are on an infinitely vaster scale than our own (analogy of proportionality) and also that God is the cause of love and of faithfulness (analogy of attribution). We have to remember that we are using our words analogically and not univocally.

AO1 activity 17

Scientists often use analogical models to help convey ideas and to help predict how things will behave. An example is the model of an atom with the nucleus at the centre orbited by electrons, like the planets orbit the Sun in the solar system. It is not a physically accurate model of what an atom looks like; it is a conceptual model that helps us to understand atoms. Can you think of any other examples of scientific models?

Analogies are considered useful in many different contexts, especially when used to communicate complex or new ideas. They can help us form pictures in our minds, associate ideas, and draw conclusions. However, they are not completely without difficulties. It is not always clear in exactly what respects two different things are being considered similar: in what respects might the love or the justice of God resemble our own, and how are they different? In Aquinas' view, it is important to remember that God cannot be wholly understood, and that we will never reach a clear understanding where we comprehend exactly what God is.

Aquinas believed that there is a real, objective God. But the analogical use of language is usually considered non-cognitive, because analogies are not truth-apt: statements like 'think of an atom as being rather like a mini-solar system', or 'think of God as being like a craftsman' are not capable of being called 'true' or 'false'.

Ian Ramsey: models and disclosure

A more modern version of the idea of speaking of God analogically comes from the philosopher Ian Ramsey, who later became Bishop of Durham. He explained his ideas in his 1957 book *Religious Language*.

Ramsey emphasised the importance of realising that critics of religious language often assume, without question, that the words in religious truth claims should be understood exactly as they are understood in a non-religious context. But he emphasised that religious language works in the way that models work in scientific language. Scientists might model their explanations of the way the world works using construction toys, balls, or drinking straws, to help people understand them. We are not expected to think that the physical world is actually made from drinking straws; we understand that we are looking at a model, not an exact replica. In the same way, Ramsey said, religious language should be understood in terms of models.

According to Ramsey, we use 'models' when we speak of God using words such as 'righteous' or 'loving'; these are words that we understand because we have a reference point in our own human experience, but it would be a mistake to apply them literally to God. Theological claims, such as the death of Christ atoned for human sin, are models. From our own human experience, we might understand atonement as replacing a precious object belonging to someone else that we damaged, paying a fine after we have broken the law, replacing an object we have stolen, or making a sacrifice to pacify an angry god. These understandings help to point us in the general direction of the significance of the death of Christ; they act as models but are not literally applicable.

However, to ensure that we do not limit God and that we recognise that his attributes are unlike our own, we also need to use 'qualifiers'. These are adjectives and adverbs such as 'everlasting' or 'perfectly'. In this way, we can anchor our ideas about God within our own experience, so that we at least know what we are talking about; and then we can show that God is different from us proportionally, by using the qualifier to point us in the right direction and remind us not to take our language too literally. We might not understand and comprehend the nature of God exactly, because qualifiers such as 'infinitely' or 'perfectly' are in many ways beyond our imagination, but it is a method of speaking about God positively that aims to avoid either limiting God or speaking incomprehensibly.

Ramsey thought that if we understand that religious language works in this way, there comes a point in religious communication when 'the penny drops'; just as, when watching someone experiment with a scientific model,

AO1 activity 18
Explain, in your own words and using your own examples, what is meant by 'analogy of attribution' and 'analogy of proportionality'.

Ramsey used the idea of models as a way of helping communicate religious ideas, just as scientists use models to aid understanding.

we might suddenly understand how the thing that the model represents works. The religious language model points us in the right direction, and (sometimes) leads to 'disclosure'. We might understand what 'infinity' means in a mathematical context, and then hear the word used in a religious context to refer to God's love or God's wisdom; mathematical infinity does not completely encapsulate the infinite nature of God, but it points us in the right direction as a model, and could lead us to disclosure, where we understand what religious believers mean when they talk of God's infinite care. Ramsey writes of disclosure as a kind of religious experience, an insight into the truth. For Ramsey, religious language both reflects and assists religious experience; when religious language is skilfully used, it can lead the listener to a point where something of God is revealed, or disclosed.

AO1 activity 19

Explain, in your own words, what Ramsey meant by:

a) models

b) qualifiers

c) disclosure.

Challenges to the use of analogy in religious language

Scientific analogies – describing an atom as 'like the solar system' or 'like a plum pudding', DNA as 'like a spiral staircase', blood vessels as 'like a road system', and the human eye as 'like a camera' – can help people to visualise something, but they can also mislead if people take them too literally. We need to know in what respects the layers of the Earth are 'like a peach' and at what point the analogy breaks down. Some people have challenged the idea that analogies are useful in religious language, arguing that God is unknowable. This makes it impossible to find points of comparison between God and anything else in a useful and meaningful way.

Hume challenged the use of analogy for discussion about God in *Dialogues concerning natural religion*, published in 1779. He was responding to the analogy of the world as a machine and the idea that just as a machine has a designer, so too does the world, namely God. He pointed out that an analogy goes only so far. It is only helpful if we know in what respect the two things being compared are similar: there are lots of ways in which an atom is not at all like a plum pudding and an eye is not at all like a camera, but there are ways in which they are similar, and those similarities make the analogy useful. However, if the analogy is between something from the physical world and God, then it will not work as an analogy because we have no way of knowing what 'God' is in order to find the point of similarity.

Ramsey could be criticised for not adding a great deal of clarity to the debate. He writes of qualifiers, which point us in the general direction of God, but God still remains a mystery. The moment of disclosure might not happen; the person listening to the analogy, with its models and qualifiers, might never get further than a vague idea of what is meant.

Synoptic link

Link to *Chapter 1: Arguments for the existence of God: inductive*. Hume is responding to William Paley's watchmaker analogy, a teleological argument for the existence of God.

How the views of Aquinas and Ramsey can be used to help understand religious teachings

Those who agree with the use of analogy in religious language could argue that analogy is a natural way of explaining difficult ideas in all kinds of contexts, and that we use it because it helps. A cookery program will use analogies to tell us when our egg white has been whipped enough, or what the roux for a white sauce should look like in the pan, and these analogies are useful. Similarly, a religious analogy can help us to see what the speaker means.

Aquinas' writings about analogy have been found useful because of their reminders that:

- God is essentially unknowable
- God is the source of all things
- God's attributes are not the same as ours, but are on an infinitely vaster scale.

Ramsey's ideas about using analogy in religious language have been found useful because:

- they make use of models, which we understand because we use them in other aspects of life
- they use qualifiers to remind us, as did Aquinas, that God's attributes are not like ours, and are essentially unknowable
- they use the idea of disclosure to emphasise the importance of religious experience and faith in discussion of God.

We do not have to understand God in the same way that we understand the physical world, using reason and sense experience, because God is not directly available to either. Instead, understanding of religious language comes when God reveals himself in that moment of disclosure.

This section of the chapter will enhance your ability to **analyse** and **evaluate** the topic and help you develop your AO2 skills. For each question, think about the different positions you might take, and decide which you find most persuasive and why. It is not enough to memorise a list of 'for and against' points; you need to develop an argument.

How successful are the solutions presented by religious philosophers for the inherent problems of using religious language?

This question invites discussion of the responses religious thinkers have made to the difficulties in religious language. You need to consider these responses made by religious thinkers, and evaluate the extent to which they are persuasive.

The view that religious thinkers have been successful in their solutions to problems inherent in religious language

It could be argued that religious thinkers have dealt successfully with the problems inherent in religious language.

Aquinas and Ramsey make an important point when they stress that religious language needs to be understood as analogical, rather than understood univocally or equivocally. If it is seen that religious language is analogical, then many of the problems inherent in its use can be overcome. If someone knows nothing of God, they can understand at least something through the use of analogy. Recognising that religious language is analogical rather than univocal avoids the problem of making God appear to be too small, because the analogical language used includes concepts of attribution and proportionality. Analogical language retains the idea that God is mysterious, while still giving people some insight.

Hick can be argued to deal successfully with problems inherent in religious language, by drawing attention to 'eschatological verification'. Although in this finite, limited world, people cannot have a full understanding of the nature or the ways of God, at the end of time, the mysteries will be resolved and a partial understanding will become a full understanding.

Basil Mitchell could be seen to deal successfully with the problems of religious language highlighted by Antony Flew. Flew thought that religious language is meaningless because it is unfalsifiable, but Mitchell argued that religious people commit to their faith without needing to have final, definite proof. Religion involves a choice about whether or not to trust, just as the partisans have to decide whether or not to trust the stranger in Mitchell's parable. Flew demands a degree of certainty that is inappropriate in the context of religion.

Some philosophers, such as William Alston, argue that the whole concept of 'religious language' is misleading. Alston argued, in his 1989 book *Divine Nature and Human Language*, that philosophers who aim to judge religious language as problematic, or even meaningless, have concentrated far too much on only one aspect of the way religious believers usually communicate. Such philosophers have focused almost entirely on truth claims, and ignored all of the other ways that religious language is used, in prayers, commandments and moral advice, thanksgiving, confession, and so on. When religious believers get together for worship, they do not spend all their time making truth claims to each other.

> *There is no language that is used only for religious purposes. 'Do you speak English, French, or religious?' … Philosophers have been narrowly selective in their approach to the field. … They have concentrated on what looked to be factual statements about God or other objects of religious worship … Many philosophers and theologians have protested against the concentration of philosophers on religious statements to the neglect of other religious uses of language. Their complaint can be briefly summed up as follows. The heart of religion is found in talk to God in prayer, worship, and liturgy. Talk about God is a secondary phenomenon that gets its religious significance by its dependence on former … the valid concerns philosophers have with statements about God can be pursued while recognising their connections with the rest of religion.*
>
> William Alston, *Divine Nature and Human Language*

Alston, then, took the view that although there can be problems with religious truth claims (and with many other truth-claims from non-religious contexts), those who wish to challenge religious language are being unfair. They concentrate too heavily on one small aspect of the whole field of religious talk, magnifying the potential problems, and failing to pay enough attention to the ways in which believers actually communicate in real life. Alston's view can be seen as successful, as instead of addressing the idea that religious truth claims are problematic, he challenges the idea that the problems in religious language are significant.

The view that religious thinkers have not been successful in their solutions to problems inherent in religious language

It can be argued that religious thinkers have been unsuccessful in their solutions to the problems of religious language.

The idea that religious language should be understood as analogical has been criticised. When we use analogy, we need to have at least some idea of what is being described for the analogy to be of any use. If I say something is 'like an avocado', the person I am talking to needs to know in what respect this mysterious thing is like an avocado. Is it the same colour, texture or weight, or does it have the same calorific content? If I say 'it is like an avocado, but on an infinite scale', can the person I am talking to really gain any understanding from my description? Analogies that use language about the infinite power or wisdom of God may not do much to solve the problems inherent in religious language.

Responses to Flew's discussion of religious language as unfalsifiable may be seen as unsuccessful. Flew himself did not think that religious thinkers such as Hare or Mitchell had offered him much of a challenge. Hare conceded that religious language is indeed unfalsifiable, and began to talk instead about religious language being non-cognitivist: a view that many religious believers would not accept. Mitchell's parable of the partisan did little to persuade Flew. The view that we will only find out later, after death or at the end of time, whether or not religious language refers to anything real, is unconvincing for those who hold that there is no life after death.

AO2 activity 1

a) Do you think William Alston is making a fair point when he says that philosophical challenges to religious language fail to recognise the ways in which religious believers use it? Give reasons to explain your answer.

b) How successfully do you think religious thinkers have tackled the problems inherent in religious language?

How significant is a consideration of the exclusive context of religious belief for an understanding of religious language?

This question invites discussion of whether religious language is best understood, or can only ever be understood, within the context of a community of believers. Religious belief and religious behaviour is different from other kinds of beliefs and behaviours, and the corresponding language also has different meanings that are particular to its religious context.

The view that religious language can only be understood by believers in that faith community

It could be argued that religious language is exclusive, and can only be understood by people within a faith community. People who support this view might argue:

- many terms used in religion have a very specific meaning that relates to other aspects of the faith in a way that outsiders cannot understand
- religious language uses words and phrases that are not used in other aspects of life, so outsiders can have no idea what they mean
- religious language relates to direct, personal experiences of God that outsiders have not had and cannot relate to
- religious terms do not always mean the same thing in different religions, so even people with faith might struggle to understand those with a different faith. For example, terms such as the 'soul', 'the afterlife', 'enlightenment', and even 'God' have very different interpretations in different religious traditions.

The view that religious language can be understood by all, and exclusivity is not a problem

It could be argued that even though religious language is meant for a particular context, anyone can understand it:

- People manage to learn other kinds of context-dependent language; for example, people learned to understand the language of epidemiology during the Covid-19 pandemic even if they had no medical background.
- People have enough imagination to understand contexts other than the ones they inhabit; writers of fantasy fiction make up entire imaginary worlds with new vocabulary, and readers can visualise them even though they do not live there.
- Religious language is about God, who exists for everyone, not just for a particular community.

People of different faiths are able to talk to one another and discuss their beliefs.

The view that there is a false dichotomy: understanding could be partial

A false dichotomy is when someone is presented with two options and invited to believe that if they reject one, they have to accept the other, when in fact more than the two options presented are available. Perhaps people are being presented with a false dichotomy when it comes to religious language: either religious language is totally incomprehensible to those outside a faith community or it is completely understandable to all.

There is a lot of ground between 'totally incomprehensible' and 'completely understandable'. We may not be able to understand completely what it means to be a believer in a faith different from our own world view, but this does not mean we cannot understand anything at all. Given that we are individuals, all with our own upbringing and genetic make-up, culture, and life experiences, perhaps we can only ever have complete understanding of our own tastes, opinions, and beliefs, and maybe even then we cannot have a total understanding of what goes on in our own heads. We might never truly understand why someone else is passionate about fishing, Harry Potter, needlework, or Formula One; we might never fully know what it means to be the parent of a child with special needs, or understand how it feels to scale a mountain and stand at the summit. Sometimes, our closest friends fall in love with someone and we struggle to understand what the attraction is. But the fact that other people's experiences, passions, and beliefs are exclusive to them does not make them totally incomprehensible to others. We might not feel what they feel, or believe what they believe, but it is still possible to see how important it is to them, and to gain at least a partial understanding by talking to them and, even more importantly, listening to them.

Also, the idea that religious language is incomprehensible to outsiders, to people who do not share the same faith, is not supported by the fact that people change their beliefs and convert to other religions. If religious language were really only comprehensible to those within the religious tradition, it would not be possible for a non-believer to convert; and yet there are plenty of people who have heard about Christianity from believers, perhaps gone to classes or to talks, or read the Bible, gained a greater understanding, and come slowly to a commitment to Christianity themselves; and there are people who have had a more dramatic conversion experience. The same applies in other religions, where people become Muslims or Buddhists, or convert to Judaism.

The phenomenological approach to the study of religion may be a step forward. Whereas, in the past, it was assumed that people would only want to study religion if they were religious themselves and probably wanted to a career in religious leadership, the phenomenological approach opened up the possibility of Religious Studies as an academic discipline that could be explored by people of any faith or none.

However, the ability of people to 'bracket out' their own beliefs and opinions and study religion objectively can be questioned. We cannot help interpreting what we experience through our own individual perspectives; we often do it unconsciously. For example, if Christians read about the Trimurti in Hinduism and see that there are three deities that are all aspects of the one Brahman, they might understand this with a Christian perspective, and think that there are similarities between this Hindu belief and the Christian belief in the Trinity. However, these beliefs are, in fact, very different. When we study belief systems that are new to us, we can make a lot of mistakes and imagine similarities with our belief systems that do not exist. We cannot look at things objectively, however hard we try, because we are subjective individuals.

This is not a problem that only affects religion and religious language, however. Historians face similar issues, when trying to understand the actions and motivations of historical characters who lived in a very different kind of society from the one we have now. It is easy to judge people from the past by the standards of today, but this could be misleading. Anthropologists, who study human cultures and societies, have to try hard not to judge very different cultures by Western standards, but this can be difficult. Perhaps Smart was overly optimistic when he suggested that people could 'bracket out' their own world views when studying the beliefs of others.

Synoptic link

Link to *Chapter 8: Religious language (part two)*. Wittgenstein's theory of language games is important for this discussion. Wittgenstein argued that language functions rather like a game, where you understand it better the more you are involved with it. Once you have studied the content of the next chapter, revisit this question, and consider the contribution that Wittgenstein makes to ideas about the exclusivity of religious language.

AO2 activity 2

a) How successfully do you think people can put aside their own world views and look at the beliefs of others objectively? Is it fairly easy, very difficult, or impossible? Explain your reasoning.

b) To what extent, if at all, do you think it is possible for an outsider to understand the beliefs of a religious person? Give reasons to explain your answer.

How persuasive are arguments asserting either the meaningfulness or meaninglessness of religious language?

This question invites discussion about the extent to which the logical positivists make convincing challenges to religious language, and also the extent to which others have provided persuasive answers to them.

How persuasive is the verification principle?

The view that the verification principle is unpersuasive

Most scholars agree that the verification principle in its original form fails. This is because, first of all, it fails to pass its own test of meaning; and also because it is too narrow in ruling out many aspects of knowledge, such as history and ethics. Those who find it unpersuasive might argue:

- It is inconsistent in its approach to language, applying rules to religious language that it does not apply to scientific language.
- It ignores the fact that language has a wide range of functions, and is not just about making truth claims.
- Hick's ideas about eschatological verification show that we do not have to be able to test a claim immediately; it could turn out to be true in the future even if we cannot test it now.
- We do not have to accept the premise that empirical testing is the best, or only, way of judging meaning; empirical testing is important in many contexts, but there could be other ways of testing truth.

The view that the verification principle is persuasive

It can be argued that the verification principle has strengths.

- It sets out clear criteria for meaning, which could help prevent religious people from making wild claims about what God is or what God wants with no evidence to support them.
- Clear criteria are important if, for example, there are disputes about whether or not to support same sex marriage or abortion. The debate will not go anywhere if people on both sides claim to know what God says but cannot evidence their claims.
- Scientific method says that claims should be open to peer review, and that we should know how we could test other people's claims if we are expected to accept them. The same rigour should be applicable to religious claims.

> **Synoptic link**
>
> Link to *Chapter 5: Religious experience (part one)*. This links with William James' pragmatic test of the validity of religious experience, where he argued that religious experience can be tested by its long-lasting results.

AO2 activity 3

Some people have suggested that Hume's own philosophical works should be 'committed to the flames' if the verification principle is correct. Think of what you already know about Hume, for example his criticisms of inductive arguments for the existence of God and his views about miracles. Do you think Hume's philosophy books would pass the test of the verification principle?

How persuasive is the falsification principle?

The view that the falsification principle is persuasive

The falsification principle put forward by Flew struck a chord with many of his listeners and readers. Flew argued that if no evidence could ever persuade religious believers to change their minds about their truth claims, then those truth claims have no genuine content; they are just empty assertions. Many people found this argument persuasive.

- Flew highlighted a flaw in religious language. Religious claims cannot mean anything if they are compatible with every state of affairs.
- Flew successfully moved away from the problems of the verification principle. Instead of setting a criterion for meaning, he talked about whether religious claims have any real content or are just 'empty'.
- Examples of evil and suffering demonstrate that religious claims about the love of God fly in the face of evidence and can, therefore, be ignored.
- Flew was right to say that a refusal to allow any counter-evidence makes some religious claims die 'a death of a thousand qualifications'. Religious believers make so many excuses for God that, in the end, their claims about God lack any meaningful content at all.

The view that the falsification principle is unpersuasive

Others disagree with Flew, and do not find the falsification principle persuasive at all.

- Hare shifted his ground because he accepted some of what Flew said, but suggested that religious language is non-cognitive, and so cannot be tested in empirical ways as it expresses a 'picture preference'. He thought Flew's mistake was in interpreting religious language cognitively.
- Mitchell argued that religious belief depends on faith rather than concrete evidence, but it is still cognitive. It is part of the nature of religious faith that people hold it even though the world is religiously ambiguous.
- Some might ask, what counter-evidence would Flew himself have accepted, to move him away from his belief that every claim must be supportable by empirical evidence? Might there be supporting evidence for belief in God that is not empirical? If Flew insisted that nothing can shake him from the belief that empirical evidence is the only kind of evidence, then his claims were unfalsifiable by his own criteria.
- Anselm could not, of course, answer Flew because he lived a thousand years before Flew, but he might have argued that Flew had misunderstood the nature and attributes of God. Flew asked, 'Under what circumstances might believers concede that God does not exist after all?', but Anselm would have argued that there is no 'might exist or might not exist after all' about the existence of God. This is because God exists necessarily. The believer cannot find potential counter-evidence to shake belief in God because there can be no such thing as counter-evidence for God.

AO2 activity 4

How persuasive do you find the falsification principle? Revisit Flew's paper 'Theology and Falsification', and think about your own response. Write one or two paragraphs explaining whether or not you agree with him. For example, does he make some points that you agree with and others that you find weaker? Explain your reasoning.

How far should Logical Positivism be accepted as providing a valid criterion for meaning in the use of language?

This question is asking for a discussion of whether Logical Positivism gives us a good way of deciding whether language is meaningful or not.

The view that Logical Positivism offers a valid criterion for meaning in the use of language

There are several arguments supporting Logical Positivism's approach to deciding whether or not language is meaningful.

- Small children, when involved in disagreements, often ask each other to 'prove it!'; it is natural for us to want some evidence to support a dubious claim, so that we can see for ourselves if it is true or not. Tests for the meaningfulness of claims allow us to ignore unsupported claims that could be harmful for society, and concentrate only on the claims that can be evidenced.
- Using tests, such as those defined by Logical Positivism, means that we can concentrate on a claim itself, looking to see whether it is true, false, or meaningless on its own merits, rather than, for example, accepting something as truth just because of the authority of the person who said it.
- Such tests could be important for changes in education, perhaps being used to support the view that religious indoctrination is inappropriate in the classroom. Teaching should stick to what is demonstrably true or false, rather than trying to instil meaningless beliefs into children.
- The tests could be seen as fair, because they are applied whatever the subject matter of the claims.

The view that Logical Positivism does not offer a valid criterion for meaning in the use of language

It could be argued that Logical Positivism does not give us a good way of deciding whether or not language is meaningful.

- The criterion for meaning offered by the logical positivists is very narrow, and rules out claims made by historians, politicians, psychologists, and those in many other fields. It concentrates too heavily on empirical sciences.

- Logical Positivism ignores all the uses of language that are not about making truth claims, such as questions, jokes, works of fiction, poetry, and expressions of emotion, which form a significant part of human communication.
- Logical Positivism suggests that there is some kind of objective way of judging meaning, but people are not objective. Everyone has a world view that colours their way of thinking, whether it is religious or scientific, or a mixture of both.
- Wittgenstein argued that meaning does not work in the way the logical positivists describe. Meaning is a relationship. A claim cannot intrinsically have meaning, or lack meaning, in a vacuum; it has to mean something to someone. It is mistaken to try to make pronouncements about what does or does not have meaning as if a claim could continue to have meaning even if there were nobody in existence.

> **AO2 activity 5**
> How convinced are you by Logical Positivism? Give reasons to support your answer.

To what extent do the challenges to Logical Positivism provide convincing arguments for non-religious believers?

This question invites an evaluation of the responses to Logical Positivism. It asks whether people who do not have religious belief are likely to find these responses persuasive. Do Hare, Mitchell, and Hick put up successful defences of religious language?

The view that the challenges to Logical Positivism lack persuasiveness for non-religious people

Logical Positivism can be challenged on the grounds that it puts too much emphasis on the empirical world, and does not recognise that there may be other ways of judging truth and meaningfulness. Non-religious people may find this challenge unpersuasive, arguing that the physical, material world is all that there is. Everything, including the human mind and human emotion, has a physical explanation. There is no other, spiritual world, and no life after death. Thinkers such as Richard Dawkins and Daniel Dennett are not persuaded by the idea that there could be other kinds of truth, or other kinds of existence, beyond the physical, and so they do not accept the challenge that Logical Positivism over-emphasises empirical testing.

Mitchell and Hare gave responses to Flew's views about falsification. Flew answered Hare and Mitchell, disagreeing with them. Non-religious people are likely to agree with Flew.

To the challenge made by Hare and his ideas about 'bliks', Flew (as a non-religious person) responded by saying that Hare's views were unorthodox, and he could not see many Christians agreeing with them. Flew said that Hare was putting forward a view of religious belief as no more than a preferred way of looking at the world, 'as if' there were a loving God. Most Christians, Flew argued, would disagree and insist that there is a real God who created the world and acts in it; God is not just 'true for me but not true for you' in the opinion of Christians. As a non-religious person, Flew was saying that Hare's response lacks persuasiveness, because Hare is not saying things that most religious believers would accept, and therefore he does not defend mainstream views successfully.

Flew also said that there was something deceitful in treating religious language as a 'blik', when religious people so often tell others how they ought to live, how God will punish them, and how God wants them to change. If someone's religious beliefs are no more than their personal world view, they would have no right to tell others how to live and what moral choices to make. As a non-religious person, Flew thought that Hare's 'blik' understanding of religious language was too generous to most religious believers, making them sound more flexible and accommodating of others' beliefs than they really are.

To Mitchell and his parable about the partisan and the stranger, Flew agreed that religious believers do not always qualify their beliefs whenever they are faced with contradictory evidence but he said that, eventually, they will have to. He thought that Mitchell's parable did not work as an analogy for the relationship between the believer and God because, in the parable, the stranger sometimes has to act as if he is on the enemy's side in order to maintain his secret identity. The stranger is forced into doing things he does not want to do. But the same is not true of God; nothing is forcing God to act as if sometimes God does not love us, and there is no good reason for God's existence or nature to be kept a secret. Flew argued that God's apparent lack of care for people who suffer is not comparable to the behaviour of people working undercover in wartime. Non-religious people are likely to agree that Mitchell's parable is not persuasive.

Hick challenged Logical Positivism by saying that empirical verification is not the only test that can determine the meaning of religious claims. Eschatological verification is also a possibility; at the end of time, we will know the answers to religious questions, even if they cannot be answered in this life. Critics of Hick, however, argue that all he has done is add another unjustifiable, meaningless claim to the debate. Asserting that everything will be testable after death is itself an untestable assertion. Non-religious people are unlikely to agree that there will be an afterlife in which religious truth-claims can be demonstrated to be true or false.

The view that challenges to Logical Positivism are convincing for non-religious people

Many non-religious people accept a logical positivist way of understanding meaning. However, some of the challenges to it can be convincing for non-religious people.

The most convincing is the challenge that Logical Positivism, especially the verification principle, does not meet its own criteria for meaningfulness. Non-religious and religious people alike may be convinced by the challenge that the logical positivists' own claims are not empirically verifiable. This undermines the principles of verification and falsification significantly.

Non-religious people may also be convinced by the challenge that Logical Positivism is too narrow in its criteria for what is meaningful. It rules out ethical claims, for example, and many will assert that ethical claims are meaningful, whether or not those people have religious belief.

Some non-religious people will also be convinced by the challenge that there could be meaningful truth that is not available to empirical observation. Claims about a person's mental state, for example, are not available to empirical observation, and yet can still be meaningful. Doctors, whether non-religious or religious, cannot empirically observe pain, but when patients report their pain levels, the doctors find the reports meaningful.

> **AO2 activity 6**
> How convincing do you find the responses to Flew made by Hare, Mitchell, and Hick?

How successful are non-cognitive interpretations as valid responses to the challenges to the meaning of religious language?

This question asks for an evaluation of non-cognitive approaches to religious language, such as analogy, or Hare's view that religious language is about an individual's 'picture-preference'.

Before evaluating non-cognitive approaches to religious language, it is important to explain why the approach to religious language you are discussing is in fact non-cognitive. Analogy is a non-cognitive use of language because it invites us to draw comparisons between different things in the hope of improving understanding. These comparisons give us pictorial ways of looking at things, but are not truth-apt.

The view that non-cognitive understandings of religious language are successful

In Aquinas' view, it was important to remember that God cannot be wholly understood, and that we will never reach a clear understanding where we comprehend exactly what God is. Up to a point at least, we have to translate the analogies into univocal language before they mean anything; we have to know how God's love relates to human love before we understand anything. This method of speaking about God still leaves us with an unclear picture, where we know something about the nature of God, but not a great deal.

But Aquinas would argue there is nothing wrong with accepting that God is mysterious and that our knowledge of God is limited, as long as the believer understands enough to be able to worship. The 'otherness' of God, described by Rudolf Otto as *mysterium tremendum et fascinans* (a fearful and fascinating mystery) is something that our language ought to convey, not disguise.

Non-cognitive understandings of religious language could be understood to be successful in the same way that poetry, art, or music is successful. It does not convey a literal truth, but instead points us towards deeper layers of human psychology and more profound aspects of what it means to be human, in a way that cognitive statements cannot do.

The view that non-cognitive understandings of religious language are unsuccessful

Analogies used in religious language could be helpful, but they could be confusing or misleading. In what respects might the love or the justice of God resemble our own, and how are they different?

Non-cognitivist views such as the one put forward by Hare when he talked about 'bliks' could be seen as unsuccessful, because many believers reject the view that all their religious language is non-cognitive. When they say there is a God who exists for all time and who created the world, they mean us to understand that what they are saying is objectively true. They do not think it is no more than picture-language. When they pray, asking for God's help or forgiveness, they intend to address an objectively existent being who has the power to do things and to answer their prayers. When they speak of life after death, they intend this to be understood as a real state of existence; they do not merely mean 'I like to live my life as if there were life after death'.

AO2 activity 7

How persuasive do you find non-cognitive interpretations of religious language? Give reasons to support your answer, and make reference to scholarly views in your discussion.

Practising AO1 questions

AO1 questions begin with one of a range of possible command words (see pages 8–9 for more detail). The following question begins with the command word 'Explain'. 'Explain' questions require you to cover the broad topic area in the question in as much detail as possible. You do not need to consider the quality of the theory, or offer any views about it.

Activity

Look at the example of a past paper question and an example paragraph from a longer answer written in response to it. This part of the answer is well written: the writer talks about Aquinas and Ramsey together, drawing attention to the things they have in common. Continue the answer with a paragraph about Aquinas and a paragraph about Ramsey, showing your understanding that Aquinas and Ramsey made related, but different, contributions to the discussion.

Explain religious language as analogy, with reference to Aquinas and Ramsey.

(Eduqas A Level Religious Studies, Summer 2019,
Component 2: Philosophy of Religion, Question 4a)

Example

Aquinas[6] and[2] Ramsey[6] both understood religious language in terms of analogy[2]. Analogy[7] is a[1] non-cognitive[7] use of language, because it is not[1] truth-apt[7]. Instead, it compares one thing with another in an attempt to clarify meaning, with the aim that the listener will gain insights into the religious ideas being explained. Aquinas[6] and[2] Ramsey[6] argued that God cannot be expressed using[2] univocal[7] language[2], with the words used having the same meaning about God as they have in the physical world. Instead, the analogy needs to convey something of the mystery of God, giving insights while at the same time emphasising the differences between God and imperfect human beings[1]. For Aquinas[6] and Ramsey[6], the way forward was through the use of analogy, in which a comparison is made between God and something from the physical world, for example a human quality such as 'loving' or 'powerful'[3].

1 The paragraph shows accurate and relevant knowledge and understanding.

2 The writer has correctly identified that the question is asking for answers that focus on two specific thinkers.

3 Examples have been used effectively to clarify meaning.

4 Sacred texts and sources or wisdom and authority are not relevant in this part of the answer, and so it is appropriate that none appear.

5 Appropriately, this paragraph does not contain connections to other areas of study.

6 The scholarly views referred to in this paragraph match the requirements of the question.

7 There is accurate and relevant use of specialist language and vocabulary.

AO1 practice question 1

Now it is your turn. Have a go at answering the following question. There are some points to remember to help you if you are not sure how to start.

> *Explain how Logical Positivism challenges the meaningfulness of religious language.*
>
> (Eduqas A Level Religious Studies, Summer 2018, Component 2: Philosophy of Religion, Question 5a)

Points to remember

- This is another 'Explain' question. It requires you to give a detailed account, but does not require you to give your own views.
- The question asks you to focus on the challenges presented by Logical Positivism to the meaningfulness of religious language. You need to concentrate on the idea that religious language is neither true nor false, but instead has no meaningful content.
- Try to give an accurate account of the views of thinkers such as Ayer and Flew.

AO1 practice question 2

Now try this question by yourself.

> *Examine the criticisms of verification and falsification in relation to religious language.*
>
> (WJEC A Level Religious Studies, Summer 2018, A2 Unit 5: Philosophy of Religion, Question 1)

Practising AO2 questions

When writing a response to an AO2 question, you must remember you are being examined on your ability to analyse and evaluate effectively. Analysis involves a detailed examination of something, and you should pick apart the concept to look for its strengths and weaknesses. Evaluation involves judging the quality or importance of the concept. You are expected to analyse and evaluate throughout the whole of your response; you are not expected to include long passages explaining knowledge and understanding.

Activity

Here is an example of a past paper question and an example paragraph, taken from a longer answer written in response to it. In this part of the answer, the writer has started to construct an argument in which they intend to support the claim that the views of Logical Positivism are indeed convincing.

Read the paragraph carefully and then continue the answer, giving more reasons to support the view that Logical Positivism is convincing, and showing why those who might hold different views are wrong (even if this is not your own view, write as though it were). Remember to make reference to scholarly points of view in your answer.

'The views of Logical Positivism are convincing.' Evaluate this view.

(WJEC A Level Religious Studies, Summer 2019, A2 Unit 5: Philosophy of Religion, Question 5)

Example

The views of Logical Positivism[2] are extremely convincing. The first reason that they are convincing is that[1] they dismiss religious belief as meaningless[6], on the grounds that it cannot be verified[6] using sense experience[6]. They are right to do this[1], because religious belief is based on superstitious, pre-scientific traditions that have no place in the modern world and hold back scientific endeavour[3]. Thinkers such as A.J. Ayer[4] persuasively[1] presented the case that, if language is to be meaningful at all, its claims should be capable of empirical testing[6]. Religious truth claims[6] are no more than empty assertions[6] with no foundation, and should not be a part of modern discourse.

1 This paragraph begins with some successful analysis and evaluation, giving a clear line of argument from the start and telling the reader they are intending to present a reasoned argument rather than just descriptive information.

2 The writer focuses clearly on the question.

3 Reasoning is given to support the point of view expressed in the paragraph.

4 There is reference to appropriate scholarly views.

5 Links with other areas of the course must not be forced, and so it is appropriate that none appear in this paragraph.

6 The student uses specialist language and vocabulary with confidence and accuracy.

AO2 practice question 1

Now it is your turn. Have a go at answering the following question. There are some points to remember to help you if you are not sure how to start.

> *'Non-cognitive interpretations of religious language are meaningful.' Evaluate this view.*
>
> (Eduqas A Level Religious Studies, Summer 2019, Component 2: Philosophy of Religion, Question 4b)

Points to remember

- Remember that for an AO2 question, you need to concentrate on evaluation and analysis, rather than giving lengthy descriptions.
- In this answer, there are opportunities to consider a variety of non-cognitive approaches to religious language, such as Aquinas and Ramsey's use of analogy, and Hare's understanding of religious language in the context of an individual's 'blik'.
- The question includes the term 'meaningful', so you need to consider what makes an interpretation meaningful; you may or may not agree with the logical positivists here.

AO2 practice question 2

Now try this question by yourself.

> *'Logical Positivism successfully shows that religious language is meaningless.' Evaluate this view.*
>
> (Eduqas A Level Religious Studies, Summer 2018, Component 2: Philosophy of Religion, Question 5b)

Mark schemes for all exam questions can be found at www.eduqas.co.uk and www.wjec.co.uk.

If you look around you, wherever you are at this moment, you will probably see some kind of symbol. It may be on your clothing, as a logo or a badge; perhaps there are symbols on the walls to indicate a fire exit or to show you that something is poisonous or flammable. If you are working online, you will see that your computer or device has symbolic icons on it. Symbols can provide a vivid and memorable way of communicating, using pictures, graphics, objects, and language in non-literal ways.

Myths similarly use non-literal ways of conveying meaning, by providing lively stories that capture the imagination while at the same time communicating significant messages. You will probably be familiar with a range of myths from your own and other cultures; you may have been introduced to them in childhood.

This chapter looks at the ways in which religious language uses symbol and myth in order to convey meaning. Symbol and myth are closely linked, as myths use symbolism to construct a thought-provoking story where the listeners know that there is a deeper meaning to find.

Continuing with the theme of non-cognitive uses of religious language, this chapter also explores the work of the philosopher Ludwig Wittgenstein, and the contribution he made to an understanding of meaning through his idea of religious language as a 'language game'.

Non-literal ways of understanding religious language can be helpful, but they also raise a lot of questions.

Symbols are used in everyday life to communicate ideas in a vivid and memorable way.

- Why do people use symbols, and are symbols helpful in communicating ideas about God?
- Is all of religious language symbolic?
- How is symbolic language in religion best understood?
- Why do religions use myths to communicate religious ideas?
- How should myths be understood?
- Does it help to think of language using the analogy of playing a game?
- Is language only properly understood within the context and world view of those who use it?

This section of the chapter will enhance your **knowledge** and **understanding** of the topic and help you develop your AO1 skills.

Religious language as non-cognitive and symbolic

The word 'symbol' comes from Greek, and means 'thrown together'. The thing being symbolised, often a concern or a focus in people's lives, is thrown together with something else to aid understanding and give insights in a way that is difficult to put into words.

People use symbols to describe God and their relationship to God, saying things like 'The Lord is my shepherd', or 'God is my rock'. They also use physical symbols, such as artwork and sacred objects, instead of language, to convey meanings that cannot readily be put into words, to evoke particular feelings, or to identify themselves as members of a particular group of believers so that they can be easily recognised by others.

Perhaps the most universal of all religious symbols is the symbol of light. It is used to represent gaining knowledge and coming to understanding (enlightenment), because in the physical world things can be more clearly perceived in the light. Darkness is used to symbolise ignorance. Flames are used to symbolise prayer, remembrance of the dead, the presence of God, and purification. Water is used as a symbol of cleansing from sin, and of purity and a life-giving force.

The Golden Temple in Amritsar is a Sikh Gurdwara. It has entrances on every side to symbolise that everyone is welcome, wherever they come from.

Religious people also use symbolism in their body language: when they kneel for prayer, prostrate themselves, or bow their heads, they remind themselves of their position in relation to God with these symbolic actions. They use symbolism in music too: in many cultures, a minor key suggests nostalgia or sadness, whereas a major key symbolises joy and triumph.

AO1 activity 1

a) Emojis have become a common part of digital communication. Why do you think people use emojis when they send each other messages, rather than sticking only to words?

b) Make a list of ten examples of symbols used in religion. You might think of symbolic foods, symbolic architecture (where the shape of the place of worship reflects an aspect of belief), symbolic dress, symbolic objects or symbolic actions, as well as symbolic language.

All language is, of course, symbolic, in the sense that we use words to stand for other things. We use the shapes of the letters to stand for particular sounds, and we use groups of letters to make words, to stand for different objects, actions, feelings, and so on. If someone uses a particular combination of sounds, and if you understand the language they are speaking, you know that they would like you to put the kettle on, or are asking what time you want to meet up.

Much language, both religious and non-religious, is figurative. It is used in a pictorial way rather than being literal. We use all kinds of figurative language in everyday conversations: 'a sea of faces' when there is no literal water involved, or 'the four corners of the Earth' although the Earth has no corners (both metaphors); 'you're not wrong' meaning that you're absolutely right (litotes); 'do I look that stupid?' when we do not genuinely want an answer (rhetoric). There are many different forms of figurative language, and symbol is one of them.

Symbol is an example of figurative language that is used in both religious language and in everyday language. A **symbol** represents, or stands for, something else, and is meant to communicate something that goes beyond a literal meaning. As well as giving understanding, it is also meant to evoke certain feelings and responses.

> **Key term**
>
> **symbol:** something that is used to stand for or represent something else, and to evoke feelings and responses, in a non-cognitive way

Religious people often use language symbolically when they are talking about their relationship with God. They might say that God 'listened' to their prayers, although they believe that God has no body and therefore no ears; they might say that God 'walks with them' even though they believe that God is always everywhere and is beyond space. The symbols convey their belief that they have a personal relationship with God, and also evokes feelings of closeness, communication, and companionship between the believer and God, in a way that literal language might not be able to achieve.

The figurative, symbolic use of language helps to create a shortcut in expressing ideas and feelings; but it can also cause problems of communication, particularly if it is not clear whether a phrase was meant as a symbolic metaphor or whether it was meant literally.

In Christianity, as in other religious traditions, symbolism is an integral part of communication. Christians believe that humanity is made in the image of God, which is a symbol; people are not literally 'in the image of God' in the sense of looking like God, but the term is used to express symbolically the idea that people have a soul that is capable of a relationship with God. The soul, Christians say, is that which gives people the ability to experience the profound realities of existence. These experiences cannot be easily expressed in words, and yet they are so important and moving that people want to share them with others. Symbols are used when Christians, in their quest to develop their relationship with God, attach a deeper spiritual significance and meaning to well-known words, actions, or things. In this way, a more profound insight is offered into God's presence in all of creation.

The symbolism is not inherent in whatever is used as a symbol; it emerges through use and association, and identification in the minds of the people who use it.

Two thinkers whose ideas have been influential for an understanding of symbol in religious language are John Herman Randall Jnr and Paul Tillich. The two scholars were contemporaries and friends, writing and discussing their ideas in the USA in the 1950s.

The period after the Second World War was a time of rebuilding and looking forward, deciding which parts of the past should be preserved or reconstructed, and which should be discarded in favour of something new. Whole cities in Europe had been bombed, and people had to think about whether they were going to reconstruct the buildings to look exactly as they had looked before the war, or whether they were going to design something fresh. Attention turned to the education system, to the welfare state, and health care: what in human society should be preserved, and where should there be a radical change of direction towards something new and fit for the modern era?

The old Coventry Cathedral was destroyed by bombing during the Second World War. The decision was made to construct a new, modern building, while preserving the ruins of the old cathedral.

Many of the leading theologians of the time thought that Christian faith should be a part of this process, and could not just carry on after the war as if nothing of significance had happened. It was a time for a new evaluation of what it meant to be a Christian in the modern world. Randall and Tillich thought that it was also time to re-evaluate the ways in which Christians conceptualised God, referred to God, and understood the symbolic nature of religious language. Meanwhile, in the UK, Ian Ramsey was looking at similar ideas with his work on religious language as analogical.

John Randall: the functions of symbols

John Herman Randall's views on the symbolic nature of religious language were closely linked with his interest in the history of ideas. Randall was an American professor with a background in history. His books focused on the ways in which different ideas in philosophy develop and come in and out of fashion, and how developments relate to what is happening in society at the time.

Randall was particularly interested in the function of religion in society, and considering the role it plays in people's individual and social lives. He explored the idea of religious language as symbolic in a book called *The Role of Knowledge in Western Religion*, first published in 1958. The book was originally written as a series of lectures, in which Randall set out to consider what 'knowledge' means in science and in religion. His conclusions were that religion is not about knowledge at all, but is non-cognitive. For Randall,

Synoptic link

Link to *Chapter 7: Religious language (part one)*. Randall and Tillich were contemporaries of Ian Ramsey, who was based in the UK and wrote about models, qualifiers, and disclosure in the context of analogy. Ramsey, Randall, and Tillich were all producing books in the 1950s.

this meant that religion could sit comfortably alongside science rather than being in competition with it, as religion and science offered humanity entirely different things and had no need to compete.

Looking at religion from this non-cognitivist, sociological perspective, Randall drew the conclusion that religion is a human creation, a human enterprise with a social function.

> *Religion is rather itself a human activity that demands careful observation and description, explanation, reflective understanding, and intelligent criticism.*
>
> John Herman Randall,
> *The Role of Knowledge in Western Religion*

Religion brings people together, and gives them common aims and values. It does not in any way give people knowledge, and it is not a set of superstitious explanations that might rival scientific claims. Instead, it functions as a means by which people can express the things that affect them deeply. Religious ceremonies and festivals serve to highlight the importance of significant times in people's lives, such as births and harvests.

Randall did not just think that religious language contains symbols. Instead, he went further and said that all religious language is symbolic in nature.

> *We can assume, therefore, that all religious beliefs without exception are 'mythology.' That is, they are all religious 'symbols.' If such symbols can be said to possess any kind of 'truth' they certainly do not possess the literal truth of the factual statements of the descriptive sciences or of common sense.*
>
> John Herman Randall,
> *The Role of Knowledge in Western Religion*

Randall did not address whether or not religion has truth in the sense that it corresponds to an objective reality. His own view of truth is known as a 'coherence' theory of truth, where something is true if it fits with other aspects of the system it is a part of. This meant that, for Randall, symbolic language can be called 'true' if it makes sense in the context of the belief system within which it operates. A Christian religious symbol is true if it makes sense within the belief system of Christianity.

Randall's interest in how aspects of society function led him to outline four functions of symbol:

1. Motivation: Symbols make people feel a certain way, and because of the emotions they evoke, they lead on to action. Symbols have a power to inspire people to do things. An example of a physical religious symbol might be a lit candle in a cathedral, as a symbol of prayer, especially a prayer for a loved one. The symbol makes people who see it feel something; they might think about loved ones in their own lives who are sick, elderly, or bereaved, and the symbol of the candle might inspire

them to call that person or to pray for them. An example of a belief that Randall would also see as a religious symbol might be belief in an afterlife, which makes people feel hopeful or comforted, and as a result, might make them more motivated towards acts of kindness.

> *[Symbols] do not, like signs, merely lead the mind to other things; they produce results in conduct.* **"**
>
> John Herman Randall,
> *The Role of Knowledge in Western Religion*

2. Co-operation: Symbols stimulate group activity. Randall mentions physical social symbols, like flags, and intellectual social symbols, like 'state' and 'liberty', which make people feel patriotic or free, and lead to group activities.
3. Communication: Symbols enable people to express shared feelings and experiences that are otherwise difficult to put into words. Randall stressed that symbols are non-cognitive, and so it is almost impossible to explain in ordinary language what they mean. They are emotional rather than factual, and provide ways of seeing rather than knowledge.
4. Revelation: All symbols share the first three characteristics, but the fourth is particular to religious symbols.

> *Religious symbols in particular can be said to 'disclose' or 'reveal' something about the world in which they function.* **"**
>
> John Herman Randall,
> *The Role of Knowledge in Western Religion*

What they reveal, Randall said, is not what we would call knowledge in the ordinary sense, but might be better described as insight or vision.

Paul Tillich: God as that which concerns us ultimately

Paul Tillich was a twentieth-century German-American theologian and philosopher, most noted for his books *Systematic Theology* and *The Courage to Be*, first published in 1951 and 1952 respectively. He was a Christian existentialist, writing in the context of the post-war years. Existentialism focuses on the needs people have, as individuals, to find their own meaning in a puzzling world, and Christian existentialism takes on this subjective, deeply personal approach to faith.

Tillich had lived in Germany all his life until 1933, when he came into conflict with the Nazis. He was dismissed from the position he held as Professor of Theology at the University of Frankfurt. Soon afterwards, he was offered a position in the USA and settled there.

Within theology, Tillich is probably best known for his 'theology of correlation'. He wanted to show that there is a correlation between the questions raised by philosophy, the arts, other world religions, psychology and history, and the answers provided by Christian theology. His aim was to correlate faith with culture, and in particular, a culture in which humanity is searching to find or create meaning. In Tillich's view, all of the big questions

---

AO1 activity 2

a) What did Randall think makes a symbol 'true'?

b) What did Randall think is the characteristic of religious symbols that makes them different from other kinds of symbols used in other contexts?

raised by people essentially come down to one question: how to make sense of human existence, what it means to live a finite human life in the context of the universe (in other words, the big existential question). This fundamental question, he thought, is the same question that Christian theology addresses and answers, and therefore Christian theology not only has a place in, but should be central to, modern life and culture.

Tillich on the symbolic language of religion

One of the main ways in which Tillich thought that faith could correlate to culture was by means of symbol. Tillich, like Randall, believed that all religious language is symbolic rather than literal, and therefore it cannot be subjected to tests such as the verification principle in order to assess its meaningfulness. He took a non-cognitive approach to religious language.

Tillich argued that metaphors and symbols help us to a better understanding of God and of religious experience. He said that symbols take us beyond the empirical world and open up new levels of reality to us, unlocking dimensions of the soul that were previously closed. The symbolic language used is intelligible and accessible to us, but it points beyond itself towards an ultimate reality, which is God. Tillich defined symbol very broadly, including visual images, as well as rituals, saints, stories, and even ideas. For Tillich, the whole of religious language should be seen more like poetry than prose, more like art than a diagram. A symbol 'participates in' that to which it points, and a religious symbol points towards God, a person's 'ultimate concern'.

Tillich thought that we use religious symbolic language as a way to come to terms with the meaning of human existence. For example, we use the symbol of God the creator to help us come to terms with our place in the universe, our ambivalent relationship with the natural world, and an understanding of our purpose. We use the symbol of Jesus as the Christ to unlock some of the mystery of the relationship between the physical and the spiritual, our tendency to sin, and our desire for freedom in a deterministic world.

In Tillich's view, people rarely use language that is not symbolic, except when they are talking about trivial things. All of our most important ideas, concerns, feelings, and experiences are expressed through symbol. He also pointed out that symbols have a shelf life; they work within particular times, places, and cultures, and can lose their power or significance when society changes or when they are seen by someone from a different culture.

Tillich claimed that to use literal language about God is unhelpful, and conveys a false impression of the nature of God. He followed Aquinas in asserting that ordinary human language is inadequate to convey ultimate truth.

In his book *Dynamics of Faith*, first published in 1957, Tillich identified six characteristics of symbols:

1. Symbols point beyond themselves to something else (in this respect, they work in the same way as signs).

> **Synoptic link**
>
> Link to *Chapter 7: Religious language (part one)*. Tillich's ideas are similar to those of Aquinas when both say that ordinary univocal language is inadequate when talking about God.

2. Symbols participate in the reality of that to which they point (this, Tillich says, makes them different from signs). He used the example of a national flag which, he said, participates in the dignity and power of the nation it represents. This participation means that symbols cannot be easily replaced, and an attack on the symbol is seen as an attack on the thing it symbolises.

3. Tillich said that symbols open up levels of reality to us that would remain closed if we relied only on literal words. The arts, especially, create symbols that do this.

4. In opening up new levels of reality to us, the symbol also opens up corresponding dimensions of the soul. The symbol gives us new vision, and also shows us something of the nature of our own being.

5. Symbols cannot be produced intentionally, but grow out of the individual or collective unconscious; Tillich was using here the Jungian idea that as human beings, we all share a deep level of the mind.

6. A consequence of the fact that symbols cannot be invented is that they grow and they die, becoming important and useful when the context is right, but fading out of use as situations change. Tillich gives the example of the symbol of kingship, which grew at a time when kings held authority and made important decisions, and died in most parts of the world when monarchy went out of fashion or kings became only figureheads. Tillich emphasised that symbols do not come into being just because people want them, and do not die just because people criticise them. Their life-span corresponds to whether or not they have power to cause a response.

> **Synoptic link**
>
> Link to *Chapter 4: Challenges to religious belief: religious belief as a product of the human mind*. Tillich used some terminology from Jung in describing how symbols deepened human understanding.

Visual symbolism is a prominent feature of religious art, but the symbols lose their impact over time. At the time of the Renaissance, strawberries symbolised righteousness and the fruits of the Holy Spirit. The owl, because it lives in darkness, represented evil. Bulrushes symbolised those who live a humble life, and the butterfly symbolised resurrection.

Tillich on distinguishing signs from symbols

Tillich said that there are differences between signs and symbols. Both 'point at something beyond', in the sense that both are meant to draw your attention to something other than themselves. For example, if someone is pointing a finger in a particular direction, you are meant to look in the direction they are pointing, and not at their finger. But, although they have this in common, signs and symbols also have significant differences:

- A sign is arbitrary, and can be replaced. We have decided that a red circle with a horizontal white line in the middle means 'no entry', but we could easily agree to change it to, for example, an open door with an X across it. Symbols, on the other hand, cannot be replaced with a different word, idea, or object, because of their participation in the thing they represent.

- Signs do not have to have a relationship with the thing they are indicating, whereas a symbol is inextricably linked with whatever it points towards. Tillich liked to use the example of a flag, which becomes a part of the national identity and provokes an emotional response.

AO1 activity 3

Explain, in your own words, what Tillich understands a symbol to be, and how he distinguishes symbols from signs.

Tillich on religious experience and symbol

For Tillich, a religious experience is an experience of something beyond the physical world, an encounter with something that cannot be encountered using the senses. The 'religious' element is subjective; someone else might have the same experience and feelings, but not interpret them in a religious way. In Tillich's view, the experience is religious if it is an experience of 'Being-Itself', which was his term for ultimate reality. A religious experience can be expressed only in symbol, and it gives a person new insights into the nature of being, helping them find meaning in the meaninglessness of human existence.

Tillich on the nature of God

Tillich was critical of traditional ways of understanding and describing God as the highest being, with characteristics such as omnipotence, omnibenevolence, and omniscience. For Tillich, even though these descriptions of God always place God as 'that than which nothing greater can be thought' (in Anselm's terminology), they still suggest that God is 'a being', and that, in the list of all the beings in the universe, God is at the top.

But, Tillich argued, this is wrong because it places God in the same category as created things. If God is 'a being', then it begs the question 'who created God and brought God into being?' God cannot be the ultimate source of all being, if God is a being too. Tillich understood God to be 'Being-Itself', the ground of all being. God does not just exist; God is existence itself, the ground of all existence, the reason why anything and everything else exists. Tillich had no time for arguments for the existence of God because they are arguments that try to settle the question of whether God does or does not exist. In Tillich's view (rather like St Anselm's), God is Being-Itself, not some 'thing' which might or might not have existence. God is that very existence.

Tillich argued that if we think of God as an existent being, then God does not give us an adequate answer to existential doubt (anxiety about our place in the universe and meaning of our lives). We end up (as symbolised by Christ on the cross) with human anxiety and fear of our own mortality, feeling that God has forsaken us and gone away. Only when we understand that God is the ground of all being, our 'ultimate concern', do we have a solid response to the big existential question.

Tillich emphasised that people have all kinds of concerns: health, relationships, money, success. But as well as these physical, material concerns, they also have spiritual concerns. The desire for the holy, for an experience of God, is humanity's ultimate concern, he thought, and this ultimate concern can only be accessed through symbol.

> **Synoptic link**
>
> Link to *Chapter 5: Religious experience (part one)*. Tillich's ideas about religious experience requiring symbolic language links with William James' description of religious experiences as 'ineffable'.

> **Synoptic link**
>
> Link to *Chapter 7: Religious language (part one)*. Tillich's ideas about God as 'Being-Itself' echo Aquinas' ideas about analogy of attribution. God is not just a living thing, but is the source of all life.

AO1 activity 4

a) What is meant by 'existential doubt'?

b) Why did Tillich choose to refer to God as 'Being-Itself'?

c) What did Tillich think were the reasons why people use symbol in religious language?

d) What did Tillich mean when he wrote of humanity's 'ultimate concern'?

Tillich on free will and Determinism

Tillich wrote that the traditional 'God is the highest being' idea creates great problems for people who are grappling with existential questions of the meaning of life and their place in the world. If God is this highest being, who holds all the cards, and decides all our fates and knows with perfect knowledge what our futures will hold, there is nothing we can do about anything … we become helpless, pointless creatures.

> *God appears as the invincible tyrant, the being in contrast with whom all other beings are without freedom and subjectivity. He is equated with the recent tyrants who with the help of terror try to transform everything into a mere object, a thing among things, a cog in a machine they control. He becomes the model of everything against which Existentialism revolted. This is the deepest root of atheism. It is an atheism which is justified as the reaction against theological theism and its disturbing implications.*
>
> Paul Tillich, *Courage to Be*

Tillich is arguing here that our existential need for freedom to make our own decisions demands that we recognise God as the ground of all being, and not as the highest being. For Tillich, this different understanding of God gets us out of the predetermined dead-end that the God of traditional theism forces upon us.

Challenges to Randall and Tillich

Both Tillich and Randall have been criticised for their lack of clarity. They use religious language (which they claim is always symbolic) in order to explain how symbol is to be understood. For example, they talk about 'opening up levels of reality to the soul', a symbol 'pointing beyond' itself and 'participating in' the thing being symbolised, without it ever being very clear what these expressions actually mean. Their use of symbol to explain symbol makes it difficult for the reader to get a firm grasp of what they are saying.

Paul Edwards criticised Tillich in a 1965 article called 'Professor Tillich's confusions'. In the article, he objected to the way in which Tillich used symbolic language to explain symbolic language but does not take us anywhere solid. He wanted Tillich to unpack the symbols and help us to know what it is they refer to. Without this, Edwards argued, the symbols take us nowhere. Tillich argued that symbols are not reducible to everyday, univocal language; but Edwards said if this is the case, Tillich's claims about symbolic language pointing beyond itself become meaningless assertions.

The philosopher William Alston criticises Tillich for using the words 'sign' and 'symbol' in ways that are different from their normal usage. Tillich rejected mathematical symbols such as '+' and '=' and insists they are signs, and Tillich would have identified a Christian making the sign of the cross as someone using a symbol. This adds to the difficulty of understanding. Tillich and Randall cannot be entirely blamed for this confusion, however;

before their books were published, other Christian writers made similar distinctions. For example:

> *A sign* represents. *It points to something, and takes its character from what is done with it. … A symbol* resembles. *It has acquired a deeper meaning than the sign, because it is more completely identified with what it represents, and its character is derived from what is known by it.*
>
> George Ferguson, *Signs and Symbols in Christian Art*

Alston also criticises Tillich for removing much, if not all, of the content from religious language. He says that when people talk about salvation, or about heaven and hell, although their language includes reference to the question of what it means to be human, they also intend their speech to have some factual content. Religious people use language to refer to things that they believe are real, not just symbolic. If they talk of Jesus dying on the cross, they mean to convey that there really was a man called Jesus who actually died on a cross. They do not merely mean to provide a symbol to show that human life is mortal and contains suffering.

John Hick similarly argued that Tillich over-emphasises the aesthetic, artistic nature of the religious symbol, making it appear very subjective and open to almost any kind of interpretation. The view seems to suggest that there is no factual content in religious language and that it is an appeal to an emotional response rather than a means of conveying knowledge. Many religious believers would not accept that, saying instead that when they make an assertion about God, they are referring to facts. Most would say that when they claim that God created the world or that God can forgive sins, they mean these assertions to be taken at face value.

Many argue that symbols leave us with no way of knowing what is a valid insight into ultimate reality, and what is not. We don't know if we are interpreting a symbol correctly. If we take a symbol to be pointing beyond itself, we don't know whether we are pointing it in the right direction, nor what we are supposed to be looking at. Tillich writes of 'genuine' religious symbols and 'idolatrous' religious symbols, but does not make it clear how the two are to be distinguished from each other. He clearly thought there was a right and a wrong way to use symbol and to interpret symbol, but does not adequately explain what makes an approach right or wrong.

Critics of Tillich argue that the idea of a symbol pointing beyond itself is not very helpful if we are not told what it is pointing to.

Randall is criticised for concentrating too heavily on the human function of religion and religious symbol, to the point where he seems to be saying that religion is no more than a human construct. He does not discuss whether there is a truth out there, to be found behind the symbol, but instead talks about symbols purely in terms of the function they perform in human expression. Randall held a coherent theory of truth, but many religious believers have a different view and think that something is true if it corresponds to an objective reality, rather than just whether it fits in with a system of belief. In academic terms, Randall is said to focus too much on the axiological side of religion (how people value religion, how religion makes them feel, and the role of religion in a human community) and not enough, if at all, on the ontological side (what is real, what exists, and where truth can be found).

Tillich's view of God has been criticised for being too radical and unbiblical. Some say that there is little difference between Tillich and atheism when he discards the God of traditional theism. Randall does not appear to have much idea of God at all, talking of religion as a function of society rather than a response to an actual divine being.

AO1 activity 5

a) Summarise the criticisms made by Alston and Hick of Tillich's approach to symbol.

b) What does it mean to say that Randall focuses too much on the axiological aspects of symbol and too little on their ontological value?

How the views of Randall and Tillich can be used to help understand religious teachings

Although Randall and Tillich have been criticised for their approach to symbol in religious language, there are also several ways in which their work can aid understanding of religious beliefs and teachings.

Their work draws attention to the richness of language, and the different ways it can be used to evoke emotion. Rather than restricting understanding to the basic 'true, false, or meaningless' categories the logical positivists attempted to impose, they recognise that language has far more uses, levels of meaning, and possibilities.

Their work helps reduce some of the conflict between scientific and religious approaches to the world, by proposing that religious language is not about establishing facts and knowledge than can be evidenced and measured, but is instead non-cognitive. It has a function that is more like poetry than science. They show how religious language can have meaning even though it cannot be reduced to truth claims that can be empirically verified or falsified.

The idea of symbols being appropriate for their cultural context, evolving and dying out, demonstrates the relevance of religious belief for the modern world. Believers are not restricted to using symbols more relevant to biblical times, but are instead able to use new ones that can change and adapt as society changes.

AO1 activity 6

The Bible is full of symbolic language. Look up these verses and then answer the questions below for each verse:

- Deuteronomy 32:18
- Psalm 118:22
- John 1:1–4
- Acts 7:55

a) What symbols are being used?

b) What are the symbols intended to convey? Can you explain the symbol in more literal language? (Do some further research if necessary.)

c) Does the symbol work well in the twenty-first century, or is it more appropriate for the time the Bible was written?

Religious language as non-cognitive and mythical

The word 'myth' is often used in ordinary conversation to refer to something that is just not true, but in religious language it has a particular meaning.

Mythical language is a kind of religious language that uses stories with layers of symbols to communicate values and insights into the purpose of human existence. Through vivid narratives, a community's belief system can be illustrated, and phenomena of importance to human life can be explored. **Myths** are non-cognitive, because they cannot be judged to be true or false; they can be effective or ineffective, but they are not about physical facts.

> ### Key term
>
> **myth:** a multi-layered traditional story full of symbolism, used to convey important truths in a non-cognitive way

There are myths in all cultures and belief systems across the world, all with their own unique qualities, but also with some common themes that serve to show how humanity is united in the same concerns even in widely different contexts. Study of mythology is important in a wide variety of disciplines, including history, literature, psychology, sociology, anthropology, and theology.

Mircea Eliade and myth

Mircea Eliade was a twentieth-century Romanian writer who did much to popularise the study of myth. He was very interested in how myths function in their cultural environments, and how they help us differentiate between what he called the sacred and the profane, or the holy and the everyday. Eliade was greatly influenced by Jung, arguing that different myths have underlying universal themes and structures, and all illustrate fundamental characteristics of the human consciousness. Eliade's work became less popular, as he was affiliated with far-right politics for a time in the 1930s, but it has nevertheless been very influential.

Different forms of myths to convey meaning

As Jung pointed out in his work on the relationship between myths and the human psyche, there are several common threads in myths that allow them to be categorised into different types.

- Creation myths tell stories of the origins of the world and the origins of humanity.
- Myths of good against evil explore the struggles people face to do the right things and to cope with suffering.
- Heroic myths provide motivation for standing up for what is right, and offer role models for people to look up to.

Creation myths

Creation myths appear in almost every culture, and are often closely related to the kind of culture they come from. Where did the universe come from? How did the world come into being? What happened in the time before our earliest records? Is there a reason why we are here? Questions like these are important to us today, and were just as important for our ancestors. Creation myths explore these questions using symbol, and often have symbols in common:

In Botticelli's painting of the Birth of Venus, the goddess emerges fully-formed from the sea.

- The symbol of water: In many creation myths from around the world, creation begins with dark and mysterious waters. Water, especially the sea, is a powerful symbol because of its many qualities. Humanity cannot live without water, and yet the sea is a dangerous place where people can drown. It gives life and it has cleansing power, but is also uncontrollable and unpredictable, sometimes calm and beautiful, sometimes stormy and destructive. In many ancient creation myths, the Earth is originally covered with water, and the first acts of the gods are to form some dry land for people to live on.
- The symbols of light and darkness: Creation myths often use darkness to symbolise chaos and ignorance. Light symbolises the opposite: control, order, peace, knowledge, and truth. In eastern mythology, the lotus flower is used as a symbol of the journey from darkness to light, as it starts first as an ugly shapeless bulb in the darkness at the bottom of a pond, and then gradually moves towards the light as it grows, until it emerges and blossoms into the beautiful, orderly flower it was always meant to be. It is used to show the human journey from ignorance to enlightenment.
- The symbol of dry land: In creation myths, the gods often create dry land, making a safe place for life to exist, protected from the waters. Dry land represents a place of security, where food can be grown, shelter can be found or built, and where things are solid and dependable.
- The creation of humanity: Humanity is given a special place in creation myths. People do not evolve, and their creation is not the same as the creation of other animals, but is given special attention by the gods.

Possibly the oldest creation myth in the world is from ancient Mesopotamia, and is known as the Enuma Elish. It is about how the world was created out of chaotic swirling water. Rival gods were born, who take control and make heaven and Earth. They decide to create humanity, to serve as helpers to the gods and maintain control of the world. Humanity is expected to recognise that the gods have brought the world into existence and be indebted to the gods for their existence, and so they are required to worship.

In Christianity, the stories of creation in the book of Genesis are the source of controversy. For some believers (sometimes called 'fundamentalists' or 'Biblical literalists'), the stories in the Bible were directly inspired by God, and are intended to be understood as literal truth. If the Bible says that God created the world in six days, then that is exactly what happened. Although scientists disagree with the accounts of the origin of the world and the origin of the species as described in the Bible, the scientists must be wrong because God does not make mistakes. Interpreting the Bible stories as myth, for some, comes far too close to saying that they are false.

Other Christians, however, point out the mythological features of the Genesis creation stories: there are unusual trees with special powers, people being made from dust and from ribs, and a talking serpent. There are close similarities with other creation myths, especially with the myths of nearby countries. These Christians understand the creation stories as myth, imagined and developed to convey the power of God and God's purposes in creation. The symbolism in the creation stories shows the responsibilities of humanity as stewards of the Earth, and the debt they owe to God for their creation. They show the inevitable disobedience of humanity in the face of God's commands, and the suffering and estrangement from God that comes as a consequence of sin.

The creation stories in Genesis have sometimes been described as 'aetiological' myths, which are myths that set out to explain the origins of puzzling features of the world. How did the world begin? Why are people here? How did the animals get their names? Why do adults leave their parents and go to form households of their own with partners? How did sin come into the world and why do we suffer? Why does the natural world make it difficult for people to grow food, and why do women have pain in childbirth? Christians who read the creation stories as myth take the view that the symbolism in the myths conveys important truths and gives new insights, but they are not meant to be understood as literal historical accounts. Understanding them as such misses the point. In addition, understanding the creation stories as myth allows Christians to accept the discoveries of science without having to abandon their Christian faith.

Myths of good against evil

Myths of good against evil take up the human concern of feeling threatened and powerless in the face of evil and suffering. They explore questions such as: Why is it that good people sometimes have unhappy lives, and bad people sometimes prosper? Will goodness win in the end? Why, as an

AO1 activity 7
Research creation myths from around the world, and make notes about some of the common themes and ideas that run through them.

AO1 activity 8
Read Genesis 1–3, and note down aspects of the stories that would be useful as examples of symbolic or mythological language.

individual, do I sometimes feel pulled in different directions, knowing what I ought to do but wanting to do the opposite? Some cultures address these questions with myths and symbols that show competing forces. Zoroastrianism is one of the world's oldest religions, and in Zoroastrian mythology, there are cosmic forces of good and evil in a constant battle, with Asha, the force of truth and light, opposing Druj, a power of deceit, and winning in the end. Manichaeism, the philosophical system that greatly influenced Augustine, similarly had myths of a dualistic universe in which the forces of goodness and light are in battle with the dark forces of evil. As well as using symbolism of darkness and light, these and other myths of good against evil often have similar recurring motifs of angels, demons, and rebellion.

John Milton's epic poem 'Paradise Lost' uses a Christian version of this mythology to tell the story of how Lucifer, one of the angels who should have been on the side of goodness, decides instead to rebel against God. He does not like the idea of having to spend his time under the rule of God, singing God's praises, and refuses to bow before the Son of God. He prefers to live in freedom even though this means permanent estrangement from heaven, and so his jealousy casts him downwards into darkness where he forms the forces of evil.

In this illustration for Paradise Lost by Doré, Lucifer falls from the light of heaven into the darkness of hell.

The idea of resurrection can also be found in myths about the battle between good and evil. In some myths, when the battle is at its height and it seems that good is losing against evil, the leader of the force for good dies and is brought back to life, in a victorious ending that shows good will always prevail. The parallels between resurrection motifs in world myths and the story of Jesus' resurrection have led some scholars to the view that Jesus' resurrection is better understood as mythological rather than as literally true.

Heroic myths

Heroic myths are closely linked with myths about the battle of good against evil. They are stories with a familiar pattern: the small, seemingly insignificant hero is confronted by what seems at first to be an impossible challenge. The hero, however, is brave and takes on the challenge despite the odds, securing an unexpected victory and saving the day. These myths occur in all cultures and in literature; the symbol of the hero becomes particularly important in times of national crisis.

In many heroic myths, the birth of the hero has special symbolic features that foreshadow what is to come. The baby hero is in mortal danger, perhaps left on a mountainside to die or threatened by an evil king or a jealous uncle, but he survives against all the odds, setting the scene for his acts of heroism in later life. Sometimes the hero has special powers, given by the gods, that are not usually used but are revealed as a secret weapon when the hero is called upon to save the people.

In the Bible, there are elements of the heroic myth. Moses, for example, narrowly escapes death as an infant when his sister Miriam hides him in the bulrushes so that he can escape being murdered by the evil Pharaoh. Later in his life, he bravely confronts the Pharaoh and demands that the Hebrew people should be set free from slavery. King David starts out as an insignificant young shepherd with a talent for music, but goes on to confront the powerful giant Goliath, and emerges as the victor.

Heroic myths are important and popular. The same themes have often been translated into modern fiction and film, because they carry symbols we enjoy and want to relate to.

Synoptic link

Link to *Chapter 4: Challenges to religious belief: religious belief as a product of the human mind.* Jung studied myths and folklore, and concluded that myths are a way for our collective unconscious to find expression through the use of archetypes.

AO1 activity 9

The motif of the hero is still popular in modern films and fiction. Why do you think people like watching films with heroes, where the hero overcomes evil at the end? What do they get out of it?

Why do religious believers use myth to communicate ideas?

Myths are an important part of belief systems, regardless of whether they are religious, social, or political. They enable us to express our fears and hopes, and give us an opportunity to explore concerns that go to the heart of what it means to be human. It is easy to dismiss myths as stories that primitive people used to explain things before modern science, but they are much more than fictional tales created to fill gaps in knowledge.

Myths help us to overcome fears of the unknown

One of the functions of myths is that they help people to confront their fears. It is natural for people to fear death, and there are myths in many cultures that address this fear. What happens after we die? Is there life after death, and if so, what can we expect? Myths provide a pictorial, symbolic way of giving people comfort. They offer ideas about the continuation of the soul, often with imagery of a crossing or a journey, and a new life to come. In Norse mythology, for example, those who die in battle go to an enormous hall decorated in gold called Valhalla, where the god Odin reigns. Those who were fearful of going to war might have been comforted by the thought that this reward awaited them if they were killed, and their families might take comfort from the idea that their soldiers had gone to this marvellous place. In Greek mythology, heroic souls go to Elysium after death, where, according to some of the Greek poets, the residents live a life of ease in shady parks, enjoying games and music.

Myths about good and evil in cosmic battles, and about the small hero who defeats the large enemy, help us to overcome our fears of being overwhelmed by evil and suffering. During difficult times, myths reassure us that even when troubles seem insurmountable, good will win in the end, and that it is worth putting up a fight, even if the enemy seems invincible.

Myths not only help us to understand our place in the world, but also help us to keep positive and purposeful as we journey through life.

Myths are an effective way to transmit religious, social, and ethical values

Another of the functions of myth is to reinforce religious, social, and ethical values. Myths are vivid and memorable, often living on in oral history for a long time after a religion itself has died out. They are good for story-telling around the fire, or for dramatising for entertainment. Through myths, the values of a group can be reinforced. Myths show what happens when you disobey the gods, or when you allow sibling rivalry to escalate uncontrollably. They show where the sin of pride or vanity can take you, how your wrongdoings will catch up with you eventually, and they show you to be careful what you wish for.

Sometimes the moral messages of myths are very obvious and straightforward, such as in Aesop's fables. In other myths, there are many interweaving messages, such as in the Hindu epic 'Ramayana', where we learn about the duties of kingship, the importance of promise-keeping, the role of the dutiful wife, and the loyalties of a faithful companion, all layered together as part of a story about good overcoming evil and darkness turning to light.

Myths are a popular subject for the visual arts, as they tell a story. The Greek myths, in particular, were popular subjects for decorated pottery, and they also captured the imaginations of the great artists of the Renaissance.

The story of Rama and Sita in the Ramayana explores many of the social, religious, and ethical values of Hinduism.

AO1 activity 10

Learn more about some of the great myths of the ancient Greeks, and think about the messages and values they illustrate. Research the myths of Pandora, King Midas, or Theseus and the Minotaur.

The challenges of myth

Myths have their challenges, particularly in religious language. One of the problems is that in religious texts, the writer does not often make it clear whether the story being told is meant to be understood as myth or as literal and accurate history. When, if at all, should a Biblical account be regarded as a myth?

The problem of competing myths

One of the difficulties of myths is that sometimes different stories give conflicting messages. If myths really do give insights into valuable truths, perhaps they should all give the same message, but this does not always happen.

If we take the example of what it means to be a good woman, there are conflicting messages to be found in mythology. Some mythical women go their own way, refuse to conform and put up a fight, such as Draupadi in the Hindu Mahabharata, and Antigone in Greek mythology. Others,

Synoptic link

Link to *Chapter 4: Challenges to religious belief: religious belief as a product of the human mind.* Jung, in his pioneering work in psychology, was fascinated by myths and the role they play in our shared understanding of what it means to be human.

such as Sita in the Ramayana, loyally do as they are told, or, like Penelope in the Odyssey, wait patiently at home for their husbands to finish their adventures. How are women supposed to know the truth about the right approach to femininity?

The different myths about creation have many similarities, but also many differences. In the Bible, the one God created the world, but in the Dreamtime mythology of indigenous Australians, the world was created by ancestral spirits. Within the Dreamtime mythology, different family groups have different versions of the creation myths, so there is not total consistency even in one country.

Perhaps the details of a myth do not matter very much, and it is the central message behind the symbolism that is important; but it is often difficult to know what the central truth actually is. How should a myth be understood? What are the central, important truths that should be distilled from it, and what is the embellishment that can safely be stripped away?

Some see these different messages in myths as competing and conflicting, but others argue that it is part of the nature of myth to have a rich variety. Just as poetry uses many different symbols for powerful concerns, such as love and sorrow, so does myth. Perhaps this richness of different perspectives is a more fruitful reflection of what it means to be human than a single, consistent narrative thread.

The problem of 'borrowed' myths

For some people, the discovery that there are striking similarities between Bible stories, written in the ancient Near East, and the mythology of countries nearby creates problems. The story of creation in Genesis is strikingly similar to the Enuma Elish from neighbouring Babylon, and to several other creation myths. It could be argued that this similarity undermines the idea that the text of the Bible is inspired by God, because it looks as though it could, instead, be a collection of local folklore. Stories of baby Moses being hidden in the bulrushes by his sister to save him from danger, or of baby Jesus being taken quickly into Egypt to save him from King Herod's murderous soldiers, could lose their impact as real historical events once it is seen that myths about babies having narrow escapes are common in many cultures.

Those who argue that there is little historical truth in Bible stories use these similarities between myths as evidence to suggest that the writers of the Bible invented their accounts to make figures such as Moses and Jesus appear more heroic than they actually were. The writers took up the myths and symbols that were already familiar to them and reworked them for the Biblical characters, to make a point rather than provide historical accuracy.

Others, however, argue that the stories in the Bible are historically true, because God does not make mistakes. Heroic characters such as Moses, David, Queen Esther, and Jesus, fit the patterns of the mythical hero because they were heroes.

AO1 activity 11
Look at the research you carried out for AO1 activity 7, and make a note of the key differences between the creation myths you found, so that you can use them as examples in a discussion about competing myths.

The meanings of myths change over time

Tillich held the view that symbols eventually 'die', and the same can be said of myths, because they are so closely related to symbols. Although myths can often be understood outside their cultural contexts, they are, nevertheless, likely to mean the most to a specific group of people in one geographical location and at one time in history. Biblical scholars refer to this cultural context as **Sitz im Leben**, a German expression that means 'situation in life'. When they study the Bible, they pay attention to the *Sitz im Leben* of the writers, so that the text can be interpreted in the way it was originally intended. In order for a myth to be understood, there should also be an understanding of the culture in which it first grew and was used.

When taken out of their *Sitz im Leben*, some of the meaning of myths may be lost, just as symbols can lose or change their meaning when taken out of context. The meaning changes because the story and the symbolic elements within it are speaking to different people, who perhaps have different concerns.

For some, this is a problem, because it means that a myth can be misunderstood or not understood at all; but others see it as part of the richness of myth, where truths from long ago gain a fresh interpretation in the modern world and offer new insights.

Demythologisation of myths results in varying interpretations

The study of myth became fashionable at the end of the nineteenth and beginning of the twentieth century, with thinkers like Freud, Jung, and Eliade providing new ways of looking at the importance of such stories. The rise of interest in Darwinism added to the debate, because of the apparent conflict between Darwin's theory of evolution through natural selection and the Biblical accounts of the creation of humanity. Those Christians who were persuaded by the evidence Darwin put forward, but who did not want to abandon their Christian faith in the Bible, looked at the idea that perhaps some of the more unlikely or unusual stories in the Bible were best interpreted as myth rather than as accurate history.

The Greek myth of Narcissus tells the story of a beautiful young man who became so obsessed with his own looks that he was unable to form relationships with anyone else. Modern people could look at the culture of taking selfies, and gain new insights from this myth.

Many Christians were able to accept the idea that the Old Testament was full of myth. Ancient stories that seemed bizarre to the modern mind, such as the turning of Lot's wife into a pillar of salt in Genesis 19, or the story of God making a bet with Satan at the beginning of the book of Job, became much more acceptable if they were understood as myth rather than as literal truth. Christians explained that some of the more difficult Old Testament stories had been written before Jesus came into the world to reveal the final and complete truth. The Old Testament writers had included obscure mythical elements in their writings because they had not yet received

Key term

Sitz im Leben: a German expression that means 'situation in life' or 'cultural context'

Synoptic link

Link to *Chapter 6: Religious experience (part two)*. Biblical scholars try to understand the miracle stories in the way that they might have been understood in first-century Palestine, the *Sitz im Leben* of the gospel writers, and of the earliest Christians.

the revelation of God in Christ. These Old Testament myths were still the word of God, and were still true, it was argued, but they had a different kind of truth. It was the central message that mattered. Humanity may have originated in the ways described by Darwin, rather than in the ways described in Genesis, but the Genesis myth contained the important truths that God is the creator of everything, that humanity has a unique place and role in creation, and that God and people have been distanced from each other because of human sin.

However, when it was suggested that there might also be myth in the New Testament, many Christians found the idea much more difficult to accept. The German theologian Rudolf Bultmann was another of the Christian existentialists, like Tillich, who was grappling with the question of what it means to be a Christian in the modern world. He recognised that rapid advances in science and communication made it increasingly difficult for Christians to accept the narrative of the Bible as literally, historically true, and he thought there was a danger that people would move away from Christianity altogether if they were expected to carry on believing (what he thought was) the impossible.

In his 1941 essay 'New Testament and Mythology', Bultmann argued that the writers of the New Testament had not been trying to make a record of accurate historical fact, but had been expressing their beliefs through the language of myth. The real point of the gospel message, for Bultmann, is the need for individuals to reach a personal decision about the direction they want their lives to take in relation to God. In Bultmann's view, the modern, intelligent, literate person could not take the supernatural elements of the Gospel stories – such as visitations by angels, the virgin birth, and miraculous events – seriously, but this did not have to mean that the whole of Christianity should be rejected. Writing at the height of the Second World War, Bultmann advocated the '**demythologising**' of the New Testament as well as the Old Testament, to enable Christianity to hold what he saw as its rightful place as an essential, vital option in a fast-changing world.

Bultmann was not the first to suggest that the New Testament contained myth. In 1835, the German Protestant theologian David Friedrich Strauss raised the idea that some of the stories in the gospels might be symbolic, mythical, or invention.

> **Key term**
>
> **demythologising:** reinterpreting a text to remove what are considered to be mythological elements

> *It is by no means conceivable that the early Jewish Christians, gifted with the spirit, that is, animated with religious enthusiasm, as they were, and familiar with the Old Testament, should not have been in a condition to invent symbolic scenes such as the temptation and other New Testament myths.*
>
> David Friedrich Strauss, *Life of Jesus Critically Examined*

Strauss' reasoning was that the story of Jesus' temptation (Luke 4:1–13) contains many mythical and symbolic elements: the forty days in the wilderness echoing the forty years spent by Moses before reaching the Promised Land, the way the Devil is presented as a character as in the book of Job, and the challenges Jesus is set. Could it be that the gospel accounts contained myth as well as, or even instead of, literal truth?

In 1977, Hick edited a book called *The Myth of God Incarnate*, to which several well-known theologians contributed chapters, and this book took up Bultmann's ideas about demythologising the New Testament. The theme of the book, as the title suggests, is that Jesus was not literally God in human form, and the idea of Jesus as God incarnate (God made into human flesh) is a myth. It is a pictorial way of expressing the importance of Jesus to God and of expressing Jesus' godliness, but statements such as 'God was in Christ' are not literally true. The book caused a great deal of shock in theological circles, as some of the writers were clergymen who seemed to be denying the most important part of Christian faith: the idea that God came into the world as a human being to save people from sin.

The writers of the book described how the idea of God becoming human is found in other myths predating the New Testament, and they claimed that the early Christians used this mythology as an aid to expressing their own ideas. However, it was a mistake to take the incarnation literally.

> *I suggest that its character is best expressed by saying that the idea of divine incarnation is a mythological idea. And I am using the term 'myth' in the following sense: a myth is a story which is told but which is not literally true, or an idea or image which is applied to someone or something but which does not literally apply, but which invites a particular attitude in its hearers. Thus the truth of a myth is a kind of practical truth consisting in the appropriateness of the attitude to its object. That Jesus was God the Son incarnate is not literally true, since it has no literal meaning, but it is an application to Jesus of a mythical concept whose function is analogous to that of the notion of divine sonship ascribed in the ancient world to a king.*
>
> John Hick, 'Jesus and the World Religions', from *The Myth of God Incarnate*

Hick and his co-authors drew attention to the *Sitz im Leben* of the first-century Christians, arguing that the way they understood the world is inappropriate today. The mythological language they used to convey their beliefs might be a hindrance, rather than a help, to modern faith.

> *The Christians of the early church lived in a world in which supernatural causation was accepted without question, and divine or spiritual visitants were not unexpected. Such assumptions, however, have become foreign to our situation. In the Western world, both popular culture and the culture of the intelligentsia has come to be dominated by the human and natural sciences to such an extent that supernatural causation or intervention in the affairs of this world has become, for the majority of people, simply incredible.'*
>
> John Hick, 'Jesus and the World Religions', from *The Myth of God Incarnate*

For many more conservative Christians, however, there are some central beliefs that should be taken literally, and not regarded as myth. Belief in the virgin birth, for example, and the literal physical resurrection of Jesus, as well as the incarnation, should not be treated as myth, but should be accepted as literal fact. It is argued that if these ideas are treated as myth, then Christianity becomes not much more than general advice to be nice to other people. They argue that it should not be taken for granted that a rationalist, scientific way of looking at the world is the best way or only way of understanding truth; if modern society has difficulty in accepting the truth of biblical ideas, then modern society should change.

AO1 activity 12

a) Summarise, in your own words, what Bultmann was trying to do by demythologising the New Testament.

b) Explain why *The Myth of God Incarnate* caused such controversy among Christians.

Myths are often incompatible with scientific understanding of the world

In the modern world, science and technology are very important. They are seen as the way forward and the disciplines that are most important for human progress. Scientific discoveries and inventions lead to things we can use: science improves our health, our economy, our transport, and our working lives. A scientific understanding of the world is clearly very important.

Myths contrast sharply with science. While scientists look at background radiation and find evidence to support the Big Bang Theory, myths talk of dark chaotic waters and the activities of the gods.

However, this contrast does not have to mean that myth and science are in a competition, and one has to be discarded. Members of the Vienna Circle talked about religion, symbol, and myth belonging to history, fit only for people who had not yet come to a better, scientific understanding of the world. They recommended that people should discard theological and symbolic interpretations of reality. Yet, both science and myth give important insights, and there is no reason why they cannot co-exist. Like the visual arts, fiction, dance, and music, myths offer us a way of exploring what it means to be human, and help us to access our deepest concerns. Meanwhile, science works on a more practical level.

Religious language as a language game

One of the most important contributions to the discussion of religious language in the twentieth century came from the philosopher Ludwig Wittgenstein, who suggested that some of the difficulties of religious language might be resolved if it is considered using the analogy of a game.

Ludwig Wittgenstein

Ludwig Wittgenstein was a fascinating character. He came from an extremely wealthy Viennese family of Jewish descent, who had made their fortune in the steel business. Ludwig was the youngest of eight gifted but complicated children, each of whom inherited a great deal of money and so were free to pursue their intellectual interests rather than work hard to make a living. When he was young, Ludwig Wittgenstein was at the same school in Linz as Adolf Hitler. According to some stories, Hitler's hatred of the Jews was sparked by an intense jealousy of the very able youngest Wittgenstein.

Wittgenstein's early work, *Tractatus Logico Philosophicus*, published in 1921, was the book that was so profoundly influential on the Vienna Circle and the logical positivist school of thought. When he wrote the book, he thought that people should confine themselves to talking only about that which can be conceptualised. There are some things that we will never know and never be able to understand, and those are the things that we will never be able to talk about meaningfully. He famously wrote: 'Whereof one cannot speak, thereof one must remain silent.'

When he wrote *Tractatus Logico Philosophicus*, Wittgenstein thought that he had found answers to many of the philosophical problems raised by language, but in later life, he realised the limitations of Logical Positivism and went in a new direction.

Ludwig Wittgenstein (1889–1951) is widely believed to be one of the greatest philosophers of the twentieth century.

One of Wittgenstein's main concerns as a philosopher was the whole concept of meaning. He recognised that there are many aspects of life that we can experience with our senses, using empirical observation, and we can talk about them using terms that are readily understood. But there are other, equally important, aspects of existence that are not available to sense experience. There are things we find hard to conceptualise, such as the nature of infinity, the concept of timelessness, or the scale of our position in the universe. Wittgenstein wanted to establish the limitations of knowledge, and the limitations of the language we can usefully employ to describe it. But he began to think that his criteria for determining meaningfulness were too narrow.

Language games

Wittgenstein's later work explores the ways in which language is rich with meaning, and can work in different ways and on different levels. He looked at how words can indicate more than one idea at a time, and how language is a process, developing and changing as society changes. He explored the idea of language usage in different contexts, showing how groups of people who are all engaged in the same activity use words with meanings they might not have in a different context.

Take, for example, the word 'plate'. A dentist uses the word in a conversation about fitting someone with dentures. A printmaker uses it to refer to the textured surface that is being inked ready for printing. A waiter uses it to mean the piece of crockery used to serve food. A geologist uses it in a conversation about plate tectonics. And a publisher uses it to mean a glossy page of illustrations.

Wittgenstein realised that the key to understanding language is to look at what is done with it while it is being used, rather than taking statements in isolation and trying to establish whether or not they are meaningful,

AO1 activity 13

Think of ways in which different groups of people might use the words 'field', 'stock', 'pole', and 'natural'.

without the context. Meaning is to do with relationships: words and statements mean something *to* someone, they are not just intrinsically meaningful. An expression or a statement can be extremely meaningful to one group of people, and almost incomprehensible to another. Similarly, language can be useful and meaningful when people are communicating in particular contexts, and not at other times, just as a tin-opener is useful if you want to open a tin but not useful if you want to mend a jumper.

Wittgenstein used the analogy of a tool box when talking about language. The tools have different uses, they are for different jobs, and they need to be handled differently. Some are easy to use, while others require experience. In the same way, language has a wide variety of functions. We do not use language only to make truth claims. Wittgenstein gave a long list of different possible ways to use language, for example to ask questions, to give directions, to express emotion and surprise, to narrate an event, and to tell a joke.

Wittgenstein invited his readers to think of language in terms of a game. He was not trying to say that language is trivial, but he thought the analogy would be useful to highlight the scope and meaningfulness of language.

We learn to play games by picking up the rules. When someone explains the rules to us, we try to follow them, but we only really understand them once we start to play. Once we are involved in the game, we recognise that some words and expressions are more important than others. When we are playing chess, we learn which moves are legitimate and which are not. We learn that a castle is also called a rook and, although this is odd, we just accept the two names and learn what to do with the piece. We learn that the queen can do a lot more than the king but that, in the end, the fate of the king decides the game. The more we play, the more we understand the subtleties of the game, and the more we start to think in the language of chess and can hold conversations about it.

Wittgenstein asked us to imagine being in the driver's cabin of a steam train. We would be able to see all sorts of levers, buttons, and pedals, and someone might tell us what each of them was, but it would only be when we tried to drive the train that we would gain a full understanding of the meaning of all these bits of machinery. We would find out which help the train go faster and which help the train go slower, and which we need in an emergency. It is in usage that meaning and understanding are to be found.

Language works in the same way as a game, argued Wittgenstein. When we use it, we have an objective to achieve. We learn to use the language of the context we find ourselves in, and the more engaged we become with the group activity, the better we understand the language; and the better we understand it, the more meaningful it is to us. Involvement in the **language game** develops a sense of commitment and loyalty to the group. Wittgenstein used the term ***Lebensform*** or 'form of life' to indicate these different contexts. Laboratory work is a *Lebensform*, as is participating in cricket or rehearsing for a ballet.

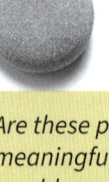

Are these pebbles meaningful? Most people would say not. But if someone had picked them up from the beach on their honeymoon and kept them on their windowsill ever since, they would be meaningful to them and still not meaningful to anyone else. Wittgenstein pointed out that meaning is contextual.

Key terms

language game: the idea that the meaning of language can only be understood if the rules of its particular context are understood; a term introduced by Ludwig Wittgenstein

Lebensform: a term Ludwig Wittgenstein used to refer to the 'form of life' that creates a context for language

So, in the case of religious language, it is not appropriate to ask 'Is this truth claim meaningful?' without any context. Instead, religious language needs to be considered in the context in which it is used. For those involved in the language game of Christianity, it is meaningful to talk about the love of God, the glory of God in creation, the forgiveness of sins, the resurrection, and life after death. For those who do not play the game, and have no interest in playing it, the words are meaningless.

Wittgenstein, then, is proposing a non-cognitive approach to religious language. Like Randall, he is adopting a coherence theory of meaning, where something is meaningful if it coheres with a set of beliefs, and not meaningful if it clashes with other beliefs, or contradicts them. Wittgenstein does not ask whether religious truth claims correspond with any facts 'out there'; the existence of God is a question that is beyond the boundaries of human comprehension. Instead, he asks how the truth claims are used, and what meaning they have for those who use them. He believed that Logical Positivism failed to capture the depth and complexities of language, concentrating far too heavily on a very small part of how it is used.

Challenges to Wittgenstein's theory of language games

Although Wittgenstein made a significant contribution to the discussion of religious language, his theory of language games has been criticised for several reasons.

Wittgenstein's view involves rejection of any true propositions in religion

Wittgenstein presented a non-cognitivist theory of religious language. In his view, therefore, religious language is about a way of looking at the world, rather than about any kind of objective truth that could be verified. For him, there is no possibility that a religious claim can be referring to something that could be known for certain. Religious claims are true within the language-game of religion, but cannot be judged to be true or false by empirical means as they are not truth-apt.

Most religious believers do not accept this. They argue that their language does refer to an external reality, and is not only true within the context of a community of believers. 'God exists' and 'God loves humanity' are, they say, factually true statements, whether you believe them or not. Religious believers argue that Wittgenstein's view reduces religious belief to a kind of private language that makes sense only within a religious community. Religious believers argue that even if there were no people in the world at all, to use any kind of language in any kind of community, God would still exist objectively.

> **AO1 activity 14**
> Explain, in your own words, what Wittgenstein meant when he suggested that language should be understood using the analogy of a game.

Wittgenstein's analogy of language being like a game is not a strong analogy

Some thinkers have challenged Wittgenstein's view by pointing out that there are significant differences between games and language usage. Although there may be some similarities between language and games, Wittgenstein has taken the analogy of 'language-games' too far. Rush Rhees, who was Wittgenstein's contemporary and friend, argued in an article called 'Wittgenstein's builders' (1959) that the analogy between language and games fails as an explanation of meaning.

● Although language follows rules, as a game follows rules, the rules are not used in the same ways or for the same reasons. In a game, the rules exist to add to the challenge and make it easier to judge the winner. So, for example, in tennis, the rules include not allowing the ball to hit the ground outside the lines, and in Scrabble, the rules include not being allowed to use proper nouns. But in language, the whole purpose is to clarify meaning and to communicate accurately so that the other person understands. Although language has rules, the rules can be ignored if it helps to achieve the aim. Poets frequently ignore rules of grammar, to good effect. This difference between language and games is important, and makes the analogy weak.

● A game can be explained to someone else, using language. If you sit down to play an unfamiliar board game with others, someone will use language to tell you how to play. But in the context of unfamiliar language, the explanation has to be given in language as there is no other way to do it. The concept of a game can be understood by using something other than the game itself, but the concept of language can only be communicated in more language.

Rhees and other critics challenged the extent to which a 'game' is a useful analogy for language and communication. Although there are some similarities, there are a great many differences. In a game, we can all easily understand that the point of the game is to get a ball into a hole, through a hoop, or into a net, more quickly or more often than the opposition. It is not nearly so easy in a religious language 'game' to understand that the point is to achieve nirvana or to fulfil the will of God.

Wittgenstein's view does not allow for meaningful conversations between different groups of language users

Wittgenstein's theory of language games might seem to suggest that it is impossible for different groups to communicate with each other. Christians are not able to talk meaningfully with non-Christians, but can only communicate with those who are part of their own belief system. Members of different religions would not be able to communicate with each other about their beliefs, if Wittgenstein is right. Possibly even sub-groups and denominations cannot understand each other, for example Methodists cannot communicate with Catholics.

In real life this is not the case, as people with different beliefs and interests communicate with each other every day. Wittgenstein is sometimes challenged on the grounds that he over-emphasises the separation of different *Lebensforms* and presents each different community as a closed unit, incapable of being understood from the outside.

This challenge could be met by pointing out that Wittgenstein was not saying that communication between different groups was always impossible. His view was that people understand more and more, the more they become immersed in a *Lebensform*. Although a beginner is not able to understand all the complexities of a language game, they can understand something, and it is enough to enable them to learn more.

Wittgenstein's view does not provide adequate meaning for the word 'God'

The theory of language games makes words like 'God' mean whatever the users choose them to mean (just as, in a game, 'winning' means whatever the maker of the game decides it means). A coherence theory of truth allows any kind of belief to be called 'true' if it fits with the rest of the belief system.

Religious believers disagree with this, arguing that God is an objective reality who can be known through religious experience, through reason and through the natural world. There are qualities and attributes that are appropriate to use as analogies to communicate about God, and helpful symbols, but there are also inappropriate analogies and symbols, because God is, in their view, a reality. If God were no more than a shared concept within a closed group, God would not be able to do things like create a universe.

It could be argued, however, that Wittgenstein's theory is entirely adequate, because it allows for the fact that religious believers from different faith communities do indeed mean different things when they talk about God. Aquinas did not accept Anselm's definition of God as 'that than which no greater can be conceived', because for Aquinas, God is unknowable and cannot be pinned down to a definition, for example. A Hindu might understand God very differently from a Muslim, as is shown in Hindu artistic depictions of deities in comparison with Islamic prohibitions about depicting God in art. Atheists might think of God as a childish invention similar to an imaginary friend, while theists will argue that God is not like that at all. Wittgenstein's theory highlights the fact that 'God' means different things in different contexts, and is therefore more adequate than any attempts at precise definition.

This section of the chapter will enhance your ability to **analyse** and **evaluate** the topic and help you develop your AO2 skills. For each question, think about the different positions you might take, and decide which you find most persuasive and why. It is not enough to memorise a list of 'for and against' points; you need to develop an argument.

How effective are the terms non-cognitive, analogical, and mythical as solutions to the problems of religious language?

This question is asking whether the problems identified in religious language are best addressed by thinking of religious language as doing something other than providing factual, demonstrable truths.

The view that non-cognitive understandings of religious language are ineffective

It could be argued that understanding religious language in a non-cognitive way does little to resolve its problems. If people are not coming from the same background and are not using language in the same cultural context, then analogies, symbols, and myths will not mean much to them.

Non-cognitive uses of language depend on people understanding what a symbol is pointing to, because they recognise it as a well-known symbol. Figurative language, such as 'the Lord is my shepherd', may not convey enough meaning to someone who comes from a modern city. For the analogy to be meaningful, we need to know that a shepherd's role is to protect sheep from danger, to find nutrition for them, to guide them in the right direction, and to keep them together. This gives us insights into how people might be in relation to God, and what people can feel confident God will do for them. If we were shepherds ourselves or knew many shepherds, the meaning would be obvious, richly layered and evocative, but someone who does not share this cultural context would miss much of the meaning of the language used.

Analogical uses of language can be of more use in everyday life than in the context of religious communication. When we use analogy in ordinary speech, people know what we are talking about when we compare one thing with another, and so they can see the similarity, and understand the point we want to make. This is not the case in religious language, and the meaning may still be unclear.

It could be argued that just as univocal language and equivocal language are not sufficient for expressing ideas about the metaphysical, non-cognitive language is also not sufficient. It still leaves us without a clear picture of what God is, or what salvation means, or what life after death might be like.

For religious believers, this is not specifically a problem of language, where a different kind of language would work better; it is because the human mind, with all its limitations, cannot fully comprehend divine mysteries. Non-cognitive language, analogy, myth, and symbol help us gain insights into the truth, but we will not gain a full understanding of religious truths in this life, whatever kind of language we use.

In 1 Corinthians 13, Paul tries to explain the unconditional love of God and what its attributes are. He offers various different ideas and symbols, and at the end of the passage, acknowledges that the disclosures given in this life are only partial. We will have to wait until the next life for a complete understanding.

> *For now we see only a reflection as in a mirror; then we shall see face to face. Now I know in part; then I shall know fully, even as I am fully known.* 99
>
> 1 Corinthians 13:12, *Holy Bible (NIV)*

The terms 'non-cognitive', 'analogical', and 'mythical' may not be effective as descriptors of religious language if the religious believer intends their language to be factual. If a Christian claims that Jesus rose from the dead, it is likely that they mean Jesus died and then came back to life again in a real historical event. Interpreting their claim as non-cognitive, analogical, or mythical is a misunderstanding of what they are saying. Many religious believers do not mean that they prefer to view the world as if there is a God who created it; they mean that there is an objectively real God, who created the world. They do not intend their miracle stories to be regarded as myth, but as factual, cognitive truth.

The view that non-cognitive understandings of religious language are effective

Understanding religious language in a non-cognitive way could be understood as effective when addressing the problems of communicating what William James calls 'the ineffable'. There are times when literal, univocal language just does not work. This is shown in everyday life, when people turn to music, poetry, and art to express their deepest emotions and experiences. It was shown in the religious context by Aquinas and Ramsey, and by Tillich. Non-cognitive language finds a way to express feelings and attitudes, and can be said to be not just effective but essential for communicating all the rich aspects of human life that go beyond our empirical experiences.

Non-cognitive language is not only used in religious contexts, but also in many other contexts too. In everyday life and in academic research, there

Synoptic link

Link to *Chapter 7: Religious language (part one)*. This links with Hick's ideas about eschatological verification.

are areas where we do not know the answer, or where we are talking about things that cannot be known using the senses. People make personal judgements which cannot be demonstrated to be cognitively true or false, for example if they work as a food or a theatre critic. And in other areas of life, we switch between cognitive and non-cognitive language all the time.

It seems unfair to religious believers to attack religious language as non-cognitive, when non-cognitive use of language is allowed in other fields, such as science. Richard Dawkins, for example, uses analogy when he writes about 'selfish' genes. Of course, genes are not really 'selfish' in the way that we use the word univocally, as they do not have egos that need to be satisfied. Dawkins uses the expression to help put into words a concept that would otherwise be more difficult to understand. Marie Curie used non-cognitive language when beginning her work into radioactivity, and her husband Pierre Curie used it to describe his symptoms of radiation sickness. J. Willard Gibbs used it when describing how thermodynamics works at an atomic level. In fact, it is hard to find a scientist who has not, at some point, resorted to non-cognitive uses of language, especially when trying to communicate the nature of a new discovery.

If religious people argue that their language is non-cognitive and not about making truth claims, then this might allow the language to skip the test of verifiability. If it is not about true-or-false facts, it does not need to be verifiable. Religious believers might argue that their claims do not have to pass anyone else's test. Tests for verifiability and falsifiability were designed by atheists, to their own advantage and to support their own case, but there is nothing to force religious people to subject their own claims to such tests. They could reject the whole idea that religious language has to pass any kind of test, and concentrate instead on using it in whatever ways they find helpful.

It could be argued, then, that different kinds of language, either cognitive or non-cognitive, are appropriate for different contexts, and people are free to use whichever they like and to change between one kind and another. Like Wittgenstein's tools in a box, language is there to be used, and we can pick whatever we feel is appropriate in the moment, when we want to communicate something, even if what we want to communicate is religious. Religious language, like all other language, can be used effectively in both cognitive and non-cognitive ways.

AO2 activity 1

How effective do you find non-cognitive language when you are learning about religion? Are symbols, analogies, and myths helpful to you when you are studying religious belief, or do you find that they add confusion? Are there stories where you are not sure whether you are meant to read them as history or as myth? Write a reflective paragraph on your own experiences of studying religious beliefs that do not match your own, concentrating on non-cognitive uses of language and their effectiveness.

How relevant are religious language issues in the twenty-first century?

This question is asking for a discussion of whether religious language issues are important or significant for modern people, or whether we have moved on to other concerns.

The view that religious language issues are relevant in the twenty-first century

People are just as interested in science as ever, if not more so. They want to know facts about the world. They expect people, including religious people, to talk sense, to use logic, and to be able to provide evidence to support their claims.

The prevalence of 'fake news' on the internet makes people more aware of spurious claims. People have increased expectations that truth claims should be capable of being supported with some kind of solid evidence, and not just asserted, so that they can distinguish truth from conspiracy theory and fiction by fact-checking. For example, there are people who claim they do not need vaccinations because God will protect them from viruses. Other people find this unacceptable, as science suggests otherwise, and they argue that unvaccinated people put everyone else at risk. They want people to provide testable evidence of their immunity from catching and spreading viruses, not just unsubstantiated truth claims. This emphasis on supportable claims makes the issues raised by logical positivists just as important in the twenty-first century as they were when they were first raised.

In the modern world, people are just as interested in religion as ever, if not more so. Now that communities are more diverse than they were in the past, people need to be able to understand the beliefs of others. Everyone needs to know how to avoid causing offence. Retailers need to know how to provide people with what they need to celebrate religious festivals, owners of leisure centres need to know how best to cater for different cultural requirements, healthcare workers need to know how best to care for a religious person at the end of life. Finding effective ways to communicate is more important than ever, especially between people who have different belief systems. Misunderstandings can quickly escalate into conflict and even violence, and can be stirred up by twenty-first century methods of communication such as social media.

The view that religious language issues are no longer relevant in the twenty-first century

The questions raised by the Vienna Circle, which seemed to be important at the time, have lost their impact, as people now realise the limitations and problems of the verification principle. Logical Positivism failed its own tests, and does not need to concern people any more.

It could be argued that people today are less interested in religion than previous generations. Atheism is more common than ever before, and people readily dismiss religion as unimportant. Even in schools, many parents show little support for Religious Studies, wanting their children instead to concentrate on 'more important' subjects.

It could also be argued that people today are much better informed about the beliefs of others than in the past, and that communication between people of different belief systems is much easier as a result. Religious Studies in schools includes the study of more than one religion, enabling all children to recognise that people have different beliefs. The internet provides people with an instant means of learning more about belief systems that are unfamiliar to them, so they can quickly check when they need information about someone else's beliefs, sensitivities, and customs.

The view that some religious language issues are relevant but have changed focus

People are still interested in knowing how to substantiate religious truth claims, or if indeed it is possible to do so. We still need to know whether there are any criteria that can help us decide if one way of thinking is true and another false. Without criteria for judging whether religious claims are true or false, some important issues remain unresolved. For example, discussions and issues about gender in relation to religion need to find a resolution. We need some way of knowing what is the 'right' religious response to such issues, rather than just having some people claiming that God wants one thing, and others claiming the opposite. When religious ethics clash with secular ethics over issues such as abortion or same-sex relationships, the need for a way to determine the truth is clear.

It could be argued that religious language issues are relevant for some people but not so much for others. Those who have regular contact with people whose beliefs are different from their own may find that they frequently need to consider how to communicate effectively, whereas those who live and work in communities with shared beliefs, or who have little contact with religious people, may find religious language is not an issue that affects them.

AO2 activity 2

How relevant do you think religious language issues are for people in the twenty-first century? Which point of view do you find most persuasive? Sketch an outline of what you would argue if you were asked to write an essay in answer to this question.

Do the strengths of language games outweigh their weaknesses?

How far can language games provide a suitable way of resolving the problems of religious language?

These two questions are closely related, and require you to make an assessment of the value of the theory of language games.

The view that the theory of language games is strong and provides a suitable way of resolving the problems of religious language

The comparison between using a language and playing a game is useful and enlightening. Not everyone has been involved in a religious community, but everyone has played games. It gives people a way in, to help them understand that it is important to consider religious language in the way that it is used by those who use it, rather than trying to judge it from the outside. It emphasises the importance of recognising when you are learning as a beginner, and of taking the time to understand gradually.

Wittgenstein moved to the theory of language games from Logical Positivism, suggesting that he could see flaws in Logical Positivism and had found a way of understanding religious language that was better and more helpful.

Wittgenstein understood that the same objects, events, and language could be more or less meaningful, depending on who is judging them. Making sweeping judgements, declaring all statements of a particular type to be meaningful and all others to be meaningless, was far too unsubtle. Language can be meaningful to someone, and meaningless to someone else, because context is very important.

It could be argued that the theory of language games does successfully resolve the problems of religious language, because of its emphasis on the importance of the *uses* of language. Challenges to the meaningfulness of religious language, such as those presented by the logical positivists, made the assumption that truth claims were the main issue. They suggested that meaningfulness could be tested, using a set of criteria. However, Wittgenstein pointed out that a claim cannot be meaningful or meaningless in a vacuum. It means something when it is used in a *Lebensform*, and it has a meaning that might be lost on people who are not engaged in that activity or community. Words that might seem like nonsense to an outsider can be meaningful to others. Instead of trying to find and refine criteria for judging meaningfulness without any context, those who want to understand religious language will learn a lot more by observing how it is used by believers.

The view that the theory of language games is weak and does not provide a suitable way of resolving the problems of religious language

The similarities between language and a game are limited. As with all analogies, there is a danger of stretching the analogy too far. Some think that categorising statements, such as 'Jesus rose from the dead', as being part of a 'game' trivialises them and suggests that they are part of an elaborate fantasy. It suggests that people can dismiss them if they do not want to play that game, just as they might decide basketball is not for them. For Christians, the meaning of the words and the decision whether or not to believe them is far more serious than that, and the same is true for members of other faith communities who similarly consider their beliefs to be objectively true.

It can be argued that the idea of language games resolves nothing, because people are looking for a commonly accepted set of criteria for meaning, and it does not offer that. People are asking, 'How can I know if what you are saying is true or false?' and the theory of language games replies 'Let's not consider true or false, but instead ask ourselves how we use what we are saying.' Those who want established criteria for meaning are merely directed to a different question.

The theory of language games implies that outsiders cannot have any understanding of what is going on within a language game, but this does not seem to be true. Academic disciplines, such as anthropology, depend on observation of different cultures and belief systems, and valuable insights are produced. People do successfully convert from atheism to religious belief, or lose their faith and move from a religious language game to a secular one. It is not impossible.

It could be argued that the theory of language games does not resolve the problems of religious language, because we are still left without any means of judging whether truth claims have a basis in reality. Many people, whether religious or not, will not be satisfied with the concept that a belief can be true for one group of people and false for another group, with no way of knowing which is right. To say that God exists is true for religious people but not true for non-religious people, seems to miss the point of what people are claiming when they say 'God exists'.

AO2 activity 3

a) Rate Wittgenstein's theory of language games out of five, where a five-star rating is the best. Then write a 'review' of the theory of language games to go with your rating. Why have you awarded the theory the number of stars that you did? What did you think was good about it, if anything, and where did it fall short, if at all?

b) Imagine, if you can, that you are Aquinas doing the same activity. What star rating do you think Aquinas would give to Wittgenstein? What does Aquinas say in his 'review'?

Can symbolic language be agreed as having adequate meaning as a form of language?

This question is asking whether symbol and myth are adequate ways to use language, which of course begs the question: 'What do we mean by 'adequate'?' What is the task we want symbolic language to perform? Is it doing the task well?

What do we mean by adequate?

Ayer and Flew would regard symbols as entirely inadequate for the task of establishing what is true and what is false, as they are unverifiable, unfalsifiable, and not truth-apt in the way that scientific statements are. Tillich, on the other hand, saw symbolic language as essential in humanity's quest for an understanding of existence.

Symbolic language can be all that we have available to us in some situations. For example, if we are trying to explain physical or mental pain to a doctor, we have to use analogies, symbols, and other kinds of picture language, because we have no other way to let the doctor know how we are feeling. Probably the answer to the question is that symbolic language has more than adequate meaning if it is used in the way it is intended, to illuminate our deepest concerns, and is inadequate for other uses of language, where straightforward, literal communication is required.

It would be overly simplistic, however, to say that symbolic language belongs in the world of metaphysics and has no place in science. Anyone who has tried to understand quantum theory or who has delved into cosmology will soon find symbolic language being used in an attempt to communicate ideas that take science in exciting new directions.

Symbolic language has many advantages

The use of symbol and myth in religious language has many advantages:

- Symbolic language can convey concepts, attitudes, feelings, and values in a way that would be difficult to express in literal language.
- Symbolic language is used in myths. Because myths tell stories, they engage the listener and are accessible to all, including children and those who cannot read.
- Symbolic language appeals to our imagination as well as to our reason. It taps into some of our deepest feelings, concerns, and emotions, accessing the part of our minds that Jung terms the 'collective unconscious'.
- Symbols are memorable and vivid, remaining a part of our cultural heritage even when the religion where they originated has died out.
- Because myths have layers of symbolic meaning, they offer people the chance to revisit them time and again and keep finding something new.
- Symbols and myths motivate us to regulate our behaviour and improve our attitudes towards life. They play out for us what might happen if we behave in one way or another, giving us warnings, encouragement, and hope.

The use of symbol and myth also has disadvantages

Symbolic language can also cause problems in understanding.

- It can be difficult for people to know what a symbol is aiming to convey. It might be necessary for someone to explain the symbol (such as when a guide in an art gallery explains features of a painting). If a symbol can be explained in literal language, we might as well dispense with the symbol and just say what we mean.

- Symbols have very different meanings in different cultures and at different times in history, making it hard for someone in the present to know how to interpret a symbol from the past, or for someone embedded in one culture to understand fully a symbol from another. The swastika is a clear example of this: in Indian culture, a swastika is a symbol of good luck and prosperity, whereas in Europe the swastika is seen as a symbol of oppression and racism.
- If there is no right way to interpret a symbol or a myth, it cannot do an adequate job of conveying truth. It can go as far as evoking emotions, and that is all.

The symbol of the swastika has very different meanings for people of different cultures.

AO2 activity 4

How helpful do you find symbolic language in developing your understanding? Do you find poetry gives you insights, or is it just puzzling? Do you think there is something to be gained from myth and, if so, what? Write a paragraph explaining your personal point of view.

How far do the works of Randall and Tillich provide a suitable counter-challenge to Logical Positivism?

This question is asking for a discussion of whether Randall and Tillich's views on religious language as symbolic successfully overcome the challenges put forward by the logical positivists.

The view that Randall and Tillich are unsuccessful in challenging Logical Positivism

It could be argued that the views of Randall and Tillich do not challenge Logical Positivism successfully:

- Logical positivists would not agree that symbolic language is a valid means of communicating meaning, as it cannot be tested empirically, and is not analytic. The logical positivists, therefore, would not concede that Randall and Tillich had challenged them successfully.
- Randall and Tillich do not offer a way of finding out whether religious claims are true or false, and it is important that we know whether they are true or false. Although Randall and Tillich talk about the role that symbolic language plays in evoking emotion and in demanding a response, they leave open the important question of whether the

language is telling us anything true. If all of religious language is symbolic, according to the logical positivists, it cannot have any meaning at all.

- If all of religious language is symbolic, there is the possibility of falling into the trap of what Flew termed a 'death by a thousand qualifications'. The religious believer might claim 'God is love'. The sceptic might reply, 'But what about childhood cancers?'. The religious believer might then have to reply, 'When I said God is love, I meant that the symbol I am calling 'God' evokes in me a response that points me towards a deeper level of my unconscious'. The sceptic is unlikely to be impressed. What began as a claim that there is a real, existent, omnipotent, and omnibenevolent being who is in control of the universe becomes something very different. The logical positivists could accuse Randall and Tillich of doing exactly what the Believer in Flew's parable was doing – qualifying what is meant by 'God' until there is nothing left of the original truth-claims.
- Symbols have some uses, but it is very difficult to find common meanings that everyone can understand and agree on.

The view that Randall and Tillich are successful in challenging Logical Positivism

It could be argued that the views of Randall and Tillich do challenge Logical Positivism successfully:

- Randall and Tillich show that language does far more than just make truth claims. They highlight some of the problems in Logical Positivism by showing that the kinds of truth that can be demonstrated by empirical testing are not the only kinds of truth. They emphasise the importance of symbol for deeper levels of understanding.
- Randall and Tillich demonstrate the significance in religion of emotion and of 'existential response', showing successfully that it is not all about science and verifiability, but instead is about personal choice, personal values, and more profound levels of reality than the levels that are observable.
- Like Wittgenstein, Randall and Tillich show that the most important aspect of language, including religious language, is the way that it is used in context. Logical Positivism ignored this, and instead concentrated entirely on truth-claims.
- Logical Positivism has been shown not to work because it fails its own tests; therefore Randall and Tillich did not need to present a direct counter-challenge, but instead showed how an understanding of religious language as symbolic is a fruitful way forward.

AO2 activity 5

Which do you find more persuasive as an explanation of meaningfulness in religious language: Logical Positivism, or Randall and Tillich's ideas about symbol? Write a paragraph or two to explain which you think is the stronger view, with your reasons.

Exam support

Practising AO1 questions

The following question begins with the command word 'Examine'. 'Examine' questions require you to look closely at a given subject, and to describe and explain it in as much detail as you can.

Activity

Here is an example of a past paper question, and an example paragraph taken from a longer answer written in response. The writer has partly met the AO1 assessment objective, but has not made reference to sacred texts or to scholarly thought. They have not used evidence and examples, and they have not made connections with other areas of study. Rewrite the paragraph, making sure that you include everything you can to meet the AO1 assessment objective.

Examine the understanding of religious language as mythical.

(WJEC A Level Religious Studies, Summer 2019, A2 Unit 5: Philosophy of Religion, Question 1)

Example

Myths are a[2] non-cognitive[7] use of language.[2] They are stories that are layered with symbol, and are used to explore ideas that are of concern to people in their quest to discover what it means to be human.[1] Although different cultures have different myths, there are many recurring themes, such as creation myths, heroic myths and myths that show the triumph of good over evil. Some scholars take the view that myths have recurring themes because they access our[1] collective unconscious[7], addressing questions that are common throughout humanity.[1] One of the key issues raised by myth for religious language is whether there are parts of the Bible that should be regarded as myth.[2]

1 The paragraph shows accurate and relevant knowledge and understanding, clearly explaining what 'myth' means in the context of religious language.

2 The paragraph focuses clearly on the question.

3 The paragraph lacks evidence and example to clarify meaning, and to demonstrate knowledge and understanding.

4 Sacred texts and sources or wisdom and authority could be relevant in an answer to this question, but the writer has not made any references to them here.

5 This paragraph does not make explicit references to other areas of study, although the term 'collective unconscious' shows that reference could usefully have been made to the views of Jung.

6 Scholarly views could have been used here, but the writer has not included any.

7 There is accurate use of specialist language and vocabulary.

AO1 practice question 1

Now it is your turn. Have a go at answering the following question. There are some points to remember to help you if you are not sure how to start.

> *Explain how Logical Positivism challenges the meaningfulness of religious language.*
>
> (Eduqas A Level Religious Studies, Summer 2018,
> Component 2: Philosophy of Religion, Question 5a)

Points to remember

- This question asks you to explain, so you need to focus on giving a full and detailed description, but you do not need to contribute your own point of view, and you do not need to include the views of those who challenged Logical Positivism.
- Remember that Logical Positivism challenged the meaningfulness of religious language, rather than its truth or falsity.
- You should be able to make reference to specific scholars in your answer.

AO1 practice question 2

Now try this question by yourself.

> *Explain how religious language can be understood as a language game.*
>
> (Eduqas A Level Religious Studies, Summer 2020,
> Component 2: Philosophy of Religion, Question 4a)

Practising AO2 questions

AO2 questions ask you to demonstrate your skills in analysis and evaluation. You need to have a clear line of argument so, when you plan your answer, decide at the start what it is that you are going to argue, and what your conclusion will be. You should not only include the views of different thinkers, but also *use* them, showing whether or not you agree with what they are saying.

Activity

Here is an example of a past paper question, and the first paragraph of an answer to it. The example paragraph is very weak. It is mainly a description rather than an argument, and some of the description is muddled. Mark it as if you are the student's teacher, pointing out the mistakes and suggesting improvements. Highlight where the AO2 assessment objective has been met, and where there are opportunities to meet it more effectively.

'The strengths of language games outweigh the weaknesses.'
Evaluate this view.

(Eduqas A Level Religious Studies, Summer 2020,
Component 2: Philosophy of Religion, Question 4b)

Example

The strengths of language games outweigh the weaknesses because the idea of language working in the same way that games work is a good one. Wittgenstein thought that language could be compared to a game. Both have special words that only make sense when you are playing the game. For example, 'offside' in football does not mean anything when you are not playing football. Wittgenstein called this *Sitz im Leben*, and compared playing games to being in the cabin of a steam train where the game is to work the different levers. People who do not know how to drive trains would be able to learn how to do it by watching the engine driver.

AO2 practice question 1

Now it is your turn. Have a go at answering the following question. There are some points to remember to help you if you're not sure how to start.

> *'Symbolic religious language is only meaningful for religious believers.' Evaluate this view.*
>
> (WJEC A Level Religious Studies, Summer 2018, A2 Unit 5: Philosophy of Religion, Question 6)

Points to remember

- This question is quite complex and subtle. There are various different points of view you could consider: the view that the statement is true; the view that symbolic religious language can be meaningful for religious and non-religious people alike; the view that symbolic religious language is meaningless for everyone; the view that the meaningfulness of symbolic religious language depends on the context in which it is used, rather than the beliefs of the people hearing it.
- The question suggests that you should consider the views of Wittgenstein, and discuss whether any religious language, whether symbolic or not, is comprehensible to those who are not involved in the 'game' of religion.
- You could include the views of thinkers such as Tillich and Randall who see all of religious language as symbolic.

AO2 practice question 2

Now try this question by yourself.

> *'Language games fail to resolve the problem of understanding religious language.' Evaluate this view.*
>
> (WJEC A Level Religious Studies, Summer 2019, A2 Unit 5: Philosophy of Religion, Question 6)

Mark schemes for all exam questions can be found at www.eduqas.co.uk and www.wjec.co.uk.

Glossary

a priori: (Latin) without, or prior to, experience; used of an argument, such as the ontological argument, which is based on acquired knowledge, independent of, or prior to, experience

a posteriori: (Latin) on the basis of experience; *a posteriori* knowledge is based on experience, observation, and empirical evidence

aesthetic: relating to beauty

agnostic: someone who does not know whether or not there is a God, or thinks it is impossible to know

analogy: a comparison between one thing and another for the purpose of clarification; saying one thing is like another in a particular respect, to aid understanding

analytic statements: these are statements where reason can tell us whether they are true or false

anthropic principle: the principle that everything in the universe has been designed to allow human existence to flourish

apologist: someone who speaks in defence of a cause, a point of view, or a belief system such as Christianity

archetypes: typical examples of something; the original form of something, from which all versions are copied; for Carl Jung, archetypes are forms or images we share in our collective unconscious, that help us to understand our experiences in the world

atheist: someone who does not believe in any God or gods

blik: a word R.M. Hare made up to describe a person's way of interpreting the world; it could be described as their 'lens' or their 'worldview'

Classical Theism: a term used to refer to belief in one eternal creator God who has attributes of omnipotence, omniscience, and omnibenevolence

cognitive: connected with thinking or mental processes relating to knowledge; a cognitive statement is a statement that can be known to be true or false

collective unconscious: a subconscious layer of the mind that Jung identified and believed was shared among humanity rather than being personal to the individual

contingency miracle: a term used by R.F. Holland to define extraordinary and beneficial coincidences that do not break the laws of nature but appear miraculous to witnesses; also known as 'coincidence miracle'

contingent: dependent on other things or other circumstances

contingent being: a being that depends upon something else for its existence; it need not be or could have been different

conversion: changing from one thing to another; in the context of religious experience, conversion refers to a radical change of belief

cosmological: to do with the universe

cosmological argument: an argument for the existence of God which claims that God's creativity is the best explanation for the existence of the universe

creatio ex nihilo: (Latin) creation out of nothing

deductive argument: an argument that relies on reason and logic; if the premises are true, then the conclusion must be true

demythologising: reinterpreting a text to remove what are considered to be mythological elements

description-related challenges: challenges to reports of experience based on the idea that the account (description) of the experience is illogical or implausible

ecstatic: when a person feels like they are transported beyond the normal range of emotions to a state of complete bliss

efficient cause: the activity that brings about changes

empirical: based on, and verifiable, using our five senses; empirical knowledge comes from things that can be experienced or observed

epistemic distance: a distance of knowledge; a phrase used by John Hick in his development of Irenaeus' theodicy to refer to the distance of knowledge between God and humankind, which allows human beings to choose freely

eschatological: to do with the end of time, life after death and judgement for humanity

falsification: the action of proving a statement to be false

falsification principle: a statement is only meaningful if it is known what would show it to be false

free will: the belief that God allows humanity the ability to choose between different courses of action

fundamentalist: a religious believer or group who follow a strict adherence to the fundamental principles of any set of beliefs, including the belief that their sacred texts are literally true

genetic fallacy: the use of faulty logic in which a proposition is attacked on the basis of where it comes from rather than evaluated on its merits

illusion: for Sigmund Freud, an illusion involves seeing reality as you wish it to be

in intellectu: (Latin) in the mind

in re: (Latin) in reality

individuation: in Carl Jung's thought, a process in which people bring together and reconcile different elements of their inner world

inductive argument: an argument based on evidence that comes from observations and experience; an argument constructed on possibly true premises reaching a logically possible and persuasive conclusion

ineffability: the quality of being difficult to express in normal vocabulary

infinite regress: a sequence that can be traced back and back but never comes to an end

inherent: being part of something as a characteristic attribute

intelligent design: the theory that the world and universe cannot have been created by chance but were made by a supernatural intelligence

Kalam cosmological argument: a form of the cosmological argument from Muslim culture; it concentrates on the idea that the universe must have had a beginning in time, and therefore must have been caused by something outside of time

kashrut (kosher): 'fit' or 'proper' in accordance with Jewish law, often used in relation to food laws

language game: the idea that the meaning of language can only be understood if the rules of its particular context are understood; a term introduced by Ludwig Wittgenstein

Lebensform: a term Ludwig Wittgenstein used to refer to the 'form of life' that creates a context for language

Logical Positivism: a philosophical position that says statements have to be either analytic or capable of empirical testing if they are to be meaningful

materialist: someone who believes that the physical world constitutes all of reality

metaphysical: relating to existence or knowledge that are non-physical, supernatural and beyond purely sensory description, such as love, truth, and God

miracle: an act of wonder; variously defined, for example, as a violation of the laws of nature (Hume) and an unusual and striking event that evokes and mediates a vivid awareness of God (Hick)

moral evil: the kinds of evil and suffering that are brought about through human agency, through wrongdoing

mysticism: religious experience in which the sense of self is lost, in an encounter with God or ultimate reality

myth: a multi-layered traditional story full of symbolism, used to convey important truths in a non-cognitive way

natural evil: the kinds of evil and suffering that are not the fault of humanity but happen because of the way the world is made

natural selection: the process by which evolution is said to take place, through the survival of the fittest who pass on their genes to the next generation

near-death experiences (NDEs): subjective experiences commonly reported when someone is close to death; these can include levitation, bright lights, and feelings of peace

necessary being: a being that is not dependent on something for its existence

necessary existence: God must exist and God's existence is necessary so it is also impossible for God not to exist

neurosis: a mental illness which results in high levels of anxiety, unreasonable fears and behaviour and, often, a need to repeat actions unnecessarily

New Atheism: a philosophical movement from the late-twentieth/early-twenty-first century which views the concept of God as a totalitarian belief that destroys individual freedom, and sees religion as a threat to the survival of the human race; sometimes referred to as antitheism because of its aggressive countering of all forms of theism

noetic: gaining special knowledge or insights that are unobtainable by the intellect alone

non-cognitive: a proposition that is not concerned with facts about the world and cannot, therefore, be known as true or false

numinous: a word coined by Rudolf Otto to refer to the feelings evoked by a non-rational sense of being in the presence of God

object-related challenge: challenges to reports of experience on the basis that the thing that was allegedly experienced (the object) is beyond credibility, does not exist, or cannot have been present

obsessional neurosis: a term once used in psychiatry to refer to obsessive compulsive disorder (OCD)

Oedipus complex: a term used by Sigmund Freud to mean that men secretly want to kill their fathers and have sexual relations with their mothers

omnibenevolent: all-loving, perfectly good

omniscient: all-knowing

omnipotent: all-powerful

ontological argument: an argument that uses the idea of God to establish the reality of God

passivity: being acted upon, rather than taking the initiative

phenomenology: an approach to study that concentrates on things that can be observed

predicate: the part of a sentence that gives information about the subject; it adds to our understanding of the subject by giving us extra detail

premise: an assumption that is claimed to be true, and is used to justify the conclusion of an argument

primal horde: a term used in the nineteenth century to refer to a very simple form of society, where prehistoric people gathered in groups to hunt together and protect each other

principle of credulity: the principle that we should, in general, believe the evidence of our senses

principle of testimony: the principle that we should, in general, believe what other people tell us

privatio boni: (Latin) a lack of goodness

Proslogion: (Latin) discourse

psyche: the name given to the human mind, and sometimes to the idea of a human soul

repression: the act of inhibiting or suppressing

ritual: a series of actions done in a prescribed order, often for religious reasons

second-order goods: virtues and qualities that can only exist if there is evil in the world, such as compassion

Sitz im Leben: a German expression that means 'situation in life' or 'cultural context'

soul-deciding theodicy: a term used to describe the kind of theodicy which proposes that evil and suffering allow people to make a personal choice about faith

soul-making theodicy: a term used to describe a theodicy that proposes people grow into spiritual maturity through encountering suffering

subject-related challenges: challenges to reports of experience based on the idea that the person who said they had the experience (the subject) is unreliable

symbol: something that is used to stand for or represent something else, and to evoke feelings and responses, in a non-cognitive way

synthetic statements: these are statements where observation of the physical world can tell us if they are true or false

teleological: from the Greek word *telos*; to do with end goals or outcomes

theodicy: an attempt to defend and justify the God of Classical Theism given that there is evil and suffering in the world

totem: a sacred object or symbol that serves as an emblem of a group of people

transcendent: having existence outside the material universe

transiency: lasting only for a short time

truth-apt: capable of being called 'true' or 'false'

unitive religious experience: when a person feels their identity is overwhelmed and they become part of God or the universe

verification principle: a principle that says analytic statements are meaningful, but some synthetic statements are meaningless if there is no possibility of supporting them with physical evidence to verify them

vision: in a religious context, seeing something either with ordinary sight or in a spiritual way, and understanding it to have deep religious significance

wish fulfilment: the satisfaction of desires and fantasies

Index

Acknowledgements

The publisher would like to thank the following for permission to use copyright material:

Dr Greg Barker who originated the ABCD paradigm quoted on page 9. Scripture quotations [marked NIV] are taken from the **Holy Bible, New International Version**®, NIV®. Copyright © 1973, 1978, 1984, 2011 by Biblica, Inc.™ Used by permission from Zondervan. All rights reserved worldwide. www.zondervan.com
The "NIV" and "New International Version" are trademarks registered in the United States Patent and Trademark Office by Biblica, Inc.™
Excerpts from *Eduqas AS Level Religious Studies, Summer 2017, Component 2: An Introduction to the Philosophy of Religion; WJEC AS Level Religious Studies, Summer 2017, AS Unit 2: An Introduction to Religion and Ethics and the Philosophy of Religion; Eduqas AS Level Religious Studies, Summer 2018, Component 2: An Introduction to the Philosophy of Religion; WJEC AS Level Religious Studies, Summer 2018, Component 2: An Introduction to the Philosophy of Religion; WJEC AS Level Religious Studies, Summer 2018, AS Unit 2: An Introduction to Religion and Ethics and the Philosophy of Religion; Eduqas A Level Religious Studies, Summer 2018, Component 2: Philosophy of Religion; Eduqas A Level Religious Studies, Summer 2018, Component 3: Religion and Ethics; WJEC A Level Religious Studies, Summer 2018, Component 2: Philosophy of Religion; WJEC A Level Religious Studies, Summer 2018, A2 Unit 5: Philosophy of Religion; Eduqas AS Level Religious Studies, Summer 2019, Component 2: An Introduction to the Philosophy of Religion; Eduqas A Level Religious Studies, Summer 2019, Component 2: An Introduction to the Philosophy of Religion; Eduqas A Level Religious Studies, Summer 2019, Component 3: Religion and Ethics; WJEC A Level Religious Studies, Summer 2019, A2 Unit 5: Philosophy of Religion; Eduqas A Level Religious Studies, Summer 2020, Component 2: Philosophy of Religion; Eduqas A Level Religious Studies, Summer 2020, Component 3: Religion and Ethics; Eduqas A Level Religious Studies, Summer 2020, Component 2: Philosophy of Religion.* Used under licence from WJEC CBAC Ltd. WJEC bears no responsibility for the example answers to questions taken from its past question papers which are contained in this publication.
Excerpts from **Tanakh: The Holy Scriptures** (Jewish Publication Society Inc., 1991). Copyright © 1985, The Jewish Publication Society, Philadelphia. Reproduced with permission from the University of Nebraska Press.
Excerpts from The Factors of Concentration, Samādhaṅga Sutta, from **Sutta Piṭaka**, Suttas from the Pāli Canon, translated by Ṭhānissaro Bhikkhu https://www.dhammatalks.org/suttas/AN/AN5_28.html Reproduced with permission from Ṭhānissaro Bhikkhu.
D. Adams: *The Salmon of Doubt (Macmillan, 2002). Reproduced with permission from Curtis Brown, London, on behalf of The Estate of Douglas Adams. © The Estate of Douglas Adams.*
St Anselm: *St Anselm's Proslogion, translated and introduced by M. J. Charlesworth (Notre Dame Press, 1979). Reproduced with permission from University of Notre Dame Press.*
T. Beattie: *The New Atheists: the Twilight of Reason and the War on Religion (Orbis Books, 2007). Reproduced courtesy of Orbis Books.*
W. L. Craig: *The Kalam Cosmological Argument (Wipf & Stock, 1979). Reproduced with* permission from Wipf and Stock Publishers.
R. Descartes: *Fifth Meditation, from The Philosophical Works of Descartes, translated by Elizabeth S. Haldane (Cambridge University Press, 1911). Reproduced with* permission from Cambridge University Press through PLSclear.
C. S. Evans: *Philosophy of Religion (InterVarcity Press, 1982). Reproduced courtesy of InterVarcity Press.*
E. E. Evans-Pritchard: *Theories of Primitive Religion (Oxford University Press, 1965). Reproduced with permission from Oxford University Press through PLSclear.*
G. Ferguson: *Signs and Symbols in Christian Art (Oxford University Press, 1954). Reproduced with permission from Oxford University Press through PLSclear.*
C. Franks Davis: *The Evidential Force of Religious Experience (Oxford University Press, 1999). Reproduced with permission from Oxford University Press through PLSclear.*
J. Hick: *Evil and the God of Love (Palgrave Press, 1966). Reproduced with permission from Springer Nature BV through PLSclear.*
J. Hick: *Jesus and the World Religions, from The Myth of God Incarnate, edited by John Hick (SCM Press, 1977). Reproduced with permission from SCM Press.*
R. F. Holland: *The Miraculous, American Philosophical Quarterly, 2:1, 1965 (John Wiley & Sons, 1965). Reproduced with permission from John Wiley & Sons, conveyed through Copyright Clearance Center, Inc.*
D. Hume: *Dialogues Concerning Natural Religion (Oxford University Press, 1779). Reproduced with permission from Oxford University Press through PLSclear.*
D. Hume: *Of Miracles, in Enquiries Concerning Human Understanding and Concerning the Principle of Morals, edited by L.A. Selby-Bigge (Clarendon Press, 1975). Reproduced with permission from Oxford University Press through PLSclear.*
D. Hume: Enquiries Concerning Human Understanding and Concerning the Principle of Morals, edited by Tom L. Beauchamp (Oxford University Press, 1999). Reproduced with permission from Oxford University Press through PLSclear.
I. Kant: *Critique of Pure Reason, translated by Norman Kemp Smith (Macmillan, 1980). Reproduced with permission from the Macmillan through PLSclear.*
C. S. Lewis: *Surprised by Joy (Collins, 1955). © copyright CS Lewis Pte Ltd 1955. Used with permission.*
R. Otto: *The Idea of the Holy, translated by John W. Harvey (Oxford University Press, 1980). Reproduced with permission from Oxford University Press through PLSclear.*
W. Paley: *Natural Theology (Cambridge University Press, 1803). Reproduced with permission from Cambridge University Press through PLSclear.*
G. S. Paul: *Theodicy's problem: a statistical look at the Holocaust of the Children and the implications of natural evil for the free will and best of all worlds hypothesis, Philosophy and Theology, Volume 19, 2007 (Philosophy and Theology, 2007). Reproduced with permission from Gregory S. Paul.*
B. Russell: *Why I am not a Christian, (George Allen and Unwin, published by Simon and Schuster, 1927). Reproduced with permission from Bertrand Russell Peace Foundation and Routledge.*
B. Russell: *What Is An Agnostic? Look Magazine, 3 November 1953, as reproduced in The Basic Writings of Bertrand Russell (Routledge, 2009). Reproduced with permission from Bertrand Russell Peace Foundation and Routledge.*
R. Swinburne: *Miracles, Philosophical Quarterly, 18:73, 1968 (Oxford University Press, 1968). Reproduced with permission from Oxford University Press.*
R. Swinburne: *The Coherence of Theism (Oxford University Press, 1977). Reproduced with permission from Oxford University Press through PLSclear.*
Teresa of Avila: *Life of St Teresa, from Complete Works St Teresa of Avila Volume 1, translated and edited by E. Allison Peers (Bloomsbury, 2002). © 2002 by Burns & Oates, 'Complete Works St Teresa of Avila Volume 1' translated by E. Allison Peers, Continuum, an imprint of Bloomsbury Publishing Plc.*
P. Tillich: *Courage to Be (Yale University Press, 1952). Reproduced with permission from Yale University Press through PLSclear.*
E. Underhill: *Mysticism (Oneworld, 1993). Reproduced with permission from Oneworld Publications through PLSclear.*

Cover photo: elodea.proteus/Shutterstock. Photos: p11: Panu Ruangjan / Shutterstock; **p12:** FotoRequest / Shutterstock; **p15:** The Picture Art Collection / Alamy Stock Photo; **p21:** STLJB / Shutterstock; **p29:** RG-vc / Shutterstock; **p33(t):** Longjourneys / Shutterstock; **p33(b):** Maria Dryfhout / Shutterstock; **p37:** Anatolii Vasilev / Shutterstock; **p41:** Danor Aharon / Shutterstock; **p51:** Vivida Photo PC / Shutterstock; **p53:** HUANG Zheng Shutterstock; **p57:** Public Domain; **p61:** Patryk Kosmider / Shutterstock; **p63:** Anton Starikov / Shutterstock; **p67:** Adamskyistudio / Shutterstock; **p79:** Willequet Manuel / Shutterstock; **p82:** incamerastock / Alamy Stock Photo; **p84:** Prometheus72 / Shutterstock; **p86:** Edward Haylan / Shutterstock; **p92:** IanDagnall Computing / Alamy Stock Photo; **p97:** Robilad Co / Shutterstock; **p108:** Great Pics - Ben Heine / Shutterstock; **p120:** Gary S. Chapman / Shutterstock; **p123:** Album / Alamy Stock Photo; **p138(tl):** AbhishekMittal / Shutterstock; **p138(tc):** Renata Sedmakova/ Shutterstock; **p138(tr):** Godong / Alamy Stock Photo; **p147(t):** Christopher Michel (CC BY 2.0); **p147(b):** Christopher Halloran / Shutterstock; **p148(t):** ATHENA PICTURE AGENCY LTD / Alamy Stock Photo; **p148(b):** Kathy deWitt / Alamy Stock Photo; **p169:** Everett Collection / Shutterstock; **p174:** Bill Perry / Shutterstock; **p176:** Stephen Dorey ABIPP / Alamy Stock Photo; **p180:** ZUMA Press, Inc. / Alamy Stock Photo; **p186:** Pictorial Press Ltd / Alamy Stock Photo; **p220:** Anna Kraynova/ Shutterstock; **p223:** incamerastock / Alamy Stock Photo; **p226:** Radiokafka / Shutterstock; **p228:** Sony Herdiana / Shutterstock; **p240:** Nicolas Economou / Shutterstock; **p249:** Pictorial Press Ltd / Alamy Stock Photo; **p259:** John Morrison / Alamy Stock Photo; **p260:** Kuz Production / Shutterstock;